DESIGN FOR
LATERAL FORCES

DESIGN FOR LATERAL FORCES

JAMES AMBROSE

DIMITRY VERGUN

University of Southern California
Los Angeles, California

A Wiley-Interscience Publication
JOHN WILEY & SONS

New York   Chichester   Brisbane   Toronto   Singapore

Library of Congress Cataloging in Publication Data:

Ambrose, James E.
  Design for lateral forces.

  1. Structural dynamics. 2. Structural design.
I. Vergun, Dimitry, 1933–   . II. Title.
III. Title: Lateral forces.
TA654.A56 1987   624.1′71   86-28929
ISBN 0-471-84889-1

Printed in the United States of America

10 9 8 7 6 5 4 3 2 1

Preface

This book deals generally with the design for the effects of lateral forces (that is, horizontal forces) in buildings. The principal sources of these forces are the effects of wind storms and earthquakes. However, there are numerous other sources as well, including horizontal earth pressures, volume changes due to change in temperature or moisture condition, and structural actions that generate horizontal effects under gravity loading—such as the thrust effect of arches. All of these effects are discussed in this book, although design for wind and earthquakes is given the most detailed development.

The book was developed with the consideration in mind of addressing a wide audience, essentially all those who have a vital interest in the design of buildings. This, of course, includes structural designers, but also many people with lesser training in engineering work. With this in mind, most of the structural computations have been presented in relatively simplified form, using simple algebra, geometry, and elementary trigonometry. The level of work is generally not beyond that developed in the typical collegiate architecture program.

While structural computations are presented for the demonstration of design examples for most of the common elements of lateral bracing systems for buildings, the book is not exclusively devoted to computational work. Numerous illustrations and much of the text discussion are devoted to explaining and discussing general effects of lateral forces, the nature and behavior of lateral bracing elements and systems, and the relations between structural problems and general architectural design problems. This approach asserts our opinion that professional design work is often largely accomplished once the problems are clearly visualized and understood, and that although structural computations are essential, they typically constitute a small fraction of the total design effort.

We gratefully acknowledge the cooperation of the Masonry Institute of America, the International Conference of Building Officials, and Building News, Inc., for their permission to reproduce materials from their publications. We are also grateful to many people for their support, their assistance, and their encouragement. We are particularly grateful to our many students and professional clients whose contacts have been essential in our own understanding of what must be explained. Finally, as always, we are grateful to our families for their continuing support, encouragement, and assistance.

JAMES AMBROSE
DIMITRY VERGUN

Los Angeles, California
March 1987

v

Contents

DESIGN FOR
LATERAL FORCES

Introduction

This book deals generally with the topic of horizontal force effects in buildings. The general term used for these effects is *lateral*, meaning sideways, which identifies them in relation to the major orientation to the effect of gravity as a vertical force. Conceptually, therefore, designing for lateral forces is typically viewed in terms of bracing a building against sideways collapse. In truth, most of the effects that produce lateral forces also generate some vertical effects and so it is of limited use to view the horizontal force effects in isolation. Even where this may be valid as an investigative technique, it must always be borne in mind that lateral effects always occur in combination with some vertical gravity effects. In the end it is the critical combined effects that must be understood and dealt with.

This is the third book that the authors have written on this topic. The first was titled *Simplified Building Design for Wind and Earthquake Forces*, which dealt with the lateral effects produced by those two major sources. Much of the material in this book relating to wind and earthquake effects, as well as the general problems of resisting horizontal forces on structures, has been redeveloped from the presentations in that book. The second book, more recently published, is titled *Seismic Design of Buildings* and deals entirely with the problems of architectural planning and structural design for earthquake-resistant buildings. That book contains treatments of some of the problems of

dealing with the incorporation of lateral bracing systems in buildings as architectural planning considerations.

In this book the problem of lateral effects is dealt with as both an architectural and a structural design problem. In addition, the general concern for lateral effects is expanded to include the effects produced by other sources, including soil pressure, structurally induced forces, thermal change, moisture change, and shrinkage. Although much material has been redeveloped from previous publications by the authors, the work in this book includes considerable new material and has been brought into a general conformance to current standards and practices.

As in our other work, an emphasis is placed on the practical concerns of the working professional designer. This is not a fundamental text on theory or investigative procedures, but is rather intended as an aid to the understanding and solving of building design problems. In the end, the solutions to those problems are seen in the form of design documentation consisting of the details of the building construction and the written specifications. While we leave to others the task of writing clear and binding specifications, we do present a considerable number of illustrations of building construction. Even so, it is not our intention to present a manual of recommended construction details. Such details are greatly subject to regional variation and the personal preferences of individual designers, builders, and permit-granting agencies. The purpose for showing construction details here is to emphasize that the design work must be carried to that level of development; this is possibly the most difficult phase of the work for most inexperienced designers.

The authors visualize this book as a beginning point for study and strongly recommend that those contemplating careers as professional designers pursue their studies considerably beyond the work given here. To that end the bibliography contains both the various sources from which materials for this book have been developed and several works of greater scope and level of intensity that may serve the readers in pursuing further studies.

Computations

In professional design firms structural computations are most commonly done with computers, particularly when the work is complex or repetitive. Anyone aspiring to participation in professional design work is advised to acquire the background and experience necessary to the application of computer-aided techniques. The computational work in this book is simple and can be performed easily with a pocket calculator. The reader who has not already done so is advised to obtain one. The "scientific" type with eight-digit capacity is quite sufficient.

For the most part, structural computations can be rounded off. Accuracy beyond the third place is seldom significant, and this is the level used in this work. In some examples more accuracy is carried in early stages of the computation to ensure the desired degree in the final answer. All the work in this book, however, was performed on an eight-digit pocket calculator.

Symbols

The following "shorthand" symbols are frequently used.

Symbol	Reading
$>$	is greater than
$<$	is less than
$\geqq$	equal to or greater than
$\leqq$	equal to or less than
$6'$	6 feet
$6''$	6 inches
Σ	the sum of
ΔL	change in L

Standard Notation

Although it would be desirable to have a standard set of symbols and letters for notation in the field of structures, this is not the case. Because many individual groups have their own special notation, structural designers must learn several different systems of notation. The following notation is used in this book and is in general conformance to that used in most of the references. The reader should also be aware that there is special notation used in the fields of wood, steel, concrete, masonry, soils, wind, and seismic investigation.

a 1. Moment arm; 2. Acceleration; 3. Increment of an area

A 1. Gross (total) area of a surface or a cross section; 2. Amplitude

b Width of a beam cross section

c Distance from the neutral axis to the edge of a beam cross section

C Base shear coefficient

d Depth of a beam cross section or overall depth (height) of a truss

D 1. Diameter; 2. Deflection

e 1. Eccentricity (dimension of the mislocation of a load resultant from the neutral axis, centroid, or simple center of the loaded object); 2. Unit elongation

E Modulus of elasticity

f 1. Computed stress; 2. Frequency

F 1. Force; 2. Allowable stress

g Acceleration of gravity

G Shear modulus of elasticity

h Height

H	Horizontal component of a force	M	1. Moment of a force ($M = F \times a$); 2. Magnitude of bending moment in a beam
I	Moment of inertia		
J	Polar moment of inertia		
K	1. Construction type coefficient (seismic); 2. End condition coefficient for column stiffness (steel); 3. Empirical coefficient for allowable compression stress in wood columns	n	Ratio of the moduli of elasticity of two materials
		N	Number of
		p	1. Percent; 2. Unit pressure
l	Length (usually in inches)	P	Concentrated load (force at a point)
L	Length (usually in feet)	q	Unit of a uniformly distributed linear load
m	Mass	r	Radius of gyration

TABLE 1.   Units of Measurement: U.S. System

Name of Unit	Abbreviation	Use
Length		
Foot	ft	Large dimensions, building plans, beam spans
Inch	in.	Small dimensions, size of member cross sections
Area		
Square feet	ft^2	Large areas
Square inches	in.^{2}	Small areas, properties of cross sections
Volume		
Cubic feet	ft^3	Large volumes, quantities of materials
Cubic inches	in.^{3}	Small volumes
Force, Mass		
Pound	lb	Specific weight, force, load
Kip	k	1000 lb
Pounds per foot	lb/ft	Linear load (as on a beam)
Kips per foot	k/ft	Linear load (as on a beam)
Pounds per square foot	lb/ft^2, psf	Distributed load on a surface
Kips per square foot	k/ft^2, ksf	Distributed load on a surface
Pounds per cubic foot	lb/ft^3, pcf	Relative density, weight
Moment		
Foot-pounds	ft-lb	Rotational or bending moment
Inch-pounds	in.-lb	Rotational or bending moment
Kip-feet	k-ft	Rotational or bending moment
Kip-inches	k-in.	Rotational or bending moment
Stress		
Pounds per square foot	lb/ft^2, psf	Soil pressure
Pounds per square inch	lb/in.^{2}, psi	Stresses in structures
Kips per square foot	k/ft^2, ksf	Soil pressure
Kips per square inch	k/in.^{2}, ksi	Stresses in structures
Temperature		
Degree Fahrenheit	°F	Temperature

R 1. Radius (of a circle, etc.); 2. Relative rigidity

s 1. Center-to-center spacing of a set of objects; 2. Distance of travel (displacement) of a moving object; 3. Strain or unit deformation

S Site–structure resonance factor (seismic)

t 1. Time; 2. Thickness

T 1. Temperature; 2. Torsional moment; 3. Period (harmoic)

v 1. Velocity; 2. Unit shear stress

V 1. Gross (total) shear force; 2. Vertical component of a force

w 1. Width; 2. Unit weight; 3. Unit of a uniformly distributed linear load (as on a beam)

W 1. Gross (total) value of a uniformly distributed load; 2. Gross (total) weight of an object

Z Region coefficient (seismic)

μ (mu)   Coefficient of friction

ϕ (phi)   Angle

θ (theta)   Angle

Units of Measurement

At the time of preparation of this edition, the building industry in the United States is still

TABLE 2.   Units of Measurement: SI System

Name of Unit	Abbreviation	Use
Length		
Meter	m	Large dimensions, building plans, beam spans
Millimeter	mm	Small dimensions, size of member cross sections
Area		
Square meters	m^2	Large areas
Square millimeters	mm^2	Small areas, properties of cross sections
Volume		
Cubic meters	m^3	Large volumes
Cubic millimeters	mm^3	Small volumes
Mass		
Kilogram	kg	Mass of materials (equivalent to weight in U.S. system)
Kilograms per cubic meter	kg/m^3	Density
Force (load on structures)		
Newton	N	Force or load
Kilonewton	kN	1000 newtons
Stress		
Pascal	Pa	Stress or pressure (one pascal = one N/m^2)
Kilopascal	kPa	1000 pascals
Megapascal	MPa	1,000,000 pascals
Gigapascal	GPa	1,000,000,000 pascals
Temperature		
Degree Celsius	°C	Temperature

in a state of confused transition from the use of English units (feet, pounds, etc.) to the new metric-based system referred to as the SI units (for Système International). Although a complete phase-over to SI units seems inevitable, at the time of this writing the construction-materials and products suppliers in the United States are still resisting it. Consequently, most building codes and other widely used references are still in the old units. (The old system is now more appropriately called the U.S. system because England no longer uses it!) Although it results in some degree of clumsiness in the work, we have chosen to give the data and computations in this book in both units as much as is practicable. The technique is generally to perform the work in U.S. units and

immediately follow it with the equivalent work in SI units enclosed in brackets [thus] for separation and identity.

Table 1 lists the standard units of measurement in the U.S. system with the abbreviations used in this work and a description of the type of the use in structural work. In similar form Table 2 gives the corresponding units in the SI system. The conversion units used in shifting from one system to the other are given in Table 3.

For some of the work in this book, the units of measurement are not significant. What is required in such cases is simply to find a numerical answer. The visualization of the problem, the manipulation of the mathematical processes for the solution, and the quantification of the answer are not re-

TABLE 3. Factors for Conversion of Units

To Convert from U.S. Units to SI Units Multiply by	U.S. Unit	SI Unit	To Convert from SI Units to U.S. Units Multiply by
25.4	in.	mm	0.03937
0.3048	ft	m	3.281
645.2	in.^{2}	mm^2	1.550×10^{-3}
16.39×10^3	in.^{3}	mm^3	61.02×10^{-6}
416.2×10^3	in.^{4}	mm^4	2.403×10^{-6}
0.09290	ft^2	m^2	10.76
0.02832	ft^3	m^3	35.31
0.4536	lb (mass)	kg	2.205
4.448	lb (force)	N	0.2248
4.448	kip (force)	kN	0.2248
1.356	ft-lb (moment)	N-m	0.7376
1.356	kip-ft (moment)	kN-m	0.7376
1.488	lb/ft (mass)	kg/m	0.6720
14.59	lb/ft (load)	N/m	0.06853
14.59	kips/ft (load)	kN/m	0.06853
6.895	psi (stress)	kPa	0.1450
6.895	ksi (stress)	MPa	0.1450
0.04788	psf (load or pressure)	kPa	20.93
47.88	ksf (load or pressure)	kPa	0.02093
$0.566 \times (°F - 32)$	°F	°C	$(1.8 \times °C) + 32$

lated to the specific units—only to their relative values. In such situations we have occasionally chosen not to present the work in dual units to provide a less confusing illustration for the reader. Although this procedure may be allowed for the learning exercises in this book, the structural designer is generally advised to develop the habit of always indicating the units for any numerical answers in structural computations.

CHAPTER ONE

Sources of Lateral Loads

This chapter describes the various sources of lateral loads and the effects that they produce. Most of these are discussed in greater detail with examples of typical problems of investigation and design in later chapters. The purpose here is to present an overall picture of the situation of horizontal force as it comes from various sources.

1.1 WIND

Wind is moving air. Air is a fluid and some general knowledge of fluid mechanics is helpful for fully understanding the various effects of wind on buildings. Our primary concern here is for the effect of wind on the lateral bracing system for the building. As a net effect this force is an aggregate of the various aspects of the fluid flow of the air around the stationary object (the building) on the ground surface. Wind effects are discussed in detail in Chapter 3 together with examples of the use of current building code criteria for investigation.

1.2. EARTHQUAKES

Earthquakes—or *seismic activity* as it is called in engineering circles—produce various disastrous effects, including tidal waves, massive ruptures along earth faults, and violent vibratory motions. It is the last effect

for which we design the lateral bracing systems for buildings, dealing mostly with the horizontal aspect of the ground motion. In a static equivalent sense the force applied to the building structure is actually generated by the momentum of the building mass as it is impelled and rapidly reversed in direction. This activity cannot be fully understood in terms of static force alone, however, as dynamic aspects of both the ground motion and the building response must be considered. Design for ground motions due to earthquakes is discussed in Chapter 4 together with examples of investigation and design using current building code criteria. For readers with a limited background in dynamics the discussion presented in Appendix A may prove useful.

1.3. SOIL PRESSURE

Basically two types of horizontal force problems relate to soil pressure. In the first type the soil itself is the load source because of some restraining action of a structure (basement wall, curb, cantilever retaining wall, etc.). The second type occurs when a horizontal force is exerted against a foundation and the soil becomes the resisting element. The problems of soil-retaining structures are discussed in Chapter 8. Horizontal forces on foundations are discussed with regard to various load sources and the problems of various types of lateral resistive structures.

7

1.4. STRUCTURAL ACTIONS

The natural action of various structures in resisting gravity loads may result in some horizontal forces on the supports of the structure even though the direction of the gravity load is vertical. Common examples of such structures are arches, gable roofs, cable structures, rigid frames, and pneumatic structures sustained by internal pressure. Examples of various structures and the problems of investigation and design for the lateral effects they generate are included in Chapter 7.

1.5. VOLUME CHANGE: THERMAL, MOISTURE, AND SHRINKAGE

Thermal expansion and contraction, moisture swelling and shrinkage, and the shrinkage of concrete, mortar, and plaster are all sources of dimensional change in the volume of building materials. Ideally, these effects are controlled through use of expansion joints, deformable joint materials, or other means. However, the potential forces that they represent must be understood and must actually be provided for in terms of structural resistance in some instances. Typical situations of these effects are discussed in Chapter 9.

1.6. RELATION OF LATERAL TO GRAVITY EFFECTS

Eventually the structural designer must deal with the potential net critical effects of the various load combinations on a structure. For the working stress method using service loads this means the establishing of the specific load combinations and the setting of critical limits for maximum stress with any applicable stress modifications for load du-

ration or other conditions. For the growingly popular strength method, modifications are made to the loads using so-called load factors. Both of these methods are in use, employed as alternatives or predominantly for some materials, types of structures, or specific loading type.

Many of the examples of investigation in this book are limited to the determination of the lateral effects alone. This is simply because this is the principal purpose of the book; a full presentation of design for all possible load combinations is beyond our space limitations here. The reader should be cautioned, however, that concentration on the resistance of a single loading condition may obscure the overall intelligent design of a structure or the building for which it exists. We do not therefore intend to overemphasize the importance of lateral effects by limiting our discussions to this single problem.

1.7. PROBLEMS OF QUANTIFICATION

A major problem in designing for lateral effects is simply that of determining the magnitudes of the loads. This is probably easiest for structurally induced effects, although approximations in determining weights of the construction and complex behaviors of highly indeterminate structures may make quantification suspect in these situations as well. Translating the fluid flow effects of the wind into so many pounds of force on a structure is a convoluted exercise in fantasy. Precisely predicting potential ground movements caused by some hypothetical earthquake at a specific site and estimating the effects of the building's response and any site/structure interaction are conjectures of ethereal proportions. Determining or controlling the conditions of a specific soil mass is a highly approximate exercise. Precisely determining the dimensional changes of complex masses of construction due to thermal or moisture variation is not possible.

This is not intended as an argument for not being serious in designing for these effects. It is merely to make the point that what we do chiefly is provide the *kind* of structure that is likely to have the character suited for its task; its *exact* capacity is a very soft target. We do our best, but cannot pretend to claim great precision.

CHAPTER TWO

Lateral Load Resistance of Buildings

2.1. APPLICATION OF WIND AND SEISMIC FORCES

To understand how a building resists the lateral load effects of wind and seismic force it is necessary to consider the manner of application of the forces and then to visualize how these forces are transferred through the lateral resistive structural system and into the ground.

Wind Forces

The application of wind forces to a closed building is in the form of pressures applied normal to the exterior surfaces of the building. In one design method the total effect on the building is determined by considering the vertical profile, or silhouette, of the building as a single vertical plane surface at right angles to the wind direction. A direct horizontal pressure is assumed to act on this plane.

Figure 2.1 shows a simple rectangular building under the effect of wind normal to one of its flat sides. The lateral resistive structure that responds to this loading consists of the following:

Wall surface elements on the windward side are assumed to take the total wind pressure and are typically designed to span

vertically between the roof and floor structures.

Roof and floor decks, considered as rigid planes (called diaphragms), receive the edge loading from the windward wall and distribute the load to the vertical bracing elements.

Vertical frames or shear walls, acting as vertical cantilevers, receive the loads from the horizontal diaphragms and transfer them to the building foundations.

The foundations must anchor the vertical bracing elements and transfer the loads to the ground.

The propagation of the loads through the structure is shown in the upper part of Figure 2.1 and the functions of the major elements of the lateral resistive system are shown in the lower part of the figure. The exterior wall functions as a simple spanning element loaded by a uniformly distributed pressure normal to its surface and delivering a reaction force to its supports. In most cases, even though the wall may be continuous through several stories, it is considered as a simple span at each story level, thus delivering half of its load to each support. Referring to Figure 2.1, this means that the upper wall delivers half of its load to the roof edge and half to the edge of the second floor. The

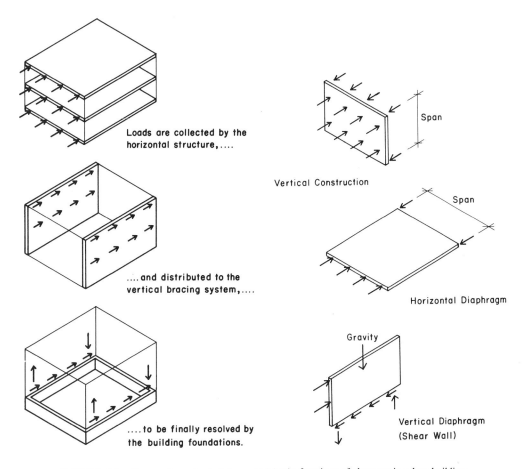

Loads are collected by the horizontal structure,....

....and distributed to the vertical bracing system,....

....to be finally resolved by the building foundations.

Vertical Construction

Horizontal Diaphragm

Vertical Diaphragm (Shear Wall)

Span

Span

Gravity

FIGURE 2.1. Propagation of wind force and basic functions of elements in a box building.

lower wall delivers half of its load to the second floor and half to the first floor.

This may be a somewhat simplistic view of the function of the walls themselves, depending on their construction. If they are framed walls with windows or doors, there may be many internal load transfers within the wall. Usually, however, the external load delivery to the horizontal structure will be as described.

The roof and second floor diaphragms function as spanning elements loaded by the edge forces from the exterior wall and spanning between the end shear walls, thus producing a bending that develops tension on

the leeward edge and compression on the windward edge. It also produces shear in the plane of the diaphragm that becomes a maximum at the end shear walls. In most cases the shear is assumed to be taken by the diaphragm, but the tension and compression forces due to bending are transferred to framing at the diaphragm edges. The means of achieving this transfer depends on the materials and details of the construction.

The end shear walls act as vertical cantilevers that also develop shear and bending. The total shear in the upper story is equal to the edge load from the roof. The total shear in the lower story is the combination of the edge loads from the roof and second floor. The total shear force in the wall is delivered at its base in the form of a sliding friction between the wall and its support. The bending caused by the lateral load produces an overturning effect at the base of the wall as well as the tension and compression forces at the edges of the wall. The overturning effect is resisted by the stabilizing effect of the dead load on the wall. If this stabilizing moment is not sufficient, a tension tie must be made between the wall and its support.

If the first floor is attached directly to the foundations, it may not actually function as a spanning diaphragm but rather will push its edge load directly to the leeward foundation wall. In any event, it may be seen in this example that only three-quarters of the total wind load on the building is delivered through the upper diaphragms to the end shear walls.

This simple example illustrates the basic nature of the propagation of wind forces through the building structure, but there are many other possible variations with more complex building forms or with other types of lateral resistive structural systems. Some of these variations are discussed in the next section of this chapter and in Chapter 5.

Seismic Forces

Seismic loads are actually generated by the dead weight of the building construction. In visualizing the application of seismic forces, we look at each part of the building and consider its weight as a horizontal force. The weight of the horizontal structure, although actually distributed throughout its plane, may usually be dealt with in a manner similar to the edge loading caused by wind. In the direction normal to their planes, vertical walls will be loaded and will function structurally in a manner similar to that for direct wind pressure. The load propagation for the box-shaped building in Figure 2.1 will be quite similar for both wind and seismic forces.

If a wall is reasonably rigid in its own plane, it tends to act as a vertical cantilever for the seismic load in the direction parallel to its surface. Thus, in the example building, the seismic load for the roof diaphragm would usually be considered to be caused by the weight of the roof and ceiling construction plus only those walls whose planes are normal to the direction being considered. These different functions of the walls are illustrated in Figure 2.2. If this assumption is made, it will be necessary to calculate a separate seismic load in each direction for the building.

For determination of the seismic load, it

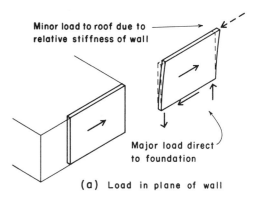

(a) Load in plane of wall

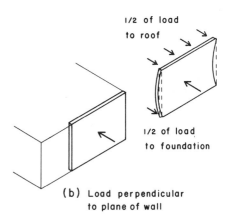

(b) Load perpendicular to plane of wall

FIGURE 2.2. Seismic loads caused by wall weight.

is necessary to consider all elements that are permanently attached to the structure. Duct-work, lighting and plumbing fixtures, supported equipment, signs, and so on, will add to the total dead weight for the seismic load. In buildings such as storage warehouses and parking garages it is also advisable to add some load for the building contents.

2.2. TYPES OF LATERAL RESISTIVE SYSTEMS

The building in the previous example illustrates one type of lateral resistive system: the box or panelized system. As shown in Figure 2.3, the general types of systems are those discussed in the following paragraphs.

The Box or Panelized System

The box or panelized system is usually of the type shown in the previous example, consisting of some combination of horizontal and vertical planar elements. Actually, most buildings use horizontal diaphragms simply because the existence of roof and floor construction provides them as a matter of course. The other types of systems usually consist of variations of the vertical bracing elements. An occasional exception is a roof structure that must be braced by trussing or other means when there are a large number of roof openings or a roof deck with little or no diaphragm strength.

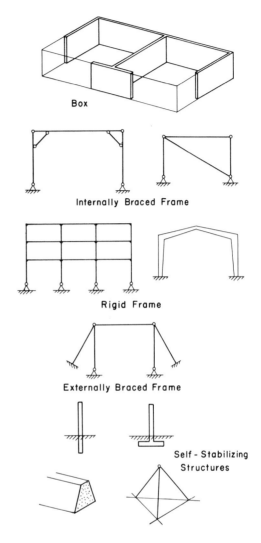

FIGURE 2.3. Types of lateral load resistive systems.

Internally Braced Frames

The typical assemblage of post and beam elements is not inherently stable under lateral loading unless the frame is braced in some manner. Shear wall panels may be used to achieve this bracing, in which case the system functions as a box even though there is a frame structure. It is also possible, however, to use diagonal members, X-bracing, knee braces, struts, and so on, to achieve the

necessary stability of the rectangular frame. The term *braced frame* usually refers to these techniques.

Rigid Frames

Although the term *rigid frame* is a misnomer since this technique usually produces the most *flexible* lateral resistive system, the term refers to the use of moment-resistive joints between the elements of the frame.

Externally Braced Frames

The use of guys, struts, buttresses, and so on, that are applied externally to the structure or the building results in externally braced frames.

Self-Stabilizing Elements and Systems

Retaining walls, flagpoles, pyramids, tripods, and so on, in which stability is achieved by the basic form of the structure are examples of self-stabilizing elements and systems.

Each of these systems has variations in terms of materials, form of the parts, details of construction, and so on. These variations may result in different behavior characteristics, although each of the basic types has some particular properties. An important property is the relative stiffness or resistance to deformation, which is of particular concern in evaluating energy effects, especially for response to seismic loads. A box system with diaphragms of poured-in-place concrete is usually very rigid, having little deformation and a short fundamental period. A multistory rigid frame of steel, on the other hand, is usually quite flexible and will experience considerable deformation and have a relatively long fundamental period. In seismic analysis these properties are used to modify the percentage of the dead weight that is used as the equivalent static load to simulate the seismic effect.

Elements of the building construction developed for the gravity load design, or for the general architectural design, may become natural elements of the lateral resistive system. Walls of the proper size and in appropriate locations may be theoretically functional as shear walls. Whether they can actually serve as such will depend on their construction details, on the materials used, on their length-to-height ratio, and on the manner in which they are attached to the other elements of the system for load transfer. It is also possible, of course, that the building construction developed only for gravity load resistance and architectural planning considerations may *not* have the necessary attributes for lateral load resistance, thus requiring some replanning or the addition of structural elements.

Many buildings consist of mixtures of the basic types of lateral resistive systems. Walls existing with a frame structure, although possibly not used for gravity loads, can still be used to brace the frame for lateral loads. Shear walls may be used to brace a building in one direction whereas a braced frame or rigid frame is used in the perpendicular direction. Multistory buildings occasionally have one type of system, such as a rigid frame, for the upper stories and a different system, such as a box system or braced frame, for the lower stories to reduce deformation and take the greater loads in the lower portion of the structure.

In many cases it is neither necessary nor desirable to use every wall as a shear wall or to brace every bay of the building frame. The illustrations in Figure 2.4 show various situations in which the lateral bracing of the building is achieved by partial bracing of the system. This procedure does require that there be some load-distributing elements, such as the roof and floor diaphragms, horizontal struts, and so on, that serve to tie the unstabilized portions of the building to the lateral resistive elements.

There is a possibility that some of the elements of the building construction that are not intended to function as bracing elements may actually end up taking some of the lateral load. In frame construction, surfacing materials of plaster, drywall, wood paneling, masonry veneer, and so on, may take some lateral load even though the frame is braced by other means. This is essentially a matter of relative stiffness, although connection for load transfer is also a consideration. What can happen in these cases is that the stiffer finish materials take the load first, and if they are not strong enough, they fail and the intended bracing system then goes to work. Although collapse may not occur, there can be considerable damage to the building con-

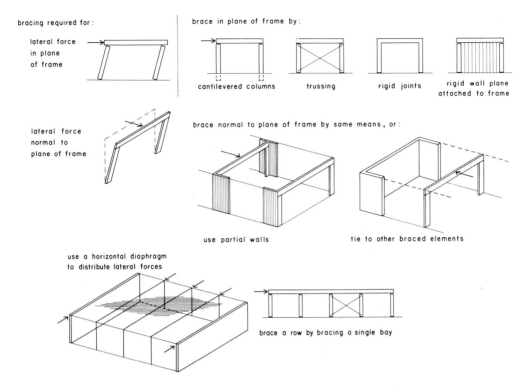

FIGURE 2.4. Bracing of framed structures for lateral loads.

struction as a result of the failure of the supposed nonstructural elements.

The choice of the type of lateral resistive system must be related to the loading conditions and to the behavior characteristics required. It must also, however, be coordinated with the design for gravity loads and with the architectural planning considerations. Many design situations allow for alternatives, although the choice may be limited by the size of the building, by code restrictions, by the magnitude of lateral loads, by the desire for limited deformation, and so on.

2.3. LATERAL RESISTANCE OF ORDINARY CONSTRUCTION

Even when buildings are built with no consideration given to design for lateral forces,

they will have some natural capacity for lateral force resistance. It is useful to understand the limits and capabilities of ordinary construction as a starting point for the consideration of designing for enhanced levels of lateral force resistance.

Wood Frame Construction

Wood structures can be categorized broadly as light frame or heavy timber. Light frames—using mostly 2 × dimension lumber for wall studs, floor joists, and roof rafters—account for the vast majority of small, low-rise buildings in the United States. In most cases the frames are covered on both surfaces by some type of surfacing material. Many of these surfacing systems have a usable, quantifiable, capacity for diaphragm resistance. Thus, without any major alteration of the basic structure, most light wood frames can be made resistive to lateral forces through the use of a combination of horizontal and vertical diaphragms.

Many of the ordinary elements of light wood frames can be utilized as parts of the lateral resistive system, serving as diaphragm chords, collectors, and edge transfer members. Wall studs, posts, sills and plates, and roof and floor framing members, occurring naturally in the structure, are often able to be utilized for these functions. Alterations necessary to make them more functional are often limited to moderate increases in sizes or to the use of some additional fastening or anchoring. When members are long and not able to be installed as a single piece (as with the top plate on a long wall), it may be necessary to use stronger splicing than is ordinarily required for gravity resistance alone.

Common practices of carpentry result in a considerable amount of fastening between members of a light wood frame. Building codes often specify minimum requirements for such fastening. (See reprint of Table 25—Q from the *Uniform Building Code* in Appendix C.) Before undertaking to design such a structure for seismic loads, it well behooves the designer to become thoroughly familiar with these requirements as well as current local practices of contractors and workmen. References with suggested details for construction become rapidly out of date as codes and construction practices and the availability of materials and equipment change.

In recent times there has been a trend toward the extensive use of sheet metal fastening devices for the assemblage of light wood structures. In general, these tend to increase resistances to lateral loads because the continuity of the frame is greater and the anchorage of members is more positive.

There is a considerable range in the diaphragm shear capability of various surfacing materials. The following are some widely used products:

Plywood. This may be used as the structural backup for a variety of finishes or may be used with a special facing as the complete surfacing. Most plywoods offer considerable potential for shear resistance. With an increase in structural quality, greater thickness than the minimum required for other functions, and a greater number of nails, it is possible to develop considerable strength for either horizontal or vertical diaphragm use.

Board Sheathing. Boards of 1-in. nominal thickness, with shiplap or tongue-and-groove edges, were once quite commonly used for sheathing. When applied in a position diagonal to the frame, they can produce some diaphragm action. Capacities are nowhere near that of plywood, however, so that for this and other reasons this type of structural covering is not much used at present.

Plaster. Portland cement plaster, applied over wire-reinforced backing and adequately secured to the framing, produces a very stiff diaphragm with load capacities equal to that of the thinner plywoods. On the exterior it is called stucco, which due to its popularity is the definitive vertical bracing material for light structures in southern and western United States.

Miscellaneous Surfacing. Gypsum drywall, gypsum plaster, nonstructural plywood, and particleboard can develop some diaphragm capacity that may be sufficient for low stress situations. Stiffness is minimal, thus narrow diaphragms should be avoided.

When the same material is applied to both sides of a wall, the code permits the use of the sum of the resistances of the two surfaces. For interior walls this is quite common and permits the utilization of low-strength surfacing. However, for exterior walls the two surfaces are seldom the same, thus the stronger (usually the exterior) must be used alone.

In the past a widely used method for bracing light wood frames consisted of diagonal bracing, typically in the form of 1-in. nominal thickness boards with their outside surfaces made flush with the face of the framing by cutting notches in the framing members (called let-in bracing). The acceptance of rated load capacities for a wider range of popular surfacing materials has made this practice largely redundant. When diagonal bracing is used today, it often consists of thin steel straps applied to the faces of the framing members.

Some of the problems encountered in developing seismic resistance with light wood frame construction follow.

1. Lack of adequate solid walls to serve as shear walls. This may be due to the building planning, with walls insufficient at certain locations or in a particular direction. Walls may also simply be too broken up in short lengths by doors and windows. For multistory buildings there may be a problem where upper level walls do not occur above walls in lower levels.

2. Lack of adequate diaphragm surfacing. Many types of surfacing have rated capacities for shear. Each, however, has its limits and some materials are not rated for code-acceptable loadings.

3. Lack of continuity of framing. Because it is often not required for gravity load conditions, members that could function as chords or collectors may consist of separate pieces that are not spliced for tension or compression continuity.

4. Lack of adequate connections. Load transfers—most notably those from horizontal to vertical diaphragms—may not be possible without modification of the construction details, involving additional framing, increased nailing, or use of special anchorage devices. Ordinary code-required minimum wall sill bolting is not acceptable for overturn resistance and is often not adequate for sliding resistance.

Wood post and beam structures can some-

times be made to function as braced frames or moment-resistive frames, the latter usually being somewhat more difficult to achieve. Often, however, these structures occur in combination with wall construction of reinforced masonry or wood frame plus surfacing so that the post and beam frame need not function for lateral bracing. Floor and roof decks are often the same as for light frames and thus are equally functional as horizontal diaphragms.

A problem with post and beam construction is often the lack of ability for load transfers between members required for resistance to lateral loads. At present this is less the case due to the increasing use of metal framing devices for beam seats, post caps and bases, and so on.

When heavy timber frames are exposed to view, a popular choice for roof or floor decks is a timber deck of 1.5 in. or greater thickness. Although such a deck has a minimal shear capacity, it is usually not adequate for diaphragm development except for small buildings. The most common and economical means for providing the necessary diaphragm resistance is to simply nail a continuous plywood surface to the top of the timber deck.

Structural Masonry

For seismic zones 3 and 4 the only masonry structural construction permitted is *reinforced masonry*. These comments are confined to structural masonry walls constructed with hollow concrete units (concrete blocks), with the voids partly or wholly reinforced and filled with grout (see Fig. 6.7).

Structural masonry walls have considerable potential for utilization as shear walls. There are, however, a number of problems that must be considered.

1. *Increased Load.* Due to their weight, stiffness, and brittleness, masonry walls must be designed for higher lateral seismic forces. The *UBC* requires an addi-

tional increase of 50% in the load for stress analysis of the wall.

2. *Limited Stress Capacity.* The unit strength and the mortar strength must be adequate for the required stress resistances. In addition, both vertical and horizontal reinforcing is required for major shear wall functions.

3. *Cracks and Bonding Failures.* Walls not built to the specifications usually used for seismic-resistive construction often have weakened mortar joints and cracking. These reduce seismic resistance, especially in walls with minimal reinforcing.

Code specifications for concrete block walls result in a typical minimum construction that has a particular limit of shear wall capacity. This limit is beyond the limit for the strongest of the wood-framed walls with plywood on a single side, and so the change to a masonry wall is a significant step. Beyond the minimum value the load capacity is increased by adding additional reinforcing and filling more of the block voids. At its upper limits the reinforced masonry wall approaches the capacity of a reinforced concrete wall.

Anchorage of masonry walls to their supports is usually simply achieved. Resistance to vertical uplift and horizontal sliding can typically be developed by the usual doweling of the vertical wall reinforcing. The anchorage of horizontal diaphragms to masonry walls is another matter and typically requires the use of more "positive" anchoring methods than are ordinarily used when seismic risk is low.

Reinforced Concrete Construction

Poured concrete elements for most structures are ordinarily quite extensively reinforced, thus providing significant compensation for the vulnerability of the tension-weak material. Even where structural demands are not severe, minimum two-way reinforcing is re-

quired for walls and slabs to absorb effects of shrinkage and fluctuation of temperature. This form of construction has considerable natural potential for lateral force resistance.

Subgrade building construction most often consists of thick concrete walls, in many cases joined to horizontal concrete structures with solid poured-in-place slabs. The typical result is a highly rigid, strong boxlike structure. Shears in the planes of the walls and slabs can be developed to considerable stress levels with minimum required reinforcing. Special attention must be given to the maintaining of continuity through pour joints and control joints and to the anchorage of reinforcing at wall corners and intersections and at the joints between slabs and walls. This does not always result in an increase in the amount of reinforcing but may alter some details of its installation.

Structures consisting of poured concrete columns used in combination with various concrete spanning systems require careful study for the development of seismic resistance as rigid frame structures. The following are some potential problems:

1. *Weight of the Structure.* This is ordinarily considerably greater than that of wood or steel construction, with the resulting increase in the total seismic force.

2. *Adequate Reinforcing for Seismic Effects.* Of particular concern are the shears and torsions developed in framing elements and the need for continuity of the reinforcing or anchorage at the intersections of elements. A special problem is that of vertical shears developed by vertical accelerations, most notably punching shear in slab structures.

3. *Ductile Yielding of Reinforcing.* This is the desirable first mode of failure, even for gravity load resistance. With proper design it is a means for developing a yield character in the otherwise brittle, tension-weak structure.

4. *Detailing of Reinforcing.* Continuity at splices and adequate anchorage at member intersections must be assured by careful layout of reinforcing installation.

5. *Tying of Compression Bars.* Column and beam bars should be adequately tied in the region of the column-beam joint.

When poured concrete walls are used in conjunction with concrete frames, the result is often similar to that of the plywood-braced wood frame, the walls functioning to absorb the major portion of the lateral loads due to their relative stiffness. At the least, however, the frame members function as chords, collectors, drag struts, and so on. The forces at the intersections of the walls and the frame members must be carefully studied to assure proper development of necessary force transfers. This is even more critical if there is an actual interaction of the wall and frame systems.

As with masonry structures, considerable cracking is normal in poured concrete structures; much of it is due to shrinkage, temperature expansion and contraction, settlement or deflection of supports, and the normal development of internal tension forces. In addition, built-in cracks of a sort are created at the cold joints that are unavoidable between successive, separate pours. Under the back-and-fourth swaying actions of an earthquake, these cracks will be magnified, and a grinding action may occur as stresses reverse. The grinding action can be a major source of energy absorption but can also result in progressive failures or simply a lot of pulverizing and flaking off of the concrete. If reinforcing is adequate, the structure may remain safe, but the appearance is sure to be affected.

It is virtually impossible to completely eliminate cracking from masonry and poured-in-place concrete buildings. Good design, careful construction detailing, and quality construction can reduce the amount of cracking and possibly eliminate some

types of cracking. However, the combination of shrinkage, temperature expansion, settlement of supports, creep, and flexural stress is a formidable foe.

Steel Frame Construction

Structures with frames of steel can often quite readily be made resistive to lateral loads, usually by producing either a braced (trussed) frame or a moment-resistive frame. Steel has the advantage of having a high level of resistance to all types of stress and is thus not often sensitive to multidirectional stresses or to rapid stress reversals. In addition, the ductility of ordinary structural steel provides a toughness and a high level of energy absorption in the plastic behavior mode of failure.

The high levels of stress obtained in steel structures are accompanied by high levels of strain, resulting often in considerable deformation. The actual magnitudes of the deformations may affect the building occupants or contents or may have undesirable results in terms of damage to nonstructural elements of the building construction. Deformation analysis is often a critical part of the design of steel structures, especially for moment-resistive frames.

The ordinary post and beam steel frame is essentially unstable under lateral loading. Typical framing connections have some minor stiffness and moment resistance but are not effective for development of the rigid joints required for a moment-resistive frame. Frames must therefore either be made self-stable with diagonal bracing or with specially designed moment-resistive connections or be braced by shear walls.

Steel frames in low-rise buildings are often braced by walls, with the steel structure serving only as the horizontal spanning structure and vertical gravity load resisting structure. Walls may consist of masonry or of wood or metal frames with various shear-resisting surfacing. For the wall-braced structure, building planning must incorporate the necessary solid wall construction for the usual shear wall braced building. In addition, the frame will usually be used for chord and collector actions; therefore, the connections between the decks, the walls, and the frame must be designed for the lateral load transfers.

The trussed steel structure is typically quite stiff, in a class with the wall-braced structure. This is an advantage in terms of reduction of building movements under load, but it does mean that the structure must be designed for as much as twice the total lateral force as a moment-resistive frame. Incorporating the diagonal members in vertical planes of the frame is often a problem for architectural planning, essentially similar to that of incorporating the necessary solid walls for a shear wall braced structure.

In the past steel frames were mostly used in combination with decks of concrete or formed sheet steel. A popular construction for low-rise buildings at present—where fire-resistance requirements permit its use—is one that utilizes a wood infill structure of joists or trusses with a plywood deck. A critical concern for all decks is the adequate attachment of the deck to the steel beams for load transfers to the vertical bracing system. Where seismic design has not been a factor, typical attachments are often not sufficient for these load transfers.

Buildings of complex unsymmetrical form sometimes present problems for the development of braced or moment-resistive frames. Of particular concern is the alignment of the framing to produce the necessary vertical planar bents. Randomly arranged columns and discontinuities due to openings or voids can make bent alignment or continuity a difficult problem.

Precast Concrete Construction

Precast concrete structures present unique problems in terms of lateral bracing. Although they share many characteristics with poured-in-place concrete structures, they lack the natural member-to-member continuity that provides considerable lateral stability. Precast structures must therefore be dealt with in a manner similar to that for post and beam structures of wood or steel. This problem is further magnified by the increased dead weight of the structure, which results in additional lateral force.

Separate precast concrete members are usually attached to each other by means of steel devices that are cast into the members. The assemblage of the structure thus becomes a steel-to-steel connection problem. Where load transfer for gravity resistance is limited to simple bearing, connections may have no real stress functions, serving primarily to hold the members in position. Under lateral load, however, all connections will likely be required to transfer shear, tension, bending, and torsion. Thus for seismic resistance many of the typical connections used for gravity resistance alone will be inadequate.

Because of their weight, precast concrete spanning members may experience special problems due to vertical accelerations. When not sufficiently held down against upward movement, members may be bounced off their supports (a failure described as dancing.)

Precast concrete spanning members are often also prestressed, rather than simply utilizing ordinary steel reinforcing. This presents a possible concern for the effects of the combined loading of gravity and lateral forces or for upward movements due to vertical acceleration. Multiple loading conditions and stress reversals tend to greatly complicate the design of prestressing.

As with frames of wood or steel, those of precast concrete must be made stable with trussing, moment connections, or infill walls. If walls are used, they must be limited to masonry or concrete. Connections between the frame and any bracing walls must be carefully developed to assure the proper load transfers.

Miscellaneous Construction

Foundations. Where considerable below-grade construction occurs—with heavy basement walls, large bearing footings, basement or sublevel floor construction of reinforced concrete, and so on—the below-grade structure as a whole usually furnishes a solid base for the above-grade building. Not many extra details or elements are required to provide for seismic actions. Of principal concern is the tying together of the base of the building, which is where the seismic movements are transmitted to the building. If the base does not hold together as a monolithic unit, the result will be disastrous for the supported building. Buildings without basements or those supported on piles or piers may not ordinarily be sufficiently tied together for this purpose, thus requiring some additional construction. Foundation design problems are discussed more thoroughly in Chapter 8.

Freestanding Structures. Freestanding structures include exterior walls used as fences as well as large signs, water towers, and detached stair towers. The principal problem is usually the large overturning effect. Rocking and permanent soil deformations that result in vertical tilting must be considered. It is generally advisable to be quite conservative in the design for soil pressure due to the overturning effects. When weight is concentrated at the top—as in the case of signs or water towers—the dynamic rotational effect is further increased. These concerns apply also to the elements that may be placed on the roof of a building.

2.4. LIMITS OF ELEMENTS AND SYSTEMS

Although the range of possibilities for development of lateral resistive structures is considerable, it is necessary to be aware of the limitations that exist. Limitations may be real, established by stress level capacities of materials or the available sizes of ordinary construction elements. Limits may also be somewhat artificial or ambiguous, established by code requirements or rules of thumb in design practice. The latter are not developed arbitrarily but rather are evolved from the collective experience and judgments of generations of professional researchers and designers. However, in time, changes in construction methods, design practices, and use of materials and products make old rules lose touch with reality.

The limits of basic types of construction are discussed in Chapter 2. The limits of typical elements of lateral resistive structural systems are discussed in Chapter 5. The following are some basic types of limits that should be recognized, although the specific quantification of data and the relative status of particular materials or systems tend to exist in a constant state of flux.

1. *Limits of Materials.* Common materials have specific stress limits; variation is typical over some range of quality or type (stress grade of wood, f'_c of concrete, etc.).

2. *Available Sizes.* Concrete is unique in its ability to form elements of virtually any size; most other materials and products have practical limits in terms of commonly available shapes and sizes.

3. *Functional Limits.* For various reasons particular materials, products, construction techniques, or details of construction are often limited to specific uses or excluded from specific uses. Unfinished bolts, which are mostly used only for temporary or minor connections, are excluded from use in braced frames. Wood-framed shear walls should not be used to brace a concrete frame. For the bolts, the limits are due to their inability to maintain a tight (nonslipping) joint. For the wood-framed wall it is simply not reasonable to brace the heavy, rigid, system with a light, deformable one.

4. *Size Limits.* Upper and lower limits of size exist—sometimes for actual reasons of the availability of products, sometimes merely for practicality, as in the case of the limits of minimum size for concrete members (wall thickness, beam width, column diameter, etc.).

5. *Aspect Ratios.* Examples of aspect ratios are the practical, or in some cases the code-specified, limits for the h/t of columns or L/d of beams. A major type of limitation is the length–to–width ratio of wood diaphragms (expressed as span-width for horizontal diaphragms and as height-width for vertical diaphragms by *UBC* Table 25—I.)

6. *Structural Behavior.* Performance of the structure is mostly limited by the assigning of values for allowable stresses (in the working stress method) or load factors (for the ultimate strength method). Except for vertical deflection of beams and lateral drift (horizontal deflection) of individual stories, codes do not provide much criteria for limitation of deformations.

2.5. DESIGN CONSIDERATIONS

The design of the lateral load resistive system for a building involves a great number of factors. The principal considerations are the following.

Determination of the Loading

Determining the loading is usually established by the satisfaction of the requirements of the building code with jurisdiction. Critical load values, as well as various requirements for the form of the structural analysis and design, are determined by the degree of local concern for extremes of wind storms or earthquakes. This concern is primarily based on the history of disasters in the area.

Selection and Planning of the Lateral Resistive System for the Building

As previously discussed, this selection and planning must be coordinated with the gravity load design and the architectural design in general. In some cases the design for lateral loads may be a major factor in establishing the building form and detail, in selection of materials, and so on. In other cases it may consist essentially of assuring the proper construction of ordinary elements of the construction.

Detailed Analysis and Design of the Elements of the Lateral Resistive System

With the loading established and the system defined the performance of the individual parts and of the system as a whole must be investigated. An important aspect of the investigation is the complete following through of the loads from their origin to their final resolution in the ground. With the internal forces and stresses determined the design of the parts of the system is usually a matter of routine, using code specifications and data from the code or from other reference sources.

Development of Structural Construction Details and Specifications

Such development constitutes essentially the documentation of the design and is a task of major importance. A thorough analytical investigation and complete set of structural calculations will be useless unless the results are translated into directives usable by the builders of the building.

Convincing the Authorities Who Grant Building Permits That the Structure Is Adequate

In most cases someone employed or retained as a consultant by the code enforcing body will review the structural calculations and the construction drawings and specifications for compliance with the local code requirements and with acceptable practices of design and construction. Although it should be expected that a competent and thorough design effort will receive a good review, there is usually some room for individual judgment and personal preference so that the potential exists for some conflict between the designer and the reviewer.

In some ways the easiest part of this process is that of the structural analysis and design. The analysis and design may be laborious if the building is large or complex, but it is usually routine in nature, with considerable information and guidance available from codes, texts, industry brochures, and so on. Some degree of training in engineering mechanics and basic structural analysis and design is necessary, but most of the work is "cookbook" in nature.

Determination of the lateral loads is also reasonably simple, at least with the use of the equivalent static load methods. One possible complication is due to the fact that the structure must be defined in some detail before the loads can be determined and their propagation through the system investigated, which is somewhat like needing to know the answer before a person can formulate the question. Some things must be known about the structure before one can analyze its behavior. As a result, the early stages of design often consist of some guessing and trying—approximating a structure and then analyzing it to see if it works. This process is easier, of course, when the designer has worked on similar problems before, or if he or she has the results of previous similar designs as a basis for a more educated first guess.

The more difficult aspects of design for lateral loads are the development of the basic systems for the lateral resistive structure and the development of the necessary construction drawings and specifications to assure proper construction. This work requires con-siderable understanding of the problems of the building design and construction in general because decisions about the basic structural scheme and some of the details of the structure may have considerable influence on the general form and detail of the building and on the economics and general feasibility of the construction.

2.6. ARCHITECTURAL DESIGN PROBLEMS

When the need to develop resistance to seismic forces is kept in mind throughout the entire process of the building design, it will have bearing on many areas of the design development. This chapter deals with various considerations that may influence the general planning as well as choices for materials, systems, and construction details.

When lateral design is dealt with as an afterthought rather than being borne in mind in the earliest decisions on form and planning of the building, it is quite likely that optimal conditions will not be developed. Some of the major issues that should be kept in mind in the early planning stages follow.

1. The need for *some kind* of lateral bracing system. In some cases, because of the building form or size or the decision to use a particular structural material or system, the choice may be highly limited. In other situations there may be several options, with each having different required features (alignment of columns, incorporation of solid walls, etc.). The particular system to be used should be established early, although it may require considerable exploration and development of the options in order to make an informed decision.

2. Implications of architectural design decisions. When certain features are desired, it should be clearly understood that there are consequences in the form of problems with regard to seismic design. Some typical sit-

uations that commonly cause problems are the following:

General complexity and lack of symmetry in the building form.

Random arrangement of vertical elements (walls and columns), resulting in a haphazard framing system in general.

Lack of continuity in the horizontal structure due to openings, multiplane roofs, split-level floors, or open spaces within the building.

Building consisting of aggregates of multiple, semidetached units, requiring considerations for linking or separation for seismic interaction.

Special forms (curved walls, sloping floors, etc.) that limit the performance of the structure.

Large spans, heights, or wall openings that limit placement of structural elements and result in high concentrations of load.

Use of nonstructural materials and construction details that result in high vulnerability to damage caused by seismic movements.

3. Allowance for seismic design work. Consideration should be given to the time, cost, and scheduling for the seismic investigation and design development. This is most critical when the building is complex or when an extensive dynamic analysis is required. Sufficient time should be allowed for a preliminary investigation of possible alternatives for the lateral bracing system, since a shift to another system at late stages of the architectural design work will undoubtedly cause problems.

4. Design styles not developed with seismic effects in mind. In many situations popular architectural design styles or features are initially developed in areas where seismic effects are not of concern. When these are imported to regions with high risk of seismic activity, a mismatch often occurs.

Early European colonizers of Central and South America and the West Coast of North America learned this the hard way. The learning goes on.

2.7. EFFECTS OF BUILDING FORM

The form of a building has a great deal to do with the determination of the effects of seismic activity on the building. This chapter discusses various aspects of building form and the types of problem commonly experienced.

Most buildings are complex in form. They have plans defined by walls that are arranged in complex patterns. They have wings, porches, balconies, towers, and roof overhangs. They are divided vertically by multilevel floors. They have sloping roofs, arched roofs, and multiplane roofs. Walls are pierced by openings for doors and windows. Floors are pierced by stairways, elevators, ducts, and piping. Roofs are pierced by skylights, vent shafts, and chimneys. The dispersion of the building mass and the overall response of the building to seismic effects can thus be complicated; difficult to visualize, let alone to quantitatively evaluate.

Despite this typical complexity, investigation for seismic response may often be simplified by the fact that we deal mostly with those elements of the building that are directly involved in the resistance of lateral forces; what we refer to as the *lateral resistive system*. Thus most of the building construction, including parts of the structure that function strictly for resistance of gravity loads, may have only minimal involvement in seismic response. These nonstructural elements contribute to the load (generated by the building mass) and may offer damping effects to the structure's motion, but may not significantly contribute to the development of resistance to lateral force.

A discussion of the issues relating to building form must include consideration of two separate situations: the form of the

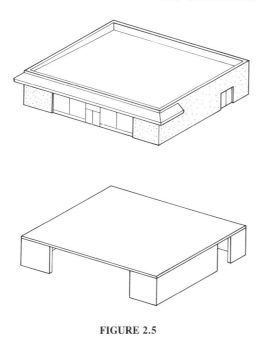

FIGURE 2.5

on the problems of lateral response, but it must be kept in mind that the architect must deal with all of these other concerns.

Development of a reasonable lateral resistive structural system within a building may be easy or difficult, and for some proposed plan arrangements may be next to impossible. Figure 2.6 shows a building plan in the upper figure for which the potentiality for development of shear walls in the north–south direction is quite reasonable but in the east–west direction is not so good as there is no possibility for shear walls on the south side. If the modification shown in the middle figure is acceptable, the building can be adequately braced by shear walls in both directions. If the open south wall is really essential, it may be possible to brace this wall by using a column and beam structure that is braced by trussing or by rigid connections, as shown in the lower figure.

building as a whole and the form of the lateral resistive system. Figure 2.5 shows a simple one-story building, with the general exterior form illustrated in the upper figure. The lower figure shows the same building with the parapet, canopy, window wall, and other elements removed, leaving the essential parts of the lateral resistive system. This system consists primarily of the horizontal roof surface and the portions of the vertical walls that function as shear walls. The whole building must be considered in determining the building mass for the lateral load, but the stripped down structure must be visualized in order to investigate the effects of lateral forces.

In developing building plans and the building form in general, architectural designers must give consideration to many issues. Seismic response has to take its place in line with the needs for functional interior spaces, control of traffic, creation of acoustic privacy, separation for security, energy efficiency, and general economic and technical feasibility. In this book we dwell primarily

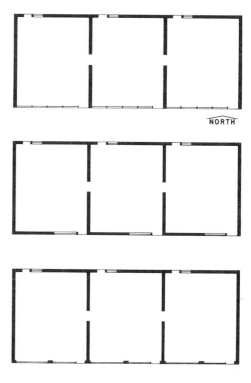

FIGURE 2.6

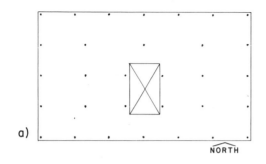

a)

NORTH

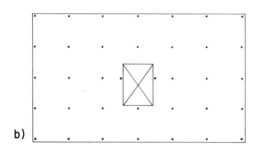

b)

FIGURE 2.7

building profiles shown in Figure 2.8*a*, *b*, and *c* represent a range of potential response with regard to the fundamental period of the building and the concerns for lateral deflection. The short, stiff building shown in (*a*) tends to absorb a larger jolt from an earthquake because of its quick response (short

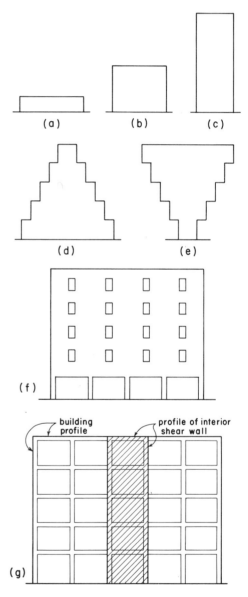

FIGURE 2.8

In the plan shown in Figure 2.7*a* the column layout results in a limited number of possible bents that may be developed as moment-resistive frames. In the north–south direction the interior columns are either offset from the exterior columns or the bent is interrupted by the floor opening; thus the two end bents are the only ones usable. In the east–west direction the large opening interrupts two of the three interior bents, leaving only three usable bents that are not disposed symmetrically in the plan. The modification shown in Figure 2.7*b* represents an improvement in lateral response, with six usable bents in the north–south direction and four symmetrically placed bents in the east–west direction. This plan, however, has more interior columns, smaller open spaces, and a reduced size for the opening—all of which may present some drawbacks for architectural reasons.

In addition to planning concerns the vertical massing of the building has various implications on its seismic response. The three period of natural vibration). The tall, slender building, on the other hand, responds slowly, dissipating some of the energy of the seismic action in its motion. However, the tall building may develop some multimodal response, a whiplash effect, or simply so much actual deflection that it may have problems of its own.

The overall inherent stability of a building may be implicit in its vertical massing or profile. The structure shown in Figure 2.8*d* has considerable potential for stability with regard to lateral forces, whereas that shown in Figure 2.8*e* is highly questionable. Of special concern is the situation in which abrupt change in stiffness occurs in the vertical massing. The structure shown in Figure 2.8*f* has an open form at its base, resulting in the so-called soft story. While this type of system may be designed adequately by the general requirements of the equivalent static force method, a true dynamic analysis will indicate serious problems, as borne out by some recent serious failures.

As with the building plan, consideration of the vertical massing must include concerns for the form of the lateral resistive system as well as the form of the whole building. The illustration in Figure 2.8*g* shows a building whose overall profile is quite stout. However, if the building is braced by a set of interior shear walls, as shown in the section, it is the profile of the shear walls that must be considered. In this case the shear wall is quite slender in profile.

Investigation of the seismic response of a complex building is, in the best of circumstances, a difficult problem. Anything done to simplify the investigation will not only make the analysis easier to perform but will tend to make the reliability of the results more certain. Thus, from a seismic design point of view, there is an advantage in obtaining some degree of symmetry in the building massing and in the disposition of the elements of the lateral resistive structure.

When symmetry does not exist, a building tends to experience severe twisting as well as the usual rocking back and forth. The twisting action often has its greatest effects on the joints between elements of the bracing system. Thorough investigation and careful detailing of these joints for construction are necessary for a successful design. The more complex the seismic response and the more complicated and unusual the details of the construction, the more difficult it becomes to assure a thorough and careful design.

Most buildings are not symmetrical, being sometimes on one axis, often not on any axis. However, real architectural symmetry is not necessarily the true issue in seismic response. Of critical concern is the alignment of the net effect of the building mass (or the centroid of the lateral force) with the center of stiffness of the lateral resistive system—most notably the center of stiffness of the vertical elements of the system. The more the eccentricity of the centroid of the lateral force from the center of stiffness of the lateral bracing system, the greater the twisting effect on the building.

Figure 2.9 shows an extreme example—the so-called *three-sided building*. In this situation the lack of resistive vertical elements on one side of the building requires that the opposite wall take all of the direct effect of the lateral force that is parallel to it. Assuming the centroid of the building mass to be approximately at the center of the plan, this results in a large eccentricity between the load and the resisting wall. The twisting action that results will be partly resisted by the two end walls that are at right angles to the

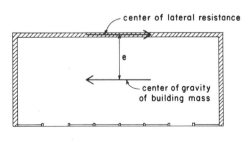

FIGURE 2.9

load, but the general effect on the building is highly undesirable. This type of structure is presently highly restricted for use in regions of high seismic risk.

When a building is not architecturally symmetrical, the lateral bracing system must either be adjusted so that its center of stiffness is close to the centroid of the mass or it must be designed for major twisting effects on the building. As the complexity of the building form increases, it may be necessary to consider the building to be multimassed.

Many buildings are multimassed rather than consisting of a single geometric form. The building shown in Figure 2.10 is multimassed, consisting of an L-shaped tower that is joined to an extended lower portion. Under lateral seismic movement the various parts of this building will have different responses. If the building structure is developed as a single system, the building movements will be very complex, with extreme twisting effects and considerable strain at the points of connection of the discrete parts of the mass.

If the elements of the tower of the building in Figure 2.10 are actually separated, as shown in Figure 2.11a or c, the independent movements of the separated elements will be different due to their difference in stiffness. It may be possible to permit these indepen-

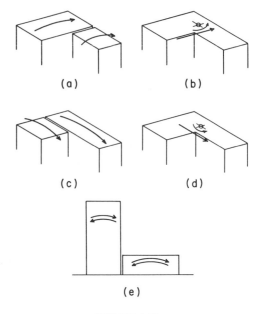

(a)   (b)

(c)   (d)

(e)

FIGURE 2.11

dent movements by providing structural connections that are detailed to tolerate the type and magnitude of the actual deformations. Thus the twisting effects on the building and the strain at the joints between the elements of the mass may be avoided.

There is also the potential for difference in response movements of the tower and the lower portion of the building, as shown in Figure 2.11e. Actual separation may be created at this connection of the masses to eliminate the need for investigation of the dynamic interaction of the separate parts. However, it may not be feasible or architecturally desirable to make the provisions necessary to achieve either of the types of separation described. The only other option is therefore to design for the twisting effects and the dynamic interactions that result from having a continuous, single structural system for the entire building. The advisability or feasibility of one option over the other is often difficult to establish and may require considerable study of alternate designs.

Figure 2.12a shows an L-shaped building in which the architectural separation of the

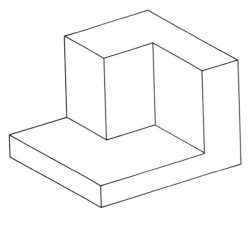

FIGURE 2.10

braced, it must be attached to one or the other of the larger elements for support, making for a quite complex study of actions at the connection of the masses.

When individual parts of multimassed buildings are joined, there are many potential problems, some of which were described in the preceding section. Figure 2.13 shows three types of action that must often be considered for such structures. When moving at the same time, as shown in Figure 2.13*a*, a problem for the separate masses becomes the actual dimension of the separation that must

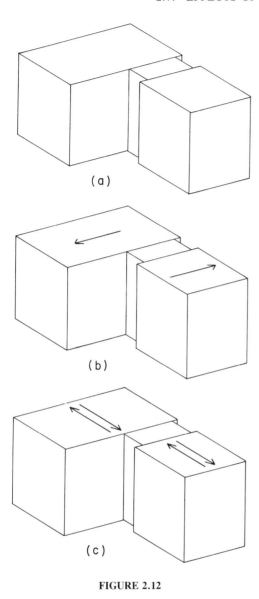

(a)

(b)

(c)

FIGURE 2.12

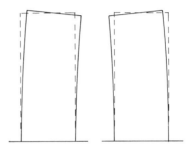

(a) differential deflection

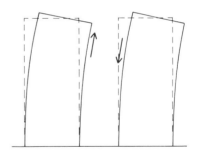

(b) vertical coupling shear

masses is accentuated. The linking element, although contiguous with the two parts, is unlikely to be capable of holding them together under seismic movements. If it cannot, there are two forms of differential movement that must be provided for, as shown in Figures 2.12*b* and *c*. In addition to providing for these movements, it is also necessary to consider the bracing of the linkage element. If it is not capable of being independently

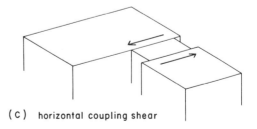

(c) horizontal coupling shear

FIGURE 2.13

be provided to prevent them from bumping each other (called *battering* or *hammering*). If they are not actually separated, their independent deflections may be a basis for consideration of the forces that must be considered in preventing them from being torn apart.

Another potential action of separately moving parts is that shown in Figure 2.13b. This involves a shearing action on the joint similar to that which occurs in laminated elements subjected to bending. For the vertically cantilevered elements shown, both the shear and lateral deflection effects vary from zero at the base to a maximum at the top. The taller the structure, the greater the actual dimension of the critical movements near the top.

A third type of action is the horizontal shearing effect illustrated in Figure 2.13c. This is probably the most common type of problem that must be dealt with, as it occurs frequently in one story structures, whereas the vertical shear and lateral deflection problems are usually severe only in taller structures.

Individual joined masses are sometimes so different in size or stiffness that the indi-

cated solution is to simply attach the smaller part to the larger and let it tag along. Such is the case for the buildings shown in Figures 2.14a and b in which the smaller lower portion and the narrow stair tower would be treated as attachments.

In some instances the tag along relationship may be a conditional one, as shown in Figure 2.14c, where the smaller element extends a considerable distance from the larger mass. In this situation the movement of the smaller part to and away from the larger may be adequately resisted by the attachment. However, some bracing would probably be required at the far end of the smaller part to assist resistance to movements parallel to the connection of the two parts.

The tag along technique is often used for stairs, chimneys, entries, and other elements that are part of a building, but are generally outside the main mass. It is also possible, of course, to consider the total structural separation of such elements in some cases.

Another classic problem of joined elements is that of coupled shear walls. These are shear walls that occur in sets in a single wall plane and are connected by the continuous construction of the wall. Figure 2.15

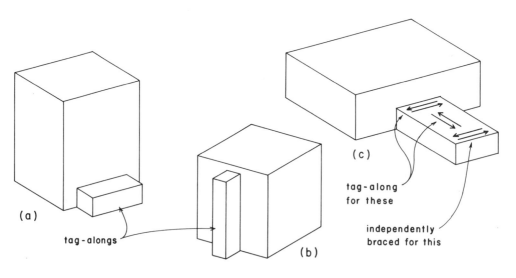

FIGURE 2.14

shear walls

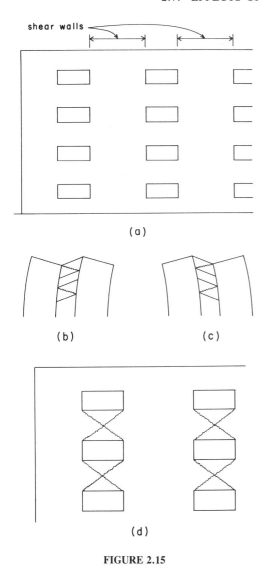

FIGURE 2.15

concrete, and stucco-surfaced buildings in regions of frequent seismic activity.

Forces applied to buildings must flow with some direct continuity through the elements of the structure, be transferred effectively from element to element, and eventually be resolved into the ground. Where there are interruptions in the normal flow of the forces, problems will occur. For example, in a multistory building the resolution of gravity forces requires a smooth, vertical path; thus columns and bearing walls must be stacked on top of each other. If a column is removed in a lower story, a major problem is created, requiring the use of a heavy transfer girder or other device to deal with the discontinuity.

A common type of discontinuity is that of openings in horizontal and vertical diaphragms. These can be a problem as a result of their location, size, or even shape. Figure 2.16 shows a horizontal diaphragm with an

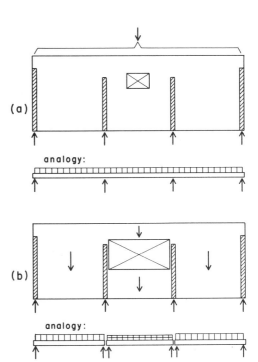

FIGURE 2.16

illustrates such a situation in a multistory building. The elements that serve to link such walls—in this example the spandrel panels beneath the windows—are wracked by the vertical shearing effect illustrated in Figure 2.13b. As the building rocks back and forth, this effect is rapidly reversed, developing the diagonal cracking shown in Figures 2.15b and c. This results in the X-shaped crack patterns shown in Figure 2.15d, which may be observed on the walls of many masonry,

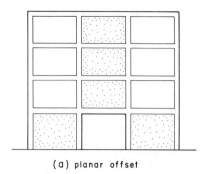

(a) planar offset

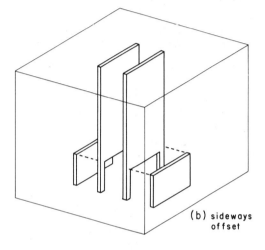

(b) sideways offset

FIGURE 2.17

opening. The diaphragm is braced by four shear walls, and if it is considered to be un-interrupted, it will distribute its load to the walls in the manner of a continuous beam. (See the discussion of flexibility of horizontal diaphragms in Section 5.1.) If the relative size of the opening is as shown in Figure 2.16*a*, this assumption is a reasonable one. What must be done to assure the integrity of the continuous diaphragm is to reinforce the edges and corners of the opening and to be sure that the net diaphragm width at the opening is adequate for the shear force.

If the opening in a horizontal diaphragm is as large as that shown in Figure 2.16*b*, it is generally not possible to maintain the continuity of the whole diaphragm. In the ex-

ample the best solution would be to consider the diaphragm as consisting of four individual parts, each resisting some portion of the total lateral force. For openings of sizes between the ones shown in Figure 2.16 judgment must be exercised as to the best course.

Another discontinuity that must sometimes be dealt with is that of the interrupted multistory shear wall. Figure 2.17 shows such a situation, with a wall that is not continuous down to its foundation. In this example it may be possible to utilize the horizontal structure at the second level to redistribute the horizontal shear force to other shear walls in the same plane. The overturn effect on the upper shear wall, however, cannot be so redirected, thus requiring that the columns at the ends of the shear wall continue down to the foundation.

It is sometimes possible to redistribute the shear force from an interrupted wall, as shown in Figure 2.17, with walls that are sidestepped rather than in the same vertical plane of the upper wall. Again, however, the overturn on the upper wall must be accommodated by continuing the structure at the ends of the wall down to the foundation.

Figure 2.18 shows an X-braced frame structure with a situation similar to that of the shear wall in Figure 2.17*a*. The individual panels of X-bracing are sufficiently similar in function to the individual panels of

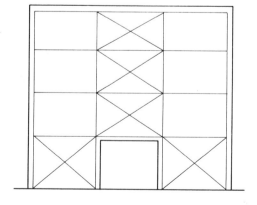

FIGURE 2.18

the shear wall to make the situation have the same general options and requirements for a solution.

Discontinuities are usually inevitable in multistory and multimassed buildings. They add to the usual problems of dissymmetry to create many difficult situations for analysis and design and require careful study for the proper assumptions of behavior and the special needs of the construction.

2.8 SPECIAL PROBLEMS

Vulnerable Elements

There are many commonly used elements of buildings that are especially vulnerable to damage due to earthquakes. Most of these are nonstructural, that is, not parts of the structural system for resistance of gravity or lateral loads. Because of their nonstructural character, they do not routinely receive thorough design study by the structural designer; thus in earthquake country they constitute major areas of vulnerability. Some typical situations are the following:

1. *Suspended Ceilings.* These are subject to horizontal movement. If not restrained at their edges, or hung with elements that resist horizontal movement, they will swing and bump other parts of the construction. Another common failure consists of the dropping of the ceiling due to downward acceleration if the supports are not resistive to a jolting action.

2. *Cantilevered Elements.* Balconies, canopies, parapets, and cornices should be designed for significant seismic force in a direction perpendicular to the cantilever. In most cases, codes provide criteria for consideration of these forces.

3. *Miscellaneous Suspended Objects.* Lighting fixtures, signs, HVAC equipment, loudspeakers, catwalks, and other items that are supported by hanging should be studied for the effects of pendulumlike movements. Supports should tolerate the movement or should be designed to restrain it.

4. *Piping.* Building movements during seismic activity can cause the rupture of piping that is installed in a conventional manner. In addition to the usual allowances for thermal expansion, provisions should be made for the flexing of the piping or for isolation from the structure that is sufficient to prevent any damage. This is obviously most critical for piping that is pressurized.

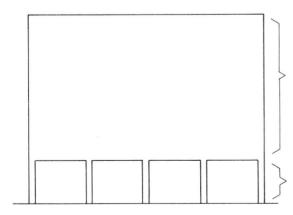

May be
· Solid wall
· Wall with few small windows
· Rigid frame with shorter story height or closer column spacing

Relatively flexible story

FIGURE 2.19. The soft story.

5. *Stiff, Weak Elements.* Any parts of the building construction that are stiff but not strong are usually vulnerable to damage. This includes window glazing, plastered surfaces, wall and floor tile (especially of ceramic or cast materials), and any masonry (especially veneers of brick, tile, precast concrete, or stone). Reduction of damage and of hazard to occupants requires careful study of installation details for attachment. In most cases extensive use of control joints is advised to permit movements without fractures.

The Soft Story

Any discontinuity that constitutes an abrupt change in the structure is usually a source of some exceptional distress. This is true for static load conditions as well, but is especially critical for dynamic loading conditions. Any abrupt increase or decrease in stiffness will result in some magnification of deformation and stress in a structure subjected to energy loading. Openings, notches, necking-down points, and other form variations produce these abrupt changes in either the horizontal or vertical structure. An especially critical situation is the so-called soft story, as shown in Figure 2.19.

The soft story could—and indeed sometimes does—occur at an upper level. However, it is more common at the ground-floor level between a rigid foundation system and some relatively much stiffer upper level system. The tall, open ground floor has both historical precedent and current popularity as an architectural feature. This is not always strictly a matter of design style, as it is often required for functional reasons.

Several failures of such structures in recent years have focused attention on their vulnerability and on the inadequacy of the equivalent static method for their design. The *UBC* presently disclaims the use of static methods for buildings with this sort of discontinuity (see Section 2312(e)3 of the 1985

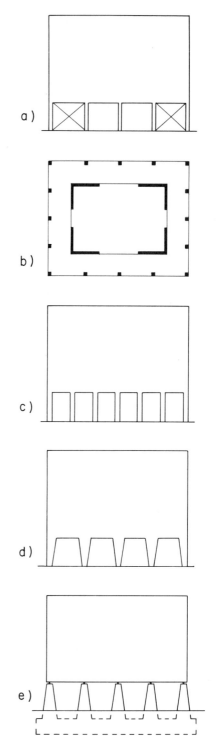

FIGURE 2.20. Some remedies for the soft story.

FIGURE 2.21. Transitional support elements used to raise the building free of the ground and create an open ground floor. (CN Park Place office building, Los Angeles. Langdon and Wilson, architects.)

edition of the *UBC*, reprinted in Appendix C). The soft story presents a strong case for a true dynamic analysis, or at the least a very conservative design with the static load method.

If the tall, relatively open ground floor is necessary, Figure 2.20 presents some possibilities for having this feature with a reduction of the soft-story effect. The methods shown consist of the following:

1. Bracing some of the open bays (Fig. 2.20*a*). If designed adequately for the forces, the braced frame (truss) should have a class of stiffness closer to a rigid shear wall, which is the usual upper structure in these situations. However, the soft story effect can also occur in rigid frames where the ''soft'' story is simply significantly less stiff.

2. Keeping the building plan periphery open while providing a rigidly braced interior (Fig. 2.20*b*).

3. Increasing the number and/or stiffness of the ground-floor columns for an all-rigid frame structure (Fig. 2.20*c*).

4. Using tapered or arched forms for the ground-floor columns to increase their stiffness (Fig. 2.20*d*).

5. Developing a rigid first story as an upward extension of a heavy foundation structure (Fig. 2.20*e*).

Figure 2.21 shows the exterior of a building with a first-story development that appears to be similar to that shown in Fig. 2.20*e*. However, the tapered first-story base elements could as well be primarily decorative (or used for recreation), and the true situation for the lateral bracing system be as that shown in Figure 2.20*b*.

The soft story is actually a method for providing critical damping or major energy absorption, which could be a *positive* factor in some situations. However, the major stress concentrations and deformations must be carefully provided for, and a true dynamic analysis is certainly indicated.

CHAPTER THREE

Wind Effects on Buildings

Wind is moving air. The air has a particular mass (density or weight) and moves in a particular direction at a particular velocity. It thus has kinetic energy of the form expressed as

$$E = \tfrac{1}{2} mv^2$$

When the moving fluid air encounters a stationary object, there are several effects that combine to exert a force on the object. The nature of this force, the many variables that affect it, and the translation of the effects into criteria for structural design are dealt with in this chapter.

3.1. WIND CONDITIONS

The wind condition of concern for building design is primarily that of a wind storm, specifically high-velocity, ground-level winds. These winds are generally associated with one of the following situations.

Tornadoes

Tornadoes occur with some frequency in the Midwest and occasionally in other parts of the United States. In coastal areas they are usually the result of ocean storms that wander ashore. Although the most violent effects are at the center of the storm, high-velocity winds in a large surrounding area often accompany these storms. In any given location the violent winds are usually short in duration as the tornado dissipates or passes through the area.

Hurricanes

Whereas tornadoes tend to be relatively short-lived (a few hours at most), hurricanes can sustain storm wind conditions for several days. Hurricanes occur with some frequency in the Atlantic and Gulf coastal areas of the United States. Although they originate and develop their greatest fury over the water, they often stray ashore and can move some distance inland before dissipating. As with tornadoes, the winds of highest velocity occur at the eye of the hurricane, but major winds can develop in large surrounding areas, often affecting coastal areas some distance inland even when the hurricane stays at sea.

Local Peculiar Wind Conditions

An example of wind conditions peculiar to one locality are the Santa Ana winds of Southern California. These winds are recurrent conditions caused by the peculiar geographic and climatological conditions of an area. They can sometimes result in local wind velocities of the level of those at the periphery of tornadoes and hurricanes and can be sustained for long periods.

Sustained Local Wind Conditions

Winds that occur at great elevations above sea level are an example of sustained local wind conditions. Such winds may possibly never reach the extremes of velocity of storm conditions, but they can require special consideration because of their enduring nature.

Local and regional meteorological histories are used to predict the degree of concern for or likelihood of critical wind conditions in a particular location. Building codes establish minimum design requirements for wind based on this experience and the statistical likelihood it implies. The map in the *UBC* Figure 4 (Appendix C) shows the variation of critical wind conditions in the United States.

Of primary concern in wind evaluation is the maximum velocity that is achieved by the wind. Maximum velocity usually refers to a sustained velocity and not to gust effects. A gust is essentially a pocket of higher velocity wind within the general moving fluid air mass. The resulting effect of a gust is that of a brief increase, or surge, in the wind velocity, usually of not more than 15% of the sustained velocity and for only a fraction of a second in duration. Because of both its

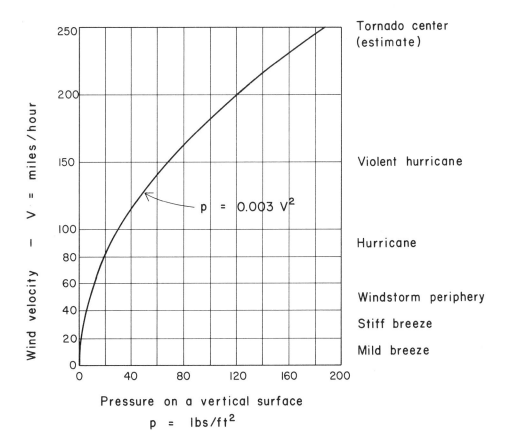

FIGURE 3.1. Relation of wind velocity to pressure on slab-sided buildings.

higher velocity and its slamming effect, the gust actually represents the most critical effect of the wind in most cases.

Winds are measured regularly at a large number of locations. The standard measurement is at 10 meters (approximately 33 ft) above the surrounding terrain, which provides a fixed reference with regard to the drag effects of the ground surface. The graph in Figure 3.1 shows the correlation between wind velocity and various wind conditions. The curve on the graph is a plot of the general equation used to relate wind velocity to equivalent static pressure on buildings, as discussed in the next section.

Although wind conditions are usually generalized for a given geographic area, they can vary considerably for specific sites because of the nature of the surrounding terrain, of landscaping, or of nearby structures. Each individual building design should consider the possibilities of these localized site conditions.

3.2. GENERAL WIND EFFECTS

The effects of wind on stationary objects in its path can be generalized as in the following discussions (see Fig. 3.2).

Direct Positive Pressure

Surfaces facing the wind and perpendicular to its path receive a direct impact effect from the moving mass of air, which generally produces the major portion of force on the object unless it is highly streamlined in form.

Aerodynamic Drag

Because the wind does not stop upon striking the object but flows around it like a fluid, there is a drag effect on surfaces that are parallel to the direction of the wind. These surfaces may also have inward or outward pressures exerted on them, but it is the drag

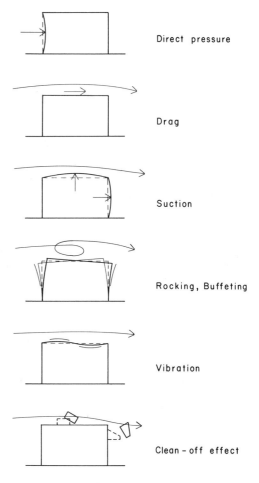

FIGURE 3.2. General effects of wind.

effect that adds to the general force on the object in the direction of the wind path.

Negative Pressure

On the leeward side of the object (opposite from the wind direction) there is usually a suction effect, consisting of pressure outward on the surface of the object. By comparison to the direction of pressure on the windward side, this is called *negative pressure*.

These three effects combine to produce a net force on the object in the direction of the wind that tends to move the object along with the wind. In addition to these there are other possible effects on the object that can occur due to the turbulence of the air or to the nature of the object. Some of them are as follows.

Rocking Effects. During wind storms, the wind velocity and its direction are seldom constant. Gusts and swirling winds are ordinary, so that an object in the wind path tends to be buffeted, rocked, flapped, and so on. Objects with loose parts, or with connections having some slack, or with highly flexible surfaces (such as fabric surfaces that are not taut) are most susceptible to these effects.

Harmonic Effects. Anyone who plays a wind instrument appreciates that wind can produce vibration, whistling, flutter, and so on. These effects can occur at low velocities as well as with wind storm conditions. This is a matter of some match between the velocity of the wind and the natural period of vibration of the object or of its parts.

Clean-Off Effect. The friction effect of the flowing air mass tends to smooth off the objects in its path. This fact is of particular concern to objects that protrude from the general mass of the building, such as canopies, parapets, chimneys, and signs.

The critical condition of individual parts or surfaces of an object may be caused by any one, or some combination, of the above effects. Damage can occur locally or be total with regard to the object. If the object is resting on the ground, it may be collapsed or may be slid, rolled over, or lifted from its position. Various aspects of the wind, of the object in the path of the wind, or of the surrounding environment determine the critical wind effects. With regard to the wind itself some considerations are the following:

The magnitude of sustained velocities.

The duration of high-level velocities.

The presence of gust effects, swirling, and so on.

The prevailing direction of the wind (if any).

With regard to objects in the path of the wind some considerations are the following:

The size of the object (relates to the relative effect of gusts, to variations of pressure above ground level, etc.).

The aerodynamic shape of the object (determines the critical nature of drag, suction, uplift, etc.).

The fundamental period of vibration of the object or of its parts.

The relative stiffness of surfaces, tightness of connections, and so on.

With regard to the environment, possible effects may result from the sheltering or funneling caused by ground forms, landscaping, or adjacent structures. These effects may result in an increase or reduction of the general wind effects or in turbulence to produce a very unsteady wind condition.

The actual behavior of an object during wind storm conditions can be found only by subjecting it to a real wind situation. Wind tunnel tests in the laboratory are also useful, and because we can create the tests more practically on demand, they have provided much of the background for data and procedures used in design.

3.3. CRITICAL WIND EFFECTS ON BUILDINGS

The major effects of wind on buildings can be generalized to some degree because we know a bracketed range of characteristics that cover the most common conditions. Some of the general assumptions made are as follows:

Most buildings are boxy or bulky in shape, resulting in typical aerodynamic response.

Most buildings present closed, fairly smooth surfaces to the wind.

Most buildings are fit snugly to the ground, presenting a particular situation for the drag effects of the ground surface.

Most buildings have relatively stiff structures, resulting in a fairly limited range of variation of the natural period of vibration of the structure.

These and other considerations allow for the simplification of wind investigation by permitting a number of variables to be eliminated or to be lumped into a few modifying constants. For unusual situations, such as elevated buildings, open structures, highly flexible structures, and unusual aerodynamic shapes, it may be advisable to do more thorough investigation, including the possible use of wind tunnel tests.

The primary effect of wind is visualized in the form of pressures normal to the building's exterior surfaces. The basis for this pressure begins with a conversion of the kinetic energy of the moving air mass into an equivalent static pressure using the basic formula

$$p = Cv^2$$

in which C is a constant accounting for the air mass, the units used, and a number of the assumptions previously described. With the wind in miles per hour (MPH) and the pressure in pounds per square foot (psf), the C value for the total wind effect on a simple box-shaped building is approximately 0.003, which is the value used in deriving the graph in Figure 3.1. It should be noted that this pressure does not represent the actual effect on a single building surface, but rather the *entire* effect of all surface pressures visualized as a single pressure on the windward side of the building.

Building codes provide data for establishing the critical wind velocity and for determining the design wind pressures for the investigation of wind effects on a particular building. Considerations involve the variables of the building size, shape, and degree of openness, of the sheltering effect of the surrounding terrain, and numerous concerns for special situations. A discussion of code criteria is given in Section 3.4.

The general effects of wind on stationary objects were described in the previous section. These effects are translated into building design criteria as explained in the following discussions.

Inward Pressure on Exterior Walls

Surfaces directly facing the wind are usually required to be designed for the full base pressure, although this is somewhat conservative, because the windward force usually accounts for only about 60% of the total force on the building. Designing for only part of the total force is, however, partly compensated for by the fact that the base pressures are not generally related to gust effects which tend to have less effect on the building as a whole and more effect on parts of the building.

Suction on Exterior Walls

Most codes also require suction on exterior walls to be the full base pressure, although the preceding comments about inward pressure apply here as well.

Pressure on Roof Surfaces

Depending on their actual form, as well as that of the building as a whole, nonvertical surfaces may be subjected to either inward or suction pressures because of wind. Actually such surfaces may experience both types of pressure as the wind shifts direction. Most codes require an uplift (suction) pressure equal to the full design pressure at the elevation of the roof level. Inward pressure is usually related to the actual angle of the surface as an inclination from the horizontal.

Overall Horizontal Force on the Building

Overall horizontal force is calculated as a horizontal pressure on the building silhouette, as previously described, with adjustments made for height above the ground. The lateral resistive structural system of the building is designed for this force.

Horizontal Sliding of the Building

In addition to the possible collapse of the lateral resistive system, there is the chance that the total horizontal force may slide the building off its foundations. For a tall building with fairly shallow foundations, this may also be a problem for the force transfer between the foundation and the ground. In both cases, the dead weight of the building generates a friction that helps to resist this force.

Overturn Effect

As with horizontal sliding, the dead weight tends to resist the overturn, or toppling, effect. In practice, the overturn effect is usually analyzed in terms of the overturn of individual vertical elements of the lateral resistive system rather than for the building as a whole.

Wind on Building Parts

The previously discussed clean-off effect is critical for elements that project from the general mass of the building. In some cases codes require for such elements a design pressure higher than the base pressure, so that gust effects as well as the clean-off problem are allowed for in the design.

Harmonic Effects

Design for vibration, flutter, whipping, multinodal swaying, and so on requires a dynamic analysis and cannot be accounted for when using the equivalent static load method. Stiffening, bracing, and tightening of elements in general may minimize the possibilities for such effects, but only a true dynamic analysis or a wind tunnel test can assure the adequacy of the structure to withstand these harmonic effects.

Effect of Openings

If the surface of a building is closed and resonably smooth, the wind will slip around it in a fluid flow. Openings or building forms that tend to cup the wind can greatly affect the total wind force on the building. It is difficult to account for these effects in a mathematical analysis, except in a very empirical manner. Cupping of the wind can be a major effect when the entire side of a building is open, for example. Garages, hangars, band shells, and other buildings of similar form must be designed for an increased force that can only be estimated unless a wind tunnel test is performed.

Torsional Effect

If a building is not symmetrical in terms of its wind silhouette, or if the lateral resistive system is not symmetrical within the building, the wind force may produce a twisting effect. This effect is the result of a misalignment of the centroid of the wind force and the centroid (called *center of stiffness*) of the lateral resistive system and will produce an added force on some of the elements of the structure.

Although there may be typical prevailing directions of wind in an area, the wind must be considered to be capable of blowing in any direction. Depending on the building shape and the arrangement of its structure, an analysis for wind from several possible directions may be required.

3.4. BUILDING CODE REQUIREMENTS FOR WIND

Model building codes such as the *UBC* (Ref. 1) and *BOCA* (Ref. 3) are not legally binding unless they are adopted by ordinances by some state, country, or city. Although smaller communities usually adopt one of the model codes, states, counties, and cities with large populations usually develop their own codes using one of the model codes as a basic reference. In the continental United States the *UBC* is generally used in the West, the Southern Building Code in the Southeast, and *BOCA* in the rest of the country.

Where wind is a major local problem, local codes are usually more extensive with regard to design requirements for wind. However, many codes still contain relatively simple criteria for wind design. One of the most up-to-date and complex standards for wind design is contained in the *American National Standard Minimum Design Loads for Buildings and Other Structures*, ANSI A58.1-1982, published by the American National Standards Institute in 1982 (Ref. 2).

Complete design for wind effects on buildings includes a large number of both architectural and structural concerns. Of primary concern for the work in this book are those requirements that directly affect the design of the lateral bracing system. The following is a discussion of some of the requirements for wind as taken from the 1985 edition of the *UBC* (Ref. 1), which is in general conformance with the material presented in the *ANSI* standard just mentioned. Reprints of some of the materials referred to are given in Appendix C.

Basic Wind Speed. This is the maximum wind speed (or velocity) to be used for specific locations. It is based on recorded wind histories and adjusted for some statistical likelihood of occurrence. For the continental United States the wind speeds are taken from *UBC*, Figure No. 4 (see the Appendix). As a reference point, the speeds are those recorded at the standard measuring position of 10 meters (approximately 33 ft) above the ground surface.

Exposure. This refers to the conditions of the terrain surrounding the building site. The *ANSI* standard (Ref. 2) describes four conditions (A, B, C, and D), although the *UBC* uses only two (B and C). Condition C refers to sites surrounded for a distance of one half mile or more by flat, open terrain. Condition B has buildings, forests, or ground surface irregularities 20 ft or more in height covering at least 20% of the area for a distance of 1 mile or more around the site.

Wind Stagnation Pressure (q_s). This is the basic reference equivalent static pressure based on the critical local wind speed. It is given in *UBC* Table No. 23-F (see the Appendix) and is based on the following formula as given in the *ANSI* standard:

$$q_s = 0.00256 V^2$$

Example: For a wind speed of 100 MPH

$$q_s = 0.00256 V^2 = 0.00256(100)^2$$

$$= 25.6 \text{ psf } [1.23 \text{ kPa}]$$

which is rounded off to 26 psf in the *UBC* table.

Design Wind Pressure. This is the equivalent static pressure to be applied normal to the exterior surfaces of the building and is determined from the formula

$$p = C_e C_q q_s I$$

(*UBC* formula 11-1, Section 2311)

in which p = design wind pressure in psf

C_e = combined height, exposure, and gust factor coefficient as given in *UBC* Table No. 23-G (see the Appendix)

C_q = pressure coefficient for the structure or portion of structure under consideration as given in *UBC* Table No. 23-H (see the appendix)

q_s = wind stagnation pressure at 30 ft given in *UBC* Table No. 23-F (see the Appendix)

I = importance factor

The importance factor is 1.15 for facilities considered to be essential for public health and safety (such as hospitals and government buildings) and buildings with 300 or more occupants. For all other buildings the factor is 1.0.

The design wind pressure may be positive (inward) or negative (outward, suction) on any given surface. Both the sign and the value for the pressure are given in the *UBC* table. Individual building surfaces, or parts thereof, must be designed for these pressures.

Design Methods. Two methods are described in the code for the application of the design wind pressures in the design of structures. For design of individual elements particular values are given in *UBC* Table 23-H for the C_q coefficient to be used in determining p. For the primary bracing system the C_q values and their use is to be as follows:

Method 1 (Normal Force Method). In this method wind pressures are assumed to act simultaneously normal to all exterior surfaces. This method is required to be used for gabled rigid frames and may be used for any structure.

Method 2 (Projected Area Method). In this method the total wind effect on the building is considered to be a combination of a single inward (positive) horizontal pressure acting on a vertical surface consisting of the projected building profile and an outward (negative, upward) pressure acting on the full projected area of the building in plan. This method may be used for any structure less than 200 ft in height, except for gabled rigid frames. This is the method generally employed by building codes in the past.

Uplift

Uplift may occur as a general effect, involving the entire roof or even the whole building. It may also occur as a local phenomenon such as that generated by the overturning moment on a single shear wall. In general, use of either design method will account for uplift concerns.

Overturning Moment

Most codes require that the ratio of the dead load resisting moment (called the restoring moment, stabilizing moment, etc.) to the overturning moment be 1.5 or greater. When this is not the case, uplift effects must be resisted by anchorage capable of developing the excess overturning moment. Overturning may be a critical problem for the whole building, as in the case of relatively tall and slender tower structures. For buildings braced by individual shear walls, trussed bents, and rigid frame bents, overturning is investigated for the individual bracing units. Method 2 is usually used for this investigation, except for very tall buildings and gabled rigid frames.

Drift

Drift refers to the horizontal deflection of the structure due to lateral loads. Code criteria for drift are usually limited to requirements for the drift of a single story (horizontal movement of one level with respect to the next above or below). The *UBC* does not provide limits for wind drift. Other standards give various recommendations, a common one being a limit of story drift to 0.005 times the story height (which is the *UBC* limit for seismic drift). For masonry structures wind drift is sometimes limited to 0.0025 times the story height. As in other situations involving structural deformations, effects on the building construction must be considered; thus the detailing of curtain walls or interior partitions may affect limits on drift. See further discussion of lateral drift in Section 9.2.

Combined Loads

Although wind effects are investigated as isolated phenomena, the actions of the structure must be considered simultaneously with other phenomena. The requirements for load combinations are given by most codes, although common sense will indicate the critical combinations in most cases. With the increasing use of load factors the combinations are further modified by applying different factors for the various types of loading, thus permitting individual control based on the reliability of data and investigation procedures and the relative significance to safety of the different load sources and effects. Required load combinations are described in Section 2303 of the *UBC*.

Special Problems. The general design criteria given in most codes are applicable to ordinary buildings. More thorough investigation is recommended (and sometimes required) for special circumstances such as the following:

Tall Buildings. These are critical with regard to their height dimension as well as the overall size and number of occupants inferred. Local wind speeds and unusual wind phenomena at upper elevations must be considered.

Flexible Structures. These may be affected in a variety of ways, including vibration or flutter as well as the simple magnitude of movements.

Unusual Shapes. Open structures, structures with large overhangs or other projections, and any building with a complex shape should be carefully studied for the special wind effects that may occur. Wind tunnel testing may be advised or even required by some codes.

Use of code criteria for various ordinary buildings is illustrated in the design examples in Chapter 6.

3.5. GENERAL DESIGN CONSIDERATIONS FOR WIND

The relative importance of design for wind as an influence on the general building design varies greatly among buildings. The location of the building is a major consideration, the basic design pressure varying by a factor of 2.4 from the lowest wind area to the highest on the *UBC* map. Other important variations include the dead weight of the construction, the height of the building, the type of structural system (especially for lateral load resistance), the aerodynamic shape of the building and its exposed parts, and the existence of large openings, recessed portions of the surface, and so on.

The following is a discussion of some general considerations of design of buildings for wind effects. Any of these factors may be more or less critical in specific situations.

Influence of Dead Load

Dead load of the building construction is generally an advantage in wind design, because it is a stabilizing factor in resisting uplift, overturn, and sliding and tends to reduce the incidence of vibration and flutter. However, the stresses that result from various load combinations, all of which include dead load, may offset these gains when the dead load is excessive.

Anchorage for Uplift, Sliding, and Overturn

Ordinary connections between parts of the building may provide adequately for various transfers of wind force. In some cases, such as with lightweight elements, wind anchorage may be a major consideration. In most design cases the adequacy of ordinary construction details is considered first and extraordinary measures are used only when required. Various situations of anchorage are illustrated in the examples in Chapter 6.

Critical Shape Considerations

Various aspects of the building form can cause increase or reduction in wind effects. Although it is seldom as critical in building design as it is for racing cars or aircraft, streamlining can improve the relative efficiency of the building in wind resistance. Some potential critical situations, as shown in Figure 3.3, are as follows:

1. Flat versus curved forms. Buildings with rounded forms, rather than rectangular forms with flat surfaces, offer less wind resistance.
2. Tall buildings that are short in horizontal dimension are more critical for overturn and possibly for the total horizontal deflection at their tops.
3. Open-sided buildings or buildings with forms that cup the wind tend to catch the wind, resulting in more wind force than that assumed for the general design pressures. Open structures must also be investigated for major outward force on internal surfaces.
4. Projections from the building. Tall parapets, solid railings, cantilevered balcon-

ies and canopies, wide overhangs, and freestanding exterior walls catch considerable wind and add to the overall drag effect on the building. Signs, chimneys, antennae, penthouses, and equipment on the roof of a building are also critical for the clean-off effect discussed previously.

Relative Stiffness of Structural Elements

In most buildings the lateral resistive structure consists of two basic elements: the horizontal distributing elements and the vertical cantilevered or braced frame elements. The manner in which the horizontal elements distribute forces and the manner in which the vertical elements share forces are critical considerations in wind analysis. The relative stiffness of individual elements is the major property that affects these relationships. The various situations that occur are discussed in Chapter 5 and illustrated in the examples in Chapter 6.

Stiffness of Nonstructural Elements

When the vertical elements of the lateral resistive system are relatively flexible, as with rigid frames and wood shear walls that are short in plan length, there may be considerable lateral force transferred to nonstructural elements of the building construction. Wall finishes of masonry veneer, plaster, or drywall can produce relatively rigid planes whose stiffnesses exceed those of the structures over which they are placed. If this is the case, the finish material may take the load initially, with the structure going to work only when the finish fails. This result is not entirely a matter of relative stiffness, however, because the load propagation through the building also depends on the attachments between elements of the construction. This problem should be considered carefully when developing the details of the building construction.

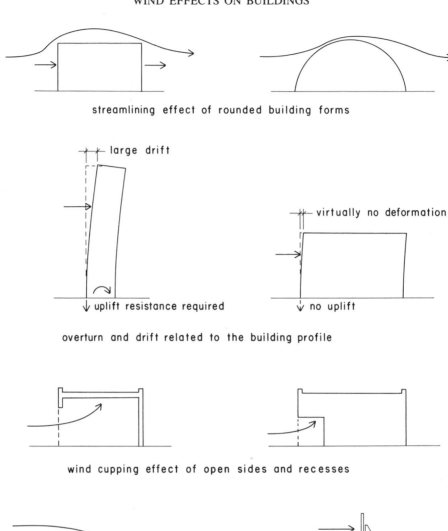

streamlining effect of rounded building forms

large drift

virtually no deformation

uplift resistance required   no uplift

overturn and drift related to the building profile

wind cupping effect of open sides and recesses

increased force on projecting elements

FIGURE 3.3.   Wind effects related to building form.

Allowance for Movement of the Structure

All structures deform when loaded. The actual dimension of movement may be insig-

nificant, as in the case of a poured-concrete shear wall, or it may be considerable, as in the case of a slender steel rigid frame. The effect of these movements on other elements of the building construction must be considered. The case of transfer of load to nonstructural finish elements, as just discussed, is one example of this problem. Another critical example is that of windows and doors. Glazing must be installed so as to allow for some movement of the glass with respect to the frame. The frame must be installed so as to allow for some movement of the structure of the building without load being transferred to the window frame.

All these considerations should be kept in mind in developing the general design of the building. If the building form and detail are determined and the choice of materials made before any thought is given to structural problems, it is not likely that an intelligent design will result. This is not to suggest that structural concerns are the most important concerns in building design but merely that they should not be relegated to afterthoughts.

CHAPTER FOUR

Earthquake Effects on Buildings

Earthquakes are essentially vibrations of the earth's crust caused by subterranean ground faults. They occur several times a day in various parts of the world, although only a few each year are of sufficient magnitude to cause significant damage to buildings. Major earthquakes occur most frequently in particular areas of the earth's surface that are called *zones of high probability*. However, it is theoretically possible to have a major earthquake anywhere on the earth at some time.

During an earthquake the ground surface moves in all directions. The most damaging effects on structures are generally the movements in a direction parallel to the ground surface (that is, horizontally) because of the fact that structures are routinely designed for vertical gravity loads. Thus, for design purposes the major effect of an earthquake is usually considered in terms of horizontal force similar to the effect of wind.

A general study of earthquakes includes consideration of the nature of ground faults, the propagation of shock waves through the earth mass, the specific nature of recorded major quakes, and so on. We do not present here a general discussion of earthquakes but concentrate on their influence on the design of structures for buildings. Some of the references following Chapter 9 may be used for a study of the general nature of earthquakes, and the reader is urged to study these if lacking such a background of knowledge.

4.1. CHARACTERISTICS OF EARTHQUAKES

Following a major earthquake, it is usually possible to retrace its complete history through the recorded seismic shocks over an extended period. This period may cover several weeks, or even years, and the record will usually show several shocks preceding and following the major one. Some of the minor shocks may be of significant magnitude themselves, as well as being the foreshocks and aftershocks of the major quake.

A major earthquake is usually rather short in duration, often lasting only a few seconds and seldom more than a minute or so. During the general quake, there are usually one or more major peaks of magnitude of motion. These peaks represent the maximum effect of the quake. Although the intensity of the quake is measured in terms of the energy release at the location of the ground fault, called the *epicenter*, the critical effect on a given structure is determined by the ground movements at the location of the structure. The extent of these movements is affected mostly by the distance of the structure from the epicenter, but they are also influenced by the geological conditions directly beneath the structure and by the nature of the entire earth mass between the epicenter and the structure.

Modern recording equipment and prac-

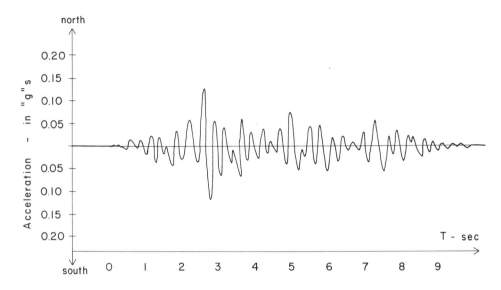

FIGURE 4.1. Characteristic form of ground acceleration graph for an earthquake.

tices provide us with representations of the ground movements at various locations, thus allowing us to simulate the effects of major earthquakes. Figure 4.1 shows the typical form of the graphic representation of one particular aspect of motion of the ground as recorded or as interpreted from the recordings for an earthquake. In this example the graph is plotted in terms of the acceleration of the ground in one horizontal direction as a function of elapsed time. For use in physical tests in laboratories or in computer modeling, records of actual quakes may be "played back" on structures in order to analyze their responses.

These playbacks are used in research and in the design of some major structures to develop criteria for design of lateral resistive systems. Most building design work, however, is done with criteria and procedures that have been evolved through a combination of practical experience, theoretical studies, and some empirical relationships derived from research and testing. The results of the current collective knowledge are put forth in the form of recommended design procedures

and criteria that are incorporated into the building codes.

Although it may seem like a gruesome way to achieve it, we advance our level of competency in design every time there is a major earthquake that results in some major structural damage to buildings. Engineering societies and other groups routinely send investigating teams to the sites of major quakes to report on the effects on buildings in the area. Of particular interest are the effects on recently built structures, because these buildings are in effect full-scale tests of the validity of our most recent design techniques. Each new edition of the building codes usually reflects some of the results of this cumulative growth of knowledge culled from the latest disasters.

4.2. GENERAL EFFECTS OF EARTHQUAKES

The ground movements caused by earthquakes can have several types of damaging effects. Some of the major effects are:

Direct Movement of Structures. Direct movement is the motion of the structure caused by its attachment to the ground. The two primary effects of this motion are a general destabilizing effect due to the shaking and to the impelling force caused by the inertia of the structure's mass.

Ground Surface Faults. Surface faults may consist of cracks, vertical shifts, general settlement of an area, landslides, and so on.

Tidal Waves. The ground movements can set up large waves on the surface of bodies of water that can cause major damage to shoreline areas.

Flooding, Fires, Gas Explosions, and so on. Ground faults or movements may cause damage to dams, reservoirs, river banks, buried pipelines, and so on, which may result in various forms of disaster.

Although all these possible effects are of concern, we deal in this book only with the first effect—the direct motion of structures. Concern for this effect motivates us to provide for some degree of dynamic stability (general resistance to shaking) and some quantified resistance to energy loading of the structure.

The force effect caused by motion is gen-

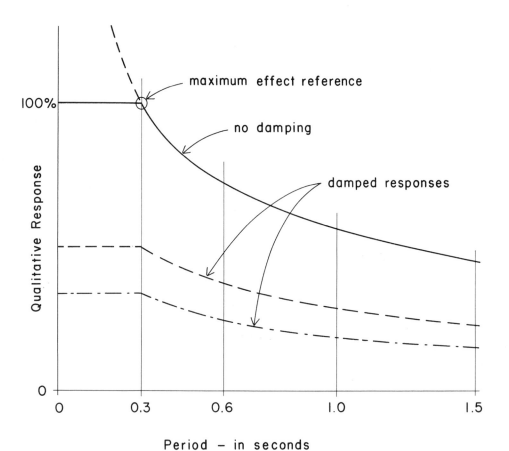

FIGURE 4.2. Spectrum response graph.

erally directly proportional to the dead weight of the structure—or, more precisely, to the dead weight borne by the structure. This weight also partly determines the character of dynamic response of the structure. The other major influences on the structure's response are its fundamental period of vibration and its efficiency in energy absorption. The vibration period is basically determined by the mass, the stiffness, and the size of the structure. Energy efficiency is determined by the elasticity of the structure and by various factors such as the stiffness of supports, the number of independently moving parts, and the rigidity of connections.

A relationship of major concern is that which occurs between the period of the structure and that of the earthquake. Figure 4.2 shows a set of curves, called *spectrum curves*, that represent this relationship as derived from a large number of earthquake "playbacks" on structures with different periods. The upper curve represents the major effect on a structure with no damping. Damping results in a lowering of the magnitude of the effects, but a general adherence to the basic form of the response remains.

The general interpretation of the spectrum effect is that the eqrthquake has its major direct force effect on buildings with short periods. These tend to be buildings with stiff lateral resistive systems, such as shear walls

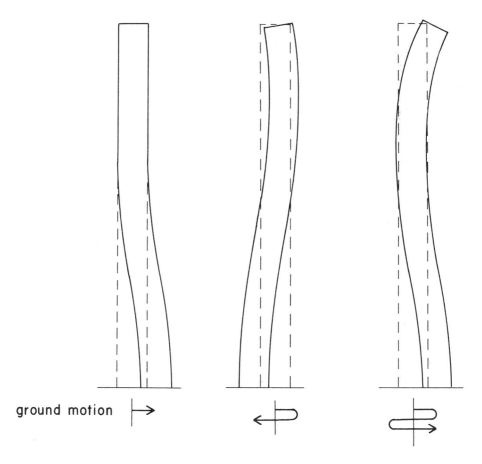

ground motion

FIGURE 4.3. Earthquake motion of a tall building.

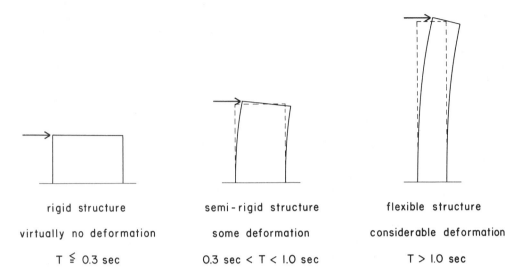

rigid structure

virtually no deformation

T ≦ 0.3 sec

semi-rigid structure

some deformation

0.3 sec < T < 1.0 sec

flexible structure

considerable deformation

T > 1.0 sec

FIGURE 4.4. Seismic response of buildings.

and X-braced frames, and buildings that are small in size and/or squat in profile.

For very large, flexible structures, such as tall towers and high-rise buildings, the fundamental period may be so long that the structure develops a whiplash effect, with different parts of the structure moving in opposite directions at the same time, as shown in Figure 4.3. Analysis for this behavior requires the use of dynamic methods that are beyond the scope of this book. The three general cases of structural response are illustrated by those shown in Figure 4.4. Referring to the spectrum curves, for buildings with a period below that representing the upper cutoff of the curves (approximately 0.3 sec), the response is that of a rigid structure with virtually no flexing. For buildings with a period slightly higher, there is some reduction in the force effect caused by the slight ''giving'' of the building and its using up some of the energy of the motion-induced force in its own motion. As the building period increases, the behavior approaches that of the slender tower, as shown in Figure 4.3.

In addition to the movement of the struc-

ture as a whole, there are independent movements of individual parts. These each have their own periods of vibration, and the total motion occurring in the structure can thus be quite complex if it is composed of a number of relatively flexible parts.

4.3. EARTHQUAKE EFFECTS ON BUILDINGS

The principal concern in structural design for earthquake forces is for the laterally resistive system of the building. In most buildings this system consists of some combination of horizontally distributing elements (usually roof and floor diaphragms) and vertical bracing elements (shear walls, rigid frames, trussed bents, etc.). Failure of any part of this system, or of connections between the parts, can result in major damage to the building, including the possibility of total collapse.

It is well to remember, however, that an earthquake shakes the whole building. If the building is to remain completely intact, the potential movement of all its parts must be considered. The survival of the structural system is a limited accomplishment if suspended ceilings fall, windows shatter, plumbing pipes burst, and elevators are derailed.

A major design consideration is that of tying the building together so that it is quite literally not shaken apart. With regard to the structure, this means that the various separate elements must be positively secured to one another. The detailing of construction connections is a major part of the structural design for earthquake resistance.

In some cases it is desirable to allow for some degree of independent motion of parts of the building. This is especially critical in situations where a secure attachment between the structure and various nonstructural elements, such as window glazing, can result in undesired transfer of force to the nonstructural elements. In these cases use must be made of connecting materials and details that allow for the holding of the elements in place while still permitting relative independence of motion.

When the building form is complex, various parts of the building may tend to move differently, which can produce critical stresses at the points of connection between the parts of the building. The best solution to this sometimes is to provide connections (or actually in some cases nonconnections) that allow for some degree of independent movement of the parts. This type of connection is called a *seismic separation joint*, and its various problems are discussed in Section 5.8.

Except for the calculation and distribution of the loads, the design for lateral loads from earthquakes is generally similar to that for the horizontal forces that result from wind. In some cases the code requirements are the same for the two loading conditions. There are many special requirements for seismic design in the *UBC*, however, and the discussion in the next section, together with the examples in Chapter 6, deal with the use of the code for analysis and design for earthquake effects.

4.4. BUILDING CODE REQUIREMENTS FOR EARTHQUAKES

The following is a discussion of the various requirements of the 1985 edition of the *UBC* for seismic design. The code for seismic design is usually quite up to date, a new edition being published every three years. The main body of material on seismic design is in Section 2312. We begin with a discussion of this section and proceed to a discussion of some materials to be found in other sections of the code. See Appendix C for reprints of the code.

General Design Requirements

In the beginning of this section are definitions of various terms and symbols used in the code. Reference should be made to this portion whenever any term or symbol is not clear to the reader.

The basic formula for determination of the lateral load on the structure is *UBC* formula 12-1:

$$V = ZIKCSW$$

in which:

Z varies from $\frac{3}{16}$ to 1, depending on the seismic zone as identified in the maps in Figures 1, 2, and 3 in the *UBC*.

I is a factor relating to the occupancy or use of the building, as given in *UBC* Table 23-K.

K is based on the type of lateral resistive

structural system and is given in *UBC* Table 23-I.

C is a factor empirically derived from the relationship of the building period to the average earthquake effect.

S is a factor that accounts for the effect of local ground conditions, which may dampen or amplify the shock.

W is the dead weight of the building.

C is determined from *UBC* formula 12-2 as

$$C = \frac{1}{15\sqrt{T}}$$

in which *T* is the fundamental period of the building in seconds.

In the words of the code, *T* is to be established by a "properly substantiated analysis." A recommended formula for this determination is given in *UBC* formula 12-3, which incorporates considerations of the seismic load distribution and the deformation characteristics of the structure. This is a somewhat complex analysis, so the code permits alternative determinations by the simpler formulas 12-3A and 12-3B.

Formula 12-3A expresses *T* as a function of the height of the structure and its depth in the direction of the lateral load.

$$T = \frac{0.05h_n}{\sqrt{D}}$$

Formula 12-3B expresses *T* simply as a function of the number of stories of the structure.

$$T = 0.10N$$

Formula 12-3B is to be used only for buildings in which the lateral resistive structure consists of a ductile rigid frame.

The *UBC* stipulates that the value of *C* need not exceed 0.12. Entering this value in the formula for *C*, we can derive a lower limit for *T*. Thus

If $$C = \frac{1}{15\sqrt{T}} = 0.12$$

Then

$$T = \left[\frac{1}{15(0.12)}\right]^2 = 0.309 \text{ sec}$$

Figure 4.5 shows a plot of *C* as a function of *T* using *UBC* formula 12-2. The form may be seen to be that of the typical spectrum curve. The maximum value for *C* is seen to correspond to the derived value of 0.309 sec for *T*. Below the graph are shown some interpretations of *UBC* formulas 12-3A and 12-3B that relate to the values for *T* in the graph.

Calculation of the *S* factor requires a determination of the fundamental period of the site (T_s) as well as of the structure. Determining T_s requires rather extensive geological information of the site conditions. In the absence of this information, the *UBC* permits the use of a maximum value for the product of *C* and *S* of 0.14. Because the code also requires a minimum value for *S* of 1.0, if the maximum value of *C* of 0.12 is used, the bracketed range for the product of *C* and *S* is between 0.12 and 0.14. The net result of this is that, unless the building project cost is high, the true *C* value is less than 0.12, or if the necessary geological information is available from previous studies in the immediate vicinity, the maximum *CS* value of 0.14 is used for most designs.

The use of the *S* factor is a fairly recent addition to the code, and there is some controversy regarding its validity as a requirement for all structures. In time the use of this factor may be more rationally developed in the code criteria so as not to amount to a de facto general increase in the required lateral load.

Subsection 2312(e) deals with the distri-

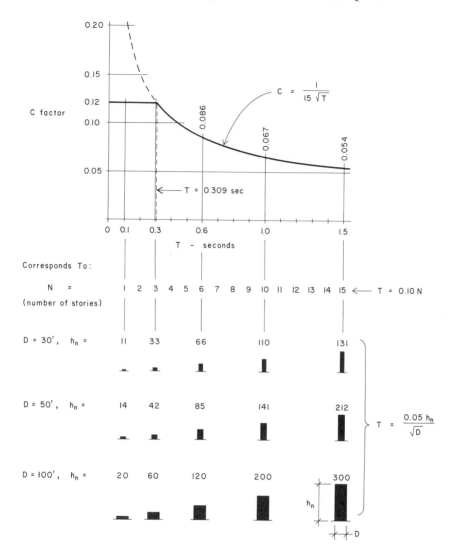

FIGURE 4.5. Relation of C and T factors.

bution of seismic loads on the structure. Formula 12-5 requires that the total load on the structure be

$$V = F_t + \sum_{i=1}^{n} F_i$$

The summation portion of this formula consists of the loads as normally calculated and applied at the various levels of the struc-

ture. F_t is an added force that must be applied at the top of the structure as well as being included in the total, and it is found using formula 12-6.

$$F_t = 0.07\,TV$$

The maximum required value for F_t is $0.25V$ and F_t may be considered to be zero where T is 0.7 sec or less. As shown in Figure 4.5, a T value this high generally occurs only with relatively tall buildings.

The value of the lateral shear force at each level of a multilevel structure (F_x) is determined from *UBC* formula 12-7. The use of this formula for the analysis of multistory structures is illustrated in the examples in Chapter 6.

The code formulas are generally applicable only to buildings that are reasonably simple in shape and have little change in their basic structural systems or their plans from top to bottom. Changes in these characteristics can result in behaviors more complex than those assumed for the general formulas and their limits. Subsection 2312(e)3 of the *UBC* requires that these more complex structures be analyzed by dynamic methods, rather than by the simpler equivalent static load method. An exception is made in subsection 2312(e)2 for setbacks of less than 25% in multistory buildings.

Subsection 2312(e)5 requires that the structure be analyzed for torsion when the center of rigidity of the structure does not coincide with the centroid of the load. Even when this eccentricity is not present, the code requires design for a minimum assumed eccentricity of 5% of the maximum plan dimension of the building when horizontal diaphragms are used to distribute the shear.

Overturning of the building or the structure is provided for in subsection 2312(f). When the lateral resistive system has a number of isolated elements (such as individual shear walls), the overturn effect is distributed to them in the same manner as for the distribution of the lateral shear forces.

Subsection 2312(g) provides that parts of the structure be designed for individual lateral forces that result from the parts' own weight. This force is calculated from formula 12-8 as

$$F_p = ZIC_pW_p$$

The C_p factor in this equation replaces the C, S, and K factors as used in the total load

for the building in formula 12-1. Values for C_p are given in *UBC* Table 23-J for various types of elements and situations.

Subsection 2312(h) limits the relative deflection of one story with respect to another (called the *drift*) to 0.5% of the story height, unless an analysis can demonstrate that more deflection is tolerable. A multiplying factor of $1/K$ must be used for the deflection calculation when K is less than 1 for the structure.

Subsection 2312(j) contains a number of requirements for the design of specific structural systems and elements. Reference is made to these requirements in the examples in Chapter 6.

Subsection 2312(k) defines essential facilities as they are listed in Table 23-K for establishment of the I factor in the lateral load formula 12-1.

Lateral Load Requirements in Other Chapters

The following is a summary of some of the requirements for lateral load design to be found in other portions of the *UBC*. In some cases these requirements apply to both wind and seismic loads.

1. *Stress Increase*: Section 2303(d). This section contains the provision for a one third increase in allowable stresses when load combinations include wind or seismic force.

2. *Load Combinations:* Section 2303(f). The highly remote possibility of a simultaneous earthquake and wind storm loading is excluded by this section.

3. *Anchorage of Masonry and Concrete Walls:* Section 2310. This section requires that the connections of masonry and concrete walls to roofs and floors that provide lateral support for the walls be designed for a minimum horizontal load of 200 lb/ft.

4. *Increase of Force on Masonry Shear*

Walls: Section 2407(h)4F(i). The third footnote to this table requires that the seismic force on reinforced masonry shear walls be increased by 50% over that required by Section 2312 when investigating shear stress in the wall.

5 *Wood Diaphragms*: Section 2513. This is an extensive section with data and requirements for plywood and board-sheathed diaphragms.

6. *Fiberboard-Sheathed Diaphragms*: Section 2514. This is a special section with design requirements for vertical diaphragms of fiberboard on a wood frame. The fiberboard referred to must meet the requirements of one of the *UBC* standards. Allowable loads for these diaphragms are given in Table 25-P.

7. *Bracing of Stud Walls*: Section 2517(g)3. This section requires that every exterior wall and main interior wall be braced at or near its ends and at least every 25 ft throughout its length. The approved methods of bracing include diagonal, let-in braces, diagonal board sheathing, plywood sheathing, fiberboard sheathing, gypsum sheathing, particleboard sheathing, gypsum drywall, and cement plaster. Reference is made to various code tables for the load capacities of these various constructions. Although all these wall constructions produce potential shear walls, the details for anchorage and load transfer must be developed in order to use them.

8. *Maximum Diaphragm Dimension Ratios for Wood Diaphragms*: Table 25-I. This table gives the limits for the span-to-width ratios of simple-span horizontal diaphragms and the height-to-width ratios for vertical diaphragms with plywood or diagonal board sheathing.

9. *Allowable Loads on Horizontal Plywood Diaphragms*: Table 25-J-1 gives the allowable shear load per foot of width for horizontal plywood diaphragms. Variables include the type and

thickness of plywood, size and spacing of nails, and details of the framing and panel layout. Table 25-J-2 gives values for particleboard diaphragms.

10. *Allowable Loads on Plywood Shear Walls*: Tables 25-K-1 and 25-K-2. These tables are similar to those for horizontal diaphragms, giving similar information for shear walls consisting of light wood framing with covering of plywood and particleboard.

11. *Minimum Nailing Requirements*: Table 25-Q. This table gives minimum nailing requirements for the various elements of light wood frame construction. Reference should be made to this table when developing the details for structural connections to assure that calculated nailing is not used when it falls below the requirements of this table.

12. *Concrete Rigid Frames*: Sections 2625 and 2626. These sections give the requirements for ductile frames of reinforced concrete.

13. *Concrete Shear Walls and Trussed Frames*: Section 2627. This section gives requirements for concrete shear walls and ''braced frames'' (trussed frames, as defined by *UBC* 2312.)

14. *Steel Rigid Frames*: Sections 2722 and 2723. These sections give the requirements for steel rigid frames used to resist seismic load.

15. *Wood-Framed Walls with Miscellaneous Sheathing*: Section 4713 and Table 47-I. This material gives requirements and data for woodframed shear walls with various materials other than plywood, diagonal boards, or fiberboard.

Although the *UBC* is reasonably well organized and indexed, it takes some time to gain a familiarity with all the material that is pertinent to structural design for wind and earthquakes. The use of much of the material just described is illustrated in the examples in

Chapter 6, but not all possible situations can be covered in a limited number of examples.

4.5. GENERAL DESIGN CONSIDERATIONS FOR EARTHQUAKE FORCES

The influence of earthquake considerations on the design of building structures tends to be the greatest in the zones of highest probability of quakes. This fact is directly reflected in the *UBC* by the *Z* factor, which varies from 3/16 to 1, or by a ratio of more than 5 to 1. As a result, wind factors often dominate the design in the zones of lower seismic probability.

A number of general considerations in the design of lateral resistive systems were discussed in Chapter 2. Most of these also apply to seismic design. Some additional considerations are included in the following discussion.

Influence of Dead Load

Dead load is in general a disadvantage in earthquakes, because the lateral force is directly proportional to it. Care should be exercised in developing the construction details and in choosing materials for the building in order to avoid creating unnecessary dead load, especially at upper levels in the building. Dead load is useful for overturn resistance and is a necessity for the foundations that must anchor the building.

Advantage of Simple Form and Symmetry

Buildings with relatively simple forms and with some degree of symmetry usually have the lowest requirements for elaborate or extensive bracing or for complex connections for lateral loads. Design of plan layouts and of the building form in general should be done with a clear understanding of the ram-

ifications in terms of structural requirements when wind or seismic forces are high. When complex form is deemed necessary, the structural cost must be acknowledged.

Following Through with Load Transfers

It is critical in design for lateral loads that the force paths be complete. Forces must travel from their points of origin through the whole system and into the ground. Design of the connections between elements and of the necessary drag struts, collectors, chords, blocking, hold downs, and so on is highly important to the integrity of the whole lateral resistive system. The ability to visualize the load paths and a reasonable understanding of building construction details and processes are prerequisites to this design work.

Use of Positive Connections

Earthquake forces often represent the most severe demands on connections because of their dynamic, shaking effects. Many means of connection that may be adequate for static force resistance fail under the jarring, loosening effects of earthquakes. Failures of a number of recently built buildings and other structures in earthquakes have been due to connection failures, even though the structures were designed in accordance with current code requirements and accepted practices. Increasing attention is being paid to this problem in the development of recommended details for building construction.

Determination of Lateral Loads. For the equivalent static load method, the determination of lateral loads consists of the following:

1. *Visualization of the Loading Pattern.* This consists of determining the manner in which the mass of various parts of the buildings become horizontal forces that are applied to the lateral resistive

structure. This varies with the form of the building and with the type and disposition of the structure.

2. *Determination of the Building Mass.* This is a matter of figuring out how much the various parts weigh, and how they aggregate as combined quantities for the loading analysis. (Example: The total mass that constitutes the lateral load applied to the roof diaphragm.)

3. *Conversion of Mass to Force.* Whether for the load on a single element or the total base shear for the building, this is a matter of using the code formulas with the various appropriate modifying factors.

4. *Redistribution (if any) of Forces.* This refers primarily to the adjustments for multistory buildings, as described in Section 2312(e) of the 1982 edition of the *UBC* (see Appendix C).

5. *Determination of Design Values for Individual Elements.* Once the load magnitudes and their patterns of application are found, this is a matter of analyzing the behavior of the particular structure— box, truss, frame, and so on.

Procedures for various types of structures are illustrated in the examples in Chapter 6. Data for the determination of the building weight are provided in Appendix E.

Calculation of Deformations. There are a few situations in seismic design in which determination of structural deformations must be made. In some cases the actual dimension of the movement is required, in other cases it is mostly a matter of establishing relative stiffness. Some common situations are the following:

1. *Lateral Drift of Frames.* This is quoted in terms of the relative horizontal movements of the levels of the frame. The code establishes limits as a percent of the story

height. (See Section 2312(h) of the 1985 edition of the *UBC*, reprinted in Appendix C.) Of concern in some situations is the effect of the frame distortion on walls in the plane of the frame. The calculation of drift for braced frames is discussed in Section 5.3, where the primary contribution is the change in length of the diagonals. Drift of rigid frames is discussed in Section 5.4.

2. *Deflection of Shear Walls.* This is mostly of concern for wood-framed walls. Empirical formulas are used for plywood walls, incorporating the various contributions of chord length change, shear distortion of the panels, and bending of the nails. Procedures for calculations are discussed in Section 5.2.

3. *Deflection of Horizontal Diaphragms.* These are mostly of concern for diaphragms that are wood framed or those that use light steel deck. Empirical formulas and available data can be used for both situations, as discussed in Section 5.1

Actual dimensions of movement may be of concern for various reasons. Satisfying code limits for story drift or determining effects on nonstructural elements—as mentioned previously—are examples. Another problem is that of providing a basis for the detailing and dimensioning of structural separation joints. In truth, however, movements calculated by the static load method are quite fictitious and considerable judgment is needed if they are used for design.

Dynamic Analysis. For the equivalent static load method, the energy loads are translated into static forces, and the analysis then proceeds in the usual manner as for real static loads. Loads are quantified in static units (pounds or kips) and the response of the structure is evaluated in static terms (stress). A more realistic dynamic analysis requires that the load be dealt with in dynamic units (energy, not force) and the structure be evaluated in dynamic terms (work done or energy absorbed).

In fact, the current application of the static load method—as specified in the *UBC*—is considerably modified by dynamic considerations. Determination of the loading is modified by dynamic responses of the structure through use of the *K*, *C*, and *S* factors. Distribution of loads for tall structures is modified to approximate the true distribution of dynamic shear. Stress magnification is required for shear in masonry walls and for forces in the members and connections of braced frames.

Nevertheless, true dynamic responses can only be determined using dynamic relationships, dynamic properties of the structure, and dynamic units for loads. This type of analysis is being increasingly done in engineering practice as the operating facilities (mostly computer software) become more readily available and usable. In time, dynamic analysis will probably be routinely done for most buildings. At present, however, it is mostly done only as a check or design adjustment after a preliminary design has been done by conventional methods. And then it is mostly only for buildings of unusual configuration, complex structural form, considerable size and cost, or where there is a heightened concern for safety (e.g., nuclear power plants).

Load Transfers between Elements. The most difficult aspect of visualizing the propagation of loads due to seismic activity is that it is essentially a three-dimensional problem. The seismic actions, the resulting forces, and the building structure are all three dimensional. Add this to the fact that the actions are dynamic and the problem is quite enough.

The difficulty of the design and investigative work may be a contributory reason for the number of failures of connections between elements of lateral resistive systems.

Neither architects nor civil engineers are, by training, well prepared to deal with three-dimensional problems of force resolution.

Load propagation in general is discussed in Section 2.1, and the actions of various elements and systems are discussed and illustrated in Chapter 5. More direct and practical applications are presented in the building design examples in Chapter 6.

Interactions in the lateral resistive system are commonly illustrated as single static load conditions for individual elements (the classic free-body diagram). Since the separate elements are usually two dimensional in character (single shear wall, single rigid bent, etc.), illustrations are simplified as two-dimensional force resolutions. The concept of the three-dimensional actions fades away when one works continuously with the relatively simple, two-dimensional problem sets.

Individual elements are not loaded individually, but rather are loaded simultaneously with all other parts of the system. Load transfers are thus a matter of load distributions (or load sharing) in an interactive, multiunit system. This is similar to the action of a continuous rigid frame in which the action of any one individual member is conditioned by the response of all the members in the system.

Anchoring and Splicing. Two functions that occur repeatedly in lateral resistive systems are those of anchoring and splicing. Anchoring is the general term for the securing of some structural entity at its boundaries. Thus a horizontal diaphragm is anchored to the vertical system, shear walls are anchored at their bases, and so on. Splicing occurs in all structures in one form or another, being generally necessary whenever continuity is required in long elements that are assembled from short individual parts.

For either anchoring or splicing there is a need for so-called positive connection. This is a somewhat nebulous term but generally means a connecting method that is relatively secure against the jolting, repetitive, multi-directional actions during an earthquake. Many connecting devices and methods that are acceptable for resistance to static gravity forces are not so qualified. The seismic behavior of ordinary connection methods is discussed in Section 2.3 and specific issues relating to typical elements of lateral resistive systems are presented in Chapter 5.

The positive character of anchorage is often a matter of degree. In some cases it may be achieved by simple redundancy, much like wearing both a belt and suspenders, or using a shotgun to kill a flea.

Figure 4.6 shows the situation of anchoring the top reinforcing for a beam in a supporting column or spandrel girder. The pos-

itive character of this connection may be increased by degrees as follows:

1. Anchorage can be achieved by simple embedment by providing a sufficient length (L in Figs. 4.6a and b) for development of bond between the bar surface and the surrounding concrete.

2. Additional anchorage is provided by adding a hook to the end of the bar, a common procedure when the length L is not sufficient. The hook substantially increases the positive character of the connection.

3. Finally, the hook may be made more effective if it is not merely made to grasp

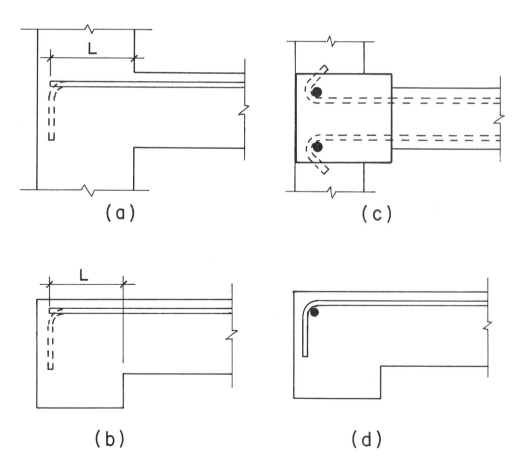

FIGURE 4.6. Progressive development of bar anchorage.

the concrete mass but is wrapped around a transverse reinforcing bar, as shown in Figures 4.6c and d.

The following are some additional considerations regarding the positive character of connections:

Screws or bolts are more positive than nails.

Nails loaded laterally are more positive than those subjected to withdrawal.

Welding of steel is more positive than bolting; high-strength friction bolts are more positive than unfinished bolts.

Lapped splices of reinforcing bars that comply with the requirements of the ACI Code are usually adequate for either tension or compression anchorage. However, some designers prefer the more positive action of welded or mechanically achieved anchorage at splice points. The latter, however, must be done by methods approved by local codes and may require special inspection during construction.

Discontinuities. In general, seismic response will be better when the flow of forces in the structure is simple, direct, and uninterrupted. The existence of various discontinuities will work to reduce all of these qualities so that the force flow becomes complex and inefficient. This is not a blank indictment for complexity, as the primary concern is for the lateral resistive structure. It is possible to have richness of form and detail in the building while still maintaining a simple, continuous, well-ordered bracing system.

Certain discontinuities in the building plan or general form, however, will often be reflected in the form of the lateral bracing system. Some of these situations are as follows:

1. *Openings.* Windows, doors, skylights, stairs, ducts, and elevators require openings. These may result in holes in horizontal or vertical diaphragms or may produce misalignment or discontinuity of rigid frame bents.

2. *Multiplane Roofs.* The farther the roof is from a single, flat, continuous plane, the less effective it will be for use as a horizontal diaphragm.

3. *Split-Level Floors.* This is the same problem as for the roof. Where this is required, the locations of level changes should be carefully worked out with the layout of the vertical elements of the bracing system so that the horizontal diaphragm does not have to try to maintain its continuity across level changes.

4. *Interrupted Shear Walls or Offset Columns.* While not uncommon, these represent major discontinuities and should be avoided if possible.

5. *Nonlinear Edges.* If the building edge is curved, saw-toothed, zigzagged, or otherwise not straight, the development of diaphragm chords and collectors may be difficult. A useful technique may be to use a line somewhat inside the actual edge as the boundary of the diaphragm and simply cantilever the edge for horizontal force.

Site–Structure Interaction. Building site problems are usually of one of the following type:

1. Subsurface conditions that complicate the building foundation design problem: weak, compressible soil deposits; high groundwater levels; highly organic materials.

2. Topographic situations: hillsides, surface water.

3. Instability conditions: collapsing soils, highly erodable soils, soils subject to dynamic liquefaction.

4. Structure–site interaction during motion that increases seismic effects on the building. (See the 1985 edition of the *UBC* for use of the S factor.)

In effect, the ground must be considered to be an element of the lateral resistive system. Once the building is set in motion, the forces induced by its momentum must be resolved into the ground, just as must be done for gravity forces. Vertical soil pressure, horizontal sliding and lateral soil pressure, pressure concentrations due to overturning, and resistance to uplift must all be given consideration in the design of the foundations. The general problems of foundation design for seismic effects are discussed in Chapter 8.

Concern for site–structure interaction in the form of vibratory relationships has only relatively recently been incorporated in code criteria. It is likely that this criterion will be further refined in future editions of the *UBC*. With more experience in the use of design criteria and the data in the form of geological studies required for its implementation, it is likely that this area of investigation will have more influence. To an extent this is a trend of concern for geological factors beyond the scale of the immediate site as traditionally reflected in ordinary shallow soil borings at the location of the building.

At present, for most small building projects, the minimum factors provided for in the code are used in lieu of obtaining the necessary geological studies to support any real investigation in this area. If the obtaining of necessary geological data becomes as routine as soil borings are now for most buildings, the code criteria are likely to become more detailed and more routinely used. As in the case of real dynamic analysis of seismic effects in general, computer-aided methods are also likely to become routine.

4.6. SPECIAL PROBLEMS

Load Sharing. A principal concern in the design of the vertical elements of the lateral bracing system is the distribution of loads to the individual elements of the system. The portion of the total horizontal force on the building that is carried by a single element will be affected by several factors. The principal considerations are as follows:

1. *Location of the Vertical Elements in the Building Plan.* This may be of significance primarily with respect to the locations of other vertical elements. If loads are distributed on a peripheral basis (also called tributary load basis), the periphery for a single element is defined by the location of adjacent elements. If the building is subject to significant torsion, the location of an element will determine its contribution to torsional resistance.

2. *Relative Stiffness.* Where elements exist in rows, such as a series of shear wall piers in a single wall surface, load sharing is on the basis of the relative stiffness of the elements in the linked series. If the distributing element (usually the horizontal diaphragm) is quite stiff, distribution to all members may be on a stiffness basis rather than on a peripheral basis. Illustrations and discussion of these situations are presented in the design examples in Chapter 6.

3. *Control Devices.* Load distribution may be controlled in part through the use of various devices such as expansion joints, seismic separation joints, pinned joints, collectors, drag struts, and ties. Natural force paths may thus be diverted or redirected to some extent.

Loads may be redistributed or shifted when staged responses occur. Initial failures, such as yielding of steel reinforcing and plastic hinging in frames, will change the relative resistance of elements so that loads may be shifted to other members in the linked system. From initial response to final failure of the entire system, load distributions will most likely shift considerably among the vertical elements.

In many cases determination of the design load for a single element of the vertical system requires some amount of judgment involving many qualifying assumptions. When a rational process seems elusive, it is not uncommon to consider a range of possibilities, to investigate each, and to provide for all the worst eventualities.

Coupling and Decoupling. It is generally desirable that the building move as a single unit in response to seismic actions. However, in the typical multimassed building, with many parts of different mass and stiffness, it is not reasonable to think of movements as simple as those of a tuning fork or a single bouncing spring. Nevertheless, it is usually a first preference to try to tie the separate elements of the building together for a single joined response if possible. This is particularly critical for the building base; thus other options are seldom considered for the foundations.

As in other situations elements of the construction may serve useful purposes for the tying together of the building. Horizontal diaphragms do the most work in this regard. Also effective are continuous spandrel beams and the continuous top plates of stud walls. If tying is a specific need, these elements often need positive splicing, although they may already be developed for use as chords or collectors.

Building corners and wall intersections are critical locations for interactions. If the presence of framing does not offer potential for tying at these locations, the wall joints themselves should be studied for this purpose.

There are times, of course, when tying elements is not practical or not even desirable. When this is the case, the construction must be designed to permit independent actions by use of flexible attachments or structural separation joints. Detachment of rigid finishes from flexible supports, decoupling of tall shear walls, and separation of separate parts of a multimassed building are examples of these instances. The judgment as to the need for separation, and the development of the construction details to facilitate the degree of required independence, is one of the most difficult parts of seismic design of buildings.

Determination of Building Weight. Translation of seismic motions into force effects involves the use of many theoretical relationships, most of which are empirical, complex, judgmental, and to say the least, mystical. One evident piece of hard data used in the process is that of the building weight. Here is a touchpoint with reality—something believable and logically determinable. However, the physical fabric of most buildings is quite complex, and the computation of building weight is typically a process that employs considerable approximation. Some of the factors that contribute to this situation are as follows:

1. The densities of many building materials vary over some range, requiring the use of *average* values, unless precise material specifications are available. "Plaster" is a description that permits considerable range of interpretation—from the very low density of sprayed-on acoustic coating of ceilings to the high density of exterior stucco.

2. Installation details vary. Thicknesses vary; required auxiliary devices, such as attachments, reinforcing, bracing, and so on, may vary; designer judgment affects many relatively common details. A simple exterior wood stud wall with drywall on the inside and plywood plus exterior finish on the outside can range over a considerable spread in terms of weight per square foot of wall surface. Variables include the size, spacing, and type of wood of the studs, the need for blocking between studs, the thickness of the plywood, the thickness of the drywall, and the type of exterior finish—from light wood siding to real brick veneer.

3. Structural design calculations are often done with information of a vague nature regarding the materials and details of the

building construction. This is simply because the definitive structural design must
often be done quite early in the design
process since the architectural designer
needs to know basic facts about the structure quite early. It is hoped that major
changes in the process of development of
the construction will be reflected in later
adjustments to the structural design.
Nevertheless, the preliminary structural
design—which often affects major decisions—is usually done with unavoidably
sketchy information.

4. Discontinuities in the construction make
   determination of material quantities difficult. Doors, windows, stairs, openings
   for ducts, and other building features
   make precise quantity takeoffs quite laborious.

In short, the determination of the building
weight is generally accepted to be an impre-
cise process that involves considerable judgment and some sheer guesswork. This does
not excuse the structural designer from trying
to do the best job possible, but the pursuit
of precision is doomed to frustration.

Data are provided in Appendix E to assist
in the determination of the weight of building construction, once some amount of detail
is known about the choices of materials and
type of construction. If the exact nature of
the construction is established (working
drawings and specifications complete), the
densities of materials provided in Table E.1
may be used to find weights. If the construction is only approximately determined—at
some midpoint of the design work—Table
E.2 may be used for average values of typical construction elements. For very early
calculations—used for quick judgments con-
cerning basic system choices and determination of approximate structural sizes—the
material in Table E.3 may prove helpful.

Distribution of Lateral Loads.   To a degree
the design requirements and the formulas and

data presented in codes are based on buildings of simple shape with lateral resistive
structures that are well ordered and free of
major discontinuities. Most real buildings are
not of this type, and the degree to which they
do not conform to simple conditions determines the relative validity of the code criteria.

A major point of consideration in this regard is the relationship between the disposition of the building mass (as generator of
lateral forces) and the arrangement of the
lateral resistive system. The idea is to try to
get the catcher positioned to catch the ball.
This may be imaged as a relationship between the entire mass and the entire resistive
system, as illustrated in Figure 2.9. In most
real situations the problem is both more
complex in nature and less subject to simple
computation.

Figure 4.7a shows an irregular building
plan with an arrangement of shear walls that
are disposed for resistance to lateral forces
in one direction. The distribution of the lateral loads to these walls on a peripheral basis
is illustrated by the zones defined by the
dashed lines on the plan. On this basis the
total building weight between the lines labeled 1 and 2 would be used to find the load
on the horizontal diaphragm in this area, and
this load would be distributed to the three
shear walls labeled H, I, and J. Even though
these three walls are not symmetrically disposed in the zone area, the stiffness of the
diaphragm and the torsional stabilizing effect
of the walls and horizontal diaphragm outside the zone would be considered adequate
to prevent any significant torsion on the affected walls.

The situation described in Figure 4.7 is
one that is subject to considerable judgmental interpretation. Some factors that could allow for different interpretations are as follows:

1. Is this a one-story or a multistory building? If it is multistory, it may be advis-

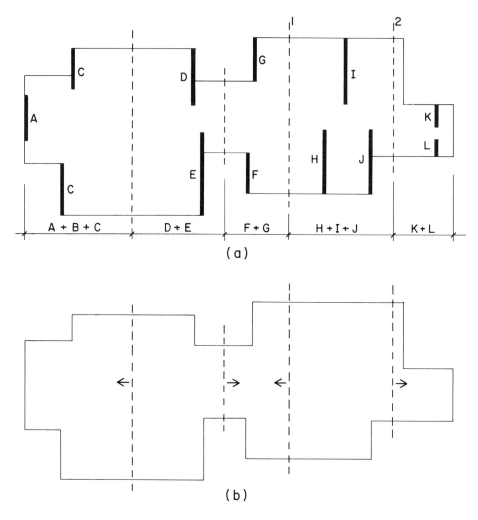

FIGURE 4.7. Load distribution in an irregular shear wall system.

able to use a seismic separation joint at one side or the other of the narrow, necked-down portion near the middle of the plan. This would alter the conditions for distribution to the shear walls near the middle of the building.

2. Are the shear walls of wood frame or of masonry or concrete construction? This relates primarily to the load distribution to individual walls. However, if the walls are of masonry or concrete, some design-

ers would move the peripheral zone boundaries slightly to acknowledge the relative stiffness of the longer walls. Possibilities for such shifting are shown in Figure 4.7b.

3. What is the construction of the horizontal diaphragm? If it is wood frame with plywood or a light-gauge metal deck, its flexibility will affect some judgments. The separation joint would be less indicated in this case, and the shift in pe-

ripheral boundaries more questionable. If the diaphragm is a poured-in-place concrete deck, the situation is reversed.

4. Should the system be designed for torsion? If the deck is flexible, and the separation joint is used, probably not. If the deck is concrete, and the separation joint *is* used, each independent half of the building should probably be investigated for torsion.

The use of the peripheral load distribution method and the procedures for consideration of torsional effects are illustrated in the design examples in Chapter 6.

CHAPTER FIVE

Elements of Lateral Resistive Systems

This chapter presents a discussion of the ordinary structural elements used to develop lateral force resistance in buildings. The primary use of the elements described here is in the development of resistance to the effects of wind and earthquakes. The general problem of structurally induced lateral effects and the structural elements utilized for various situations of such effects are discussed in Chapter 7. The general problem of lateral forces on foundations is discussed in Chapter 8. Design examples of building structures utilizing the elements discussed in this chapter are included in Chapter 6.

5.1. HORIZONTAL DIAPHRAGMS

Most lateral resistive structural systems for buildings consist of some combination of vertical elements and horizontal elements. The horizontal elements are most often the roof and floor framing and decks. When the deck is of sufficient strength and stiffness to be developed as a rigid plane, it is called a *horizontal diaphragm*.

General Behavior

A horizontal diaphragm typically functions by collecting the lateral forces at a particular level of the building and then distributing them to the vertical elements of the lateral resistive system. For wind forces the lateral loading of the horizontal diaphragm is usually through the attachment of the exterior walls to its edges. For seismic forces the loading is partly a result of the weight of the deck itself and partly a result of the weights of other parts of the building that are attached to it.

The particular structural behavior of the horizontal diaphragm and the manner in which loads are distributed to vertical elements depend on a number of considerations that are best illustrated by various example cases in Chapter 6. Some of the general issues of concern are discussed in the following sections.

Relative Stiffness of the Horizontal Diaphragm. If the horizontal diaphragm is relatively flexible, it may deflect so much that its continuity is negligible and the distribution of load to the relatively stiff vertical elements is essentially on a peripheral basis. If the deck is quite rigid, on the other hand, the distribution to vertical elements will be essentially in proportion to their relative stiffness with respect to each other. The possibility of these two situations is illustrated for a simple box system in Figure 5.1.

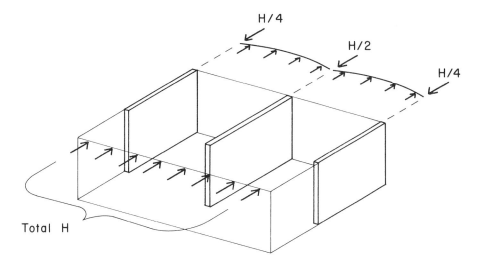

Peripheral distribution – flexible horizontal diaphragm

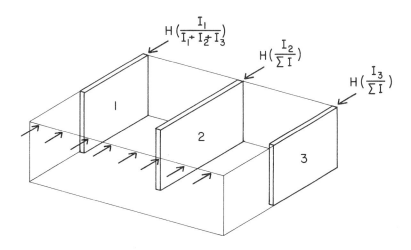

Proportionate stiffness distribution – rigid horizontal diaphragm

FIGURE 5.1. Peripheral distribution versus proportionate stiffness distribution.

Torsional Effects. If the centroid of the lateral forces in the horizontal diaphragm does not coincide with the centroid of the stiffness of the vertical elements, there will be a twisting action (called *rotation effect* or *torsional effect*) on the structure as well as the direct force effect. Figure 5.2 shows a structure in which this effect occurs because of a lack of symmetry of the structure. This effect is usually of significance only if the horizontal diaphragm is relatively stiff. This stiffness is a matter of the materials of the construction as well as the depth-to-span ratio of the horizontal diaphragm. In general, wood and

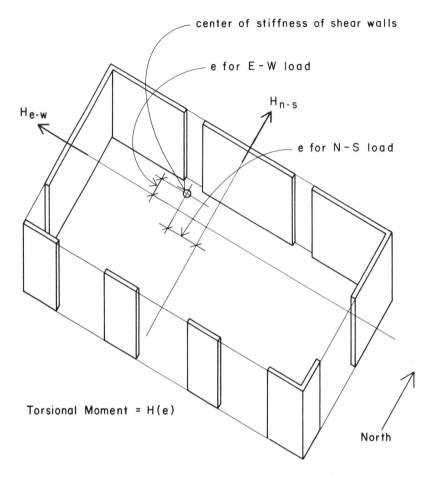

FIGURE 5.2. Torsional effect of lateral load.

metal decks are quite flexible, whereas poured concrete decks are very stiff.

Relative Stiffness of the Vertical Elements.
When vertical elements share load from a rigid horizontal diaphragm, as shown in the lower figure in Figure 5.1, their relative stiffness must usually be determined in order to establish the manner of the sharing. The determination is comparatively simple when the elements are similar in type and materials such as all plywood shear walls. When the vertical elements are different, such as a mix of plywood and masonry shear walls or of some shear walls and some braced frames,

their actual deflections must be calculated in order to establish the distribution, and this may require laborious calculations.

Use of Control Joints. The general approach in design for lateral loads is to tie the whole structure together to assure its overall continuity of movement. Sometimes, however, because of the irregular form or large size of a building, it may be desirable to control its behavior under lateral loads by the use of structural separation joints. In some cases these joints function to create total separation, allowing for completely independent motion of the separate parts of the building.

In other cases the joints may control movements in a single direction while achieving connection for load transfer in other directions. A general discussion of separation joints is given in Section 5.8.

Design and Usage Considerations

In performing their basic tasks, horizontal diaphragms have a number of potential stress problems. A major consideration is that of the shear stress in the plane of the diaphragm caused by the spanning action of the diaphragm as shown in Figure 5.3. This spanning action results in shear stress in the material as well as a force that must be transferred across joints in the deck when the deck is composed of separate elements such as sheets of plywood or units of formed sheet metal. The sketch in Figure 5.4 shows a typ-

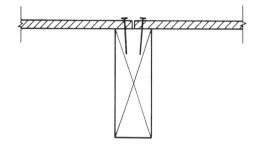

FIGURE 5.4.

ical plywood framing detail at the joint between two sheets. The stress in the deck at this location must be passed from one sheet through the edge nails to the framing member and then back out through the other nails to the adjacent sheet.

As is the usual case with shear stress, both diagonal tension and diagonal compression are induced simultaneously with the shear stress. The diagonal tension becomes critical in materials such as concrete. The diagonal compression is a potential source of buckling in decks composed of thin sheets of plywood or metal. In plywood decks the thickness of the plywood relative to the spacing of framing members must be considered, and it is also why the plywood must be nailed to intermediate framing members (not at edges of the sheets) as well as at edges. In metal decks the gauge of the sheet metal and the spacing of stiffening ribs must be considered. Tables of allowable loads for various deck elements usually incorporate some limits for these considerations.

Diaphragms with continuous deck surfaces are usually designed in a manner similar to that for webbed steel beams. The web (deck) is designed for the shear, and the flanges (edge-framing elements) are designed to take the moment, as shown in Figure 5.5. The edge members are called *chords*, and they must be designed for the tension and compression forces at the edges. With diaphragm edges of some length, the

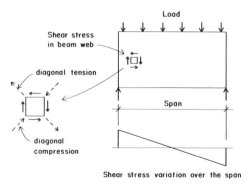

Beam Analogy

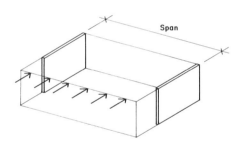

FIGURE 5.3. Function of a horizontal diaphragm.

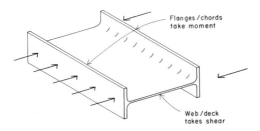

FIGURE 5.5. Horizontal diaphragm functions—beam analogy.

latter function usually requires that the edge members be spliced for some continuity of the forces. In many cases there are ordinary elements of the framing system, such as spandrel beams or top plates of stud walls, that have the potential to function as chords for the diaphragm.

In some cases the collection of forces into the diaphragm or the distribution of loads to vertical elements may induce a stress beyond the capacity of the deck alone. Figure 5.6 shows a building in which a continuous roof diaphragm is connected to a series of shear walls. Load collection and force transfers require that some force be dragged along the dotted lines shown in the figure. For the outside walls it is possible that the edge framing used for chords can do double service for this purpose. For the interior shear wall, and possibly for the edges if the roof is canti-

levered past the walls, some other framing elements may be necessary to reinforce the deck.

The diaphragm shear capacities for commonly used decks of various materials are available from the codes or from load tables prepared by deck manufacturers. Loads for plywood decks are given in the *UBC* (see Appendix C). Other tabulations are available from product manufacturers, although care should be exercised in their use to be certain that they are acceptable to the building code of jurisdiction.

A special situation is a horizontal system that consists partly or wholly of a braced frame. Care may be required when there are a large number of openings in the roof deck, or when the diaphragm shear stress is simply beyond the capacity of the deck. In the event of a deck with no code-accepted rating for shear, the braced frame may have to be used for the entire horizontal system.

The horizontal deflection of flexible decks, especially those with high span-to–depth ratios, may be a critical factor in their design. Calculation of actual deflection dimensions may be required to determine the effect on vertical elements of the building construction or to establish positively whether the deck must be considered as essentially flexible or rigid, as discussed previously.

The use of subdiaphragms may also be required in some cases, necessitating the design of part of the whole system as a separate diaphragm, even though the deck may be continuous.

Typical Construction

The most common horizontal diaphragm is the plywood deck for the simple reason that wood frame construction is so popular and plywood is mostly used for roof and floor decks. For roofs the deck may be as thin as $\frac{3}{8}$ in., but for flat roofs with waterproof membranes decks are usually $\frac{1}{2}$ in. or more. At-

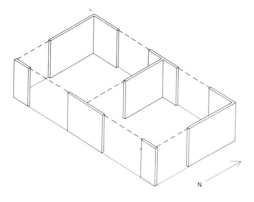

FIGURE 5.6. Collector functions in the box system.

tachment is typically by nailing, although glued floor decks are used for their added stiffness and to avoid nail popping and squeaking. Mechanical devices for nailing may eventually become so common that shear capacities will be based on some other fastener; at present the common wire nail is still the basis for load rating.

Attachment of plywood to chords and collectors and load transfers to vertical shear walls are also mostly achieved by nailing. Code-acceptable shear ratings are based on the plywood type and thickness, the nail size and spacing, and features such as size and spacing of framing and use of blocking. Load capacities for plywood decks are given in *UBC* Table 25-J, which is reprinted in Appendix C.

In general, plywood decks are quite flexible and should be investigated for deflection when spans are large or span–depth ratios are high.

Decks of boards or timber, usually with tongue-and-groove joints, were once popular but are given low rating for shear capacity at present. Where the exposed plank-type deck is desired, it is not uncommon to use a thin plywood deck on top of it for lateral force development.

Steel decks offer possibilities for use as diaphragms for either roof or floors. Acceptable shear capacities should be obtained from the supplier for any particular product, as capacities vary considerably and code approval is not consistent. Stiffnesses are generally comparable with those of plywood decks. Floor decks receive concrete fill, which significantly increases the stiffness of the deck. In some situations it is practical to use the concrete as the basic shear-resisting element.

Poured-in-place concrete decks provide the strongest and stiffest diaphragms. Precast concrete deck units, as well as the slab portions of precast systems, can be used for diaphragms. Precast units must be adequately attached to each other and to supporting members for diaphragm actions; if designed only for gravity, ordinary attachments will usually not be adequate for lateral forces. As with steel deck, concrete fill is sometimes placed on top of precast units, which both stiffens and strengthens the system.

Many other types of roof deck construction may function adequately for diaphragm action, especially when the required unit shear resistance is low. Acceptability by local building code administration agencies should be determined if any construction other than those described is to be used.

Stiffness and Deflection. As spanning elements, the relative stiffness and actual dimensions of deformation of horizontal diaphragms depend on a number of factors such as:

The materials of the construction.

The continuity of the spanning diaphragm over a number of supports.

The span-to-depth ratio of the diaphragm.

The effect of various special conditions, such as chord length changes, yielding of connections and influence of large openings.

In general, wood and light-gauge metal decks tend to produce quite flexible diaphragms, whereas poured concrete decks tend to produce the most rigid diaphragms. Ranging between these extremes are decks of lightweight concrete, gypsum concrete, and composite constructions of lightweight concrete fill on metal deck. For true dynamic analysis the variations are more complex because the weight and degree of elasticity of the materials must also be considered.

With respect to their span-to-depth ratios, most horizontal diaphragms approach the classification of deep beams. As shown in Figure 5.7, even the shallowest of diaphragms, such as the maximum 4 to 1 case allowed for a plywood deck by the *UBC*, tends to present a fairly stiff flexural member. As the span-to-depth ratio falls below

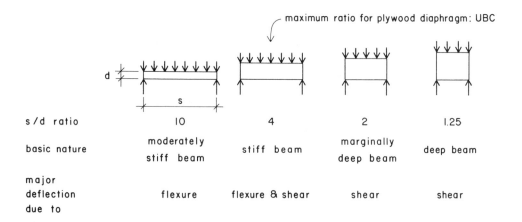

FIGURE 5.7. Behavior of horizontal diaphragms related to depth-to-span ratios.

about 2, the deformation characteristic of the diaphragm approaches that of a deep beam in which the deflection is primarily caused by shear strain rather than by flexural strain. Thus the usual formulas for deflection caused by flexural strain become of limited use.

The following formula is used for the calculation of deflection of simple-span plywood diaphragms:

$$\Delta = \frac{5vL^3}{8EAb} + \frac{vL}{4Gt}$$

$$+ 0.094Le_n + \sum \frac{(\Delta_c X)}{2b}$$

in which the four terms account for four different contributions to the deflection, as follows:

Term 1 accounts for the length change of the chords.

Term 2 accounts for the shear strain in the plywood panels.

Term 3 accounts for the lateral bending of the nails.

Term 4 accounts for additional change in the chord lengths caused by slip in the chord splices.

The deflection of steel deck diaphragms is discussed and illustrated in the *Inryco Lateral Diaphragm Data Manual 20-2* published by Inryco, Inc. The formula used for calculating the deflection of a simple span deck is

$$\Delta_t = \frac{5\ WL_s^4 \times 1728}{384\ E \times I} + q$$

$$\times F \times \frac{L_s}{2} \times 10^{-6}$$

in which the first term accounts for flexural deflection caused by the length change of the chords and the second term for shear strain and panel distortion in the diaphragm web.

The quantities q and F vary as a function of the type and gauge of the deck, the fastening patterns and methods used, and the possible inclusion of concrete fill.

As with deck load capacities, deflections and the relative stiffness of deck systems are generally based on materials presented in the *Diaphragm Design Manual*, published by the Steel Deck Institute. For a specific product, however, designers should obtain information from the product supplier and verify that any data or procedures used are acceptable to the building permit-approving agency for the work.

5.2. VERTICAL DIAPHRAGMS

Vertical diaphragms are usually the walls of buildings. As such, in addition to their shear wall function, they must fulfill various architectural functions and may also be required to serve as bearing walls for the gravity loads. The location of walls, the materials used, and some of the details of their construction must be developed with all these functions in mind.

The most common shear wall constructions are those of poured concrete, masonry, and wood frames of studs with surfacing elements. Wood frames may be made rigid in the wall plane by the use of diagonal bracing or by the use of surfacing materials that have sufficient strength and stiffness. Choice of the type of construction may be limited by the magnitude of shear caused by the lateral loads, but will also be influenced by fire code requirements and the satisfaction of the various other wall functions, as described previously.

General Behavior

Some of the structural functions usually required of vertical diaphragms are the following (see Fig. 5.8):

1. *Direct Shear Resistance.* This usually consists of the transfer of a lateral force in the plane of the wall from some upper level of the wall to a lower level or to the bottom of the wall. This results in the typical situation of shear stress and the accompanying diagonal tension and compression stresses, as discussed for horizontal diaphragms.

2. *Cantilever Moment Resistance.* Shear walls generally work like vertical can-

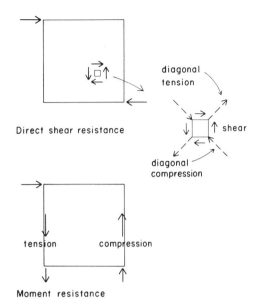

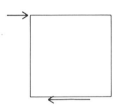

FIGURE 5.8. Functions of a shear wall.

tilevers, developing compression on one edge and tension on the opposite edge, and transferring an overturning moment (M) to the base of the wall.

3. *Horizontal Sliding Resistance.* The direct transfer of the lateral load at the base of the wall produces the tendency for the wall to slip horizontally off its supports.

The shear stress function is usually considered independently of other structural functions of the wall. The maximum shear stress that derives from lateral loads is compared to some rated capacity of the wall construction, with the usual increase of one third in allowable stresses because the lateral load is most often a result of wind or earthquake forces. For concrete and masonry walls the actual stress in the material is calculated and compared with the allowable stress for the material. For structurally surfaced wood frames the construction as a whole is generally rated for its total resistance in pounds per foot of the wall length in plan. For a plywood-surfaced wall this capacity depends on the type and thickness of the plywood; the size, wood species, and spacing of the studs; the size and spacing of the plywood nails; and the inclusion or omission of blocking at horizontal plywood joints.

The analysis and design of shear walls of concrete and reinforced masonry are illustrated in the examples in Chapter 6. For walls of concrete the procedures are based on the requirements of the American Concrete Institute (ACI) Code (Ref. 5). For walls of reinforced hollow concrete block construction the procedures are based on the requirements in Chapter 24 of the *UBC*.

For wood stud walls the *UBC* provides tables of rated load capacities for several types of surfacing, including plywood, diagonal wood boards, plaster, gypsum drywall, and particleboard. This material is included in the *UBC* reprints in Appendix C.

Although the possibility exists for the buckling of walls as a result of the diagonal compression effect, this is usually not critical because other limitations exist to constrain wall slenderness. The thickness of masonry walls is limited by maximum values for the ratio of unsupported wall height or length-to-wall thickness. Concrete thickness is usually limited by forming and pouring considerations, so that thin walls are not common except with precast construction. Slenderness of wood studs is limited by gravity design and by the code limits as a function of the stud size. Because stud walls are usually surfaced on both sides, the resulting sand-

wich–panel effect is usually sufficient to provide a reasonable stiffness.

As in the case of horizontal diaphragms, the moment effect on the wall is usually considered to be resisted by the two vertical edges of the wall acting as flanges or chords. In the concrete or masonry wall this results in a consideration of the ends of the wall as columns, sometimes actually produced as such by thickening of the wall at the ends. In wood-framed walls the end-framing members are considered to fulfill this function. These edge members must be investigated for possible critical combinations of loading because of gravity and the lateral effects.

The overturn effect of the lateral loads must be resisted with the safety factor of 1.5 that is required by the *UBC*. The form of the analysis for the overturn effect is as shown in Figure 5.9. If the tiedown force is actually required, it is developed by the anchorage of the edge-framing elements of the wall.

Resistance to horizontal sliding at the base of a shear wall is usually at least partly resisted by friction caused by the dead loads. For masonry and concrete walls with dead loads that are usually quite high, the frictional resistance may be more than sufficient.

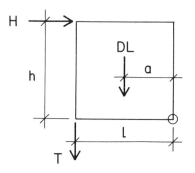

To determine T:

$$DL(a) + T(l) = 1.5\left[H(h)\right]$$

FIGURE 5.9. Determination of tiedown requirements for a shear wall.

If it is not, shear keys must be provided. For wood-framed walls the friction is usually ignored and the sill bolts are designed for the entire load.

Design and Usage Considerations

An important judgment that must often be made in designing for lateral loads is that of the manner of distribution of lateral force between a number of shear walls that share the load from a single horizontal diaphragm. In some cases the existence of symmetry or of a flexible horizontal diaphragm may simplify this consideration. In many cases, however, the relative stiffnesses of the walls must be determined for this calculation.

If considered in terms of static force and elastic stress–strain conditions, the relative stiffness of a wall is inversely proportionate to its deflection under a unit load. Figure 5.10 shows the manner of deflection of a shear wall for two assumed conditions. In (a) the wall is considered to be fixed at its top and bottom, flexing in a double curve with an inflection point at midheight. This is the case usually assumed for a continuous wall of concrete or masonry in which a series of individual wall portions (called *piers*) are connected by a continuous upper wall or other structure of considerable stiffness. In (b) the wall is considered to be fixed at its bottom only, functioning as a vertical cantilever. This is the case for independent, freestanding walls or for walls in which the continuous upper structure is relatively flexible. A third possibility is shown in (c) in which relatively short piers are assumed to be fixed at their tops only, which produces the same deflection condition as in (b).

In some instances the deflection of the wall may result largely from shear distortion, rather than from flexural distortion, perhaps because of the wall materials and construction or the proportion of wall height to plan length. Furthermore, stiffness in resistance to dynamic loads is not quite the same as stiffness in resistance to static loads. The fol-

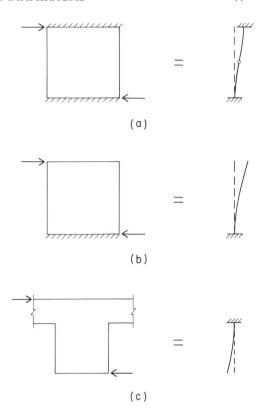

FIGURE 5.10. Shear wall support conditions: (a) fixed top and bottom; (b) and (c) cantilevered.

lowing recommendations are made for single-story shear walls:

1. For wood-framed walls with height–to-length ratios of 2 or less, assume the stiffness to be proportional to the plan length of the wall.

2. For wood-framed walls with height–to-length ratios over 2 and for concrete and masonry walls, assume the stiffness to be a function of the height–to-length ratio and the method of support (cantilevered or fixed top and bottom). Use the values for pier rigidity given in Appendix D.

3. Avoid situations in which walls of significantly great differences in stiffness share loads along a single row. The short walls will tend to receive a small share

of the loads, especially if the stiffness is assumed to be a function of the height–to-length ratio.

4. Avoid mixing of shear walls of different construction when they share loads on a deflection basis.

Item 4 in the preceding list can be illustrated by two situations as shown in figure 5.11. The first situation is that of a series of panels in a single row. If some of these panels are of concrete or masonry and others of wood frame construction, the stiffer concrete or masonry panels will tend to absorb the major portion of the load. The load sharing must be determined on the basis of actual calculated deflections. Better yet is a true dynamic analysis, because if the load is truly dynamic in character, the periods of the two types of walls are of more significance than their stiffness.

In the second situation shown in Figure 5.11, the walls share load from a rigid horizontal diaphragm. This situation also requires a deflection calculation for determining the distribution of force to the panels.

In addition to the various considerations

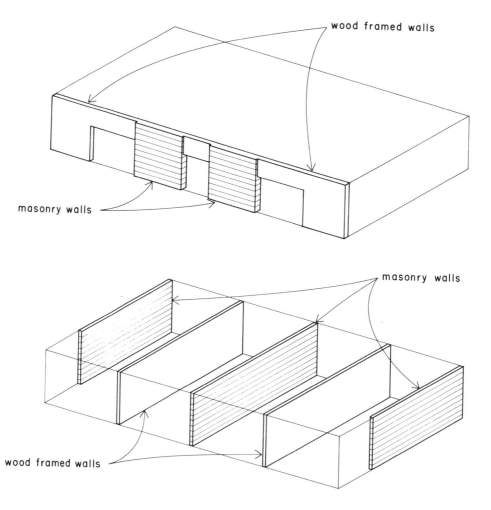

FIGURE 5.11. Interacting walls of mixed construction.

mentioned for the shear walls themselves, care must be taken to assure that they are properly anchored to the horizontal diaphragms. Problems of this sort are illustrated in the examples in Chapter 6.

A final consideration for shear walls is that they must be made an integral part of the whole building construction. In long building walls with large door or window openings or other gaps in the wall, shear walls are often considered as entities (isolated, independent piers) for their design. However, the behavior of the entire wall under lateral load should be studied to be sure that elements not considered to be parts of the lateral resistive system do not suffer damage because of the wall distortions.

An example of this situation is shown in Figure 5.12. The two relatively long solid portions are assumed to perform the bracing function for the entire wall and would be designed as isolated piers. However, when the wall deflects, the effect of the movement on the shorter piers, on the headers over openings, and on the door and window framing must be considered. The headers must not be cracked loose from the solid wall portions or pulled off their supports.

Typical Construction

The various types of common construction for shear walls mentioned in the preceding

FIGURE 5.13.   Wood frame diaphragms. Garage with side wall of stucco fastened directly to studs, end wall of plywood, let-in bracing for temporary use to brace structure during construction (and to give courage to those who worry about relying on stucco alone).

section are wood frames with various surfacing, reinforced masonry, and concrete. The only wood frame wall used extensively in the past was the plywood-covered one. Experience and testing have established acceptable ratings for other surfacing, so that plywood is used somewhat less when shear loads are low (see Fig. 5.13).

For all types of walls there are various considerations (good carpentry, fire resistance, available products, etc.) that establish a certain minimum construction. In many situations this "minimum" is really adequate for low levels of shear loading, and the only additions are in the area of attachments and joint load transfers. Increasing wall strength beyond the minimum usually requires increasing the size or quality of units, adding or strengthening attachments, developing supporting elements to function as chords or collectors, and so on. It well behooves the designer to find out the standards for basic construction to know what the minimum consists of so that added strength can be developed when necessary— but using methods consistent with the ordinary types of construction.

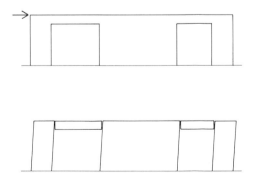

FIGURE 5.12.   Effect of shear wall deformation on headers.

Load Capacity.   Load capacities for ordinary wood-framed shear walls are given in the load tables in the *UBC*. For seismic actions the only masonry construction ordinarily acceptable is that of reinforced masonry, of which the most common form is one using hollow precast concrete units (concrete blocks). The design of masonry construction should be done with the references that present material acceptable to the building code of jurisdiction. The reprints from the 1985 *UBC* in Appendix C give some criteria for masonry, but the complete design guide is in Chapter 24 of the code.

Most concrete design is based on the current edition of the ACI Code (*Building Code Requirements for Reinforced Concrete*, Ref. 5), although local codes are sometimes slow in accepting new changes in the ACI Code editions. The current edition of the ACI Code provides some criteria for seismic design, but recent developments—mostly in the form of suggested details for construction—are more stringent for areas of high seismic risk. Concrete design in general and seismic design in particular have become quite sophisticated and complex, and there are few simple guides. The shear wall is a relatively simple concrete element, but its design should be done in conformance with the latest codes and practices.

Stiffness and Deflection. As with the horizontal diaphragm, there are several potential factors to consider in the deflection of a shear wall. As shown in Figure 5.14*a*, shear walls also tend to be relatively stiff in most cases, approaching deep beams instead of ordinary flexural members.

The two general cases for the vertical shear wall are the cantilever and the doubly fixed pier. The cantilever, fixed at its base, is the most commonly used. Fixity at both the top and bottom of the wall usually affects deflection only when the wall is relatively short in length with respect to its height. Walls with long lengths in proportion to their height fall into the deep beam category in which the predominant shear strain is not affected by the fixity of the support.

As shown in Figure 5.14*b*, if the doubly fixed pier is assumed to have an inflection point at its midheight, its deflection can be approximated by considering it to be the sum of the deflections of two half-height cantilevered piers. Yielding of the supports and flexure in the horizontal structure will produce some rotation of the assumedly fixed ends, which will result in some additional deflection.

The following formula is used for calculating deflection of cantilevered plywood shear walls similar to that for the plywood horizontal diaphragm:

$$\Delta = \frac{8vh^3}{EAb} + \frac{vh}{Gt} + 0.376he_{\text{n}} + d_{\text{a}}$$

in which the four terms account for the following:

Term 1 accounts for the change in length of the chords (wall end framing).

Term 2 accounts for the shear strain in the plywood panels.

Term 3 accounts for the nail deformation.

Term 4 is a general term for including the effects of yield of the anchorage.

The formula can also be used for calculating the deflection of a multistory wall, as shown in Figure 5.14*c*. For the loading as shown in the illustration, a separate calculation would be made for each of the three loads (Δ_1, Δ_2, and Δ_3). To these would be added the deflection at the top of the wall caused by the rotation effects of the lower loads (d_1 and d_2). Thus the total deflection at the top of the wall would be the sum of the five increments of deflection.

Rotation caused by soil deformation at the base of the wall can also contribute to the deflection of shear walls (see Fig. 5.14*d*). This is especially critical for tall walls on isolated foundations placed on relatively compressible soils, such as loose sand and

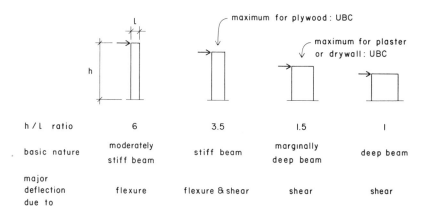

h/L ratio	6	3.5	1.5	1
basic nature	moderately stiff beam	stiff beam	marginally deep beam	deep beam
major deflection due to	flexure	flexure & shear	shear	shear

(a) Behavior of cantilvered elements related to height-to-length ratios

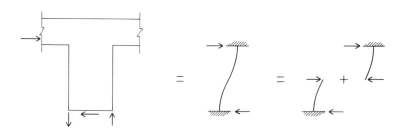

(b) Deflection assumption for a fully fixed masonry pier

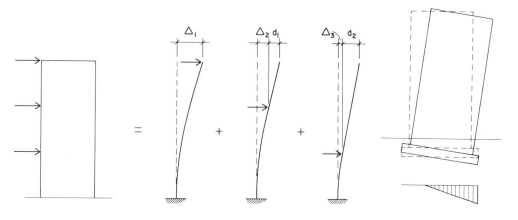

(c) Deflection of a multistory shear wall

(d) Shear wall tilt caused by uneven soil pressure

FIGURE 5.14. Aspects of deflection of shear walls.

soft clay—a situation to be avoided if at all possible.

5.3. BRACED FRAMES

Although there are actually several ways to brace a frame against lateral loads, the term *braced frame* is used to refer to frames that utilize trussing as the primary bracing technique. In buildings, trussing is mostly used for the vertical bracing system in combination with the usual horizontal diaphragms. It is also possible, however, to use a trussed frame for a horizontal system, or to combine vertical and horizontal trussing in a truly three-dimensional trussed framework. The latter is more common for open tower structures, such as those used for large electrical transmission lines and radio and television transmitters.

Use of Trussing for Bracing

Post and beam systems, consisting of separate vertical and horizontal members, may be inherently stable for gravity loading, but they must be braced in some manner for lateral loads. The three basic ways of achieving this are through shear panels, moment-resistive joints between the members, or by trussing. The trussing, or triangulation, is usually formed by the insertion of diagonal members in the rectangular bays of the frame.

If single diagonals are used, they must serve a dual function: acting in tension for the lateral loads in one direction and in compression when the load direction is reversed (see Fig. 5.15a). Because long tension members are more efficient than long compression members, frames are often braced with a crisscrossed set of diagonals (called X-bracing) to eliminate the need for the compression members. In any event the trussing causes the lateral loads to induce only axial forces in the members of the frame, as compared to the behavior of the rigid frame. It also generally results in a

frame that is stiffer for both static and dynamic loading, having less deformation than the rigid frame.

Single-story, single-bayed buildings may be braced as shown in Figure 5.15a. Single-story, multibayed buildings may be braced by bracing less than all of the bays in a single plane of framing, as shown in Figure 5.15b. The continuity of the horizontal framing is used in the latter situation to permit the rest of the bays to tag along. Similarly, a single-bayed, multistoried, towerlike structure, as shown in Figure 5.15c, may have its frame fully braced, whereas the more common type of frame for the multistoried building, as shown in Figure 5.15d, is usually only partly braced. Since either the single diagonal or the crisscrossed X-bracing causes obvious problems for interior circulation and for openings for doors and windows, building planning often makes the limited bracing a necessity.

Just about any type of floor construction used for multistoried buildings usually has sufficient capacity for diaphragm action in the lateral bracing system. Roofs, however, often utilize light construction or are extensively perforated by openings, so that the basic construction is not capable of the usual horizontal, planar diaphragm action. For such roofs or for floors with many openings, it may be necessary to use a trussed frame for the horizontal part of the lateral bracing system. Figure 5.15e shows a roof for a single-story building in which trussing has been placed in all the edge bays of the roof framing in order to achieve the horizontal structure necessary. As with vertical trussed frames, the horizontal trussed frame may be partly trussed, as shown in Figure 5.15e, rather than fully trussed.

For single-span structures, trussing may be utilized in a variety of ways for the combined gravity and lateral load resistive system. Figure 5.15f shows a typical gable roof with the rafters tied at their bottom ends by a horizontal member. The tie, in this case, serves the dual functions of resisting the out-

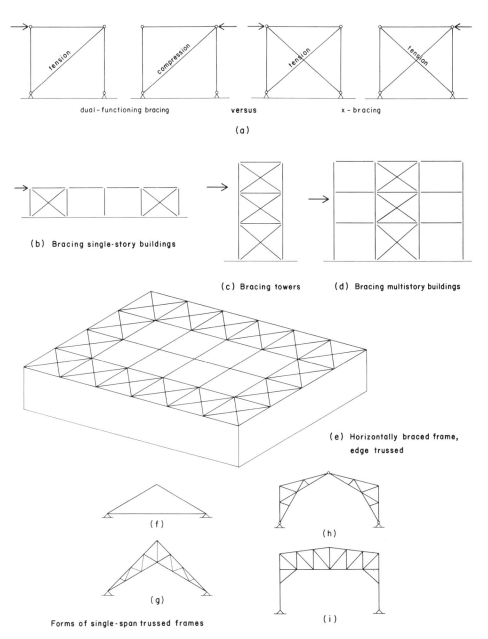

dual-functioning bracing   versus   x-bracing

(a)

(b) Bracing single-story buildings

(c) Bracing towers   (d) Bracing multistory buildings

(e) Horizontally braced frame, edge trussed

(f)

(g)

(h)

(i)

Forms of single-span trussed frames

FIGURE 5.15. Considerations of braced frames.

ward thrust due to gravity loads and of one of the members of the single triangle, trussed structure that is rigidly resistive to lateral loads. Thus the wind force on the sloping roof surface, or the horizontal seismic force caused by the weight of the roof structure, is resisted by the triangular form of the rafter–tie combination.

The horizontal tie shown in Figure 5.15f may not be architecturally desirable in all cases. Some other possibilities for the single-span structure—all producing more openness beneath the structure—are shown in Figures 5.15*g*, *h*, and *i*. Figure 5.15*g* shows the so-called scissors truss, which can be used to permit more openness on the inside or to permit a ceiling that has a form reflecting that of the gable roof. Figure 5.15*h* shows a trussed bent that is a variation on the three-hinged arch. The structure shown in Figure 5.15*i* consists primarily of a single-span truss that rests on end columns. If the columns are pin-jointed at the bottom chord of the truss, the structure lacks basic resistance to lateral loads and must be separately braced. If the column in Figure 5.15*i* is continuous to the top of the truss, it can be used in rigid frame action for resistance to lateral loads. Finally, if the knee-braces shown in the figure are added, the column is further stiffened, and the structure has more load resistance and less deflection under lateral loading.

The knee-braces shown in Figure 5.15*i* can also be used with a simple post and beam structure, as shown in Figure 5.16, transforming it essentially into a rigid frame. The advantage of the knee-braces over other techniques for producing moment-resistive joints is that the jointing can be of simple pin type. This advantage is most significant for members for which moment-resistive jointing is difficult to develop.

A special type of bracing is that shown in Figure 5.17 called K-bracing (from the form described by the diagonal and horizontal members). As with knee-bracing, the action of this structure involves a combination of truss and rigid frame actions. The principal advantage—and reason for its current popularity—of K-bracing is in its ultimate energy capacity, which typically involves the development of plastic hinging in the frame. Figure 5.17 shows the use of K-bracing for a peripheral bracing system for a low-rise office building, with diagonals of round steel pipe.

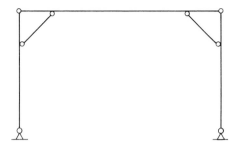

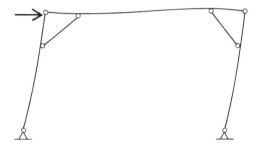

FIGURE 5.16. The knee-braced bent.

Planning of Bracing. Some of the problems to be considered in using braced frames are the following:

1. Diagonal members must be placed so as not to interfere with the action of the

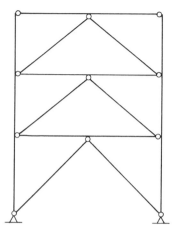

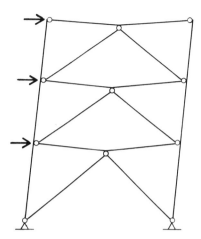

FIGURE 5.17. Use of K-bracing.

gravity-resistive structure or with other building functions. If the bracing members are designed essentially as axial stress members, they must be located and attached so as to avoid loadings other than those required for their bracing functions. They must also be located so as not to interfere with door, window, or roof openings or with ducts, wiring, piping, light fixtures, and so on.

2. As mentioned previously, the reversibility of the lateral loads must be considered. As shown in Figure 5.15*a*, such consideration requires that diagonal members be dual functioning (as single diagonals) or redundant (as X-bracing) with one set of diagonals working for load from one direction and the other set working for the reversal loading.

3. Although the diagonal bracing elements

usually function only for lateral loading, the vertical and horizontal elements must be considered for the various possible combinations of gravity and lateral load. Thus the total frame must be analyzed for all the possible loading conditions, and each member must be designed for the particular critical combinations that represent its peak response conditions.

4. Long, slender bracing members, especially in X-braced systems, may have considerable sag due to their own dead weight, which requires that they be supported by sag rods or other parts of the structure.

5. The trussed structure should be "tight." Connections should be made in a manner to assure that they will be initially free of slack and will not loosen under the load reversals or repeated loadings. This means generally avoiding connections that tend to loosen or progressively deform such as those that use nails, loose pins, and unfinished bolts.

6. To avoid loading on the diagonals, the connections of the diagonals are sometimes made only after the gravity-resistive structure is fully assembled and at least partly loaded by the building dead loads.

7. The deformation of the trussed structure must be considered, and it may relate to its function as a distributing element, as in the case of a horizontal structure, or to the establishing of its relative stiffness, as in the case of a series of vertical elements that share loads. It may also relate to some effects on nonstructural parts of the building, as was discussed for shear walls.

8. In most cases it is not necessary to brace every individual bay of the rectangular frame system. In fact, this is often not possible for architectural reasons. As shown in Figure 5.15b, walls consisting of several bays can be braced by trussing

only a few bays, or even a single bay, with the rest of the structure tagging along like cars in a train.

The braced frame can be mixed with other bracing systems in some cases. Figure 5.18a shows the use of a braced frame for the vertical resistive structure in one direction and a set of shear walls in the other direction. In this example the two systems act independently, except for the possibility of torsion, and there is no need for a deflection analysis to determine the load sharing.

Figure 5.18b shows a structure in which the end bays of the roof framing are X-braced. For loading in the direction shown, these braced bays take the highest shear in the horizontal structure, allowing the deck to be designed for a lower shear stress.

Figure 5.18c shows a low-rise office building in which X-braced steel bents are used in combination with wood-framed shear walls for the lateral bracing system. The detail shown in Figure 5.18d illustrates the typical use of steel gusset plates welded to the vertical and horizontal framing members for attachment of the diagonal braces. In this case the diagonal members consist of steel channel sections turned back-to-back to form the X-braces.

Although buildings and their structures are often planned and constructed in two-dimensional components (horizontal floor and roof planes and vertical wall or framing bent planes), it must be noted that the building is truly three dimensional. Bracing against lateral forces is thus a three-dimensional problem, and although a single horizontal or vertical plane of the structure may be adequately stable and strong, the whole system must interact appropriately. While the single triangle is the basic unit for a planar truss, the three-dimensional truss may not be truly stable just because its component planes are braced.

In a purely geometric sense the basic unit for a three-dimensional truss is the four-sided

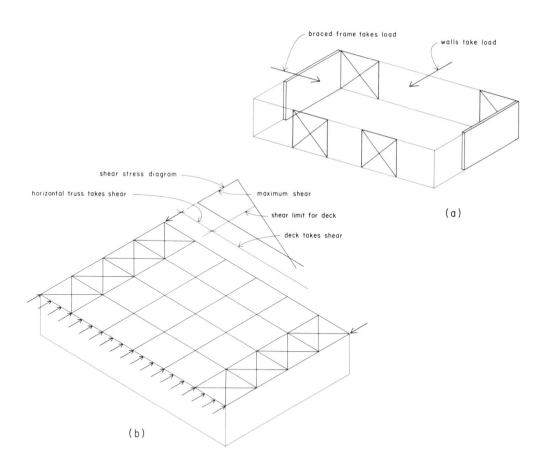

FIGURE 5.18. Use of braced systems: (*a*) mixed vertical elements for lateral resistance; (*b*) mixed horizontal diaphragm and braced frame; (*c*) X-braced bents used in a mixed steel and wood system; (*d*) joint detail for bent in (*c*).

(d)

FIGURE 5.18.   (*Continued*)

figure called a tetrahedron. However, since most buildings consist of spaces that are rectangular boxes, the three-dimensional trussed building structure usually consists of rectangular units rather than multiples of the pyramidal tetrahedral form. (See Fig. 5.19). When so used, the single planar truss unit is much the same as a solid planar wall or deck unit, and general reference to the box-type system typically includes both forms of construction.

Typical Construction

Development of the details of construction for trussed bracing is in many ways similar to the design of spanning trusses. The materials used (generally wood or steel), the form of individual truss members, the type of jointing (nails, bolts, welds, etc.), and the magnitudes of the forces are all major considerations. Since many of the members of the complete truss serve dual roles for grav-

ity and lateral loads, member selection is seldom based on truss action alone. Quite often trussed bracing is produced by simply adding diagonals (or X-bracing) to a system already conceived for the gravity loads and for the general development of the desired architectural forms and spaces.

Figure 5.20 shows some details for wood framing with added diagonal members. Wood-framing members are most often rectangular in cross section and metal connecting devices of various form are used in the assembly of frameworks. Figure 5.20*a* shows a typical beam and column assembly with diagonals consisting of pairs of wood members bolted to the frame. When X-bracing is used, and members need take only tension forces, slender steel rods may be used; a possible detail for this is shown in Figure 5.20*b*. For the wood diagonal an alternative to the bolted connection is the type of joint in Figure 5.20*c*, employing a gusset plate to attach single members all in a single plane. If architectural detailing makes the protruding members shown in Figure 5.20*a* or even the protruding gussets in Figure 5.20*c* undesirable, a bolted connection like that shown in Figure 5.20*d* may be used.

As discussed in the next section, a contributing factor in the deformation of the bracing under loading may be movements within the connections. Bolted connections are especially vulnerable when used in shear resistance, since both oversizing of the holes and shrinkage of the wood contribute to a lack of tightness in the joints. In some cases

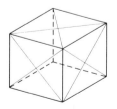

single tetrahedron   the trussed box

FIGURE 5.19.   Three-dimensional trussing.

wood, sheet steel, or steel plate, depending mostly on the magnitude of the loads. Plywood joints should be glued or the nails should be ring or spiral shafted to increase the joint tightness. Steel plate gussets are usually attached by either lag screws or through bolts. Thin sheet metal gussets are either nailed or screwed in place, the latter being preferred for maximum tightness.

Figure 5.21 shows some details for the incorporation of diagonal bracing in steel frames. As with wood structures, bolt loosening is a potential problem. For bolts used in tension—or for the threaded ends of round steel rods—loosening of nuts can be prevented by welding them in place or by scarring the threads. For shear-type connections, highly tensioned, high-strength bolts are preferred over ordinary, unfinished bolts. A completely welded connection will produce the stiffest joint, but on-site bolting in the field is usually preferred over welding.

Various steel elements can be used for diagonal members, depending on the magnitude of loads, the problems of incorporating or exposing the members in the construction, and the requirements for attachment to the structural frame. Figure 5.21d shows an interior view of a building in which a system of exposed truss bents is used for the roof structure as well as the lateral bracing system. Columns are round steel pipes and truss members are mostly double angles with welded gusset plate joints, as shown in the detail in Figure 5.21e.

Use of round steel pipe diagonals is shown in Figure 5.17c. Steel channels are used for X-bracing in the building shown in Figure 5.18d.

Stiffness and Deflection. As has been stated previously, the braced frame is typically a relatively stiff structure. This is based on the assumption that the major contribution to the overall deformation of the structure is the shortening and lengthening of the members of the frame as they experience the

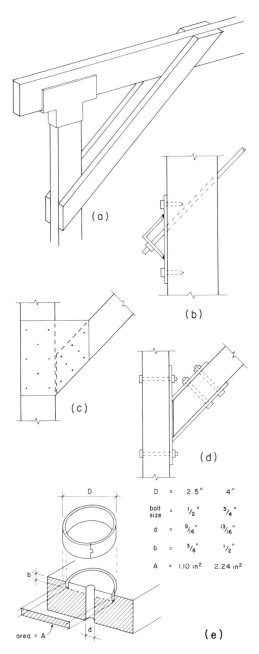

FIGURE 5.20. Framing of trussed bents in wood.

it may be possible to increase the tightness of the joints by using some form of shear developer such as steel split rings (see Fig. 5.20e).

Gusset plates ordinarily consist of ply-

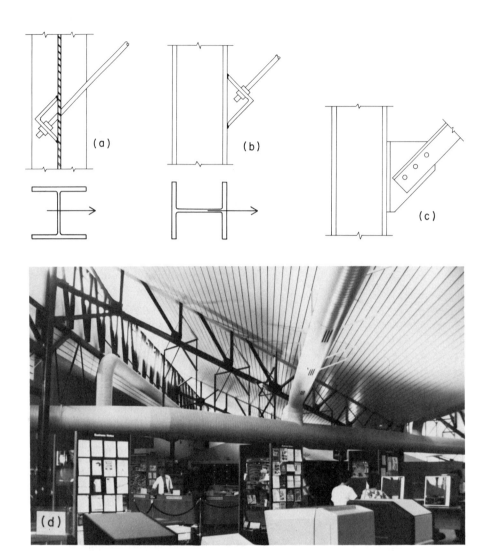

FIGURE 5.21. Use of trussed steel systems: (a), (b), and (c) framing details for *H* columns; (d) and (e) building with an exposed steel structure consisting of a two-way trussed bent system with round pipe columns. (Public library for City of Thousand Oaks, CA. Albert Martin, architect.)

tension and compression forces due to the truss action. However, the two other potentially significant contributions to the movement of the braced frame, with either or both of major concern, are:

1. *Movement of the Supports.* This includes the possibilities of deformation of the foundations and yielding of the anchorage connections. If the foundations rest on compressible soil, there will be some movement due to soil stress. Deformation of the anchorage may be due to a combination of lengthening of anchor bolts and bending of column base plates.

2. *Deformation in the Frame Connections.* This is a complex problem having to do with the general nature of the connection (e.g., welds or glue versus bolts or nails) as well as its form and layout and the deformation of the parts being connected.

It is good design practice in general to study the connection details for braced frames with an eye toward reduction of deformation within the connections. As has been mentioned previously, this generally favors the choice of welding, gluing, high-strength bolts, wood screws, and other fastening techniques that tend to produce stiff, tight joints. It may also favor the choice of materials or form of the frame members as these choices may affect the deformations within the joints or the choice of connecting methods.

The deflection, or drift, of single-story X-braced frames is usually caused primarily by the tension elongation of the diagonal X members. As shown in Figure 5.22a, the elongation of one diagonal moves the rectangular-framed bay into a parallelogram form. The approximate value of the deflection, d in Figure 5.22a, can be derived as follows.

Assuming the change in the angle of the diagonal, $\Delta\Theta$ in the figure, to be quite small, the change in length of the diagonal may be

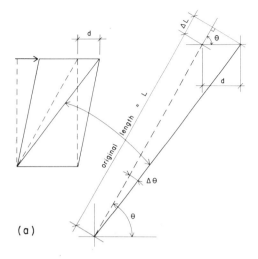

(a)

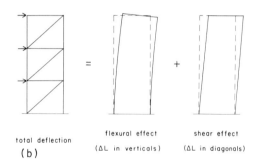

total deflection
(b)

flexural effect
(ΔL in verticals)

shear effect
(ΔL in diagonals)

FIGURE 5.22. Deflection of trussed bents.

used to approximate one side of the triangle of which d is the hypotenuse. Thus

$$d = \frac{\Delta L}{\cos \Theta} = \frac{TL/AE}{\cos \Theta} = \frac{TL}{AE \cos \Theta}$$

in which T = the tension in the X caused by the lateral load

A = the cross-sectional area of the X

E = the elastic modulus of the X

Θ = the angle of the X from the horizontal

The deflection of multistory X-braced frames has two components, both of which may be significant. As shown in Figure 5.22*b*, the first effect is caused by the change in length of the vertical members of the frame as a result of the overturning moment. The second effect is caused by the elongation of the diagonal X, as discussed for the single-story frame. These deflections occur in each level of the frame and can be calculated individually and summed up for the whole frame. Although this effect is also present in the single-story frame, it becomes more pronounced as the frame gets taller with respect to its width. These deflections of the cantilever beam can be calculated using standard formulas such as those given in the beam diagrams and formulas in Section 2 of the *Manual of Steel Construction* (Ref. 4).

5.4. MOMENT-RESISTIVE FRAMES

There is some confusion over the name to be used in referring to frames in which interactions between members of the frame include the transfer of moments through the connections. In years past the term most frequently used was *rigid frame*. This term came primarily from the classification of the connections or joints of the frame as *fixed* (or rigid) versus *pinned*, the latter term implying a lack of capability to transfer moment through the joint. As a general descriptive term, however, the name was badly conceived, since the frames of this type were generally the most deformable under lateral loading when compared to trussed frames or those braced by vertical diaphragms. The *UBC* (Ref. 1) uses the specific term *ductile moment-resisting space frame* and gives various qualifications for such a frame when it is used for seismic resistance. With apologies to the *UBC*, although we will assume the type of frames they thus define, we prefer not to use this rather cumbersome mouthful of a term, so will use the simpler term of rigid frame in our discussions.

General Behavior

In rigid frames with moment-resistive connections, both gravity and lateral loads produce interactive moments between the members. The *UBC* requires that a rigid frame designed for seismic loading be classified as a ''ductile moment-resistive space frame.'' Generally, frames of steel possess this character, but frames of reinforced concrete require special consideration of the reinforcing in order to meet this qualification.

In most cases rigid frames are actually the most flexible of the basic types of lateral resistive systems. This deformation character, together with the required ductility, makes the rigid frame a structure that absorbs energy loading through deformation as well as through its sheer brute strength. The net effect is that the structure actually works less hard in force resistance because its deformation tends to soften the loading. This is somewhat like rolling with a punch instead of bracing oneself to take it head on.

Most moment-resistive frames consist of either steel or concrete. Steel frames have either welded or bolted connections between the linear members to develop the necessary moment transfers. Frames of concrete achieve moment connections through the monolithic concrete and the continuity and anchorage of the steel reinforcing. Because concrete is basically brittle and not ductile, the ductile character is essentially produced by the ductility of the reinforcing. The type and amount of reinforcing and the details of its placing become critical to the proper behavior of rigid frames of reinforced concrete.

A complete presentation of the design of moment-resistive ductile frames for seismic loads is beyond the scope of this book. Such design can be done only by using plastic design for steel and ultimate strength design for reinforced concrete. We present only a brief discussion of this type of structure. For wind loading the analysis and design may be somewhat more simplified. However, if the structure is considerably indeterminate, an accurate analysis requires a complex and laborious calculation. We show some examples in Chapter 6, but limit the analysis to approximate methods.

For lateral loads in general, the rigid frame offers the advantage of a high degree of freedom in architectural terms. Walls and interior spaces are freed of the necessity for solid diaphragms or diagonal members. For building planning as a whole, this is a principal asset. Walls, even where otherwise required to be solid, need not be of a construction qualifying them as shear walls.

When seismic load governs as the critical lateral load, the moment-resistive frame has the advantage of being required to carry less load than other types of lateral resistive systems. Table 23-I in the *UBC* gives the value of *K* for a rigid frame as 0.67 versus 1.33 for a box system with shear walls or braced frames. Thus the rigid frame is required to carry only half the load specified for the box system. Even when the rigid frame is interactive with a box system, and the rigid frame is capable of carrying at least 25% of the lateral load, the *K* factor is reduced to 0.80, or 40% less than that for a box system alone.

Deformation analysis is a critical part of the design of rigid frames because such frames tend to be relatively deformable when compared to other lateral resistive systems. The deformations have the potential of causing problems in terms of movements of a disturbing nature that can be sensed by the building occupants or of damage to nonstructural parts of the building, as previously discussed. The need to limit deformations often results in the size of vertical elements of the frame being determined by stiffness requirements rather than by stress limits.

Loading Conditions

Unlike shear walls or X-bracing, rigid frames are not generally able to be used for lateral bracing alone. Thus their structural actions induced by the lateral loads must always be combined with the effects of gravity loads. These combined loading conditions may be studied separately in order to simplify the work of visualizing and quantifying the structural behavior, but it should be borne in mind that they do not occur independently.

Figure 5.23*a* shows the form of deformation and the distribution of internal bending moments in a single-span rigid frame, as induced by vertical gravity loading. If the frame is not required to resist lateral loads, the singular forms of these responses may be assumed, and the various details of the structure may be developed in this context. Thus the direction of rotation at the column base, the sign of moment at the beam-to-column joint, the sign of the bending moment and nature of the corresponding stresses at midspan of the beam, and the location of inflection points in the beam may all relate to choices for the form and details of the members and development of any connection details. If the frame is reasonably symmetrical, the only concerns for deflection are the outward bulging of the columns and the vertical sag of the beam.

Under action of lateral loading due to wind or seismic force, the form of deformation and distribution of internal bending moment will be as shown in Fig. 5.23*b*. If the gravity and lateral loadings are combined, the net effect will be as shown in Figure 5.23*c*. Observing the effects of the combined loading, we note the following:

1. Horizontal deflection at the top of the frame (called drift) must now be considered, in addition to the deflections mentioned previously for gravity load alone.

2. The maximum value for the moment at the beam-to-column connection is increased on one side and reduced on the other side of the bent. The increased moment requires that the beam, the column,

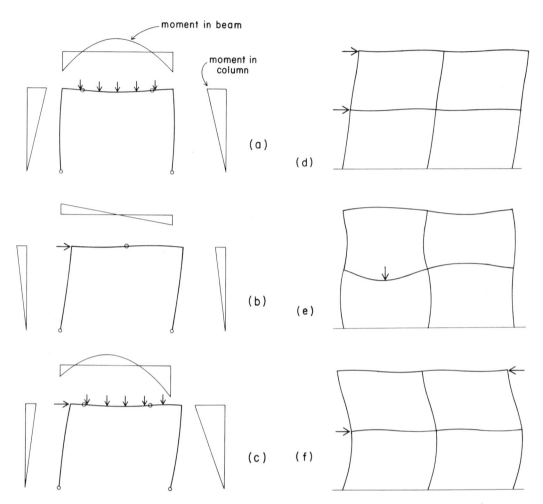

FIGURE 5.23. Behavior of rigid frames: (*a*) under gravity load; (*b*) under lateral load; (*c*) under combined gravity and lateral loading; (*d*) lateral load on a multistory bent; (*e*) effect of single gravity loading in a multiunit bent; (*f*) effects of rapid reversal of lateral loads.

and the connection at the joint must all be stronger for the combined loading.

3. If the lateral load is sufficient, the minimum value for the moment at the beam-to-column joint may be one of opposite sign from that produced by gravity loading alone. The form of the connection, and possibly the design of the members, may need to reflect this reversal of the sense of the moment.

4. The direction of the lateral load shown in Figure 5.23*b* is reversible so that two

combinations of load must be considered: gravity plus lateral load to the right and gravity plus lateral load to the left.

While single-span rigid frames are often used for buildings, the multispan or multistory frame is the more usual case. Figures 5.23*d* and *e* shows the response of a two-bay, two-story frame to lateral loads and to a gravity-type load applied to a single beam. The response to lateral loads is essentially similar to that for the single bent in Figure

5.22. For gravity loads the multiunit frame must be analyzed for a more complex set of potential combinations, because the live load portion of the gravity loads must be considered to be random, and thus may or may not occur in any given beam span.

Lateral loads produced by winds will generally result in the loading condition shown in Figure 5.23*d*. Because of its relative flexibility and size, however, a multistory building frame may quite likely respond so slowly to seismic motions that upper levels of the frame experience a whiplashlike effect; thus separate levels may be moving in opposite directions at a single moment. Figure 5.23*f* illustrates a type of response that may occur if the two-story frame experiences this action. Only a true dynamic analysis can ascertain whether this action occurs and is of critical concern for a particular structure.

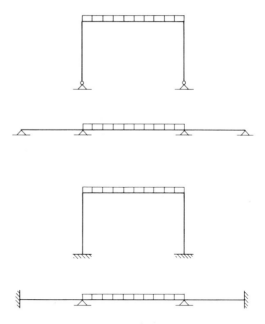

FIGURE 5.24. Continuous beam analogy for a single-span frame.

Approximate Analysis for Gravity Loads.
Most rigid frames are statically indeterminate and require the use of some method beyond simple statics for their analysis. Simple frames of few members may be analyzed by some *hand* method using handbook coefficients, moment distribution, and so on. If the frame is complex, consisting of several bays and stories, or having a lack of symmetry, the analysis will be quite laborious unless performed with some computer-aided method.

For preliminary design it is often useful to have some approximate analysis, which can be fairly quickly performed. Internal forces, member sizes, and deflections thus determined may be used for a quick determination of the structural actions and the feasibility of some choices of systems and components. For the simple, single-bay bent shown in Figure 5.24, the analysis for gravity loads is quite simple, since a single-loading condition exists (as shown) and the only necessary assumption is that of the relative stiffnesses of the beam and columns. For the frame with pin-based columns the analogy is

made to a three-span beam on rotation-free supports. If the column bases are fixed, the end supports of the analogous beam are assumed fixed.

For multibayed, multistoried frames, an approximate analysis may be performed using techniques such as that described in Chapter 8 of the ACI Code (Ref. 5). This is more applicable to concrete frames, of course, but can be used for quick approximation of welded steel frames as well.

Even when using approximate methods, it is advisable to analyze separately for dead and live loads. The results can thus be combined as required for the various critical combinations of dead load, live load, wind load, and seismic load. (See UBC Sec. 2303f in Appendix C.)

Approximate Analysis for Lateral Loads.
Various approximate methods may be used for the analysis of rigid frames under statically applied lateral loading. For ordinary frames, whether single-bay, multibay, or

even multistory, approximate methods are commonly used for loading due to wind or as obtained from an equivalent static load analysis for seismic effects. More exact analyses are possible, of course, especially when performed by computer-aided methods.

For frames that are complex—due to irregularities, lack of symmetry, tapered members, and so on—analysis is hardly feasible without the computer. This is also true for analyses that attempt to deal with the true dynamic behavior of the structure under seismic load. With the increasing availability of the software, and the accumulation of experience with its use, this type of analysis is becoming more widespread in use. For quick approximations for preliminary design, however, approximation methods are likely to continue in use for some time.

For the simple bent shown in Figure 5.25, the effects of the single lateral force may be quite simply visualized in terms of the deflected shape, the reaction forces, and the variation of moment in the members.

If the columns are assumed to be pin based and of equal stiffness, it is reasonable to assume that the horizontal reactions at the base of the columns are equal, thus permitting an analysis by statics alone. If the column bases are assumed to be fixed, the frame is truly able to be analyzed only by indeterminate methods, although an approximate analysis can be made with an assumed location of the inflection point in the column. In truth, the column bases will most likely be somewhere between these two idealized conditions. Approximate designs are sometimes done by combining the results from both idealized conditions (pinned and fixed bases) and designing for both. Adjustments are made when the more precise nature of the condition is established by the detailed development of the base construction.

For multibayed frames, such as those shown in Figure 5.26, an approximate analysis may be done in a manner similar to that for the single-bay frame. If the columns are all of equal stiffness, the total load is simply divided by the number of columns. Assumptions about the column base condition would

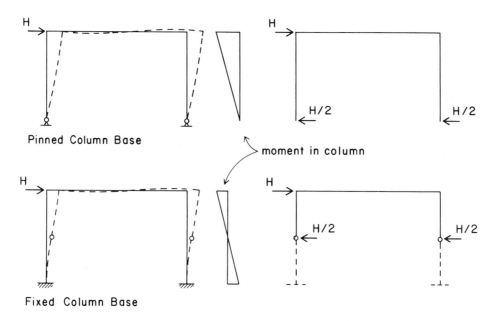

FIGURE 5.25. Effects of column base conditions on a single-span frame.

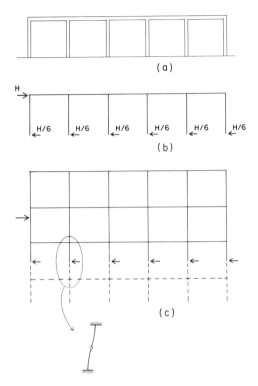

FIGURE 5.26. Distribution of lateral load in a multiunit frame.

over shear walls or braced (trussed) frames by requiring less design load due to the lower assigned K value. For large frames the combination of slow reaction time (because of long fundamental period of vibration) and various damping effects means that forces tend to dissipate rapidly in the remote portions of the frame.

Architecturally, the rigid frame offers the least potential for interference with planning of open spaces within the building and in exterior walls. It is thus highly favored by architects whose design style includes the use of ordered rectangular grids and open spaces of rectangular or cubical form. Geometries other than rectangular ones are possible also; what remains as the primary advantage is the absence of the need for diagonal bracing or solid walls at determined locations.

Some of the disadvantages of rigid frames are the following:

1. Lateral deflection, or drift, of the structure is likely to be a problem. As a result, it is often necessary to stiffen the frame—mostly by increasing the number and/or size of the columns.

2. Connections must be stronger, especially in steel frames. Addition of heavily welded steel joints, of additional reinforcing for bar anchorage, shear, and torsion in concrete frames, and for cumbersome moment-resistive connections in wood frames can add appreciably to the construction cost and time.

3. For large frames dynamic behavior is often quite complex, with potential for whiplash, resonance, and so on. Dynamic analysis is more often required for acceptable design when a rigid frame is used. In time, dynamic analysis may be routine and easily performed with available aids on all structures; at the present it is quite expensive and time consuming.

When rigid frames are to be used for the lateral bracing system for a building, there

be the same as for the single-bay frame. If the columns are not all of the same stiffness, an approximate distribution can be made on the basis of relative stiffness.

Figure 5.26c illustrates the basis for an approximation of the horizontal shear forces in the columns of a multistory building. As for the single-story frame, the individual column shears are distributed on the basis of assumed column stiffnesses. For the upper columns the inflection point is assumed to occur at midheight, unless column splice points are used to control its location.

General Design Considerations

From a purely structural point of view, there are many advantages of the rigid frame as a lateral bracing system for resisting seismic effects. The current codes tend to favor it

must be a high degree of coordination between the planner of the building form and
the structural designer. As illustrated in the
examples in Chapter 6, the building plan
must accommodate some regularity and
alignment of the columns that constitute the
vertical members of the rigid frame bents.
This may not include *all* of the building columns, but those that function in the rigid
frames must be aligned to form the planes
of the bents. Openings in floors and roofs
must be planned so as not to interrupt beams
that occur as horizontal members of the
bents.

There must, of course, be a coordination
between the designs for lateral and gravity
loads. If a rigid frame is used for bracing, it
will in most cases be used in conjunction
with some type of framed floor and roof systems. Horizontal members of the floor and
roof systems designed for gravity loads will
also be used as horizontal elements of the
rigid frames. However, in some cases, much
of the horizontal structure may be used only
for gravity loads. In the system that utilizes
only the bents that occur in exterior walls,
none of the interior portion of the framing is
involved in the rigid frame actions; thus its
planning is free of concerns for the bent development.

Selection of members and construction
details for rigid frames depends a great deal
on the materials used. The following discusses separately the problems of bents of
steel and reinforced concrete.

Steel Frames. Steel frames with moment-
resistive connections were used for early
skyscrapers. Fasteners consisted of rivets,
which were widely used until the development of high-strength bolts. Today, rigid
frame construction in steel mostly utilizes
welded joints, although bolting is sometimes
used for temporary connection during erec-
tion. Figure 5.27 shows the erected frame
for a low-rise office building, using a steel

FIGURE 5.27. Steel frame structure with a peripheral
bracing system of rigid bents.

frame for both gravity and lateral load resistance. The principal members of the frame
are wide flange (I-shape) rolled steel sections, and moment connections are welded.
This is the most common form of steel rigid
frame for building construction.

Another form of steel rigid frame is the

trussed bent. A single-span bent is illustrated in Figure 5.15i, and the use of a two-span bent is described in the building design study in Figure 6.32.

For tall buildings a currently popular system is one that uses a peripheral bracing arrangement with closely spaced, stiff steel columns and heavy spandrel beams. This type of structure offers a major advantage in its overall stiffness in resistance to lateral drift (horizontal deflection). Figure 5.28 shows the erected frame for such a structure. Note that the exterior rigid bents are discontinuous at the corners, thus avoiding the high concentration of forces on the corner col-

umns, especially those due to torsional action of the building.

Reinforced Concrete Frames. Poured-in-place frames with monolithic columns and beams have a natural rigid frame action. For seismic resistance both columns and beams must be specially reinforced for the shears and torsions at the member ends. Beams in the column-line bents ordinarily use continuous top and bottom reinforcing with continuous loop ties that serve the triple functions of resisting shear, torsion, and compression bar buckling. Figure 5.29 shows two buildings with exposed concrete frames

FIGURE 5.28. Use of closely spaced columns and stiff spandrels in a peripheral bent system.

FIGURE 5.29. Exposed concrete frames.

that are of this type of construction. It is possible, of course, to brace such a building with poured concrete shear walls and to use the frame strictly for gravity resistance, except for collector and chord functions.

Precast concrete structures are often difficult to develop as rigid frames, unless the precast elements are developed as individual bent units instead of the usual, single, linear members. Moment-resistive joints for these structures are usually quite difficult to develop, the more common solution being to use a shear wall system for lateral bracing.

5.5. INTERACTION OF FRAMES AND DIAPHRAGMS

Most buildings consist of combinations of walls and some framing of wood, steel, or concrete. The planning and design of the lateral-resistive structure require some judgments and decisions regarding the roles of the frame and the walls. This section discusses some of the issues relating to this aspect of design.

Coexisting, Independent Elements

Most buildings have some solid walls, that is, walls with continuous surfaces free of openings. When the gravity load-resistive structure of the building consists of a frame, the relationship between the walls and the frame has several possibilities with regard to action caused by lateral loads.

The frame may be a braced frame or a moment-resistive frame designed for the total resistance of the lateral loads, in which case the attachment of walls to the frame must be done in a manner that prevents the walls from absorbing lateral loads. Because solid walls tend to be quite stiff in their own planes, such attachment often requires the use of separation joints or flexible connections that will allow the frame to deform as necessary under the lateral loads.

The frame may be essentially designed for gravity resistance only, with lateral load resistance provided by the walls acting as shear walls. (See Fig. 5.30.) This method requires that some of the elements of the frame function as collectors, stiffeners, shear wall end members, or diaphragm chords. If

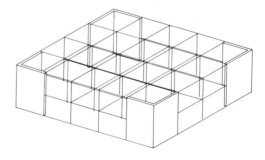

FIGURE 5.30. Wall-braced frame structure.

the walls are intended to be used strictly for lateral bracing, care must be exercised in the design of construction details to assure that beams that occur above the walls are allowed to deflect without transferring loads to the walls.

Load Sharing. When walls are firmly attached to vertical elements of the frame, they usually provide continuous lateral bracing in the plane of the wall, thus permitting the vertical frame elements to be designed for column action using their stiffness in the direction perpendicular to the wall. Thus 2 × 4 studs may be designed as columns using h/d ratios based on their larger dimension.

In some cases both walls and frames may be used for lateral load resistance at different

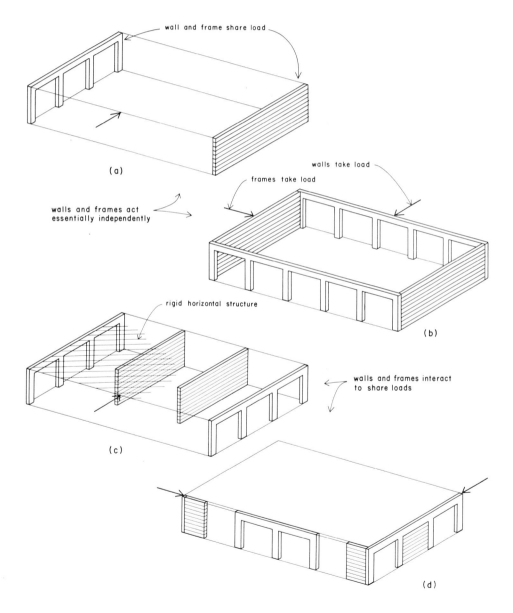

FIGURE 5.31. Mixed shear walls and rigid frames.

locations or in different directions. Figure 5.31 shows two such situations. In Figure 5.31a a shear wall is used at one end of the building and a frame at the other end for the wind from one direction. In Figure 5.31b walls are used for the lateral loads from one direction and frames for the load from the other direction. In both cases the walls and frames do not actually interact, that is, they act independently with regard to load sharing.

Figure 5.31c shows a situation in which walls and frames interact to share a direct load. The interior walls and the end frames share the total load from a single direction. If the horizontal structure is a rigid diaphragm, the load sharing will be on the basis of the relative stiffness of the vertical elements. This relative stiffness must be established by the calculated deflection resistance of the elements, as previously discussed.

Figure 5.31d shows a situation in which the walls and frames interact to share a single direct load. This represents a highly indeterminate situation. Case 3 in Table 23-I of the *UBC* describes such a situation, called a "dual bracing system," that consists of shear walls and a moment-resistive frame. The *UBC* requires that the shear walls in this system be capable of resisting the entire lateral load but that the frame be capable of resisting 25% of the load by itself. This is an apparent redundancy in the design, but the advantage gained is that the K factor for the seismic load may be reduced from 1.33 for the walls alone to 0.80 for the dual system.

Structures of the type illustrated in Figure 5.31 should be analyzed using dynamic methods to determine the load distribution and ultimate or plastic strength analysis for the behavior of the elements of the system. If the simpler equivalent static load method is used and the elements are designed using working stress analysis, the stiffer elements of the system should be designed quite conservatively, because they will tend to take more loading than the static analysis implies.

5.6. COLLECTORS AND TIES

Transfer of loads from horizontal to vertical elements in laterally resistive structural systems frequently involves the use of some structural members that serve the functions of struts, drags, ties, collectors, and so on. These members often serve two functions—as parts of the gravity-resistive system or for other functions in lateral load resistance.

Figure 5.32 shows a structure consisting of a horizontal diaphragm and a number of exterior shear walls. For loading in the north–south direction the framing members labeled A serve as chords for the roof diaphragm. In most cases they are also parts of the roof edge or top of the wall framing. For the lateral load in the east–west direction they serve as collectors. This latter function permits us to consider the shear stress in the roof diaphragm to be a constant along the entire length of the edge. The collector "collects" this constant stress from the roof and distributes it to the isolated shear walls, thus functioning as a tension/compression member in the gaps between the walls.

In the example in Figure 5.32 the collector A must be attached to the roof edge to develop the transfer of the constant shear stress. The collector A must be attached to the individual shear walls for the transfer of the total load in each wall. In the gaps between walls the collector gathers the roof edge load and functions partly as a compression member, pushing some of the load to the forward wall, and partly as a tension member, dragging the remainder of the collected load into the rearward wall.

Collectors B and C in Figure 5.32 gather the edge load from the roof deck under the north–south lateral loading. Their function over the gap reverses as the load switches direction. They work in compression for load in the northerly direction, pushing the load into the walls. When the load changes to the southerly direction, they work in tension, dragging the load into the walls.

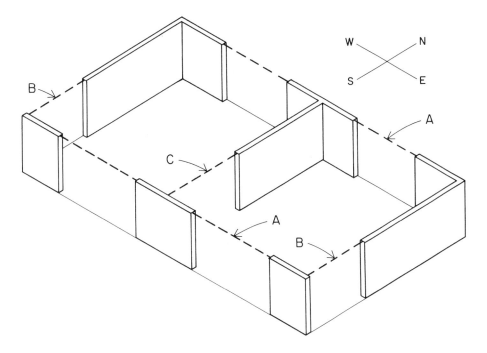

FIGURE 5.32. Collector functions in a box system.

The complete functioning of a lateral resistive structural system must be carefully studied to determine the need for such members. As mentioned previously, ordinary members of the building construction will often serve these functions: top plates of the stud walls, edge framing of roofs and floors, headers over openings, and so on. If so used, such members should be investigated for the combined stress effects involved in their multiple roles.

5.7. ANCHORAGE ELEMENTS

The attachment of elements of the lateral resistive structure to one another, to collectors, or to supports usually involves some type of anchorage element. There is a great variety of these, encompassing the range of situations with regard to load transfer conditions, magnitude of the forces, and various mate-

rials and details of the structural members and systems.

Tiedowns

Resistance to vertical uplift is sometimes required for elements of a braced- or moment-resistive frame for the ends of shear walls, or for light roof systems subject to the force of upward wind suction. For concrete and reinforced masonry structures, such resistance is most often achieved by doweling and/or hooking of reinforcing bars. Steel columns are usually anchored by the anchor bolts at their bases. The illustrations in Figure 5.33 show some of the devices that are used for anchoring wood structural elements. In many cases these devices have been load tested and their capacities rated by their manufacturers. When using them, it is essential to determine whether the load ratings have been accepted by the building code

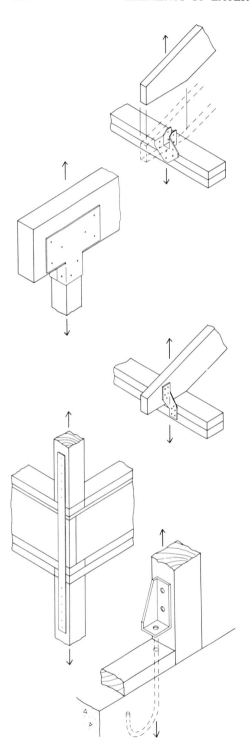

agency with jurisdiction for a specific building design.

The term *tiedown* or *hold-down* is used mostly to describe the type of anchor shown in the lower right corner of Figure 5.33.

Horizontal Anchors. In addition to the transfer of vertical gravity load and lateral shear load at the edges of horizontal diaphragms, there is usually a need for resistance to the horizontal pulling away of walls from the diaphragm edge. In many cases the connections that are provided for other functions also serve to resist this action. Codes usually require that this type of anchorage be a "positive" one, not relying on such things as the withdrawal of nails or lateral force on toe nails. Figure 5.34 shows some of the means used for achieving this type of anchorage.

Shear Anchors. The shear force at the edge of a horizontal diaphragm must be transferred from the diaphragm into a collector or

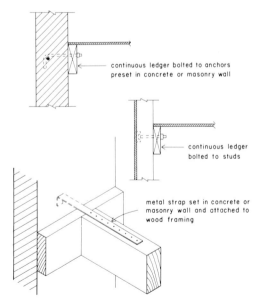

continuous ledger bolted to anchors preset in concrete or masonry wall

continuous ledger bolted to studs

metal strap set in concrete or masonry wall and attached to wood framing

FIGURE 5.33. Anchoring of wood frames.

FIGURE 5.34. Anchoring of horizontal diaphragms.

some other intermediate member, or directly into a vertical diaphragm. Except for poured-in-place concrete structures, this process usually involves some means of attachment. For wood structures the transfer is usually achieved through the lateral loading of nails, bolts, or lag screws for which the codes or industry specifications provide tabulated load capacities. For steel deck diaphragms the transfer is usually achieved by welding the deck to supporting steel framing.

If the vertical system is a steel frame, these members are usually parts of the frame system. If the vertical structure is concrete or masonry, the edge transfer members are usually attached to the walls with anchor bolts set in the concrete or in solid-filled horizontal courses of the masonry. As in other situations, the combined stresses on these connections must be carefully investigated to determine the critical load conditions.

Another shear transfer problem is that which occurs at the base of a shear wall in terms of a sliding effect. For a wood-framed wall some attachment of the wall sill member to its support must be made. If the support is wood, the attachment is usually achieved by using nails or lag screws. If the support is concrete or masonry, the sill is usually attached to preset anchor bolts. The lateral load capacity of the bolts is determined by their shear capacity in the concrete or the single shear limit in the wood sill. The *UBC* Section 2907(f) gives some minimum requirements for sill bolting, which should be used as a starting point in developing this type of connection.

For walls of concrete and masonry, in which there is often considerable dead load at the base of the wall, sliding resistance may be adequately developed by friction. Doweling provided for the vertical wall reinforcing also offers some lateral shear resistance. If a more positive anchor is desired, or if the calculated load requires it, shear keys may be provided by inserting wood blocks in the concrete, as shown in Figure 5.35.

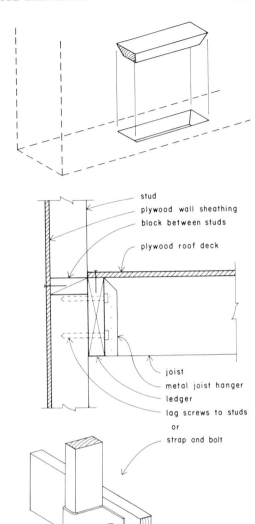

FIGURE 5.35. Transfer of lateral loads between horizontal and vertical elements.

Transfer of Forces

The complete transfer of force from the horizontal to the vertical elements of the lateral-resistive system can be quite complex in some cases. Figure 5.35 shows a joint between a horizontal plywood diaphragm and a vertical plywood shear wall. For reasons other than lateral load resistance, it is desired that the studs in the wall run continuously past the level of the roof deck. This necessitates the use of a continuous edge-framing member, called a *ledger*, that serves as the vertical support for the deck as well as the chord and edge collector for the lateral forces. This ledger is shown to be attached to the faces of the studs with two lag screws at each stud. The functioning of this joint involves the following:

1. The vertical gravity load is transferred from the ledger to the studs directly through lateral load on the lag screws.

2. The lateral shear stress in the roof deck is transferred to the ledger through lateral load on the edge nails of the deck. This stress is in turn transferred from the ledger to the studs by horizontal lateral load on the lag screws. The horizontal blocking is fit between the studs to provide for the transfer of the load to the wall plywood which is nailed to the blocking.

3. Outward loading on the wall is resisted by the lag screws in withdrawal. This is generally not considered to be a good positive connection, although the load magnitude should be considered in making this evaluation. A more positive connection is achieved by using the bolts and straps shown in the lower sketch in Figure 5.35.

5.8. SEPARATION JOINTS

During the swaying motions induced by earthquakes, different parts of a building tend to move independently because of the differences in their masses, their fundamental periods, and variations in damping, support constraint, and so on. With regard to the building structure, it is usually desirable to tie it together so that it moves as a whole as much as possible. Sometimes, however, it is better to separate parts from one another in a manner that permits them a reasonable freedom of motion with respect to one another.

Figure 5.36 shows some building forms in which the extreme difference of period of adjacent masses of the building makes it preferable to cause a separation. Designing the building connection at these intersections must be done with regard to the specific situation in each case. Some of the considerations to be made in this are the following.

The Specific Direction of Movements. In generally rectangular building forms, such as those shown in the examples in Fig. 5.36, the primary movements are in the direction

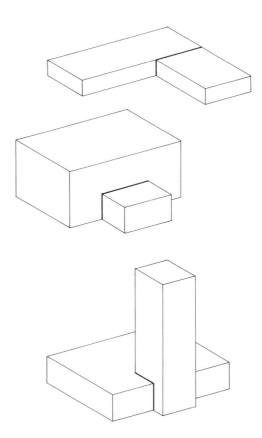

FIGURE 5.36. Potential situations requiring separation joints.

of the major axes of the adjacent masses. Thus the joint between the masses has two principal forms of motion: a shear effect parallel to the joint, and a together–apart motion perpendicular to the joint. In building forms of greater geometric complexity, the motions of the respective masses are more random and the joint action is much more complex.

The Actual Dimensions of Movement at the Joint. If the joint is to be truly effective and if the adjacent parts are not allowed to pound each other, the actual dimension of the movements must be safely tolerated by the separation. The more complex the motions of the separate masses, the more difficult it is to predict these dimensions accurately, calling for some conservative margin in the dimension of the separation provided.

Detailing the Joint for Effective Separation. Because the idea of the joint is that structural separation is to be provided while still achieving the general connection of the adjacent parts, it is necessary to make a joint that performs both of these seemingly contradictory functions. Various techniques are possible using connections that employ sliding, rolling, rotating, swinging, or flexible elements that permit one type of connection while having a freedom of movement for certain directions or types of motion. The possibilities are endless, and the specific situation must be carefully analyzed in order to develop an effective and logical joint detail. In some cases the complexity of the motions, the extreme dimension of movement to be facilitated, or other considerations may make it necessary to have complete separation— that is, literally to build two separate buildings very close together.

Facilitating Other Functions of the Joint. It is often necessary for the separation joint to provide for functions other than those of the seismic motions. Gravity load transfer may be required through the joint.

Nonstructural functions, such as weather sealing, waterproofing, and the passage of wiring, piping, or ductwork through the joint, may be required. Figure 5.37 shows two typical cases in which the joint achieves structural separation while providing for a closing of the joint. The upper drawing shows a flexible flashing or sealing strip used to achieve weather or water tightness of the joint. The lower drawing symbolizes the usual solution for a floor in which a flat element is attached to one side of the joint and is allowed to slip on the other side.

Figure 5.38 shows a number of situations in which partial structural separation is achieved. The details of such joints are often quite similar to those used for joints designed to provide separation for thermal expansion. Figure 5.38*a* shows a key slot, which is the type of connection usually used in walls

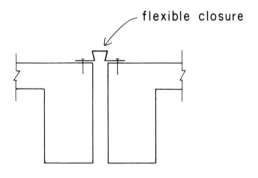

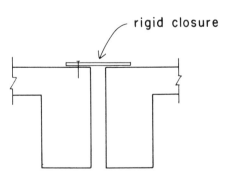

FIGURE 5.37.   Closure of horizontal separation joints.

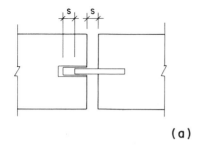

(a)

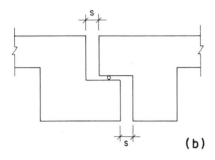

(b)

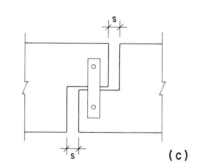

(c)

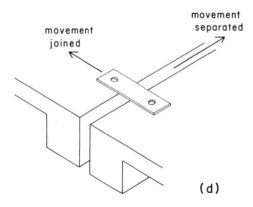

(d)

FIGURE 5.38. Means for achieving partial separation.

where the separation is required only in a direction parallel to the wall plane. Figures 5.38*b* and *c* show means for achieving the transfer of vertical gravity forces through the joint while permitting movement in a horizontal direction. Figure 5.38*d* shows a means for achieving a connection in one horizontal direction while permitting movement in the perpendicular direction.

5.9. FOUNDATIONS

This section presents a discussion of some of the concerns for foundations relating to the development of the lateral resistive systems for wind and earthquake effects. A more complete discussion of the problems of lateral forces on foundations is presented in Chapter 8.

General Considerations

Foundation design problems have considerable variety because of the wide range of possible soil conditions, load magnitudes, building size and shape, and type of structural system. For any building it is wise to have a subsoil investigation, lab tests on representative soil samples, and a recommendation from an engineer with experience in soil behaviors and foundation problems. We illustrate some of the ordinary and simple design problems in the examples in Chapter 6, but do not attempt to deal with all the special problems that can occur in the design of foundations for lateral loads.

For seismic load the foundations have a dual role. Initially, they are the origin point for load on the building, being directly attached to the ground and used by the ground to shake the building. In our analysis procedures, however, the seismic load is considered to be a result of the inertial effect of the moving building mass. From this viewpoint the loading condition becomes similar to that for the wind load. Thus we visualize the horizontal inertial force as being transmitted through the building structure into the foundation, and finally into the ground, which is now considered to offer passive resistance, as it does actually to the wind force.

For seismic loads it is usually desirable that the entire building foundation act essentially as a single rigid unit. If elements of the foundation are isolated from one another, as in the case of individual column footings, it may be necessary to provide struts or grade walls to tie the structure into a unit. Where they exist, of course, the ordinary elements such as basement walls, grade walls, wall footings, and grade-level framing members may be used for this tying function.

For wind loads the foundations function essentially as an anchor for the building superstructure, resisting the overturn, uplift, and horizontal sliding effects. The predominant effects on the foundations depend on the magnitude of the wind load, the type of foundation system, the ground conditions, and the relative magnitude of the weight of the building construction. For very light construction, for example, the principal problems may be the resistance of uplift and overturn. For a building on deep foundations (piles or piers) with no basement, the principal problem may be the simple resistance to horizontal movement. For a building of heavy masonry or concrete construction, the wind load on the foundations may be negligible and the predominant concern be that for vertical soil pressure.

Design Criteria and Data. Chapter 29 of the *UBC* provides some data and recommendations for use in designing for sliding or lateral passive resistance of soil. The *UBC* material is quite conservative in most cases, and a complete soils investigation and report may provide more rational data and permit a less conservative design. In many cases soil conditions are general local phenomena,

and local building codes often have special requirements and procedures for foundation design. Local design and construction procedures are sometimes based more on histories of successes and failures than on scientific analysis or engineering judgment.

Deep Foundations. Buildings on deep foundations consisting of long piles or piers offer special problems in design for lateral loads. The entire lateral force must usually be developed by the passive resistance of soil because the sliding friction present on the bottom of shallow bearing footings is not available. When the upper soil strata are considerably deformable, the fundamental period of the building and its general dynamic behavior may be significantly affected by the lateral movement of the foundation. It is highly recommended that the design of these foundations and the structures supported by them be done by an engineer with experience in these problems.

Special Problems

Many seismic load failures of building structures are precipitated or aggravated by soil movements in fill or other highly compressible soil deposits. An especially hazardous situation is that which occurs when different parts of the foundation are placed on soil of significantly different compressibility, as may occur because of a hilly site, variations in the level of the foundations, extensive regrading, or nonhorizontal soil strata. Subsidence of the fill, major differences in settlements, or lateral movement of the soil mass can produce various critical situations. Figure 5.39 illustrates some of the possibilities that can produce structural failures for both gravity and lateral load conditions.

For buildings with exceptional uplift or overturn effects, the foundation must usually provide an anchor through its own sheer dead weight. For a large building with shallow

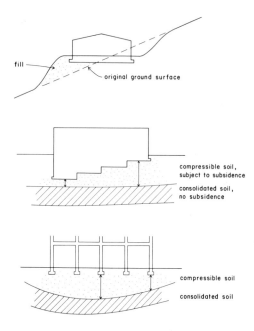

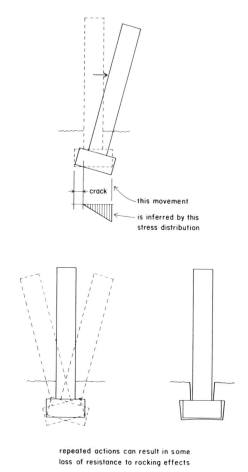

FIGURE 5.39.　Potential foundation problems.

foundations and no basement, the necessary dead load may not exist in the foundations designed for gravity loads alone. This situation may require some additional mass in the foundation itself or the use of soil weight in the form of backfill over the foundation.

Another problem with shallow foundations is that they often bear on relatively compressible soil. Figure 5.40 illustrates the effect that can occur with a large lateral load and a strong overturning moment. With repeated applications and reversals of such a load, the soil beneath the foundation edges becomes compressed, resulting in an increasing tendency for the structure to rock, thus producing a loss of stability or a significant change in the dynamic load behavior of the structure. When the bearing strata of soil are very compressible, it is generally advisable to avoid the extreme condition of soil stress shown in the illustration.

Figure 5.41 illustrates the typical problem of tying isolated footings, which is done primarily for the purpose of ensuring that the building structure move as a single mass with

FIGURE 5.40.　Potential effect of repeated lateral forces.

respect to the ground. It is also sometimes done to allow for the sharing of the lateral load when the load on a single footing cannot be resisted by that footing alone.

In many cases the existence of basement

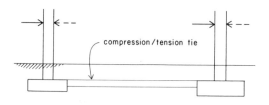

FIGURE 5.41.　Tying of isolated footings.

walls, grade walls, wall footings, or other parts of the building substructure makes the addition of ties unnecessary. When individual footings are truly isolated, the tie member is designed as both a tension and a compression member. The required size of the concrete cross section and the main reinforcing is usually determined by the column action in compression. The tension tie is provided by extending the tie reinforcing into the footings in dowel action.

When calculated lateral loads exist for the footings, they may be used as the design loads on the ties. Section 2312(j)3.B of the *UBC* requires ties for pile caps and caissons to be designed for a minimum load of 0.10 of the vertical load on the heaviest loaded element. For isolated footings under structural elements that are not part of the lateral resistive structural system, there is no quantifiable basis for the tie design. Such footings are usually designed using the minimum requirements for concrete compressive members.

For foundations that do not use bearing footings, there are some special problems with regard to lateral loads. Figure 5.42 shows three such situations: drilled caissons, driven piles, and pole-type structures. Direct resistance to horizontal movement by the ground in all these situations can be developed only as a passive lateral soil pressure. Where the upper soil strata are highly compressible, which is usually what causes piles and caissons to be used, this resistance is

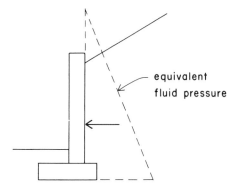

lateral soil pressure
for gravity design

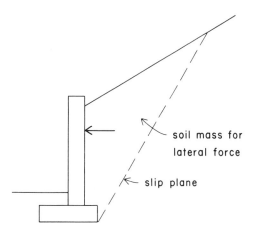

lateral soil pressure
for seismic design

FIGURE 5.43. Lateral load conditions for tall retaining walls, with gravity plus seismic loads.

quite limited. In addition, the construction of all three types of foundation shown results in considerable disturbance of the upper ground mass, which further lowers its effectiveness for passive resistance.

The tying of the pole structure is usually performed above the level of the ground by the rest of the structure or by added ties and struts. The use of piles and caissons usually involves two considerations: the actual lat-

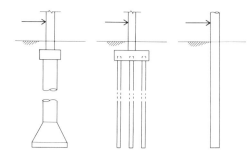

FIGURE 5.42. Deep, penetration-type foundations.

eral load and the need for lateral stability under the vertical load. Tying is required for both of these reasons, and the previously cited *UBC* requirement is based on the latter problem—that of stability under the vertical load. Any calculated lateral loads delivered to the tops of the pile and caisson foundations should be carried away to other parts of the construction for development of the actual lateral resistance, which is essentially similar to the procedure used for isolated footings.

Another special soil problem occurs when there is a seismic load on retaining walls. As shown in Fig. 5.43, when designing for gravity loads, a lateral soil pressure is usually assumed on the basis of an equivalent horizontal fluid pressure. If a surcharge exists, or if the ground slopes to the wall as shown in the illustration, the level of the equivalent fluid is assumed to be somewhere above the true ground level at the back of the wall.

When lateral load has been caused by seismic movement, the earth mass behind the wall has the potential of delivering a horizontal force while simultaneously offering gravity resistance to the overturn of the wall. The lower illustration in Figure 5.43 shows the usual assumption for the soil failure mechanism that defines the potential mass whose weight develops the lateral seismic force. In a conservative design for the anal-

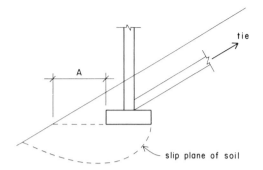

FIGURE 5.44. Bearing footings in hillside conditions.

ysis of the wall, this force should be added to the lateral seismic forces of the wall and footing weights.

Figure 5.44 illustrates the situation of a footing in a hillside location that could be a wall footing or an isolated column footing. The dimension A in the figure, called the *daylight dimension*, must be sufficient to provide resistance to the failure of the soil as shown. Lateral load on the footing will further aggravate this type of failure if A is too small. The preferred solution, if the construction permits it, is to use a tension tie to transfer the lateral effect to some other part of the structure. Otherwise, the level of the footing should be lowered until a conservative distance is developed for the daylight dimension.

CHAPTER SIX

Design for Wind and Earthquake Effects

This chapter contains a number of examples of the design of building structures for the effects of wind and seismic actions. The examples have been chosen to illustrate relatively common situations with regard to size and to building construction type. A few example buildings have been used repetitively, resulting in the presentation of alternative solutions for the lateral bracing system for the same basic building form. The examples are limited to low-rise buildings with relatively simple forms; for this category the use of the equivalent static load method is reasonably acceptable. Buildings of greater size, more complex form, unique construction, or with heightened concern for damage will require more rigorous investigation and more knowledgeable design procedures.

6.1. PROCESS OF DESIGN

Design is essentially a continuing task of inquiry and decision. The inquiry continues as long as potential questions can be brought up; decisions must be made with much judgment and with the weighing of the importance of many factors, some of which are usually in opposition. Final design solutions for complex systems, such as those for building structures, often contain many compromises and many relatively arbitrary

choices. The most economical, most fire-resistive, most quickly erected, most handsome, or most architecturally accommodating structure is only accidentally likely to be the optimal choice for the resistance of lateral forces. We cannot pretend to show the complete process of structural design in these examples, although consideration of factors other than lateral force actions is frequently mentioned. The design solutions developed are thus unavoidably somewhat simplistic and myopic in their concentration on the lateral force problem.

In general, with regard to the lateral force resistive system, the design process incorporates the following:

1. *Determination of the Basic Scheme.* This includes the choice of type and layout of the basic elements of the system.
2. *Determination of Loads.* This involves the establishment of criteria and the choice of investigative methods.
3. *Determination of the Load Propagation.* This consists of the tracing of the load through the structure, from element-to-element of the system, until it is finally resolved into the supporting ground.
4. *Design of Individual Elements.* Based on their load-sharing roles, each separate element of the system must be investigated and designed.

5. *Design for Interactions.* Connections between elements of the structure, and between structural and nonstructural parts of the building, must be investigated and designed.

6. *Design Documentation.* Because the design as such is essentially only an imagined idea, all the information necessary to clearly and unequivocally communicate the idea must be documented.

In the discussions of the examples that follow, all of these aspects of the design process are given some treatment.

6.2. EXAMPLE 1—BUILDING A

The upper part of Figure 6.1 shows the plan, partial elevation, and partial section for a one-story building. We will refer to this building as Building A, and in this example will design it with a light wood frame with plywood wall sheathing and roof deck. The following criteria will be used:

For wind: basic wind speed = 80 MPH [145 km/h]. (See *UBC* map, Figure No. 4, in the Appendix.) Assume exposure condition *C*.

For seismic: *UBC* map zone 3. (See *UBC* map, Figure No. 1, in the Appendix.)

Building construction:

Roof: with ceiling, suspended items, DL = 20 psf.

Walls: 2X frame, plywood + stucco on exterior, gypsum drywall on interior, DL = 18 psf for exterior, 10 psf for interior.

Materials for design: framing is Douglas Fir-Larch, No. 1; plywood is fir, structural grade.

Assume that equipment for an air exchange system used for heating and cooling will be installed on the roof with a total equipment weight of 5 k [22 kN].

It is quite common, when designing for both wind and seismic forces, to have some parts of the structure designed for wind and others for seismic effects. In fact, what is necessary is to investigate for both effects and to design each element of the structure for the condition that produces the greater effect.

The *UBC* Section 2311(d) defines the *design wind pressure* as

$$p = C_e C_q q_s I \qquad (UBC \text{ formula } 11\text{-}1)$$

In this formula the factor C_e combines concerns for the height above ground level, exposure conditions, and gust effects. From *UBC* Table 23-G (see the Appendix), assuming exposure condition *C*, $C_e = 1.2$ for the height zone from zero to 20 ft above the ground surface.

The quantity q_s is the *wind stagnation pressure* at the standard measuring height of 10 meters (approximately 30 ft) above ground. From *UBC* Table 23-F (see the Appendix) the q_s value for a wind speed of 80 MPH is ~~17~~ psf [0.8 kPa]. 21

The importance factor *I* is given in *UBC* Table 23-K (see the Appendix). We will assume for this example that the building use does not qualify for the heightened concerns indicated in the table and will therefore use a value of 1.0 for *I*.

The factor C_q is the pressure coefficient for the structure or portion of structure under consideration, as given in *UBC* Table 23-F (see the Appendix). Values are given for individual building elements, such as the exterior walls and roof surfaces, as well as for items such as parapets, eaves, and canopies. For design of the building structural system (called the *primary frame and system* in the code), two methods are given. The first, called method 1 or the normal force method, consists of applying individual forces to the

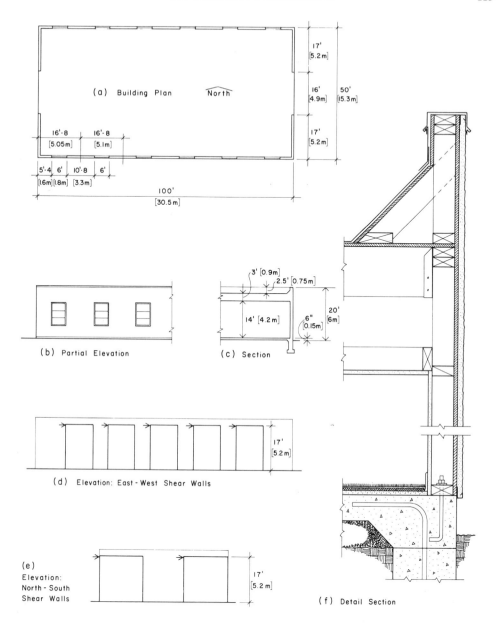

FIGURE 6.1. Example 1—Building A

various components of the building surface. This method is required for gable frames and optional for other cases. The second method, called method 2 or the projected area method, may be used for any building less than 200 ft high, except those with ga-

bled frames. Method 2 is applied by considering the projected building profile as a single vertical or horizontal surface acted on by direct pressure. (See Fig. 6.2.) We will demonstrate the use of method 2 in this example.

The wind pressures and total wind forces

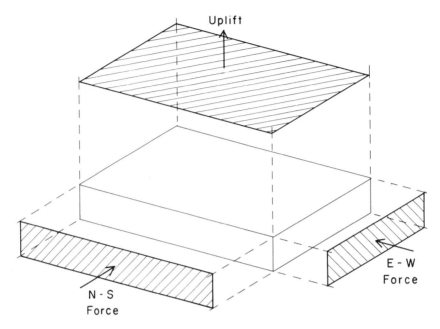

FIGURE 6.2. Generation of wind forces—Building A.

must be considered for a number of situations, including the following:

Direct pressure effects on walls and roof surfaces, affecting design of rafters and studs as well as the consideration of window glazing, attachment of cladding, and so on.

Uplift effect of wind on the roof that is possibly critical for lifting of the roof structure or even the entire building if construction is very light.

Horizontal sliding of the building or some part of the foundation, or sliding of the foundation where depth of penetration below grade is shallow.

Overturning of the entire building.

Horizontal force effects on the various elements of the lateral bracing system.

All of these, plus other possible concerns, must be investigated for a complete building design. Because our concern here is with the design of the lateral bracing system, we will

limit our involvement to considerations of the major elements of that system. Figure 6.3 shows the basic elements of the lateral bracing system and the manner in which wind forces are applied as lateral effects. We observe that the exterior walls function in spanning vertically between the floor slab and the edge of the roof structure. There are two possibilities for the function of the parapet structure, as described in the illustration. We will assume the parapet to be cantilevered from the roof structure and the wall studs to be simple spans, as shown for Case 2 in Figure 6.3a. For this situation, the critical design consideration will most likely be that occurring under the combined wind and gravity loads, with the columns subjected to combined axial compression and bending.

We will assume that the roof functions and the wall construction produce a design gravity load of 200 lb/ft of the wall length. With the studs at 16-in. centers, the load on a single stud is thus $1.33 \times 200 = 267$ lb [1.19 kN]. For the wind loading, the critical condition is that of direct inward pressure for

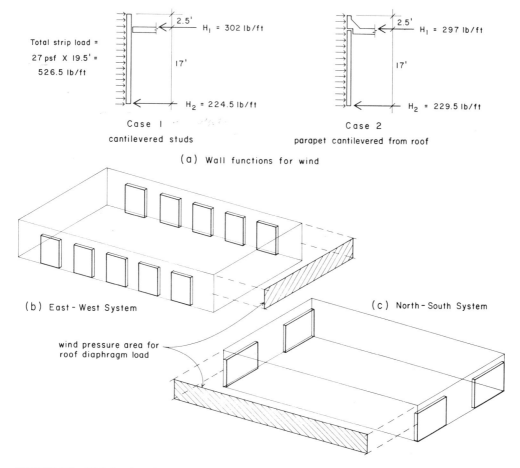

Total strip load =
27 psf X 19.5' =
526.5 lb/ft

2.5' H_1 = 302 lb/ft

17'

H_2 = 224.5 lb/ft

Case 1
cantilevered studs

2.5' H_1 = 297 lb/ft

17'

H_2 = 229.5 lb/ft

Case 2
parapet cantilevered from roof

(a) Wall functions for wind

(b) East-West System

(c) North-South System

wind pressure area for
roof diaphragm load

FIGURE 6.3. Wall functions for wind—Building A: (*a*) direct pressure effects; (*b*) east–west shear wall system; (*c*) north–south shear wall system.

which *UBC* Table 23-H yields a value of C_q = 1.1. Thus, using the other data established previously, the wind pressure on the wall is determined as

$$p = C_e C_q q_s I$$

$$= (1.2)(1.1)(17)(1.0)$$

$$= 22.44 \text{ psf}$$

$$\text{say 23 psf } [1.1 \text{ kPa}]$$

and the load on a single stud will be 1.33 × 23 = 30.6 lb/ft [0.14 kN/m].

Assuming the studs to have a clear height

of 17 ft, the simple beam moment will thus be

$$M = \frac{w(L)^2}{8}$$

$$= \frac{30.6(17)^2}{8}$$

$$= 1105 \text{ ft-lb } [1.5 \text{ kN-m}]$$

For an investigation of the studs we will assume them to be of Douglas Fir-Larch, No. 1 grade, for which we will use the following data:

$$F_b = 1750 \text{ psi } [12.1 \text{ MPa}]$$

(repetitive member use)

$$F_c = 1250 \text{ psi } [8.6 \text{ MPa}]$$

$$E = 1,800,000 \text{ psi } [7.6 \text{ GPa}]$$

For the combined compression plus bending we use the formula

$$\frac{f_c}{F'_c} + \frac{f_b}{F'_b - Jf_c} \gtrless 1$$

For the 17-ft height the minimum stud will be a 2 × 6. We will thus investigate the stress condition for a nominal 2 × 6 for which $A = 8.25 \text{ in.}^2$ and $S = 7.563 \text{ in.}^3$

For the axial stress,

$$f_c = \frac{P}{A} = \frac{267}{8.25} = 32.4 \text{ psi } [0.22 \text{ MPa}]$$

$$\frac{L}{d} = \frac{17 \times 12}{5.5} = 37.1$$

$$K = 0.671 \sqrt{\frac{E}{F_c}} = 25.46$$

$$F'_c = F_c \left[1 - \frac{1}{3} \left(\frac{L/d}{K} \right)^4 \right]$$

$$= 1250 \left[1 - \frac{1}{3} \left(\frac{37.1}{25.46} \right)^4 \right]$$

$$= 643 \text{ psi } [4.43 \text{ MPa}]$$

For the bending stress,

$$f_b = \frac{M}{S} = \frac{1105 \times 12}{7.563}$$

$$= 1754 \text{ psi } [12.1 \text{ MPa}]$$

$$F_b = 1750 \text{ psi } [12.1 \text{ MPa}] \quad \text{(as given)}$$

For bending stress adjustment we assume $J = 1$. Then the combined actions, incorporating the usual increase of one third in the allowable stresses, are as follows:

$$\frac{f_c}{F'_c} + \frac{f_b}{F'_b - Jf_c}$$

$$= \frac{32.4}{1.33(643)}$$

$$+ \frac{1754}{1.33(1750 - 32.4)}$$

$$= 0.3123 + 0.7642 = 1.0765$$

The investigation thus demonstrates that an overstress condition exists, calling for some remedy. Possibilities for this include:

A check of the data for accuracy, as the overstress is quite low. If some dimensions are not accurate, or loads are overestimated, the overstress may not be real. Increase the stress grade of the wood to obtain some higher design values for F_c, F_b, and E.

Place the studs on 12-in. centers to lower the loading on individual studs.

Increase the stud size to 3 × 6 or 2 × 8.

Install kick braces from the bottom of the roof structure to the stud just above the ceiling. This will reduce the L/d ratio and the span for bending.

As we are not designing the whole building structure, we will pass on this decision and move on to consider the other elements of the lateral bracing system.

Referring again to Figure 6.3, we note that the lateral bracing system for wind in a north–south direction consists of the roof deck acting as a horizontal diaphragm, and the four end shear walls acting as vertical diaphragms and providing the reactions for the simple span of the roof diaphragm. On the basis of the functioning of the wall as shown for Case 2 in Figure 6.3a, the wind load delivered to the edge of the roof diaphragm is thus (see Fig. 6.3b)

$$H_{ns} = p \times 100 \text{ ft} \times 11 \text{ ft} = 1100p$$

in which p is the design wind pressure.

From *UBC* Table 23-H (see the Appendix) the value of C_q to be used finding p in this case is 1.3. Thus, using the other data as established previously, the design pressure is

$$p = C_e C_q q_s I = (1.2)(1.3)(17)(1.0)$$

$$= 26.52 \text{ psf say } 27 \text{ psf } [1.29 \text{ kPa}]$$

and the north–south load to the roof diaphragm is thus

$$H_{ns} = 1100p = 1100(27)$$

$$= 29,700 \text{ lb } [132 \text{ kN}]$$

Similarly, the force applied to the roof diaphragm by wind in the east–west direction is determined as (see Fig. 6.3c)

$$H_{ew} = 27 \times 50 \times 11$$

$$= 14,850 \text{ lb } [66 \text{ kN}]$$

The action of the roof deck as a simple beam subjected to the uniformly distributed loading is illustrated in Figure 6.4. This indicates the condition for north–south loading, with the reactions representing the loads to the end shear walls, and the shear and moment representing actions of the roof diaphragm. Before proceeding with the wind investigation we will determine the seismic loading to see which loading is critical for the various elements of the system.

For the seismic load we consider the building mass as a horizontally impelled force. Thus the weight of the roof and any items on top of it or hung directly from it will constitute load to the roof diaphragm. Added to this will be the portions of the walls that depend on the roof for lateral support.

As discussed in Section 2.1 and illustrated in Figure 2.3, the wall function for seismic load depends on the direction of the load with respect to the plane of the wall surface. As with wind load, the parapet on the exterior wall has two possibilities, and we will again assume Case 2 as shown in Figure 6.3a. With these considerations, the building weight used for the determination of the loads to the roof diaphragm are tabulated in Table 6.1. Note that the wall loads

TABLE 6.1. Building Weights for the Roof Diaphragm Loads

	Load Direction			
	N–S		E–W	
Load Source and Computation	(kips)	(kN)	(kips)	(kN)
Roof Dead Load				
20 psf × 50 ft × 100 ft	100	445	100	445
East and West Exterior Walls				
20 psf × 11 ft × 50 ft × 2			22	98
North and South Exterior Walls				
20 psf × 11 ft × 100 ft × 2	44	196		
Interior Walls				
10 psf × 7 ft × 100 ft	7	31	7	31
Rooftop HVAC Unit	5	22	5	22
Total weights	156	694	134	596

are included only when the load direction is perpendicular to the wall. For the tabulation we have assumed a nominal amount of interior partition wall using a light-framed wall weight of 10 psf.

Using the weights from Table 6.1, the horizontal seismic loads to the edges of the roof diaphragms are thus:

$$V = ZIKCSW$$

$$= (0.75)\,(1.0)\,(1.0)\,(0.14)\,(156)$$

$$= 16.38 \text{ k in the north–south direction}$$

$$[72.9 \text{ kN}]$$

and

$$V = (0.75)(1.0)(1.0)(0.14)(134)$$

$$= 14.07 \text{ k in the east–west direction}$$

$$[62.6 \text{ kN}]$$

in which Z = 0.75 for seismic risk zone 3
                    is assumed to be 1.0
      K = 1.0 for the wood-framed box
               system
     CS = 0.14 (assumed)

In both directions these loads are less than those determined previously for wind. We thus proceed with the design of the bracing system using the wind loadings.

Figure 6.4 shows the function of the roof diaphragm as a simple span beam with uniformly distributed load. The maximum shear is one half the total load and results in a unit shear in the roof deck of

$$v = \frac{\text{maximum shear}}{\text{deck width}} = \frac{29{,}700/2}{50}$$

$$= 297 \text{ lb/ft } [4.33 \text{ kN/m}]$$

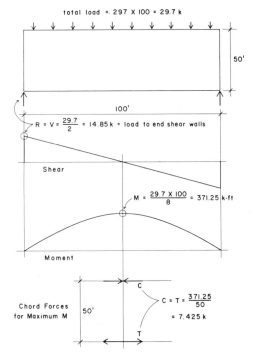

FIGURE 6.4. Beam actions of the roof diaphragm—Building A.

and the maximum chord force is

$$C = T = \frac{\text{maximum moment}}{\text{building width}}$$

$$= \frac{(29.7 \times 100)/8}{50}$$

$$= 7.425 \text{ k} [33 \text{ kN}]$$

For the roof deck, referring to *UBC* Table 25-J-1 (see the Appendix), one option is

Nominal $\frac{1}{2}$-in. (actually $\frac{15}{32}$-in.) plywood, Structural II grade.

8d nails at 4 in. at diaphragm boundary and any continuous panel edges parallel to the load, and at 6 in. at other panel edges.

Table load value: 320 lb/ft with 2× framing.

For the chord we will assume a Douglas Fir-Larch No. 2 grade to be used for the double 2 × 6 top plate. With an allowable tension stress of 625 psi, the capacity of a single 2 × 6 is thus 625 × 8.25 = 5.3625 k [23.8 kN]. This indicates that the single 2 × 6 is not enough for continuity at the splices. Options are to design a splice joint with bolts or steel straps to develop the full double plate as a continuous member, or to use a larger member or higher stress grade wood to obtain enough capacity from a single member. If a single member is adequate, and the joints in the two plates are staggered a sufficient distance, a splice joint is probably not necessary.

Depending on the details of the construction at the joint between the roof and wall, it is also possible that some other part of the framing may be used for the chord. It must, of course, be something to which the roof deck is nailed to develop the shear transfer at the boundary edge.

Although the roof must also function as a diaphragm for the load in the east–west direction, it is obvious that the unit shear in the deck will be much lower in that direction and the chord force will be quite small. Thus the deck and chord design are of primary concern for the north–south loading.

The wind loading condition for the end shear wall is shown in Figure 6.5a. The end force in the roof deck is divided between the pair of walls at one end. The total shear force to the wall is thus 7.425 k and the unit shear in the wall is computed as

$$v = \frac{\text{shear force}}{\text{wall length}} = \frac{7.425}{17}$$
$$= 437 \text{ lb/ft } [6.37 \text{ kN/m}]$$

Referring to *UBC* Table 25-K-1 (see the Appendix), options for the wall are:

A $\frac{3}{8}$-in. Structural I plywood with 8d nails at 3 in. at all panel edges. Capacity: 1.20

× 460 = 552 lb/ft [8.05 kN/m]. Note that the table footnote allows a 20% increase in the table values for $\frac{3}{8}$-in. plywood for certain conditions.

Nominal $\frac{1}{2}$-in. (actually $\frac{15}{32}$-in.) Structural II plywood with 10d nails at 4 in. Capacity: 460 lb/ft [6.71 kN/m].

For overturning of the wall, we consider the moment of the lateral force about the wall base as opposed by the moment of the wall dead weight plus any other dead load carried by the wall. The code requires that the restoring moment (due to dead load) be at least one and one half times the overturning moment; if it is not, anchorage must be provided. Referring to Figure 6.5a, the investigation is as follows:

Overturning moment:
$$7.425 \times 17 \times 1.5 = 189.3 \text{ k-ft}$$

Restoring moment:
$$12.63 \times 8.5 = \underline{-107.4}$$

Net moment for anchor force
$$= 81.9 \text{ k-ft}$$

Anchor force required: $T = \dfrac{81.9}{17} = 11.7 \text{ k}$

For the investigation, the overturning moment is multiplied by the safety factor of 1.5; if the restoring moment equals or exceeds this, no anchorage is required. In the example, the net force is what must be supplied by the anchorage for assistance of the dead load moment. Because the safety factor is already included, this force is really not a service load, although most designers treat it as such.

Note that some roof dead load is assumed to be carried by the wall. Note also that the determination of this effect must include consideration for the wind uplift force on the roof. (See Fig. 6.2.)

If anchorage must be provided, it may be possible to use a device such as that shown

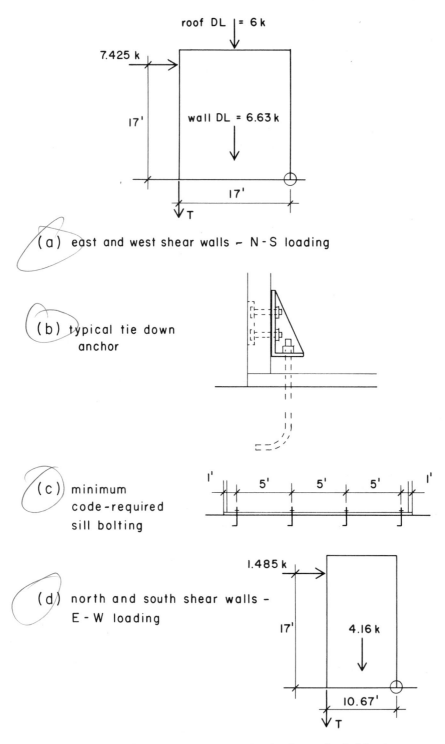

roof DL = 6 k

7.425 k

17'

wall DL = 6.63 k

17'

T

(a) east and west shear walls – N-S loading

(b) typical tie down anchor

(c) minimum code-required sill bolting

1' 5' 5' 5' 1'

1.485 k

(d) north and south shear walls – E-W loading

17'

4.16 k

10.67'

T

FIGURE 6.5. Design considerations for the shear walls—Building A.

in Figure 6.5*b*. This device is bolted to the member that forms the end framing of the wall and is secured by an anchor bolt in the foundation. It is also possible that anchorage is not really required. At the building corner, for example, the end wall is attached to the wall on the north or south side. If both are adequately attached to the end framing at the corner, anchorage is probably redundant. At the other end of the wall the wall may be constituted as a post for support of a header over the opening or for a beam from the roof-framing system. If the dead load delivered by such framing is sufficient, anchorage at this point may also be redundant.

For the design of the end-framing members in the wall any investigation should include the force generated by the chord function due to the overturning moment. For this consideration the uplift effect should probably not be included.

Another consideration for the wall is that of the sliding at the base due to the lateral force. From *UBC* Section 2907(f) the minimum bolting of the wall sill to the foundation must be done with $\frac{1}{2}$-in. bolts a maximum of 6 ft on center, with one bolt not more than 12 in. from each end of the wall. In this case, this minimum bolting could be provided by four bolts, as shown in Figure 6.5*c*. With a Douglas Fir-Larch No. 2 2×6 sill and $\frac{1}{2}$-in. bolts, *UBC* Table 25-f (see the Appendix) gives a value for one bolt in single shear of 470 lb. The four bolts will thus provide a total resistance of $1.33 \times 4 \times 470 = 2500$ lb [11.2 kN], which is considerably less than lateral force of 7425 lb. If we increase the sill size to 3×6 and use a $\frac{3}{4}$-in. bolt, the number of bolts required is

$$N = \frac{7425}{1.33 \times 1155} = 4.8 \text{ or } 5$$

This is a reasonable solution, although others are also possible. With five bolts the spacing will be 3 ft 9 in., which is quite

reasonable. However, the concrete contractor may prefer to set fewer bolts, and a larger bolt allowing the 5-ft spacing could be used.

In the east–west direction the wind load is half of that in the north–south direction and there are five shear walls on each side. The load on each wall is thus quite low, although the shorter wall will result in some increased overturn effect due to the shorter moment arm for the restoring moment. The loading condition for this wall is as shown in Figure 6.5*d*. The unit shear in the wall is

$$v = \frac{1485}{10.67} = 139 \text{ lb/ft } [2.03 \text{ kN/m}]$$

This is quite a low stress, and if plywood is used, the thinnest, lowest grade plywood with minimum nailing is more than adequate. (See *UBC* Table 25-K-1 in the Appendix.) Other wall treatments are also possible including the following:

From *UBC* Table 25-K-2 (see the Appendix): $\frac{5}{16}$-in. particleboard with 6d nails at 6 in. Capacity = 180 lb/ft.
From *UBC* Table 47-I (see the Appendix):
  Stucco: capacity = 180 lb/ft.
  Gypsum sheathing board: $\frac{1}{2}$-in., blocked edges, 4-in. nail spacing. Capacity = 180 lb/ft.
  Gypsum wallboard or veneer base: $\frac{1}{2}$ in. with blocked edges, 5d nails at 4 in. Capacity = 150 lb/ft.

A final consideration for the shear walls is the wall foundation. If there is a net overturning moment, it must be resisted by the foundation, and the foundation design should include this together with the gravity loads. The general problem of shear wall foundations is discussed in Chapter 8. We will not deal with the design here as we are not designing the complete building structure.

Building A, as described in Figure 6.1,

has a symmetrical plan layout of its shear wall system. If the disposition of the building weight affecting the roof diaphragm is also symmetrical, there is in theory no torsional effect on the building during seismic actions. However, *UBC* Section 2312(e)4 requires that the seismic force be considered to have an accidental torsion with an eccentricity equal to 5% of the maximum building dimension. This provision is intended mostly for multistory buildings and rigid horizontal diaphragms, and not for the single-story building with a light wood frame and a plywood diaphragm. If rigidly interpreted, however, the procedure is to compute the torsional moment as the seismic force times the eccentricity and to determine the torsional rigidity of the shear wall system. The added stress to the shear walls is then determined as for a cross section in torsion. This procedure is demonstrated in Section 6.5 for Building B, which has an unsymmetrical shear wall layout—a case that clearly calls for such an investigation.

6.3. EXAMPLE 2—BUILDING A

This example uses the same basic building form as in Example 1, with a difference consisting of the use of masonry shear walls and a steel deck roof in place of the all wood structure. The slightly modified plan and the typical construction for this example are shown in Figure 6.6. A pilaster is used on the inside of the wall piers on the north and south sides to create a column for the roof beams. In addition, this pilaster provides a brace, permitting the use of a thinner wall, for the approximately 16-ft unbraced height would otherwise probably require a 12-in. masonry wall with hollow concrete units.

The light steel-framed roof structure should have a dead load close to that of the wood structure. However, the masonry walls will be considerably heavier than the wood-framed ones. Rather than computing the actual loads, we will assume the lateral seismic

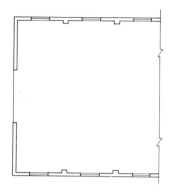

(a) partial plan - with masonry walls

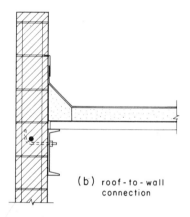

(b) roof - to - wall
connection

(c) wall with isolated piers

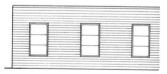

(d) continuous wall

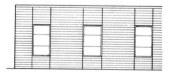

(e) continuous wall with control joints

FIGURE 6.6. Masonry wall details—Example 2, Building A.

loads to be 50% greater than those deter-mined for the wood example. It should be noted that the *K* factor for the seismic shear force will be 1.33 for the masonry walls, which is the normal value for shear walls. With the all wood structure the *UBC* permits an exception and the *K* value is reduced to 1.0.

With the building exterior form and di-mensions the same, the wind loads on this example are the same as those in Example 1. The lateral forces for this example are thus as follows with regard to the load to the roof diaphragm:

Wind, N–S: 29.7 kips [132 kN]

Wind, E–W: 14.85 kips [65 kN]

Seismic, N–S: $1.5 \times 16.38 = 24.57$ kips [109 kN]

Seismic, E–W: $1.5 \times 14.07 = 21.1$ kips [93.9 kN]

From these computations observe that the wind load is still critical for the design of the lateral bracing in the north–south direc-tion, but the seismic force is now critical for the east–west direction. The loading for the design of the roof deck will therefore be the same as in Example 1. Design of the end shear walls for anchorage and chord forces and the design of the load transfer connec-tions between the roof and the end walls will use the same forces as in Example 1. How-ever, the *UBC* Section 2407(h)4(F) requires that the seismic force be increased by 50% when considering shear stresses or diagonal tension in the masonry wall. This will make the seismic force critical for this single con-cern in the north–south direction.

The steel deck diaphragm is similar in many ways to the plywood diaphragm. In-dividual panels of decking must be attached to each other and to the supports to achieve the continuous diaphragm surface structure. A wide variety of deck units is marketed, although a few basic types are quite widely used. The details in the illustrations for this example show a common unit in which ribs are formed on 6-in. centers in a panel that usually comes in 2-ft-wide units and can be obtained in lengths up to about 30 ft. Edges of the panels have a slip-fit interlock and ends are simply overlapped. Units are typi-cally welded to steel supports by placing a thick washer in the bottom of the corrugation and welding the inside hole of the washer to the support by burning through the thin deck material.

Diaphragm shear capacity and relative stiffness of steel decks depend on a number of considerations, including the following:

1. *Thickness (Gauge) of the Deck Sheet.* Decks can be obtained in a range of weights, but the thinner gauges are most often used for cost reduction.

2. *Form of the Deck Corrugation, Depth of the Ribs, and Spacing of the Ribs.*

3. *Spacing of the Welded Connections to Supports.*

4. *Enhancement of the Edge Connection Be-tween Units.* This is equivalent to pro-viding blocking for a plywood deck. The interlocking joint can be crimped (pinched and twisted) to make a mechan-ical fastening.

Rating of decks for shear capacity and relative stiffness is the responsibility of in-dividual producers, and information must be obtained from the manufacturer or marketer for an individual product. Design criteria are developed by the Steel Deck Institute, but building structural designers usually rely on the manufacturers to obtain code approval of design values for their products.

As with the plywood diaphragm, a com-plete design also includes the development of diaphragm chords, the provision for trans-fer of forces to vertical bracing elements of the lateral resistive system, and the devel-opment of any collectors, drag struts, and so on. Because steel deck units are most often used with a steel-framing system, the various components of the framing system will usually serve to form the chords and help in the transfer of forces.

Masonry shear walls consist most often of walls made from units of precast concrete (concrete blocks). Other forms of masonry are possible, but the most widely used construction is that with hollow units of concrete with both horizontal and vertical reinforcing. The reinforcing usually consists of small size steel reinforcing rods installed in continuous voids in the wall which are filled with concrete. The filled voids and reinforcing rods literally form a reinforced concrete rigid frame within the hollow block wall. (See Fig. 6.7.) Although less heavily reinforced construction is also possible, the reinforced masonry described is the only type permitted by codes in the higher risk seismic zones.

The code requires minimum reinforcing and grouting of voids and the various special requirements for doweling of vertical reinforcing, added reinforcing at ends, tops, and around opening in walls; the attachment of walls to roofs and floors result in a "minimum" construction with a capacity usually already above that of the heaviest plywood shear wall. Unlike the plywood wall, however, the masonry wall is most often also a bearing wall for gravity loads and its complete design must consider the full range of load combinations. Choice of the units, the

FIGURE 6.7. Reinforced masonry construction with hollow concrete blocks.

type of mortar joints, the pattern of the unit arrangement, and other considerations are also of some concern when the wall is exposed to view.

In this example we will limit our concern to that for the shear walls on the north and south sides of the buildings. Three possibilities for the form of these walls are shown in Figure 6.6. In Figure 6.6c the walls consist of individual masonry panels separated by the window units that are formed by light frame construction. The masonry shear walls thus function as isolated piers that resist force independently, although they are linked together by the rest of the wall and roof structure and thus have the same deflection under lateral load. This form of behavior is illustrated in Figure 6.8a and is the same as that which was assumed for the plywood walls in Example 1. Shear stress is constant throughout the height of the wall and overturn, sliding, and any critical chord force effects are investigated as for the plywood walls.

Another possibility for the masonry wall is to build it as a continuous wall with openings for the windows as shown in Figure 6.6d. In this case, the wall functions under lateral loading as shown in Figure 6.8b. The portions of wall between openings function as fixed end columns, inflecting at midheight, with end restraint provided by the upper and lower portions of the wall. There are two values of unit shear to consider in the wall: that in the continuous upper and lower portions and that in the portions of wall between openings.

From the loadings previously determined, total E–W seismic load = 21.1 kips [93.9 kN] Ignoring torsion, the total load on the north or south wall is

$$\frac{21.1}{2} = 10.55 \text{ kips } [47 \text{ kN}]$$

The load in the wall is then divided between the various elements in the wall plane. For the cantilevered, isolated piers (Fig.

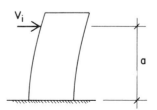

(a) wall as linked isolated piers

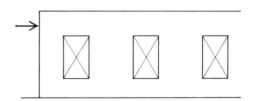

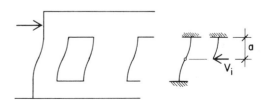

(b) continuous wall

FIGURE 6.8. Functioning of the masonry shear walls.

6.8a), considering only the larger intermediate piers, the load per pier is thus

$$\frac{10.55}{5} = 2.11 \text{ kips } [9.39 \text{ kN}]$$

and the unit shear force in the 10-ft 8-in. long pier is

$$\frac{2110}{10.67} = 198 \text{ lb/ft } [2.89 \text{ kN/w}]$$

This is a very low stress for the reinforced masonry wall and will most likely be developed with the minimum construction required by codes. Stresses in the individual piers between window openings with the continuous wall (Fig. 6.8*b*) will be the same—again, if the shorter end piers are ignored. Stress will be even lower in the continuous wall above and below the windows. The low stress condition does not make the construction a poor choice, but it leaves little concern for further consideration of this example. We will therefore use some later examples to discuss additional concerns for masonry walls.

As with the plywood walls, a major concern may be the development of the foundations, especially for the isolated piers. Anchorage is usually adequately provided for the wall by the doweling of the vertical reinforcing, particularly that installed at the ends of the walls. What the cantilevered piers are cantilevered from, however, is the foundation. If this is a shallow-bearing grade beam-type footing, it must be designed for the shears and moments induced by the cantilevered walls as well as the effects of gravity loading. As we are not designing the whole building structure, we will again dodge this problem, although some discussion is given in Section 8.9 on shear wall foundations.

Transfer of loads from the roof deck to the walls is usually achieved through the connections of the steel framing to the masonry. With the parapet wall, as shown in Figure 6.6*a*, a steel ledger (braced angle or channel) is usually bolted to the wall using anchor bolts set in the masonry. This member and its connections to the wall must be designed for the loading combinations possible with these three different loads:

1. The transfer of the roof diaphragm shear from wind or seismic force.

2. The bracing of the wall against outward force normal to the wall plane—wind suction effect or seismic force due to the weight of the wall.

3. Vertical load transfer of the roof gravity loads.

For seismic anchorage, especially item 2 above, the bolts should be set in a concrete-filled horizontal course of the block wall and preferably hooked around a reinforcing rod, as shown in Figure 6.6*b*.

If the wall construction is as shown in Figure 6.8*b*, the construction between the isolated masonry piers must be adequate to connect the piers for combined action. Framing at the roof will most likely be developed for the roof diaphragm shear collection and serve as the connector between piers.

6.4. EXAMPLE 3—BUILDING A

In this example Building A is considered to have the same general form as indicated in Figure 6.1 with the structure consisting of a light steel frame. Lateral bracing of the vertical structure consists of trussing developed with X-bracing between members of the steel frame. Figure 6.9 shows a possible development for such a bracing system. For resistance in the north–south direction the east and west walls are braced with the diagonals in the same walls that were used as shear walls in Example 1. In the other direction, however, only two walls on each side (north and south) are used so that there are a total of four walls with diagonals. (See Fig. 6.9*b*.) It is assumed that the diagonal members and their connections to the steel frame can be adequately developed with only four trussed bays in each direction.

Some considerations for the design of this system are as follows:

1. For lateral deflection and general dynamic response the trussed system is consid-

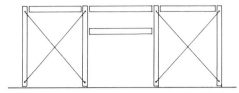

(a) east and west walls

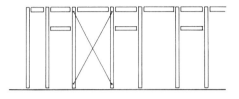

(b) north and south walls

FIGURE 6.9. Braced frame scheme—Example 3, Building A.

ered to be equivalent to the shear wall system. The codes recognize this by assigning the same K factor for determination of the seismic load.

2. Connections stressed during lateral force actions should be tight and nonloosening (generally called *positive*), for the buffeting during wind storms and shaking during earthquakes will tend to shake them loose. Rigid frames will normally have such connections, but the simple pinned connections used routinely for trussing do not always have this character.

3. Although trussed structures are normally quite stiff, there are a number of things that may contribute to lateral deflection. These include the shortening and lengthening of the truss members, the deformation of connections, and the deformation of column anchorage. For the X-braced structure, a major contribution is that of the tension elongation of the X members, as these will be quite highly stressed and are usually the longest members of the truss system.

4. Planning of trussing is often a major architectural problem. Although trussing di-

agonals may be exposed if fire codes permit, they are frequently incorporated in wall constructions. Locating solid walls at points that are strategically useful to the lateral bracing system may be difficult.

The following computations demonstrate the process of investigation and design for the simple X-braced system. We consider the case of seismic loading in the east–west direction, using the load as determined for Example 1:

total east–west seismic force

$$= 14.07 \text{ kips } [62.6 \text{ kN}]$$

load to north and south walls

$$= \frac{14.07}{2} = 7.035 \text{ kips } [31.3 \text{ kN}]$$

With two bents in the wall, the load per bent is thus one half of the total load in the wall, or 3.52 kips [15.65 kN]

Assuming the bent layout as shown in Figure 6.10, tne tension force in the diagonal is thus

$$T = \frac{1}{0.53} \times 3.52 = 7.0 \text{ kips } [31 \text{ kN}]$$

The code requires that this force be increased by 25% for the design of the member and its connections. (See *UBC* Section 2312(j)1G.) We thus design for a force of $1.25(7) = 8.75$ kips [38.9 kN]. If a round rod of A36 steel is used and design is based on the maximum stress of 22 ksi in the rod, the area of rod required is

$$A = \frac{T}{1.33 \, F_t} = \frac{8.75}{1.33 \times 22}$$

$$= 0.299 \text{ in.}^2 \, [193 \times 10^3 \text{ mm}^2]$$

It is possible therefore to use a $\frac{5}{8}$-in. diameter

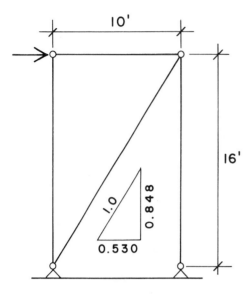

FIGURE 6.10. Layout of the east–west bent—Example 3.

rod with a gross cross-sectional area of 0.307 in.^{2} If this size rod is used, the lateral deflection of the top of the bent due only to the tension stretching of the rod will be (see Section 5.3, Fig. 5.22)

$$d = \frac{TL}{AE \cos \theta}$$

$$= \frac{8.75 \times (10 \times 12)/0.53}{0.306 \times 29,000 \times 1/0.53}$$

$$= 0.19 \text{ in. or about } \tfrac{3}{16} \text{ in. [3 mm]}$$

This indicates a very small deflection, even with the use of the relatively small diameter rod. The true deflection will be larger, as discussed previously, but should not be more than two or three times that computed. Most designers, however, would consider this rod to be too skinny, and would increase it for some more stiffness as well as to reduce stress and elongation.

It is also possible to use other types of steel members for the X-braces, although the

simple round rod is often used when forces are low. (See Figs. 5.17, 5.18, and 5.21.)

Overturning, sliding, and anchorage must also be considered, essentially in the same manner as for the shear walls in Example 1.

6.5. EXAMPLE 4—BUILDING A

The illustrations in Figure 6.11 show a variation for Building A in which the roof structure consists of a series of rigid frame bents.

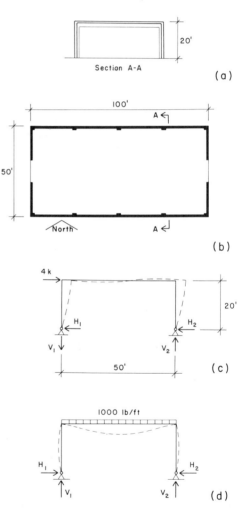

FIGURE 6.11. Example 4—Building A: (*a*) building section; (*b*) building plan; (*c*) lateral loading of the bents, (*d*) gravity loading of the bents.

There is a bent at each of the building ends and at 25-ft intervals in the center portion of the building. We will assume that the total lateral seismic force delivered to the roof edge in the north–south direction is 20 kips [90 kN], or 200 lb/ft [2.92 kN/m]. If the roof diaphragm is flexible, this load is distributed to the bents on a peripheral basis and the bent loads are:

load in end bent

$$= 12.5 \times 200$$

$$= 2500 \text{ lb/bent } [11.25 \text{ kN}]$$

load in intermediate bent

$$= 25 \times 200$$

$$= 5000 \text{ lb/bent } [22.5 \text{ kN}]$$

If the roof diaphragm is considered to be reasonably rigid, it tends to distribute the loads to the bents in proportion to the bent stiffnesses. Thus, if they are of approximately equal stiffness, the load on each bent is

$$\frac{200 \times 100}{5} = 4000 \text{ lb/bent } [18 \text{ kN}]$$

We assume the latter to be the case and design the bents for the 4000-lb load, applied as a concentrated load at the top of the bent.

Figure 6.11c shows the free-body diagram of the bent with the loads and reactions. The deflected shape under load is shown by the dashed line. Although this problem is essentially indeterminate, if we assume the bent to be symmetrical, we may reasonably assume the two horizontal reactions to be equal. In any event the vertical reactions are statically determinate and may be determined as follows:

$$V_1 = V_2 = \frac{4 \times 20}{50} = 1.6 \text{ k}$$

On the basis of this analysis for the reac-

tions, the distribution of internal forces is shown in the illustrations in Figure 6.12. These forces must be combined with the forces caused by the gravity load to determine the critical design conditions for the bents.

Figure 6.11d shows the bent as loaded by a uniform load of 1000 lb/ft on top of the horizontal member. This effect is based on an assumption that the roof framing delivers an approximately uniform loading with a total dead plus live load of 40 psf as an average for the roof construction, including the weight of the horizontal bent member. As with the lateral load, the vertical reactions may be found on the basis of the bent symmetry to be

$$V_1 = V_2 = \frac{1 \times 50}{2} = 25 \text{ k each}$$

Determination of the horizontal reactions in this case, however, is indeterminate and must consider the relative stiffness (I/L) of the bent members. For the pin-based columns it will be found that the horizontal reactions will each be

$$H = \frac{wL^3 I_c}{8 I_g h^2 + 12 I_c h L}$$

In this calculation we may use the relative, rather than actual, values of the column and girder stiffness (I_c and I_g in the formula). If we assume the girder to be approximately 1.5 times as stiff as the column, the horizontal reaction will be

$$H = \frac{(1)(50)^3(1)}{8(1.5)(20)^2 + 12(1)(20)(50)}$$

$$= \frac{125,000}{4800 + 12,000} = 7.44 \text{ k}$$

With these values for the reactions the free-body diagrams and distribution of internal forces for the gravity loading are as

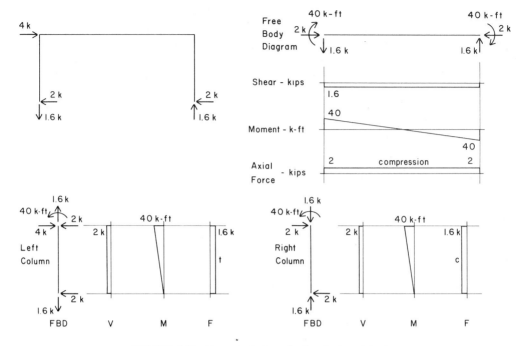

FIGURE 6.12. Example 4—investigation for lateral load.

shown in Figure 6.13. These must next be combined with the previously determined lateral forces, as shown in Figure 6.14. The design conditions for the individual bent members would be selected from the maximum values of Figure 6.13 (gravity only) or three-quarters of the maximum values of the combined loading, as shown in Figure 6.14. The adjustment of three-quarters for the comparison is based on the increased allowable stress for the combined forces that include the seismic load.

We may now proceed to make a preliminary design of the column and girder, based on these analyses. For the illustration we will design the bent in steel, using standard rolled sections, and then discuss other possibilities for its construction. For the column the critical condition is that of the leeward column, which must be designed for the compression plus bending. We assume the following for the first trial design:

A36 steel, rolled WF sections

Design for M = 148.8 k-ft, axial compression = 25 k

(Combined loading is not critical; no increase in allowable stresses.)

Assume the wall to brace the column continuously on its y axis.

We may now try a section by picking one from the S_x tables in the *American Institute of Steel Construction Manual* (Ref. 4) with a moment capacity slightly higher than 148.8 k-ft, based on the assumption that the axial load is not very important because of the relatively high stiffness on the unbraced x axis. We thus will try a W 16 × 57, with a listed moment capacity of 184 k-ft with F_v = 36 ksi. Checking this with formula 1.6–2 from the steel design specification of the *AISC Manual*, we get

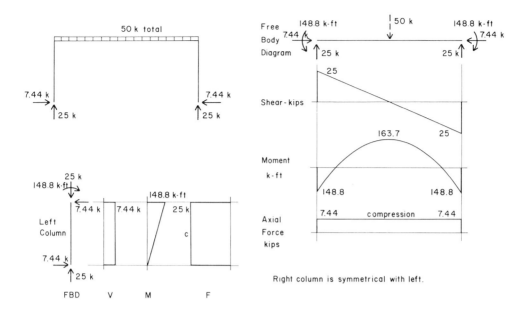

FIGURE 6.13. Example 4—investigation for gravity load.

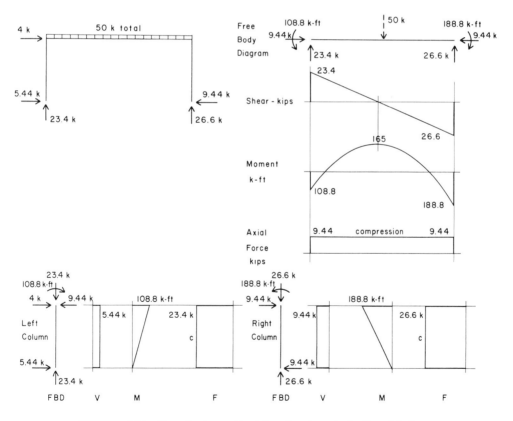

FIGURE 6.14. Example 4—combined lateral and gravity loading of the bents.

133

$$\frac{f_a}{F_a} + \frac{f_b}{F_b} \leq 1$$

where

$$f_a = \frac{25}{6.8} = 1.49 \text{ ksi}$$

$$\frac{KL}{r_x} = \frac{2(240)}{6.72} = 71.4$$

$$F_a = 16.29 \text{ ksi (from } AISC \\ Manual, \text{ p. 5-74)}$$

$$f_b = \frac{M}{S} = \frac{(148.8 \times 12)}{2.2} = 19.36 \text{ ksi}$$

$$F_b = 24 \text{ ksi}$$

Then

$$\frac{f_a}{F_a} + \frac{f_b}{F_b} = \frac{1.49}{16.29} + \frac{19.36}{24}$$

$$= 0.09 + 0.81 = 0.90$$

which indicates that the section is adequate on a stress basis.

There are two additional design considerations for the column that have some importance. One has to do with the connection of the column to the girder. If the connection is to be a fully welded connection, the flange widths of the two members should be reasonably matched. The other consideration has to do with the lateral deflection, or drift, of the bent, which is discussed later.

For the girder design we assume the following:

A36 steel, rolled WF section

Design for M: 163.7 k-ft (positive moment at midspan)

Axial compression is negligible, based on the column design.

Assume roof-framing braces the girder on 6-ft centers.

Once again using the S_x tables from the *AISC Manual*, we try a $W\,21 \times 50$ with a listed moment capacity of 189 k-ft. This will make the f_b/F_b ratio in the combined stress formula

$$\frac{163.7}{189} = 0.866$$

Then

$$f_a = \frac{7.44}{14.7} = 0.506 \text{ ksi}$$

$$\frac{KL}{r_y} = \frac{1(72)}{1.30} = 55$$

$$F_a = 17.90 \text{ ksi}$$

which clearly indicates that the combined stress is not critical.

Two deflection problems should be considered. The first is that of the vertical deflection of the girder, which is most critical for the end bent because the details of the end wall construction must tolerate at least the deflection due to the live load. If we assume the live load to be approximately half of the total load, this deflection will be something less than

$$\frac{5WL^3}{384EI} = \frac{5(25)(50)^3(1728)}{384(29,000)(984)} = 2.4 \text{ in.}$$

which is the simple beam deflection based on no end moments.

The end moment will produce an upward deflection equal to $ML^2/8EI$. Using half of the calculated end moment for the live load deflection, this reduction amounts to

$$\frac{ML^2}{8EI} = \frac{(74.4)(50)^2(1728)}{8(29,000)(984)} = 1.4 \text{ in.}$$

resulting in a net midspan deflection of approximately 1 in.

The other deflection consideration is that of the lateral drift caused by wind, as mentioned previously. Again, this is most critical for the end wall construction. As shown in Figure 6.15a, the lateral deflection (Δ in the figure) may be calculated in two parts. The first part consists of the simple cantilever deflection of the column (t_1 in the figure). The

second part is caused by the rotation at the top of the column (t_2 in the figure). The determination of this combined deflection is

$$\Delta = t_1 + t_2$$

$$= \frac{Hh^3}{3EI_c} + \frac{Hh^2L}{8EI_g}$$

$$= \frac{(2)(20)^3(1728)}{3(29,000)(758)}$$

$$+ \frac{(2)(20)^2(50)(1728)}{8(29,000)(984)}$$

$$= 0.41 + 0.30 = 0.71 \text{ in.}$$

Although these are live load deflections and consequently quite theoretical, the end wall construction, as well as any interior cross wall construction, should be designed to tolerate movements of this order of magnitude.

Connection of the column and girder rolled sections is done with some combination of bolting and welding. Figure 6.15b shows two possibilities, both based on the assumption that the bent cannot be transported from the fabricating shop to the site in one piece. In the upper part of the figure welded plates extend beneath the girder and are bolted to each side of the column. In the lower part of the figure the column-to-girder connection is fully welded, and the field connection consists of a splice in the girder at the approximate location of the inflection point under gravity load. The web plates of this connection are designed for the girder shear and the flange plates are designed for the seismic moment plus some amount of the gravity moment, because unbalanced live load would produce some moment at this theoretical zero moment point.

Although we do not illustrate their design, Figure 6.16 shows details for four other possible constructions of the bents. Figure 6.16a shows a bent built up from flat plates

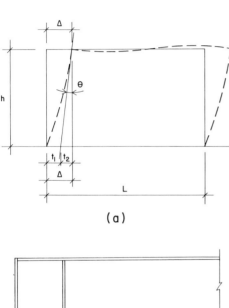

(a)

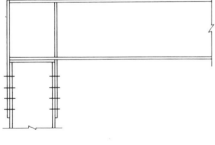

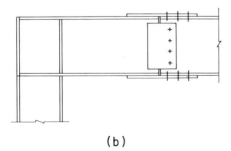

(b)

FIGURE 6.15. Example 4—design considerations: (a) lateral deflection; (b) joint details.

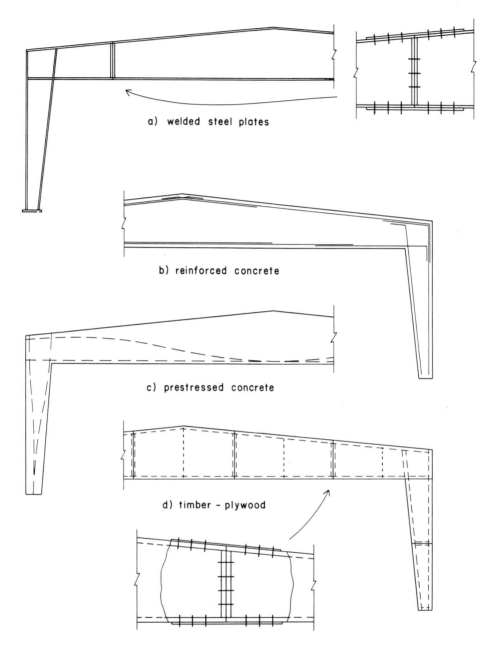

FIGURE 6.16. Example 4—optional construction for the bents.

of steel, producing the same basic I-shaped cross section for the members. An advantage of this construction, as well as of the others in the figure, is that the members may be tapered in length. This offers the possibility of designing the girder for the required depths at the midpoint and ends and the possibility of providing for roof drainage while maintaining a flat bottom on the girder. And it offers the advantage of reducing the size of the column at the floor level where the moment capacity is not required.

Figures 6.16b and c illustrate construction of the bent in concrete with either conventional reinforcing or prestressing with steel cables. If the bents are cast flat on the site and tilted in place, they could be built in one piece.

Figure 6.16d shows the possibility of a plywood and timber box-type construction for the bent. Such bents would most likely be primarily shop-built, using field splices similar to those for the steel bents. The sketch in the figure shows a possibility for a joint placed near the girder inflection point.

6.6. EXAMPLE 5—BUILDING B

Building B is a simple, rectangular, one-story building that is similar to Building A, except that the walls on the front and rear are different, resulting in a lack of symmetry in the lateral resistive system. This applies only to the east–west loading and we will limit our concern in this example to the problems of the north and south walls. The general building plan and details are shown in Figures 6.17 and 6.18.

As shown in the roof-framing plan and the wall sections, the roof structure consists of large steel beams supporting 6 ft on center steel purlins, which in turn support a steel-formed deck. The walls consist of reinforced masonry with hollow concrete units. The walls provide both vertical and lateral support. We will consider the design of the walls for direct wind load plus vertical gravity load and for their actions as shear walls resisting the east–west seismic force on the building.

We will consider the concrete units to be medium weight, Grade N, ASTM C90 with $f'_m = 1350$ psi [9.3 MPa] laid with type S mortar. Reinforcing is Grade 40, with $f_y = 40$ ksi [276 MPa].

We assume that the walls will consist of reinforced, hollow concrete blocks with finishes of stucco (cement plaster) on the exterior and gypsum drywall on wood furring strips on the interior. We assume this construction to weigh approximately 70 psf of wall surface.

The exterior walls must be designed for the following combinations of vertical gravity and lateral wind or seismic forces (see Fig. 6.19.):

1. Gravity dead plus live loads.
2. Gravity vertical dead load plus bending due to lateral load.
3. Horizontal shear and overturn due to shear wall actions.

We first consider the long expanses of wall at the building ends and rear. For the end wall the laterally unsupported height varies because of roof slope. We assume it to be a maximum of 15 ft at the end of the solid wall portion nearest the front of the building. With an 8-in. block thickness, the maximum h/t of the wall is thus $(15 \times 12)/7.625 = 23.6$, which is just short of the usual limit of 25.

Assuming that code-required inspection is not provided during construction, the maximum stress for vertical compression is

$$F_a = 0.10 f'_m \left[1 - \left(\frac{h}{42t} \right)^3 \right]$$

$$= 0.10(1350) \left[1 - \left(\frac{180}{42 \times 7.625} \right)^3 \right]$$

$$= 111 \text{ psi } [0.77 \text{ MPa}]$$

and the maximum allowable bending stress is

$$F_b = 0.166 f'_m = 224 \text{ psi } [1.54 \text{ MPa}]$$

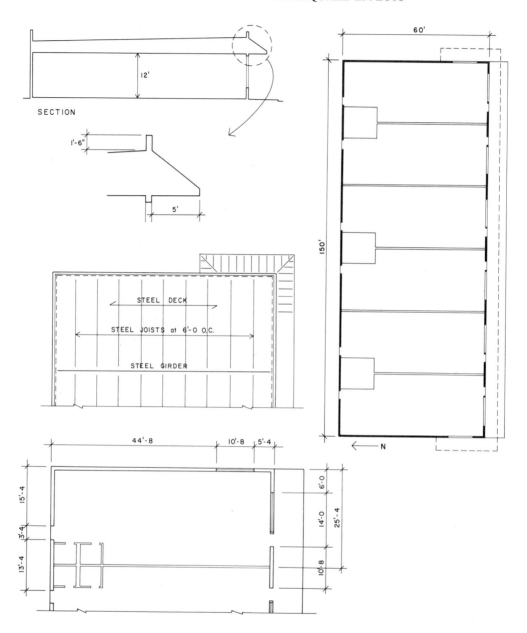

FIGURE 6.17. Example 5—Building B.

For a total wall height of 18 ft the wall dead load is 18 × 70 = 1260 lb/ft [18.4 kN/m]. Assuming the clear purlin span to be 24 ft, the loads from the purlins are:

dead load = 12 × 25 psf

= 300 lb/ft [4.38 kN/m]

live load = 12 × 20 psf

= 240 lb/ft [3.50 kN/m]

The total gravity vertical load on the wall is thus 1800 lb/ft and the average net compression stress, assuming the wall to be 65% solid, is

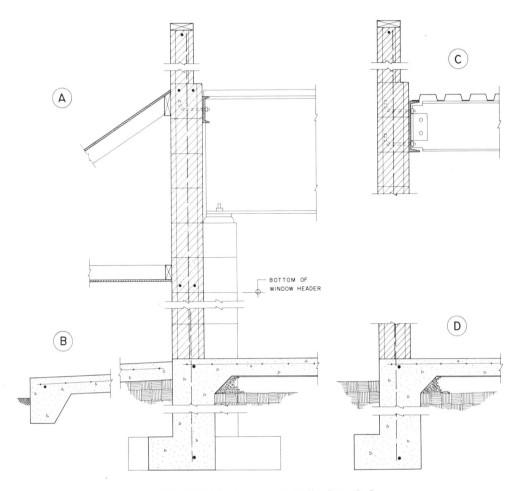

FIGURE 6.18. Construction details—Example 5.

$$f_a = \frac{P}{A} = \frac{1800}{0.65(12 \times 7.625)}$$

$$= 30.3 \text{ psi } [0.21 \text{ MPa}]$$

Assuming the purlins to be supported by a ledger that is bolted to the wall surface, the roof loading will cause a bending moment equal to the load times one half the wall thickness; thus

$$M = 540 \times \frac{7.625}{2}$$

$$= 2059 \text{ in.-lb per foot of wall length}$$

Using Figure D.1, Appendix D, we find an approximate bending stress as follows.

Assume an average reinforcing with No. 5 bars at 40-in. centers. Thus

$$p = \frac{(0.31)(12/40)}{12 \times 7.625} = 0.001$$

$$np = 44 \times 0.001 = 0.045$$

$$K = \frac{M}{bd^2} = \frac{2059}{12(3.813)^2} = 11.8$$

From the graph, $f_m = \pm 90 \text{ psi} = f_b$ [0.62 MPa]. Then

$$\frac{f_a}{F_a} + \frac{f_b}{F_b} = \frac{30.2}{111} + \frac{90}{224}$$

$$= 0.27 + 0.40 = 0.67$$

GRAVITY
DL + LL

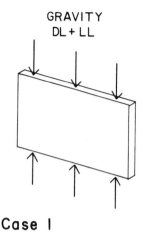

Case 1

GRAVITY
DL + % of LL

WIND OR
SEISMIC

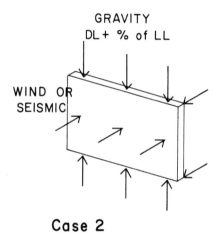

Case 2

GRAVITY
DL ONLY

WIND OR
SEISMIC

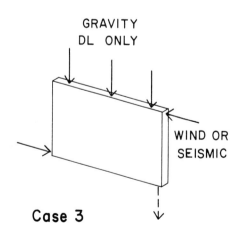

Case 3

FIGURE 6.19. Load cases for the walls—Example 5.

Because this is less than 1.0, the wall is adequate for the vertical gravity load alone. For the case of gravity plus lateral bending we must determine the maximum bending moment due to wind pressure or seismic load. For seismic action the code requires a force in the direction perpendicular to the wall surface equal to 30% of the wall weight, or 0.30 × 70 psf = 21 psf. Because this slightly exceeds the wind pressure of 20 psf, we use it for the bending. The wall spans the vertical distance of 15 ft from the floor to the roof. The doweling of the reinforcing at the base plus the cantilever effect of the wall above the roof will reduce the positive moment at the wall midheight. We thus use an approximate moment for design of

$$M = \frac{qL^2}{10} = \frac{(21)(15)^2}{10}$$

$$= 473 \text{ ft-lb } [0.64 \text{ kN-m}]$$

To this we add the moment due to the eccentricity of the roof dead load; thus

$$M = 300 \times \frac{7.625}{2 \times 12}$$

$$= 95 \text{ ft-lb } [0.13 \text{ kN-m}]$$

and we now design for a total moment of 568 ft-lb [0.77 kN-m]. Assuming an approximate value of $j = 0.85$, we find that the required reinforcing is

$$A_s = \frac{M}{f_s jd} = \frac{0.568 \times 12}{(1.33 \times 20)(0.85)(3.813)}$$

$$= 0.079 \text{ in.}^2/\text{ft}$$

We try No. 5 at 32 in.

$$A_s = (0.31)(12/32) = 0.116 \text{ in.}^2/\text{ft}$$

Then

$$p = \frac{A_s}{bd} = \frac{0.116}{12 \times 3.813} = 0.0025$$

$$np = 44 \times 0.0025 = 0.112$$

$$K = \frac{M}{bd^2} = \frac{568 \times 12}{12(3.813)^2} = 39$$

From Figure D.1, Appendix D, $f_m = \pm 240$ psi. For axial compression due to dead load only,

$$f_a = \frac{1560}{0.65(12 \times 7.625)}$$

$$= 26.2 \text{ psi } [0.18 \text{ MPa}]$$

and

$$\frac{f_a}{F_a} + \frac{f_b}{F_b} = \frac{26.2}{111} + \frac{240}{224}$$

$$= 0.24 + 1.07 = 1.31$$

This indicates a combination close to the limit of 1.33. However, the analysis is conservative because the axial stress used is actually that at the bottom of the wall and the tension resistance of the masonry is ignored.

The rear walls have less load from the roof and a slightly shorter unsupported height. For these walls it is possible that the minimum reinforcing required by the code is adequate. The code requirements are:

1. Minimum of 0.002 times the gross wall area in both directions (sum of the vertical and horizontal bars).
2. Minimum of 0.0007 times the gross area in either direction.
3. Maximum spacing of 48 in.
4. Minimum bar size of No. 3.
5. Minimum of one No. 4 or two No. 3 bars on all sides of openings.

With the No. 5 bars at 32 in., the gross percentage of vertical reinforcing is

$$p_g = \frac{0.116}{12 \times 7.625} = 0.00127$$

To satisfy the requirement for total reinforcing, it is thus necessary to have a minimum gross percentage for the horizontal reinforcing of

$$p_g = 0.002 - 0.00127 = 0.00073$$

which requires an area of

$$A_s = p_g \times A_g = (0.00073)(12 \times 7.625)$$

$$= 0.067 \text{ in.}^2/\text{ft}$$

This can be provided by

$$\text{No. 4 at 32 in.,} \quad A_s = 0.20 \times \frac{12}{32}$$

$$= 0.075 \text{ in.}^2/\text{ft.}$$

$$\text{No. 5 at 48 in.,} \quad A_s = 0.31 \times \frac{12}{48}$$

$$= 0.0775 \text{ in.}^2/\text{ft.}$$

Choice of this reinforcing must also satisfy the requirements for shear wall functions.

At the large wall openings the headers will transfer both vertical and horizontal loads to the ends of the supporting walls. The ends of these walls will be designed as reinforced masonry columns for this condition. Figure 6.20 shows the details and the loading condition for the header columns. In addition to this loading the columns are part of the wall and must carry some of the axial load and bending as previously determined for the typical wall.

Figure 6.21 shows a plan layout for the entire solid front wall section between the window openings. A pilaster column is provided for the support of the girder. Because of the stiffness of the column, it will tend to take a large share of the lateral load. We will thus assume the end column to take only a 2-ft strip of the wall lateral load. As shown

LOADS ON HEADER   LOADS ON HEADER COLUMNS

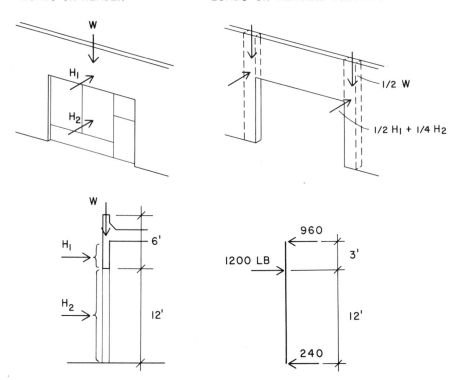

FIGURE 6.20. Loads on the headers and columns— Example 5.

in Figure 6.21, the end column is a doubly reinforced beam for the direct lateral load.

The gravity dead load on the header is:

Roof = 100 lb/ft

Wall = (70 psf)(6 ft)

     = 420 lb/ft

Canopy = <u>100</u> lb/ft (assumed)

Total load = 620 lb/ft [9.05 kN/m]

For the lateral load we will use the wind pressure of 20 psf because the weight of the window wall will produce a low seismic force. Assuming the window mullions span vertically, the wind loads are as shown in Figure 6.20.

$H_1 = (20 \text{ psf})(2 \text{ ft} \times 15 \text{ ft})$

$\quad = 600 \text{ lb } [2.67 \text{ kN}]$

$H_2 = (20 \text{ psf})(12 \text{ ft} \times 15 \text{ ft})$

$\quad = 3600 \text{ lb } [16.0 \text{ kN}]$

Thus the column loads from the header are:

vertical load = $(620 \text{ plf})(15/2)$

$\quad = 4650 \text{ lb } [20.7 \text{ kN}]$

horizontal load = $(\tfrac{1}{2}H_1 + \tfrac{1}{4}H_2)$

$\quad = 300 + 900$

$\quad = 1200 \text{ lb } [5.4 \text{ kN}]$

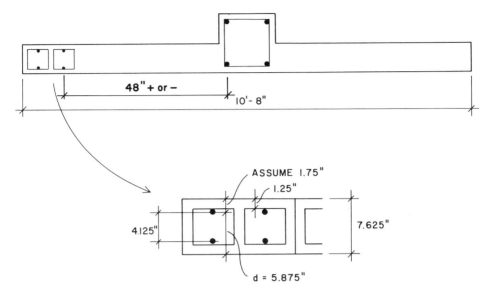

FIGURE 6.21. Details of the front wall—Example 5.

$$\text{moment} = 960(3)$$
$$= 2880 \text{ ft-lb } [3.9 \text{ kN-m}]$$
$$(\text{see Fig. } 6.20)$$

For the direct wind load on the wall we assume a 15-ft vertical span and a 2-ft-wide strip of wall loading. Thus

$$M = \frac{wL^2}{8} = \frac{(20 \text{ psf})(2)(15)^2}{8}$$
$$= 1125 \text{ ft-lb } [1.53 \text{ kN-m}]$$

These two moments do not peak at the same point; thus without doing a more exact analysis we assume a maximum combined moment of 3800 ft-lb. Then, for the moment alone, assuming a j of 0.85,

$$\text{required } A_s = \frac{M}{f_s jd} = \frac{3.8(12)}{26.7(0.85)(5.9)}$$
$$= 0.34 \text{ in.}^2 [219 \text{ mm}^2]$$

$$\text{approximate } f_m = \frac{M}{bd^2}\frac{2}{kj}$$
$$= \frac{3800(12)(2)}{(16)(5.9)^2(0.4)(0.85)}$$
$$= 482 \text{ psi } [3.32 \text{ MPa}]$$

Although f_m appears high, we have ignored the effect of the compressive reinforcing in the doubly reinforced member. The following is an approximate analysis based on the two moment theory with two No. 5 bars on each side of the column.

For the front wall it is reasonable to consider the use of a fully grouted wall because the pilaster and the end columns already constitute a considerable solid mass. For the fully grouted wall we may use $f'_m = 1500$ psi, and the allowable bending stress thus increases to

$$F_b = 1.33 \times 0.166 \times 1500$$
$$= 331 \text{ psi } [2.28 \text{ MPa}]$$

Assuming the axial load to be almost negligible compared to the moment, we analyze for the full moment effect only. With a maximum stress of 331 psi we first determine the moment capacity with tension reinforcing only as

$$M_1 = \frac{f_m(bd^2)(k)(j)}{2}\left(\frac{1}{12}\right)$$

$$= \frac{331(16)(5.9)^2(0.4)(0.85)}{2(12)}$$

$$= 2612 \text{ ft-lb } [3.54 \text{ kN-m}]$$

This leaves a moment for the compressive reinforcing of

$$M_2 = 3800 - 2600$$

$$= 1200 \text{ ft-lb } [1.63 \text{ kN-m}]$$

If the compressive reinforcing is two No. 5 bars, then

$$f'_s = \frac{M_2}{A'_s(d - d')}$$

$$= \frac{1200(12)}{(0.62)(4.125)}$$

$$= 5630 \text{ psi } [38.8 \text{ MPa}]$$

This is a reasonable stress even with the assumed low k value of 0.4. As shown in Figure 6.22, if k is 0.4 and f_m is 331, the compatible strain value for f'_s will be

$$f'_s = 2n(f_c) = 2(40)(3.31)\left(\frac{0.61}{2.36}\right)$$

$$= 6844 \text{ psi } [47.2 \text{ MPa}]$$

As shown by the preceding calculation, the stress in the tension reinforcing will not be critical. This approximate analysis indicates that the column is reasonably adequate for the moment. The axial load capacity should

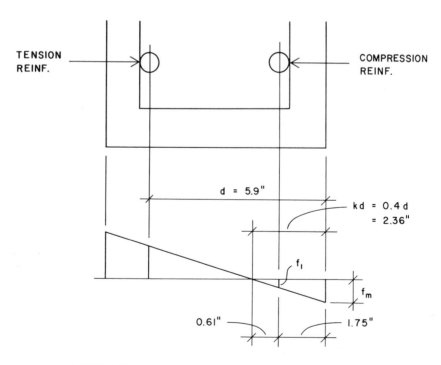

FIGURE 6.22. Stress investigation of the header column—Example 5.

also be checked, using the procedure shown later for the pilaster design.

Window Header

As shown in Figure 6.23, the header consists of a 6-ft-deep section of wall. This section will have continuous reinforcing at the top of the wall and at the bottom of the header. In addition there will be a continuous reinforced bond beam in the wall at the location of the steel ledger that supports the edge of the roof deck.

Using the loading previously determined, and an approximate design moment of $wL^2/10$, the steel area required for gravity alone will be

$$A_s = \frac{M}{f_s(jd)}$$

where $M = wL^2/10 = 620(15)^2/10$

$$= 13{,}950 \text{ ft-lb } [18.9 \text{ kN-m}]$$

$$d = \text{approximately 68 in.}$$
$$[1.727 \text{ m}]$$

Then

$$A_s = \frac{13.95(12)}{(20)(0.85)(68)}$$

$$= 0.145 \text{ in.}^2 [94 \text{ mm}^2]$$

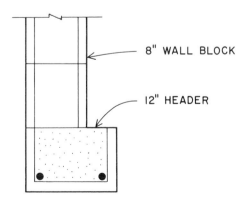

FIGURE 6.23. Alternate header detail—Example 5.

8" WALL BLOCK

12" HEADER

This indicates that the minimum reinforcing at the top of the wall may be two No. 3 bars or one No. 4 bar. This should be compared with the code requirement for minimum wall reinforcing. The *UBC* Section 2407(h)4 calls for a minimum of 0.0007 times the gross cross-sectional area of the wall in either direction and a sum of 0.002 times the gross cross-sectional area of the wall in both directions. Thus

$$\text{minimum } A_s = 0.007(7.625)(12)$$

$$= 0.064 \text{ in.}^2/\text{ft of width}$$

$$\text{or height}$$

With two No. 3 bars $A_s = 0.22 \text{ in.}^2$

$$\text{required spacing} = \frac{0.22}{0.064}$$

$$= 3.44 \text{ ft or } 41.3 \text{ in.}$$

The minimum horizontal reinforcing would then be two No. 3 bars at 40 in., or every fifth block course.

At the bottom of the header there is also a horizontal force consisting of the previously calculated wind load plus some force from the cantilevered canopy. Estimating this total horizontal force to be 250 lb/ft, we add a horizontal moment as

$$M = \frac{wL^2}{10} = \frac{0.25(15)^2}{10}$$

$$= 5.625 \text{ k-ft } [7.63 \text{ kN-m}]$$

for which we require

$$A_s = \frac{M}{f_s(jd)} = \frac{5.625(12)}{(26.7)(0.85)(5.9)}$$

$$= 0.504 \text{ in.}^2 [325 \text{ mm}^2]$$

This must be added to the previous area required for the vertical gravity loads:

$$\text{total } A_s = 0.504 + \frac{(\tfrac{1}{2})(0.145)}{1.33}$$

$$= 0.504 + 0.055$$

$$= 0.559 \text{ in.}^2 \ [361 \text{ mm}^2]$$

The requirement for vertical load is divided by two because it is shared by both bottom bars. It is divided by 1.33, since the previous calculation did not include the increase of allowable stresses for wind loading. If this total area is satisfied, the bottom bars in the header would have to be two No. 7s. An alternative would be to increase the width of the header at the bottom by using a 12-in.-wide block for the bottom course, as shown in Figure 6.23. This widened course would be made continuous in the wall.

The Pilaster Column

To permit the wall construction to be continuous, the girder stops short of the inside of the wall and rests on the widened portion of the wall called a *pilaster*. As shown in Figure 6.24, the pilaster and wall together form a 16-in. square column. The principal gravity loading on the column is due to the end reaction of the girder. Since this load is

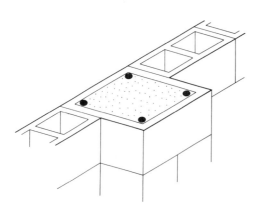

FIGURE 6.24. The pilaster column—Example 5.

eccentrically placed, it produces both axial force and bending on the column. The parapet, canopy, and column weight add to the axial compression.

Because of its increased stiffness, the column tends to take a considerable portion of the wind pressure on the solid portion of the wall. We will assume it to take a 6-ft-wide strip of this load. As shown in Figure 6.25, the direct wind pressure on the wall (pushing inward on the outer surface) causes a bending moment of opposite sign from that due to the eccentric girder load. The critical wind load is therefore due to the outward wind pressure (suction force) on the wall. For a conservative design we will take this to be equal to the inward pressure of 20 psf. The combined moments are thus

$$\text{wind moment} = \frac{wL^2}{8} = \frac{(20)(6)(13.33)^2}{8}$$

$$= 2665 \text{ ft-lb } [3.61 \text{ kN-m}]$$

Assuming an eccentricity of 4 in. for the girder (see Fig. 6.18),

$$\text{girder moment} = \frac{23.5(4)}{12}$$

$$= 7.833 \text{ k-ft or } 7833 \text{ ft-lb}$$

$$[10.62 \text{ kN-m}]$$

For the combined wind plus gravity loading we have used only half the live load. With the allowable stress increase, it should be apparent that this loading condition is not critical, so we will design for the gravity loads only. For this we will redetermine the girder-induced moment with full live load:

$$\text{girder } M = \frac{27.6(4)}{12}$$

$$= 9.2 \text{ k-ft } [12.48 \text{ kN-m}]$$

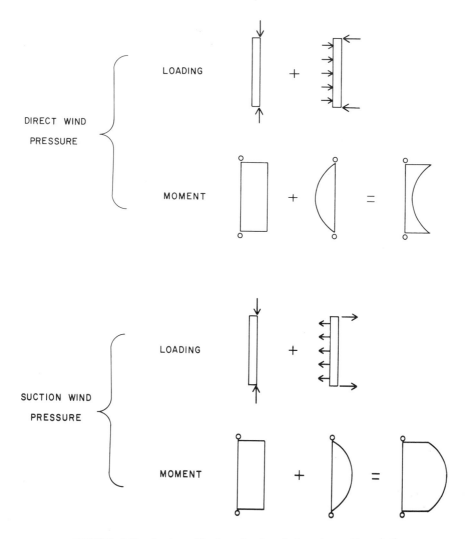

FIGURE 6.25. Load combinations for the pilaster column—Example 5.

The gravity loads of the canopy, parapet, roof edge, and column must be added. We will therefore assume a total vertical design load of approximately 35 kips. With this total load the equivalent eccentricity for design will be

$$e = \frac{M}{N} = \frac{9.2(12)}{35} = 3.15 \text{ in. } [80 \text{ mm}]$$

The *UBC* Section 2418(k)1 requires a minimum percentage of reinforcing of 0.005 of the gross column area. Thus

$$\text{minimum } A_s = 0.005(16)^2$$

$$= 1.28 \text{ in.}^2 \ [826 \text{ mm}^2]$$

With four No. 7 bars $A_s = 2.40$ in.^{2} [1548 mm^2]. Then from *UBC* Section 2406(c)2B the allowable axial load is

$$P = \tfrac{1}{2}\left(0.20\, f'_m A_e + 0.65\, A_s F_{sc}\right)$$

$$\times \left[1 - \left(\frac{h'}{42t}\right)^3\right]$$

for which

A_e = the total area of the fully grouted column

$$= (15.625)^2 = 244 \text{ in.}^2$$

$F_{sc} = 0.40 \qquad F_y = 16 \text{ ksi}$

h' = effective (unbraced) height of the column

$$= 13.3 \text{ ft or } 160 \text{ in.}$$

$$P = \tfrac{1}{2}\left\{(0.20 \times 1.5 \times 244)\right.$$

$$+ (0.65 \times 2.40 \times 16)\}$$

$$\times \left[1 - \left(\frac{160}{42(15.6)}\right)^3\right]$$

$$= 48.4 \text{ kips } [215 \text{ kN}]$$

Ignoring the compression steel, the approximate moment capacity is

$$M = A_s f_s (jd) = \frac{1.20(20)(0.85)(13.5)}{12}$$

$$= 22.95 \text{ k-ft } [31.1 \text{ kN-m}]$$

and for the combined effect

$$\frac{\text{actual } P}{\text{allowable } P} + \frac{\text{actual } M}{\text{allowable } M}$$

$$= \frac{27.6}{48.4} + \frac{9.2}{22.95} = 0.55 + 0.40 = 0.95$$

Note that the one half factor has been used with the axial load formula, assuming no special inspection during construction. Although a more exact analysis should be performed, this indicates generally that the col-

umn is reasonbly adequate for the axial load and the moment previously determined.

The Shear Walls

The calculation of the loads applied to the roof diaphragm is shown in Table 6.2. In the north–south direction the load is symmetrically placed, the shear walls are symmetrical in plan, and the long diaphragm is reasonably flexible, all of which results in very little potential torsion. Although the code requires that a minimum torsion be considered by placing the load off center by 5% of the building long dimension, the effect will be very little on the shear walls.

At the ends of the building the shear stress in the edge of the diaphragm will be

north–south total $V = 0.1862(535)$

$$= 99 \text{ kips } [440 \text{ kN}]$$

$$\text{maximum } v = \frac{49{,}500}{60}$$

$$= 825 \text{ plf } [12 \text{ kN/m}]$$

This is a very high shear for the metal deck. It would require a heavy gauge deck and considerable welding at the diaphragm edge. Although it would probably be wise to reconsider the general design and possibly use at least one permanent interior partition, we assume the deck to span the building length for the shear wall design.

In the other direction the shear in the roof deck will be considerably less:

east–west total $V = 0.1862(410)$

$$= 76.5 \text{ kips } [340 \text{ kN}]$$

$$\text{maximum } v = \frac{38{,}250}{150}$$

$$= 255 \text{ plf } [3.72 \text{ kN/m}]$$

TABLE 6.2. Loads to the Roof Diaphragm

Load Source and Calculation	North–South Load (kips)	East–West Load (kips)
Roof Dead Load		
150 × 60 × 29 psf	261	261
East and West Exterior Walls		
50 × 11 × 70 psf × 2	0	77
10 × 6 × 70 psf × 2	0	9
10 × 6 × 10 psf × 2	0	1
North Wall		
150 × 12 × 70 psf	126	0
South Wall		
65.3 × 10 × 70 psf	46	0
84 × 6 × 70 psf	35	0
84 × 6 × 10 psf	5	0
Interior North–South Partitions		
60 × 7 × 10 psf × 5	21	21
Toilet Walls		
Estimated 250 × 7 × 10 psf	17	17
Canopy		
South: 150 × 100 plf	15	15
East and west: 40 × 100 plf	4	4
Rooftop HVAC Units (estimate)	5	5
Total load	535	410
	[2380 kN]	[1824 kN]

This is very low for the deck, so if any interior shear walls are added, the deck gauge could probably be reduced to that required for the gravity loads only.

In the north–south direction, with no added shear walls, the end shear forces will be taken almost entirely by the long solid walls because of their relative stiffness. The shear force will be the sum of the end shear from the roof and the force due to the weight of the end wall. For the latter we compute the following:

Wall weight

= 18 ft × 50 ft × 70 psf

$$\times \ 63,000 \ \text{lb}$$

6 ft × 10.67 ft × 70 psf

$$= 4,481 \ \text{lb}$$

12 ft × 10.67 ft × 5 psf

$$= \underline{640}$$

Total   = 68,121 lb [303 kN]

Lateral force $= 0.1862W = 0.1862 \times 68$

$$= 12.7 \text{ k } [56.5 \text{ kN}]$$

The total force on the wall is thus $12.7 + 49.5 = 62.2$ k $[277$ kN$]$ and the unit shear is

$$v = \frac{62,200}{44.67} = 1392 \text{ lb/ft } [20.3 \text{ kN/m}]$$

The code requires that this force be increased by 50% for shear investigation. (*UBC* Section 2407(g)4.F(i)). Assuming a 60% solid wall with 8-in. blocks, the unit stress on the net area of the wall is thus

$$v = \frac{1392 \times 1.5}{12 \times 7.625 \times 0.60}$$

$$= 38 \text{ psi } [262 \text{ kP/a}]$$

From the *UBC*, with the reinforcing taking all shear and no special inspection, the allowable shear stress is dependent on the value of M/Vd for the wall. This is determined as

$$\frac{M}{Vd} = \frac{(49.5 \times 15) + (12.7 \times 9)}{62.2 \times 44.67}$$

$$= 0.308$$

Interpolating between the table values for M/Vd of 0 and 1.0,

allowable $v = 35 + 0.69(25) = 52$ psi

This may be increased by the usual one third for seismic load to $1.33(52) = 69$ psi $[476$ kPa$]$. This indicates that the masonry stress is adequate, but we must check the wall reinforcing for its capacity as shear reinforcement. With the minimum horizontal reinforcing determined previously—No. 5 at 48 in.—the load on the bars is

$$V = 1392 \left(\frac{48}{12}\right) (1.5)$$

$$= 8352 \text{ lb } [37 \text{ kN}] \text{ per bar}$$

and the required area for the bar is

$$A_s = \frac{V}{f_s} = \frac{8352}{26,667}$$

$$= 0.31 \text{ in.}^2 [200 \text{ mm}^2]$$

This indicates that the minimum reinforcing is just adequate. Some additional stress will be placed on these walls by the effects of torsion, so that some increase in the horizontal reinforcing is probably advisable.

Overturn is not a problem for these walls because of their considerable dead weight and the natural tiedown provided by the doweling of the vertical wall reinforcing into the foundations. These dowels also provide the necessary resistance to horizontal sliding.

In the east–west direction the shear walls are not symmetrical in plan, which requires that a calculation be made to determine the location of the center of rigidity so that the torsional moment may be determined. The total loading is reasonably centered in this direction, so we will assume the center of gravity to be in the center of the plan.

The following analysis is based on the examples in the *Masonry Design Manual* (Ref. 10.) The individual piers are assumed to be fixed at top and bottom and their stiffnesses are found from Table D.2, Appendix D. The stiffness of the piers and the total wall stiffnesses are determined in Figure 6.26. For the location of the center of stiffness we use the values determined for the north and south walls:

$$\bar{y} = \frac{(R \text{ for the S wall})(60 \text{ ft})}{(\text{sum of the } R \text{ values for the N and S walls})} = \frac{2.96(60)}{17.57}$$

$$= 10.11 \text{ ft } [3.08 \text{ in.}]$$

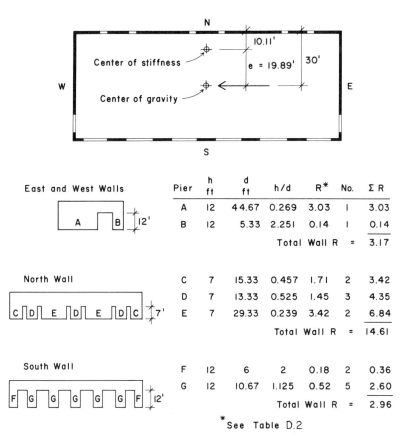

FIGURE 6.26. Stiffness analysis of the masonry walls—Example 5.

The torsional resistance of the entire shear wall system is found as the sum of the products of the individual wall rigidities times the square of their distances from the center of stiffness. This summation is shown in Table 6.3. The torsional shear load for each wall is then found as

$$V_W = \frac{Tc}{J}$$

$$= \frac{(V)(e)(c)(\text{the } R \text{ for the wall})}{(\text{the sum of the } Rd^2 \text{ for all walls})}$$

In the north–south direction   *UBC*

TABLE 6.3.   Torsional Resistance of the Masonry Shear Walls

Wall	Total Wall R	Distance from Center of Stiffness (ft)	$R(d)^2$
South	2.96	49.89	7,367
North	14.61	10.11	1,495
East	3.17	75	17,831
West	3.17	75	17,831
Total torsional moment of inertia (J)			44,524

2312(e)5 requires that the load be applied with a minimum eccentricity of 5% of the building length, or 7.5 ft. Although this produces less torsional moment than the east–west load, it is additive to the direct north–south shear and therefore critical for the end walls. The torsional load for the end walls is thus

$$V_w = \frac{(99)(7.5)(75)(3.17)}{44,524}$$

$$= 3.96 \text{ kips } [17.6 \text{ kN}]$$

As mentioned previously, this should be added to the direct shear of 49,500 lb for the design of these wall:

For the north wall:

$$V_w = \frac{(76.5)(19.89)(10.11)(14.61)}{44,524}$$

$$= 5.05 \text{ kips } [22.5 \text{ kN}]$$

This is actually opposite in direction to the direct shear, but the code does not allow the reduction and thus the direct shear only is used.

For the south wall:

$$V_w = \frac{(76.5)(19.89)(49.89)(2.96)}{44,524}$$

$$= 5.05 \text{ kips } [22.5 \text{ kN}]$$

The total direct east–west shear will be distributed between the north and south walls in proportion to the wall stiffnesses:

For the north wall:

$$V_w = \frac{76.5(14.61)}{17.57} = 63.6 \text{ kips } [283 \text{ kN}]$$

For the south wall:

$$V_w = \frac{76.5(2.96)}{17.57} = 12.9 \text{ kips } [57.4 \text{ kN}]$$

The total shear loads on the walls are therefore

north: $V = 63.6$ kips $[283 \text{ kN}]$

south: $V = 5.05 + 12.9$

$$= 17.95 \text{ kips } [79.8 \text{ kN}]$$

The loads on the individual piers are then distributed in proportion to the pier stiffnesses (R) as determined in Figure 6.26. The calculation for this distribution and the determination of the unit shear stresses per foot of wall are shown in Table 6.4. A comparison with the previous calculations for the end walls will show that these stresses are not critical for the 8-in. block walls.

In most cases the stabilizing dead loads plus the doweling of the end reinforcing into the foundations will be sufficient to resist

TABLE 6.4. Shear Stresses in the Masonry Walls

Wall	Shear Force on Wall (kips)	Wall R	Pier	Pier R	Shear Force on Pier (kips)	Pier Length (ft)	Shear Stress in Pier (lb/ft)
North	63.6	14.61	C	1.71	7.44	15.33	485
			D	1.45	6.31	13.33	473
			E	3.42	14.89	29.33	508
South	17.95	2.96	F	0.18	1.09	6	182
			G	0.52	3.15	10.67	296

TOTAL DL = 23000 LB

7440 LB

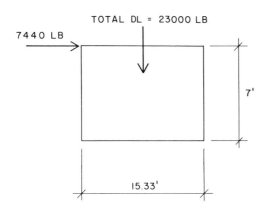

7'

15.33'

FIGURE 6.27. Stability of wall C—Example 5.

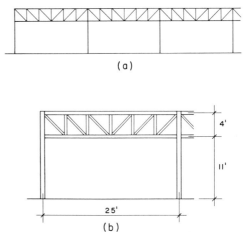

(a)

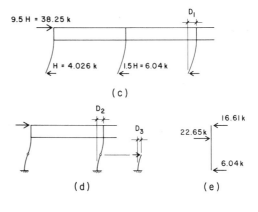

(b)

overturn effects. The heavy loading on the header columns and the pilasters will provide considerable resistance for most walls. The only wall not so loaded is wall *C*, for which the loading condition is shown in Figure 6.27. The overturn analysis for this wall is as follows:

$$\text{overturn } M = (7440)(7.0)(1.5)$$

$$= 78{,}120 \text{ ft-lb } [106 \text{ kN-m}]$$

$$\text{stabilizing } M = 23{,}000 \left(\frac{15.33}{2}\right)$$

$$= 176{,}295 \text{ ft-lb } [239 \text{ kN-m}]$$

This indicates that the wall is stable without any requirement for anchorage even though the wall weight in the plane of the shear wall was not included in computing the overturning moment.

6.7. EXAMPLE 6—BUILDING B

In this example a full steel frame is provided for the building whose general plan was shown in Figure 6.17. One reason for the frame might be the desire for more open space in the exterior walls. The trussed bent structure shown in Figure 6.28*a* is suggested

9.5 H = 38.25 k

H = 4.026 k   1.5 H = 6.04 k

D₁

(c)

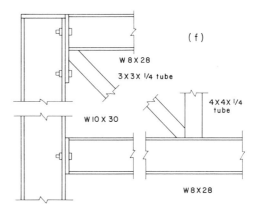

(d)   (e)

(f)

W 8 X 28

3 X 3 X 1/4 tube

4 X 4 X 1/4 tube

W 10 X 30

W 8 X 28

FIGURE 6.28. Example 6—Building B: (*a*) layout of the south wall bents; (*b*) form of the single bent unit; (*c*) bent loading; (*d*) assumed function of the bents; (*e*) column loading; (*f*) bent details.

for the front wall, resulting in the elimination of the need for either the solid shear walls (Example 5) or the diagonals for an X-braced scheme. The bracing of the remainder of the building, however, may be achieved with shear walls or braced bays of the framing.

For seismic design, a problem that arises when a mixed system is used is what to use for the K factor in the equation for design shear: $V = ZIKCSW$. If the trussed bent as shown in Figure 6.28 is used only on the front of the building, and the rest of the construction remains essentially as described for Example 5, the seismic load in the east–west direction will be shared by the front bents and the rear shear walls. Although the trussed bents may be classified as moment-resistive frames, allowing a K of 0.67, the usual practice would be to use the K of 1.33 required for the shear walls to find the load for the whole building.

Let us assume that the construction is in general the same as for Example 5, except for the use of the bents on the front wall. If the K of 1.33 is used for the east–west seismic force, the design load to the roof diaphragm will then be the same as was determined for Example 5: a total of 76.5 kips [340 kN]. If a simple peripheral distribution is assumed, the total load to the six-span front bent is thus one half of this, or 38.25 kips [170 kN].

If the columns are pin based, and the intermediate columns are assumed to be 50% stiffer than the end columns, the bent action is as shown in Figure 6.28c. The moment on an intermediate column is thus

$$M = 6.04 \times 11 = 66.44 \text{ k-ft } [90 \text{ kN-m}]$$

Although the column must be designed for the combined actions of bending plus axial compression, the bending due to the lateral load is by far the major action. If a section is chosen that is slightly stronger than required for this moment, it will serve as a reasonable first try. In fact, because the crit-

ical concern is the more likely for lateral deflection, stress concerns may be secondary. Let us try a column consisting of a W 10×30 wide flange section, which has a moment capacity approximately one third larger than that required for the computed lateral moment alone. We then consider the lateral deflection (D_1 in Fig. 6.28c) based on the cantilever action of the intermediate column. Although there is also some lateral deflection due to the rotation at the bottom of the truss, the general stiffness of the bent will be primarily indicated by the cantilever action of the column. Using the W 10×30 with an I_x of 170 in.[4], and the deflection formula for a simple fixed cantilever with a concentrated load at its end, we determine the deflection as

$$D_1 = \frac{PL^3}{3\,EI} = \frac{6.04 \times (11 \times 12)^3}{3 \times 29,000 \times 170}$$

$$= 0.939 \text{ in. } [23.85 \text{ mm}]$$

Although there is no generally accepted limit for such deflection, this compares reasonably with a value of one half of 1% of the story height ($0.005h$) that is frequently used for frame drift. In this case

$$0.005h = 0.005(16 \times 12) = 0.96 \text{ in.}$$

In this situation, however, it is possible that the drift of approximately 1 in. may cause problems with the distortions resulting in the wall construction. In addition, with the mixed bent and shear wall system, it is usually desirable to maintain relatively rigid bents for a more favorable load sharing with the stiff shear walls. We may therefore consider stiffening the bent by one of two means. The first is to simply choose a stiffer section. Although the W 10×30 is close to a square and generally of the usual form for a column, we may chose a section that is more of the proportions of a beam. This is not unreasonable as the major action is that of the lateral bending moment. Care should be used, however, to avoid having too low a stiffness on the minor axis (r_y) for the column action.

Let us consider the use of a $W\ 16 \times 31$ section, which has an I_x of 375 in.^{4} and an r_y of 1.17. The increase in stiffness will reduce the deflection to

$$D_1 = \frac{170}{375} \times 0.939 = 0.426 \text{ in.}$$

The r_y value of the $W\ 16 \times 31$ is slightly lower than that of the $W\ 10 \times 30$, but is possibly still not a critical concern, as the axial load is probably quite low.

The other means for stiffening the bent is to develop a moment-resistive connection at the column base, as shown in Figure 6.28d. If we assume the top and bottom of the column to be fully fixed, the column will inflect at midheight. The cantilever length of the column is thus one half the height and for comparison with the pin-based bent, we observe the following:

$$D_2 = \text{twice the deflection}$$
$$\text{of the half height column}$$

$$D_3 = \frac{P(L/2)^3}{3\ EI} = \frac{PL^3}{24\ EI} = \frac{1}{8} D_1$$

$$D_2 = 2D_3 = \tfrac{1}{4} D_1$$

This indicates a significant stiffening effect, although in reality the effect is lessened by some rotation at the top and at the base due to distortions in the connections. Nevertheless, the fixed base is a major means for stiffening the frame. It does, of course, require a foundation capable of developing the necessary resistance to the moments and shears caused by the fixed bases.

Investigation of the equilibrium of the intermediate column indicates the development of forces in the chords of the trusses as shown in Figure 6.28e. To develop the lateral resistance of the bents, the trusses

must be assembled as a continuous system. If we assume an approximate gravity load of 1500 lb/ft [22 kN/m] and a maximum moment of $wL^2/10$, the maximum chord force due to gravity load is

$$T = C = \frac{wL^2}{10\ d}$$
$$= \frac{1.5\ (25)^2}{10 \times 4} = 23.4 \text{ kips } [104 \text{ kN}]$$

Adding this to the force determined in the bottom chord due to lateral load (Fig. 6.28e) produces a total of approximately 46 kips [205 kN]. Although the top chord of the truss will most likely be braced laterally by the roof system, the bottom chord may be unbraced for the entire distance between columns. With these assumptions, a possible choice for the bottom chord is a $W\ 8 \times 28$ whose flange width is close to that of the $W\ 16 \times 31$ column.

Some possible details for the truss assembly are shown in Figure 6.28f. The trusses are shop assembled with web members of tubular sections that are cut to fit and directly welded to the flanges of the wide flange chords. Column connections are achieved with plates welded to the ends of the chords of the trusses and field bolted to the column flanges. A cap plate at the top of the column and web stiffening plates at the bottom chord of the truss should be used to brace the thin web of the column.

6.8. EXAMPLE 7—BUILDING C

This building is similar to Building B, except for the plan dimensions which result in a very long, narrow plan form shown in Figure 6.29. We will investigate the possibility of a plywood deck with a light wood frame for the building with no interior shear walls. The following data will be used:

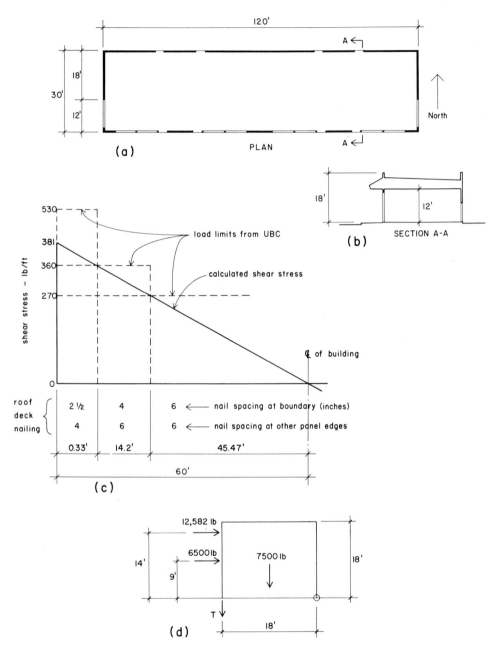

FIGURE 6.29. Example 7—Building C: (*a*) building plan; (*b*) building section; (*c*) zoned nailing for the roof diaphragm; (*d*) stability of the end shear wall.

Seismic zone 4 (considered critical, $Z = 1$)

Roof, ceiling, and supported items = 16 psf [0.77 kN/m^2]

Exterior walls = 20 psf [0.96 kN/m^2]

Canopy added to wall = 200 lb/ft [2.92 kN/m]

Rooftop HVAC units = 15 kips total [67 kN]

Obviously the critical concern is for the north–south load; thus we limit our investigation to this condition and to the resulting effects on the roof deck and the two end shear walls. Table 6.5 presents the summary of the building weights for determination of the north–south seismic load to the edge of the roof diaphragm. As in Example 4, we determine the design load as

$$V = ZIKCSW = (1)(1)(1)(0.14)(163.4)$$

$$= 22.88 \text{ kips } [102 \text{ kN}]$$

$$\text{maximum shear in the roof deck} = \frac{22.88}{2}$$

$$= 11.44 \text{ kips } [51 \text{ kN}]$$

$$\text{maximum unit shear} = \frac{11,440}{30}$$

$$= 301 \text{ lb/ft } [4.39 \text{ kN/m}]$$

To compound matters, we may consider the addition of stress due to the code-re-quired 5% eccentricity (*UBC* Section 2312(e)5). For this computation the main portion of J will be due to the end shear walls; considering these only,

$$J = 2 \times 18 \times (60)^2 = 129,600 \text{ ft}^3$$

$$= [12 \times 10^3 \text{ m}^2]$$

and the added shear is

$$v = \frac{Fec}{J}$$

$$= \frac{22,880 \times (0.05 \times 120) \times 60}{129,600}$$

$$= 64 \text{ lb/ft } [0.934 \text{ kN/m}]$$

This should be added to the end shear wall shear stress. Without the torsion the end shear wall stress is

$$v = \frac{11,440}{18} = 636 \text{ lb/ft } [9.28 \text{ kN/m}]$$

and the maximum stress with accidental torsion is

$$v = 636 + 64 = 700 \text{ lb/ft } [10.2 \text{ kN/m}]$$

Using Douglas fir plywood for the roof deck (see Appendix C for *UBC* Table 25-J), some options are as follows:

TABLE 6.5 Building Weights for the Roof Diaphragm Loads—North–South Direction

Load Source and Computation	Load (kips)
Roof and Ceiling 16 psf × 120 ft × 30 ft	57.6
East and West Exterior Walls 20 psf × 240 ft × 11 ft	52.8
Interior Walls 10 psf × 200 ft × 7 ft	14.0
Canopy 200 lb/ft × 120 ft	24.0
Rooftop HVAC Units	15.0
Total	163.4k
	[727 kN]

$\frac{1}{2}$-in. Structural II with $2\times$ framing, blocking, and 8d nails at $2\frac{1}{2}$ in. at boundaries and at 4 in. at other edges.

$\frac{5}{8}$-in. Structural II with $3\times$ framing, blocking, and 10d nails at 4 in. at boundaries and at 6 in. at other edges.

$\frac{1}{2}$-in. Structural I with $3\times$ framing, blocking, and 10d nails at 4 in. at boundaries and at 6 in. at other edges.

Because the high stresses occur only near the ends of the building, it is reasonable to consider the possibility of zoning the deck nailing in this case. By using the $\frac{1}{2}$-in. Structural II plywood, it is possible to use two fewer nail spacings, as given in the *UBC* table. Thus the range of nail spacings and corresponding load ratings are the following:

8d at $\frac{1}{2}$ in. at boundaries, 4 in. at other edges: load = 530 lb/ft.

8d at 4 in. at boundaries, 6 in. at other edges: load = 360 lb/ft.

8d at 6 in. at all edges: load = 270 lb/ft.

In Figure 6.29c these allowable loads are plotted on the graph of stress variation in the deck to permit the determination of the areas in which the various nailing spacings are usable. The maximum nailing is seen to be required on only a very small area at each end of the roof. The actual dimensions of the specified nailing zones may be adjusted slightly to correspond to modules of the roof framing and plywood sheet layouts as long as the limits of the calculated zone boundaries are not exceeded.

Using Douglas fir plywood for the wall sheathing (see Appendix C for *UBC* Table 25-K), possible options are:

$\frac{1}{2}$-in. Structural II with $3\times$ boundary framing and 10d nails at 2 in. at all edges: load = 770 lb/ft.

$\frac{3}{8}$-in. Structural I with 8d nails at 2 in. at all edges: load = 610 (1.2) = 732 lb/ft.

(See footnote No. 3 in the *UBC* table in Chapter 28.)

$\frac{1}{2}$-in. Structural I with $3\times$ boundary framing and 10d nails at $2\frac{1}{2}$ in. at all edges: load = 770 lb/ft.

And if it is possible to have plywood on both sides of the wall, use:

$\frac{3}{8}$-in. Structural II, both sides, with 8d nails at 4 in. at all edges: load = 2(320)(1.2) = 768 lb/ft.

Although technically permitted by the code, none of the foregoing is desirable. The closely spaced heavy nailing is likely to cause some splitting of framing members. Placing plywood on both sides of the wall can entail some difficulty in the framing details and in the installation of wiring or other elements within the wall cavity. The heavy shear load on the wall is also likely to be a problem in terms of stress on the wall boundary framing.

Figure 6.29d shows the loading for the end shear wall. The required tiedown force is considerable and requires a very heavy anchorage device, heavy end framing in the wall, and a strong foundation. Development of sliding resistance for the total load requires heavy bolting of the wall sill to the foundation. Although the chord force can be developed with ordinary framing members, the length of the building will result in several splices, each of which needs considerable bolting to maintain the continuity of the chord.

A final consideration is the horizontal deflection of the roof diaphragm at the center of the 120-ft span. The diaphragm depth-to-span ratio of 4 to 1 is just at the limit permitted by the *UBC* (see *UBC* Table 25-I in Appendix C). Even though the diaphragm is within the code limit, the actual dimension of the deflection should be determined and its possible effect on interior partitions considered.

We abandon this example without attempting to solve all its problems because we actually consider it to be a poor solution. It was presented to show what bad planning can produce in the way of difficult situations and not as an illustration of proper design.

This example presents a situation in which a strong argument can be made for the use of at least one interior shear wall. Figure 6.30 shows a modification of the plan with the introduction of a central north–south wall extending from the full width of the build-

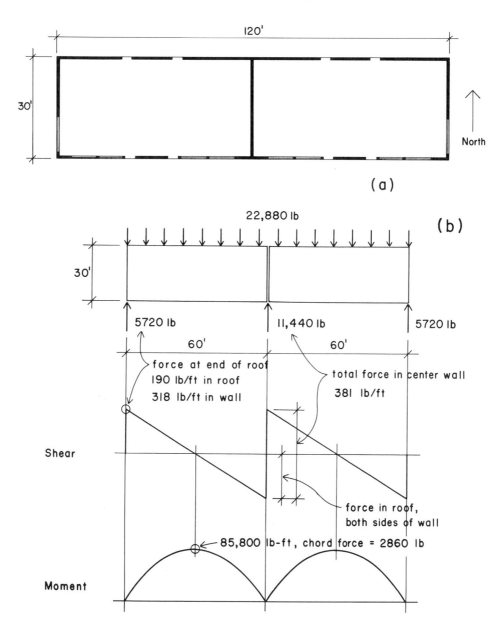

FIGURE 6.30. Modification of Building C with interior shear wall: (*a*) building plan; (*b*) load investigation of the roof diaphragm.

ing. Using the same loading as in the previous computation, the analysis for the north–south seismic loading of the roof diaphragm is as shown in Figure 6.30*b*. In this analysis the roof deck is assumed to be sufficiently flexible to justify an assumption of distribution of load to the vertical elements on a peripheral basis. This is consistent with the usual practice for a wood diaphragm with the depth-to-span ratio in the example. With this assumption half of the total load is taken by the center wall, and the load on the end walls is reduced to one half that in the preceding computations.

Ignoring torsional effects, the maximum stress in the roof diaphragm drops to 190 lb/ft, occurring at the ends and at both sides of the interior wall. This is less than the lowest rated capacity for $\frac{1}{2}$-in. plywood with edge blocking and minimum nailing as given in *UBC* Table 25-J (see Appendix C). Nail zoning is therefore not a consideration, unless it is acceptable to use an unblocked diaphragm for some portions of the roof.

The shear stress in the end wall drops to 318 lb/ft. This is still a significant stress, but it can be achieved with $\frac{3}{8}$-in. Structural II plywood with 8d nails at 4 in. at all panel edges, which is quite reasonable. The overturn and tiedown requirement are also considerably reduced.

The center shear wall must carry a considerable force—the same as that on the end shear walls in the previous example. However, the wall is longer in plan, which results in a lower shear stress and less overturn effect. The design of this wall must include the full consideration of its use in the building. Possible issues are its use for fire separation, acoustic separation, and load bearing for the roof structure. For our analysis we consider it to be a single stud wall and to serve as a bearing wall. If it were not a bearing wall, the net overturning effect would be higher. It happens in this example that the same plywood and nailing can be used for the end walls and the interior wall. From

the *UBC* table, the capacity is 384 lb/ft, which includes the allowable 20% increase noted in the footnote to the table.

If the interior wall is not a bearing wall, there may be some tiedown requirement. However, the connection of this wall to the walls at the front and the rear of the building should be adequate for this function.

If sliding friction is ignored and the entire horizontal force is taken on the sill bolts, the choice is whether to use a lot of small bolts or a few large ones. This is a matter of individual preference by designers and builders. If the maximum code spacing of 6 ft is used, the two walls will have a minimum of four bolts in the end wall and six in the center wall. Thus the minimum required capacity for this minimum number of bolts is as follows:

$$\text{End wall:} \quad \text{load} = \frac{5720}{4}$$

$$= 1430 \text{ lb/bolt}$$

$$\text{Center wall:} \quad \text{load} = \frac{11440}{6}$$

$$= 1907 \text{ lb/bolt}$$

If the bolt size required for these loads is not excessive, the minimum number of bolts may be used—which is the usual preference of both the concrete and framing contractors.

A construction detail that must be developed for this example is the connection between the roof diaphragm and the center shear wall. This connection must transfer the total force from the roof to the wall. Because there are several options for both the roof and the wall construction, the potential variations for this connection become quite numerous. Figure 6.31 illustrates some of the possibilities based on the assumption that the wall is a single stud wall and that the roof framing consists of joists perpendicular to and supported by the wall. There are three basic structural functions to be considered

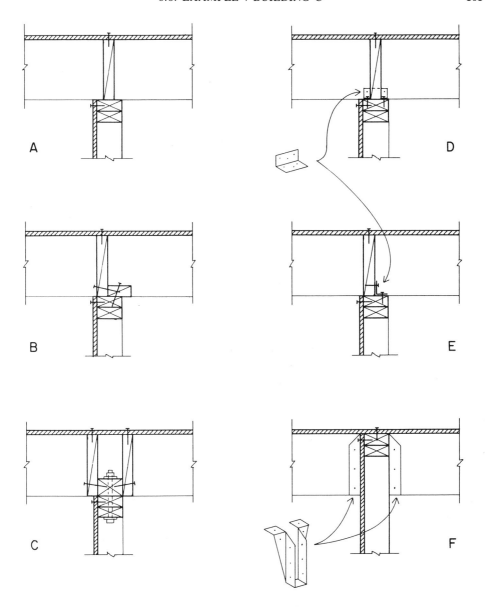

FIGURE 6.31. Connection details—roof to interior wall.

for this situation: the vertical gravity load transfer, the hold-down against wind uplift, and the transfer of diaphragm force parallel to the wall.

Detail A in Figure 6.31 shows the ordinary construction used if the gravity load alone is considered. The joists are either but-ted end to end, or they are lapped on top of the wall and are toe nailed to the top plate. Vertical blocking is usually provided between the joists for their stability as well as to provide a nailer for the plywood edges perpendicular to the joists. This joint provides only minor resistance to uplift (relying on withdrawal of the toenails) and virtually no capacity for transfer of the shear.

In detail B of Figure 6.31, a second horizontal block is added to facilitate the transfer of diaphragm shear. The vertical block is nailed to the horizontal block, and the horizontal block is nailed to the top plate. With the roof deck nailed to the top of the vertical block, the transfer is achieved from the roof deck to the top plate of the wall. With the wall surfacing nailed to the top plate, the transfer from horizontal to vertical diaphragms is then complete.

It should be noted that, although the stress in the roof deck is only 190 lb/ft at this location (see Fig. 6.30b), the total load transfer to the wall is twice this, resulting from a delivery of load to both sides of the wall by the deck. Thus all the nailing shown in detail B of Figure 6.31—the deck to the vertical block, the blocks to one another, and the block to the top plate—must be designed for the load transfer of 381 lb/ft. If a roof plywood panel edge occurs at this point, the nailing will be adequate because there will actually be two edge nailings at the joint. If this is an interior support point for a plywood panel, the usual minimum nailing with nails at 12-in. centers will not be sufficient, and a nailing must be specified that is capable of the load transfer. It is questionable whether the nailing of the blocks for this load magnitude could be achieved without splitting the blocks, so this option is probably not the best for the example.

A variation on detail B is shown in detail C of Figure 6.31. A second vertical block is added, and the horizontal block is bolted to the top plate. This results in an extended range of load capacity because there are now two rows of nails and the bolts are much stronger than nails in lateral load resistance. However, with fairly closely spaced joists, this detail would require a considerable number of bolts through the top plates.

Another approach to this connection is shown in details D and E of Figure 6.31 in which metal framing anchors are used for the attachment to the top plates. In detail D the anchors are attached to the joists, and in detail E they are attached to the blocks. Assuming that the anchor devices used have a rated load capacity adequate for the load transfer, either of these options is acceptable for the wind shear function. Detail D is slightly better for wind uplift because there is more attachment between the roof deck and the joists than there is between the deck and the blocks.

A third technique for this connection is shown in detail F of Figure 6.31 in which the top plate of the wall is raised to the level of the roof deck. This procedure allows for the simplest transfer of the wind shear because both the roof deck and the wall sheathing are directly nailed to the top plate. The joists are supported by saddle-type metal hangers hung from the top plate. One problem with this detail is that the upper panels of the wall sheathing must be installed before the roof framing can be placed, which is not the usual sequence of the construction.

We do not attempt to judge which of these, or of other possible options, is the best solution for this connection. From the viewpoint of structural design, anything that "works" is all right. In real situations there are many issues to consider in addition to the necessary structural functions. Thus the influence of roof drainage, wall surface finishes, ceiling construction, ductwork installation, and so on, may provide the deciding factors for choice between viable alternatives.

6.9.   EXAMPLE 8—BUILDING D

The plan and section in Figure 6.32 show a building with two symmetrical wings connected by a narrowed central portion. The presence of solid walls permits the consideration of the development of a shear wall system for lateral resistance, except for the

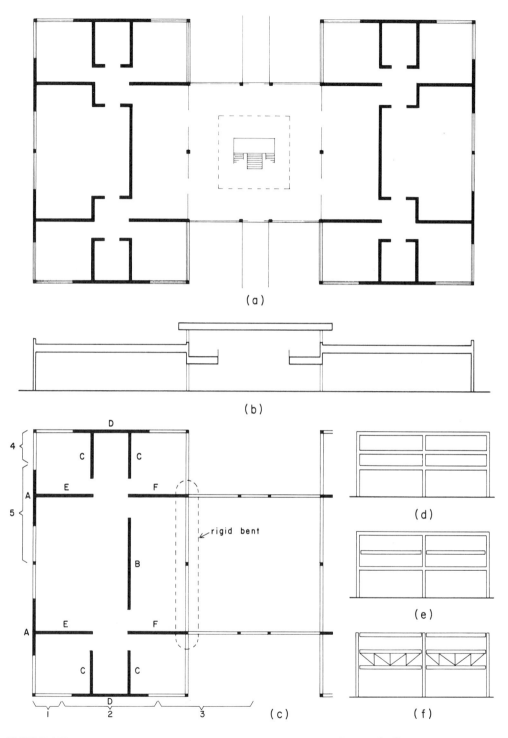

FIGURE 6.32. Example 8—Building D: (*a*) building plan; (*b*) building section; (*c*) loading zones for the shear walls and bents; (*d*) and (*e*) alternate forms for the rigid bents; (*f*) form of the trussed bent.

163

center portion with respect to north–south loading. A possible solution in this situation is the use of a rigid frame bent at the east and west sides of the center section, as shown in the plan in Figure 6.32c.

Unless the roof deck diaphragms are exceptionally rigid (as in the case of a poured-in-place concrete structural deck), the usual method of determining the distribution to the mixed vertical elements in this situation would be on the basis of peripheral distribution. For this distribution, the zones are as shown in Figure 6.32c.

As the section shows, there are three upper levels of framing in the bent. The bents may thus take one of the two forms shown in Figures 6.32d and e. In (d) the frame is developed as a three-story rigid bent, whereas in (e) the roof of the wings is developed with shear-type connections only and the bent is only two stories.

Figure 6.32f illustrates an alternative means of achieving the braced bent, that is, through the use of a trussed bent, which may be simpler for fabrication and more economical in general if the truss depth is adequate. Discussion of such a bent is presented in Example 6 in Section 6.7 and illustrated in Figure 6.28. In this case, if the trussing is incorporated in a solid portion of the wall, it offers no intrusion in the architectural form or detail of the building.

As with other systems involving the mixing of shear walls and bents, it is necessary for the bents to be made quite stiff. Otherwise the peripheral distribution will not be valid. The more rigid the shear walls, the more this condition is critical. If the walls are of reinforced masonry or concrete, and are quite long in plan with respect to their heights, the mixing for a peripheral distribution may be questionable.

We will not proceed with any computations or design of the elements for this example. Other examples show the methods for using the peripheral distribution and the design of shear walls and multistory rigid bents.

6.10. EXAMPLE 9—BUILDING E

Building E is a small three-story office building. Assuming the building is to be built for investment, with a speculative rental occupancy or a sale for undetermined purpose, a feature typically desired is the adaptability of the building to change. With regard to the structure, this usually means an emphasis on minimizing permanent elements of the construction—notably on the interior of the building. In this instance the permanent elements are limited to the exterior walls and the core elements (stairs, elevators, duct shafts, rest rooms) with a few interior free-standing columns. (See Fig. 6.33.)

The following will be used for consideration of lateral actions:

Wind: map speed = 80 mph;
    exposure B [129 km/h]
Seismic: zone 3
Assumed construction loads:
    Floor finish = 5 psf [0.24 kPa]
    Ceiling, lights, ducts = 15 psf [0.72 kPa]
Walls (average surface weight):
    Interior partitions = 25 psf [1.20 kPa]
    Exterior curtain wall = 25 psf [1.20 kPa]

Fire codes permitting, the most economical structure for the building will be one that makes the most use of light wood frame construction. It is unlikely that the building would use all wood construction of the type illustrated in Example 1, but a mixed system is quite possible. It is also possible to use steel, masonry, or concrete construction and eliminate wood, except for nonstructural uses. In addition to code requirements, consideration must be given to the building owners' preferences and to design criteria or standards for acoustic privacy, thermal control, and so on.

The plan as shown, with 30-ft square bays and a general open interior, is an ideal arrangement for a beam and column system in either steel or reinforced concrete. Other types of systems may be made more effective

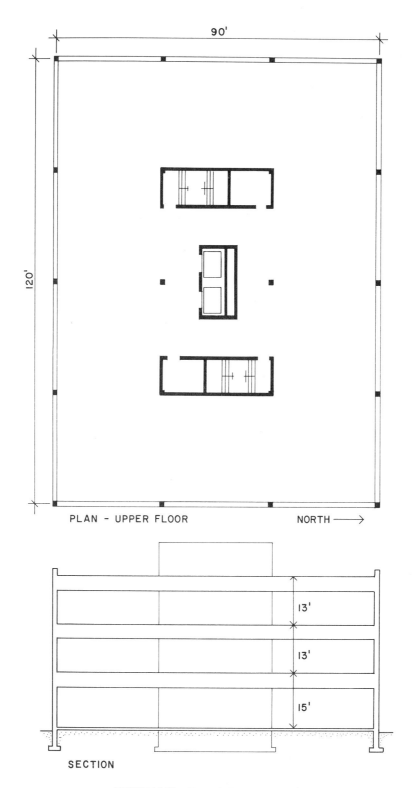

90'

120'

PLAN - UPPER FLOOR

NORTH ⟶

13'

13'

15'

SECTION

FIGURE 6.33. Example 9—Building E.

165

if some modifications of the basic plans are made. These changes may affect the planning of the building core, the plan dimensions for the column locations, the articulation of the exterior wall, or the vertical distances between the levels of the building.

The general form and basic type of the structural system must relate to both the gravity and lateral force problems. Considerations for gravity require the development of the horizontal spanning systems for the roof and floors and the arrangement of the vertical elements (walls and columns) that provide support for the spanning structure. Vertical elements should be stacked, thus requiring coordinating the plans of the various levels.

The most common choices for the lateral bracing system would be the following (see Fig. 6.34):

1. *Core Shear Wall System* (Fig. 6.34*a*). This consists of using solid walls to produce a very rigid central core. The rest of the structure leans on this rigid interior portion, and the roof and floor construction outside the core—as well as the exterior walls—are somewhat more free of concerns for lateral forces as far as the structure as a whole is concerned.

2. *Truss-Braced Core.* This is similar in nature to the shear wall-braced core, and the planning considerations would be essentially similar. The solid walls would be replaced by bays of trussed framing (in vertical bents) using various possible patterns for the truss elements.

3. *Peripheral Shear Walls* (see Fig. 6.34*b*). This in essence makes the building into a tubelike structure. Because doors and

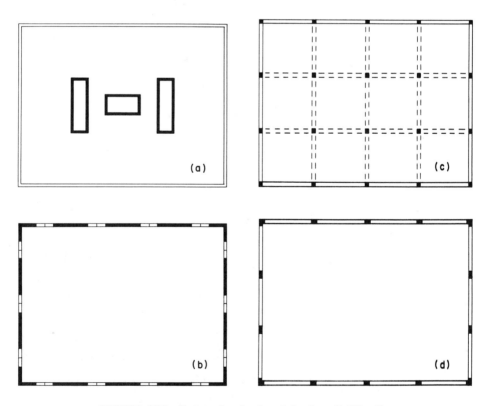

FIGURE 6.34. Options for the lateral bracing— Building E.

windows must pierce the exterior, the peripheral shear walls usually consist of linked sets of individual walls (sometimes called piers).

4. *Mixed Exterior and Interior Shear Walls.* This is essentially a combination of the core and peripheral systems.

5. *Full Rigid Frame System* (see Fig. 6.34c). This is produced by using the vertical planes of columns and beams in each direction as a series of rigid bents. For this building there would thus be four bents for bracing in one direction and five for bracing in the other direction. This requires that the beam–to–column connections be moment resistive.

6. *Peripheral Rigid Frame System* (see Fig. 6.34d). This consists of using only the columns and beams in the exterior walls, resulting in only two bracing bents in each direction.

In the right circumstances any of these systems may be acceptable. Each has advantages and disadvantages from both structural design and architectural planning points of view. The braced core schemes were popular in the past, especially for buildings in which wind was the major concern. The core system allows for the greatest freedom in planning the exterior walls, which are obviously of major concern to the architect. The peripheral system, however, produces the most torsionally stiff building—an advantage for seismic resistance.

The rigid frame schemes permit the free planning of the interior and the greatest openness in the wall planes. The integrity of the bents must be maintained, however, which restricts column locations and planning of stairs, elevators, and duct shafts so as not to interrupt any of the column-line beams. If designed for lateral forces, columns are likely to be large, and thus offer more intrusion in the building plan.

Other solutions are also possible, limited only by the creative imagination of design-

ers. In the chapters that follow we will illustrate the design of two possible structures for the building. We do not propose that these are ideal solutions, but merely that they are feasible alternatives. They have been chosen primarily to permit illustrating the design of the elements of the construction.

A structural framing plan for one of the upper floors of Example 9 is shown in Figure 6.35a. The plan indicates major use of structural masonry walls for both bearing walls and shear walls. The lateral bracing scheme is a combination of the core and peripheral systems. The floor—and probably the roof—structures consist of deck–joist–beam systems that are supported mostly by the interior and exterior bearing walls. The material in this section consists of the design of the major elements of this system.

For wind it is necessary to establish the design wind pressure, defined by the code as

$$p = C_e C_q q_s I$$

where C_e is a combined factor including concerns for the height above grade, exposure conditions, and gusts. From *UBC* Table 23-G (see Appendix C), assuming exposure B:

$$C_e = 0.7 \text{ from 0 to 20 ft above grade}$$
$$= 0.8 \text{ from 20 to 40 ft}$$
$$= 1.0 \text{ from 40 to 60 ft}$$

and C_q is the pressure coefficient. Using the projected area method (method 2), we find from *UBC* Table 23-H (see Appendix C) the following.

For vertical projected area:

$$C_q = 1.3 \text{ up to 40 ft above grade}$$
$$= 1.4 \text{ over 40 ft}$$

For horizontal projected area (roof surface):

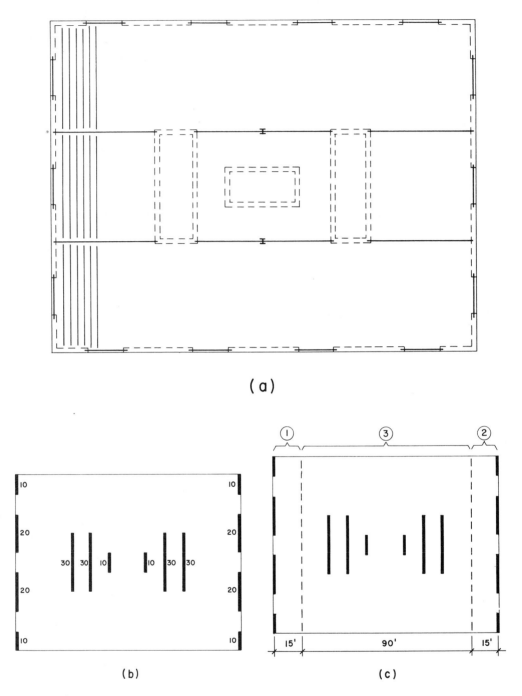

FIGURE 6.35. Masonry shear wall system—Example 9: (*a*) floor-framing plan; (*b*) north–south shear wall system; (*c*) load zones for the shear walls; (*d*) relative stiffness of the walls.

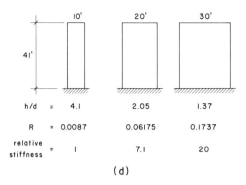

	10'	20'	30'
h/d =	4.1	2.05	1.37
R =	0.0087	0.06175	0.1737
relative stiffness =	1	7.1	20

(d)

FIGURE 6.35. (*Continued*)

$C_q = 0.7$ upward

The symbol q_s is the wind stagnation pressure at the standard measuring height of 30 ft. From *UBC* Table 23-F the q_s value for a speed of 80 mph is 17 psf.

For the importance factor *I* (*UBC* Table 23-K) we use a value of 1.0.

Table 6.6 summarizes the foregoing data for the determination of the wind pressures at the various height zones for Example 9. For the analysis of the horizontal wind effect on the building, the wind pressures are applied and translated into edge loadings for the horizontal diaphragms (roof and floors) as shown in Figure 6.36. Note that we have rounded off the wind pressures from Table 6.6 for use in Figure 6.36.

Figure 6.35*b* shows a plan of the building with an indication of the masonry walls that offer potential as shear walls for resistance to north–south lateral force. The numbers on the plan are the approximate plan lengths of the walls. Note that although the core construction actually produces vertical tubular-shaped elements, we have considered only the walls parallel to the load direction. The walls shown in Figure 6.35*b* will share the total wind load delivered by the diaphragms at the roof, third-floor, and second-floor levels (H_1, H_2, and H_3, respectively, as shown in Figure 6.36). Assuming the building to be a total of 122-ft wide in the east–west direction, the forces at the three levels are:

$$H_1 = 195 \times 122 = 23{,}790 \text{ lb } [106 \text{ kN}]$$

$$H_2 = 234 \times 122 = 28{,}548 \text{ lb } [127 \text{ kN}]$$

$$H_3 = 227 \times 122 = 27{,}694 \text{ lb } [123 \text{ kN}]$$

and the total wind force at the base of the shear walls is the sum of these loads, or 80,032 lb [356 kN].

Although the distribution of shared load to masonry walls is usually done on the basis of a more sophisticated analysis for relative stiffness (as was done for Example 5 in Section 6.6), if we assume for the moment that the walls are stiff in proportion to their plan lengths (as is done with plywood walls), we may divide the maximum shear load at the base of the walls by the total of the wall plan lengths to obtain an approximate value for the maximum shear stress. Thus

TABLE 6.6.   Design Wind Pressures for Example 9

Height above Average Level of Adjoining Ground (ft)	C_e	C_q	Pressure[a] p (psf)
0–20	0.7	1.3	15.47
20–40	0.8	1.3	17.68
40–60	1.0	1.4	23.80

[a]Horizontally directed pressure on vertical projected area: $p = C_e \times C_q \times 17$ psf.

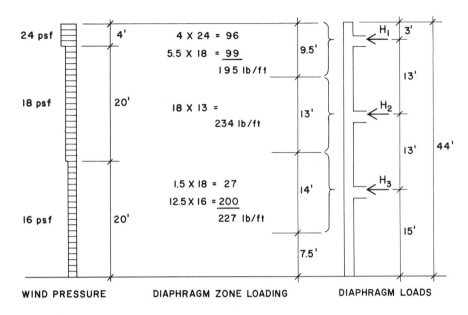

WIND PRESSURE   DIAPHRAGM ZONE LOADING   DIAPHRAGM LOADS

FIGURE 6.36. Generation of wind loads—Example 9.

$$\text{maximum shear: } v = \frac{80,032}{260}$$

$$= 308 \text{ lb/ft of wall length } [4.49 \text{ kN/m}]$$

This is quite a low force for a reinforced masonry wall, which tells us that if wind alone is of concern we have considerable overkill in terms of total shear walls. However, because we will find that the seismic forces are considerably greater for our example, we will reserve final judgment on the structural scheme.

Table 6.7 presents the analysis for determining the building weight to be used for the computation of the seismic effects in the north—south direction. In the tabulation we have included the weights of all the walls, which eliminates the necessity for adding the weights of the shear walls in any subsequent analysis of individual walls. Tabulations are done separately for the determination of loads to the three upper diaphragms (eventually producing three forces similar to H_1, H_2, and H_3, as determined for the wind loading). Ex-

cept for the shear walls, the weight of the lower half of the first-story walls is assumed to be resisted by the first-floor-level construction (assumed to be a concrete structure poured directly on the ground) and is thus not part of the distribution to the shear wall system.

For the determination of the base shear we now use *UBC* formula 12-1:

$$V = ZIKCSW$$

For seismic zone 3: $Z = \frac{3}{4}$.

For our building as for wind: $I = 1.0$.

For the masonry shear wall structure: $K = 1.33$.

For the three-story building with S not determined, we use the maximum value of the product of $CS = 0.14$.

Thus

$$V = \tfrac{3}{4}(1.0)(1.33)(0.14)(2775.9)$$

$$= 388 \text{ k } [1724 \text{ kN}]$$

TABLE 6.7. Dead Load for the North–South Seismic Force

Level	Source of Load	Unit Load (psf)	Load (kips)
Roof	Roof and ceiling	25	$120 \times 90 \times 25 = 270$
	Masonry walls	60	$480 \times 9.5 \times 60 = 273.6$
	Window walls	15	$140 \times 9.5 \times 15 = 20.0$
	Interior walls	10	$200 \times 5 \times 10 = 10.0$
	Penthouse + equipment (estimate total)		$= 25.0$
	Subtotal		598.6
Third floor	Floor	55	$120 \times 90 \times 55 = 594.0$
	Masonry walls	60	$480 \times 13 \times 60 = 374.4$
	Window walls	15	$140 \times 13 \times 15 = 27.3$
	Interior walls	10	$200 \times 9 \times 10 = 18.0$
	Subtotal		1013.7
Second floor	Floor	55	$120 \times 90 \times 55 = 594.0$
	Masonry walls	60	$480 \times 14 \times 60 = 403.2$
	Window walls	15	$140 \times 14 \times 15 = 29.4$
	Interior walls	10	$200 \times 10 \times 10 = 20.0$
	Subtotal		1046.6
First floor	Shear walls	60	$260 \times 7.5 \times 60 = 117.0$
	(Remainder of first floor direct to ground)		
	Total dead load for base shear		$= 2775.9$
			$[12.347 \times 10^3 \text{ kN}]$

This total force must be distributed to the roof and second floor in accordance with the requirements of Section 2312(e) of the *UBC*. The force at each level F_x is determined from formula 12-7 as

$$F_x = (V)(w_x h_x) / \sum_{i=1}^{n} w_i h_i$$

where F_x = the force to be applied at each level x

  w_x = the total dead load at level x

  h_x = the height of level x above the base of the structure

(Notice that F_t has been omitted from the formula because T is less than 0.7 sec.)

The determination of the F_x values is shown in Table 6.8. Distribution of the total forces at each level to the individual shear walls requires two considerations. The pri-mary concern is for the functioning of the horizontal diaphragms. First, if these are considered to be infinitely stiff, then the distribution to the individual walls will be strictly in terms of their relative stiffness or deflection. Second, if the horizontal diaphragms are considered to be quite flexible (in their diaphragm spanning actions), then the distribution to the shear walls will be on a peripheral basis.

Figure 6.35c shows the building plan with the north–south shear walls and a breakdown of peripheral distribution assuming the flexible horizontal diaphragm. On this basis, the end shear walls each carry one eighth of the total shear and the core walls carry three fourths of the shear. In this approach the next step would be to consider the relative stiffness of the group of walls in each of the zones and to distribute forces to the individual walls.

TABLE 6.8. Seismic Loads: Example 9

Level	w_x (kips)	h_x (ft)	$w_x h_x$	$F_x{}^a$ (kips)
Roof	598.6	41	24,543	138.8
Third floor	1013.7	28	28,384	160.5
Second floor	1046.6	15	15,699	88.7
			68,626	

$${}^aF_x = \frac{388}{68,626}(w_x h_x)$$

In truth, the nature of the diaphragms is most likely somewhere between the two extremes described (just as most structural connections are neither pinned nor fully fixed but actually partially fixed). It is thus not uncommon in practice for designers to investigate both conditions and to incorporate data from both analyses into their designs.

For either approach it is necessary to consider the relative stiffness of the walls of various plan length. The most common means for doing this is the method illustrated in Example 5, Section 5.6. Figure 6.35d shows an analysis for the relative stiffness of the walls with the three plan lengths of 10 ft, 20 ft, and 30 ft. The walls are assumed to be cantilevered from fixed bases and the distributions shown are for the roof load for which the wall height (h in the table and figure) is 41 ft. For a precise analysis separate distributions should be made for the distribution of the floor diaphragm loads using the shorter wall heights. If this is done, it will be found that the percent of load carried by the shorter walls will be considerably increased.

Referring to Figure 6.35c, if we consider the group of core walls in peripheral zone 3, their total combined stiffness is

$$4 \times 0.1737 = 0.6948$$

$$2 \times 0.0087 = \underline{0.0174}$$

$$\text{Total} \quad = 0.7122$$

The portion of load carried by a single 10-ft-long wall will thus be

$$\frac{0.0087}{0.7122} = 0.0122 \text{ or barely more than } 1\%$$

It is therefore reasonable to assume that the 30-ft walls carry the entire load to the core zone. For a single pair of walls constituting one stair plus a rest room tower, the portion of the full lateral load will thus be

$$\tfrac{1}{2} \times \tfrac{3}{4} \times F_x = \tfrac{3}{8} \times F_x$$

Referring to Table 6.8 and Figure 6.37, the loads for a single tower are:

$$H_1 = \tfrac{3}{8} \times 138.8 = 52.05 \text{ k } [232 \text{ kN}]$$

$$H_2 = \tfrac{3}{8} \times 160.5 = 60.2 \text{ k } [268 \text{ kN}]$$

$$H_3 = \tfrac{3}{8} \times 88.7 = 33.3 \text{ k } [148 \text{ kN}]$$

and the total overturning moment about the base of the wall at the first floor level is:

$$
\begin{array}{llll}
H_1 \times 41 & = 52.05 \times 41 & & \\
 & = 2134 \text{ k-ft} & [2894 \text{ kN-m}] \\
H_2 \times 28 & = 60.2 \times 28 & & \\
 & = 1686 & & 2286 \\
H_3 \times 15 & = 33.3 \times 15 & & \\
 & = \underline{500} & & 678 \\
\text{Total} & = 4320 \text{ k-ft} & [5858 \text{ kN-m}]
\end{array}
$$

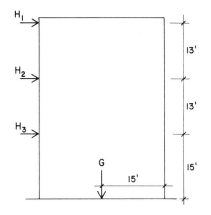

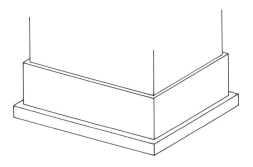

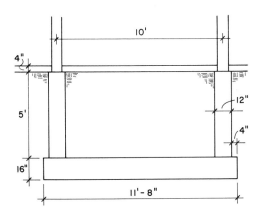

FIGURE 6.37. Loading and form of the stair tower wall and its foundation.

For the dead load moment that resists this overturn effect we make the following assumptions:

1. The walls are 8-in. concrete block weighing 60 psf of wall surface. For the en-tire tower the total weight is thus approximately

$$80 \times 41 \times 60 = 196.8 \text{ k } [875 \text{ kN}]$$

2. As bearing walls, the tower walls carry approximately 1800 ft² of roof or floor periphery, which results in a supported dead load of

$$55 \times 1800$$

$$= 99 \text{ k/floor or } 198 \text{ k total } [881 \text{ kN}]$$

$$25 \times 1800$$

$$= 45 \text{ k of roof load } [200 \text{ kN}]$$

This results in a total load (G in Fig. 6.37) of 439.8 k [1956 kN] and a restoring dead load moment of

$$439.8 \times 15 = 6597 \text{ k-ft } [8946 \text{ kN}]$$

The safety factor against overturn is thus

$$\frac{6597}{4320} = 1.53$$

which indicates that there is no real need for a tiedown force.

There will, of course, be a considerable tiedown developed in the form of the doweling of the wall reinforcing into the foundation. If the tower foundation is as shown in Figure 6.37, the construction results in an additional dead weight of approximately 150 k, not including the earth fill. For an investigation of the footing, the total dead load is thus approximately 690 k, and the unit soil pressure for dead load is

$$q = \frac{690,000}{11.7 \times 31.7} = 1860 \text{ psf } [89 \text{ kPa}]$$

The equivalent eccentricity of the dead load caused by the seismic overturn force is

$$e = \frac{4320}{690} = 6.26 \text{ ft } [1.91 \text{ m}]$$

which is slightly less than the kern limit of $D/6$ ($41.7/6 = 6.95$ ft); thus the maximum soil stress due to dead load plus seismic load will be approximately 3500 psf. This should not be a problem unless the soil is highly compressible.

At the base of the tower the total lateral shear ($H_1 + H_2 + H_3$) is 145.5 kips. This will be shared by the two walls, although the shear stress will be slightly higher in the wall with the door openings. If we assume the 30-ft wall to be reduced to a net width of 22 ft by the openings and an 8-in. wall with 40% voided blocks, the shear analysis is:

$$\text{unit shear force: } \frac{1.5 \times 145,500}{2 \times 22}$$

$$= 4960 \text{ lb/ft } [72.4 \text{ kN/m}]$$

$$\text{unit stress: } f_v = \frac{4960}{7.5 \times 12 \times 0.60}$$

$$= 92 \text{ psi } [845 \text{ kPa}]$$

This is a bit high, but not beyond the capacity of the reinforced masonry wall. (Note the increase of shear force by 50% per *UBC* 2407(h)4F(i).)

Because of their relative stiffness, the core walls carry the major portion of the lateral force in this building. If the building is designed only for the lower wind force, it would be possible to use the core alone and to eliminate the exterior shear walls. For seismic load, however, the exterior walls add significantly to the torsional resistance, thus making the core-braced scheme less desirable. Core bracing is common where wind is the critical lateral force, but is less used for seismic resistance.

6.11. EXAMPLE 10-BUILDING E

If Building E is built with a column and a beam frame, it is possible to use trussed

bracing for lateral resistance. The planning of such bracing is in many ways similar to that required for the shear wall schemes, and planes of trussed bracing could be substituted for some of the shear walls indicated in the preceding example. Because the trussing is produced ordinarily by using the columns and beams of the gravity resistive system and simply adding diagonals, the planning of both systems must be tightly coordinated.

Figure 6.38 shows some possibilities for use of X-bracing for Building E. In Figure 6.38a is shown the use of a large single brace in place of the 30-ft core shear walls. If overturning and anchorage can be solved, two of these trussed bents can easily brace the building in place of the shear wall towers in Section 6.10.

Figure 6.38b shows the use of a series of peripheral bents corresponding to the locations of the exterior shear walls shown in the plan in Figure 6.35a. Again, if overturning can be dealt with, it would be possible to use fewer braced bents, with not every wall unit braced. As with the systems using peripheral shear walls, the location of peripheral X-bracing is significant to the development of torsion and an advantage in seismic force resistance.

A particularly strategic location for either shear walls or trussed bents on a building such as this is at the building's exterior corners. In Figures 6.38 c, d, and e are three possibilities for the use of peripheral trussing at the building corners. Figure 6.38c shows a single width vertical bent—the simplest and most direct solution. Figure 6.38d shows a scheme in which the number of bents is increased by one for each lower story. Although this adds some complexity, it produces a form which is reflective of the relative magnitude of the shear and the overturning effects at each level.

Figure 6.38e shows the use of a single large diagonal that extends from the corner at the roof level down through all three stories, producing a single triangular form. This is actually a very direct solution that is com-

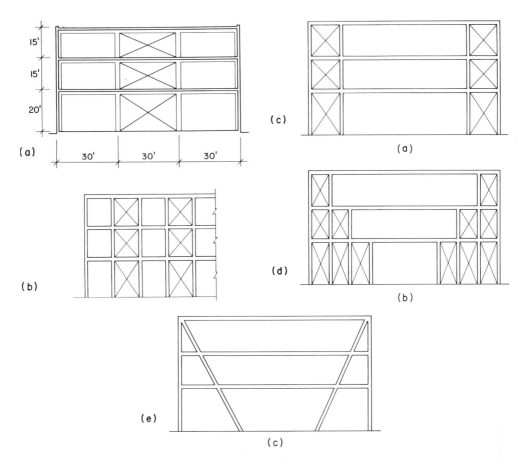

FIGURE 6.38. Considerations of trussed bracing—Example 10: (*a*) core bracing; (*b*) peripheral bents; (*c*) corner bents; (*d*) stepped corner bents; (*e*) multistory corner diagonal brace.

monly used in structures other than those for buildings.

In most cases trussed bracing would not be used for both core and peripheral locations in the same building. However, there is nothing wrong with such an application if some reasonable means can be used to determine the distribution of forces to the individual bents. As was indicated with the examples of one-story buildings, it may also be possible to mix systems of shear walls and some trussed or rigid frame bents.

6.12. EXAMPLE 11-BUILDING E

Referring to the plan for Building E, as shown in Figure 6.33, observe that there is

a series of columns arranged in rows in each direction defining a column bay system of 30-ft by 30-ft bays. Another way to visualize this system is in terms of the vertical planar bents that are defined by the columns in a single row associated with the beams that connect them at the three upper levels of the building: the second floor, the third floor, and the roof. These bents, as shown in Figure 6.39, may be used to brace the building in both directions if the beam-to-column connections can be made moment resistive and the columns are vertically continuous. If the latter is achieved and the system is utilized for lateral bracing, it is in the words of the *UBC* (Ref. 1), "a moment-resistive space frame," or, in the more commonly used reference, a rigid frame system.

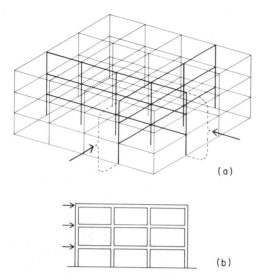

FIGURE 6.39. Vertical beam and column bents—Example 11: (*a*) form of the individual bents; (*b*) loading of a single bent.

For the structure as defined in Figure 6.33, there are four bents in the east–west direction, each having five columns connected at each level by four beams. In the north–south direction there are five bents, each with four columns connected at each level by three beams. The form of the individual bents is as shown in Figure 6.39*a*. The horizontal roof and the floor deck diaphragms deliver the lateral loads to the bents as shown for the north–south bent in Figure 6.39*b*. The lateral loading develops shear, bending, and axial force in all the members of the frame; the investigation for these effects is a statically indeterminate problem.

There are many ways in which rigid frames can be utilized for lateral resistance in different situations. Example 8 in Section 6.9 shows the use of a pair of frames employed selectively for part of the bracing system for the building, with the rest of the frame structure limited to simple post-and-beam functions. This can be achieved in steel framing by simply using moment-resistive connections only where moment resistance is desired. It is somewhat less able to be

controlled in poured-in-place concrete frames, for moment continuity of the frame members is a natural attribute.

If the structure defined in Figure 6.33 utilizes steel beams and columns, then any, all, or none of the frame bents can be made "rigid" through the use of moment-resistive connections; the remainder of the frame functions as a post–and–beam system for gravity loads only. If the structure is of poured-in-place reinforced concrete, and the columns are all square and close to the same size, all of the defined bents will function as rigid frames for both lateral and gravity loading.

Plywood shear walls and X-bracing represent elements that function primarily for lateral load resistance, leaving other elements to develop gravity load resistance. Structural masonry walls, trussed bents, and rigid frames represent elements that are usually by their nature and the means of employing them used for both vertical and lateral load resistance. Although a rigid frame may be visualized primarily as such for its lateral load resistance potential, it must also be designed for the combined effects that include the vertical loads due to gravity.

For a building such as Building E, there are several possible schemes for using rigid frames for lateral load resistance. The basic techniques include the following:

1. *The Full Rigid Frame.* This consists of using all of the bents defined by the alignment of columns and having continuous beams at all levels.

2. *Selected Frames.* This consists of choosing only some of the potential bents for use as lateral bracing. This may be controlled by use of the type of connections (in steel) or by the selection of the member sizes for stiffness. As in any load-sharing situation, the stiffer bents will take the greater share of the total load.

3. *The Braced Core.* As with shear wall

or trussed frames, the permanent construction around stairs, elevators, duct shafts and pipe chases, or stacked rest rooms may become the location of lateral bracing.

4. *Peripheral Bracing.* This consists of using only the bents that occur in the planes of the exterior walls that are defined by the exterior columns and the spandrel beams.

Many structural and architectural issues are to be considered in choosing one of these schemes over the other. A currently popular system is one using the peripheral bents. Structurally, this has the principal advantage of providing the most torsional resistance—of particular concern for seismic load. Architecturally, it offers the freedom of the entire interior structure from concerns for lateral resistance. However, any of the other schemes—plus other more imaginative possibilities—may be logical for a given situation. The following example illustrates a design of a peripheral bent system for Building E, with no particular intention of prejudice.

Design of Peripheral Bent System

Figure 6.40a shows a structural-framing plan for a reinforced concrete beam and slab system for one of the upper floors of Building E. The construction detail section in Figure 6.40b shows the condition at the building exterior, indicating the use of an exposed spandrel beam and column. The columns and column–line beams constitute a three-dimensional rigid frame, with the three typical column–beam joint conditions as shown in Figure 6.40c.

The plan arrangements and beam layouts for this system permit considering using either a full rigid frame system or a peripheral bent system. For the poured-in-place concrete frame it is actually somewhat difficult to avoid the full rigid frame action. One technique that can be used is to manip-

ulate the distribution of lateral forces to the individual bents by the choice of the member shapes and sizes. In this case, it has been decided to use the exterior wall bents (peripheral bents) as the main bracing system. To increase the stiffness of these bents the exterior columns are made oblong, with their large dimension in the direction of the wall plane and their interacting beams made excessively deep. (See Figures 6.40a and b.) With the square interior columns and the much shallower interior beams, the other bents will be much less stiff.

For an initial approximate design we will consider the peripheral bents to take the entire lateral load. This is not quite true, of course, and a final, more exact, investigation—preferably a true dynamic one—would indicate some minor forces in the other bents. However, as all the bents will be designed for gravity loading, it is reasonable to expect that the lateral forces on the interior bents may quite likely not be critical if the usual stress increase of one third is considered.

It is not reasonable, of course, to design the bents for lateral forces only. Although we do not present it, some values for internal forces generated by gravity loads must be added to the effects of the lateral loads, requiring a complete combined loading investigation. These values have been approximated and are included where required in the example.

The lateral force resisting systems for the building are shown in Figure 6.41. For force in the east–west direction the resistive system consists of the horizontal roof and floor slabs and the exterior bents (columns and spandrel beams) on the north and south sides. For force in the north–south direction the system utilizes the bents on the east and west sides.

If the lateral load is the same in both directions, the stress in the slab (shear in the horizontal diaphragm) is critical for the north–south loading because the slab has less width for resistance to this loading. The loads are not equal, however. Wind force will be

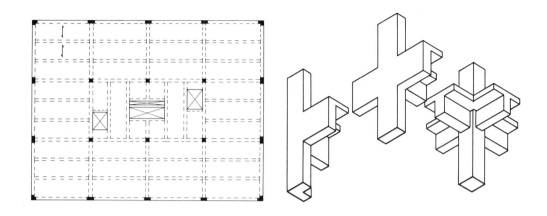

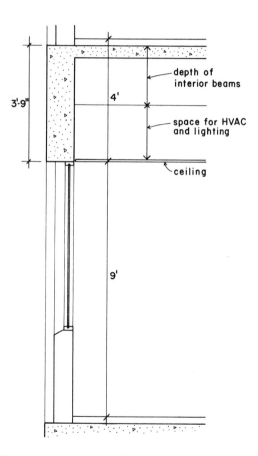

FIGURE 6.40. Form and details of the concrete structure for Example 11.

178

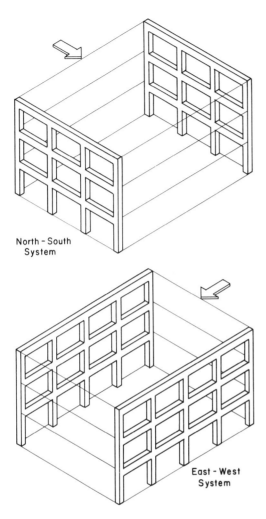

North - South
System

East - West
System

FIGURE 6.41.   The peripheral bent system—Example 11.

greater in the north and south directions because the building has a greater profile in this direction. This makes it even more obvious that this will be the loading critical for the slab in design for wind. However, for seismic load, a true dynamic analysis reveals that the load effect is greater in the east–west direction because the resistive bents are slightly stiffer in this direction. In any event, it is unlikely that the 5-in.-thick slab with properly anchored edge reinforcing at the spandrels will be critically stressed for any loading.

Our considerations for lateral load will be limited to the seismic loading in the north–south direction and to investigations of the effects on the columns and spandrel beams on the east and west sides. Both the wind and seismic loadings were determined for the masonry and steel structure in Section 6.10. The wind loading is the same for the concrete structure, but the seismic effects will be modified by the difference in building weight caused by the heavier concrete structure and the different value to be used for the K factor.

Review of the designs for the floor systems indicate that the total weight of the horizontal construction in the concrete building is more than twice that in the masonry and steel building. Assuming other elements of the construction to be approximately the same in both buildings, inspection of the weight tabulation in Table 6.7 indicates that the total weights are approximately 25% higher for the concrete building. Thus, for use in the *UBC* formula for seismic load, the values for W should be increased by 25%.

On the other hand, the *UBC* gives a value of only 0.67 for K for the building with a rigid frame system. This is one half of that for the shear wall (box system). Thus a 50% reduction is effected. Note that the K of 0.67 is to be used only for a building with a "ductile moment-resisting space frame" that requires a great number of special considerations in both the design and the construction detailing for the concrete frame.

With the approximate adjustments for weight and different bracing, we may use the values determined in Table 6.8 with an adjustment of $1.25 \times 0.5 = 0.625$. Figure 6.42 shows the typical total loading in the north–south direction. As there are two bents, the values from Figure 6.42a are divided by two for the design of the bent. Note that even with the reductions the seismic loading is still higher than the wind loading determined in Section 6.10.

For an approximate analysis we consider the individual stories of the bent to behave

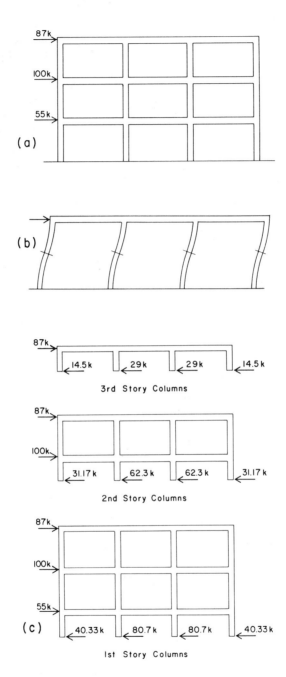

FIGURE 6.42. Loading and investigation of the north–south bents—Example 11. (*Note:* Loads shown are the total building loads which must be distributed to the bents.)

as shown in Figure 6.42b, with the columns developing an inflection point at their mid-height points. Because the columns all move the same distance, the shear load in a single column may be assumed to be equal to the cantilever deflecting load and the individual shears to be proportionate to the stiffnesses of the columns. If the columns are all of equal stiffness in this case, the total load would be simply divided by four. However, the end columns are slightly less restrained as there is a beam on only one side. We will assume the net stiffness of the end columns to be one half that of the interior columns. Thus the shear force in the end columns will be one sixth of the load and that in the interior columns one third of the load. The column shears for each of the three stories are thus as shown in Figure 6.42c.

The column shear forces produce moments in the columns. With the column inflection points assumed at midheight, the moment produced by a single shear force is simply the product of the force and half the column height. These moments must be resisted by the end moments in the rigidly attached beams, and the actions are as shown in Figure 6.43a. These effects due to the lateral loads may now be combined with the effects of gravity loads for an approximate design of the columns and beams.

For the columns, we combined the axial compression forces with any gravity-induced moments and first determine that the load condition without lateral effects is not critical. We may then add the effects of the moments caused by lateral loading and investigate the combined loading condition for which we may use the one third increase in allowable stress. Gravity-induced beam moments are taken from Figure 6.45 and are assumed to induce column moments as shown in Figure 6.43b. The summary of design conditions for the corner and interior column is shown in Table 6.9. The design values for axial load and moment and approximate sizes and reinforcing are shown in

Figure 6.44. Column sizes and reinforcing were obtained from the tables in the *CRSI Handbook* (Ref. 8) using concrete with $f'_c = 4$ ksi and Grade 60 reinforcing.

The spandrel beams (or girders) must be designed for the combined shears and moments due to gravity and lateral effects. Using the values given for gravity-induced moments and the values for lateral load moments from Figure 6.43a, the combined moment conditions are shown in Figure 6.45a. For design we must consider both the gravity only moment and the combined effect. For the combined effect we use three fourths of the total combined values to reflect the allowable stress increase of one third.

Figure 6.45b presents a summary of the design of the reinforcing for the spandrel beam at the third floor. If the construction that was shown in Figure 6.40 is retained with the exposed spandrel beams, the beam is quite deep. Its width should be approximately the same as that of the column without producing too massive a section. The section shown is probably adequate, but several additional considerations must be made as will be discussed later.

For computation of the required steel areas we assume an effective depth of approximately 40 in. and use

$$A_s = \frac{M}{f_s jd} = \frac{M \times 12}{(24)(0.9)(40)} = 0.0139\,M$$

Because the beam is so deep, it is advisable to use some longitudinal reinforcing at an intermediate height in the section—especially on the exposed face.

Shear design for the beams should also be done for the combined loading effects. The closed tie form for the shear reinforcing—as shown in Figure 6.45b—is used for considerations of torsion as well as the necessity for tying the compressive reinforcing.

With all of the approximations made, this should still be considered to be a very pre-

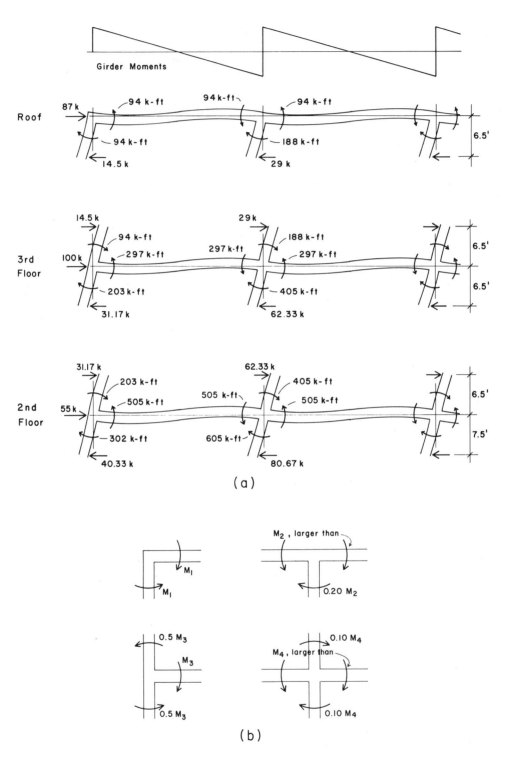

FIGURE 6.43. Investigation for beam and column shears and moments—Example 11.

182

TABLE 6.9 Summary of Design Data for the Bent Columns

	Column	
	Intermediate	Corner
Axial Gravity Design Load (kips)		
Third story	90	55
Second story	179	117
First story	277	176
Assumed Gravity Moment on Bent Axis (k-ft)		
Third story	60	120
Second story	40	100
First story	40	100
Moment from Lateral Force (k-ft) from Figure 6.43		
Third story	94	47
Second story	203	102
First story	302	151

	Intermediate Column					Corner Column				
	Axial Load	Moment	e	Column Dimensions	Reinforcing	Axial Load	Moment	e	Column Dimensions	Reinforcing
	(kips)	(k-ft)	(in.)	(in.)	No. – Size	(kips)	(k-ft)	(in.)	(in.)	No. – Size
Roof										
	90 X 3/4 = 68	154 X 3/4 = 115	20	20 X 28	6 - 9	55 X 3/4 = 41	167 X 3/4 = 125	36	20 X 24	6 - 10
3										
	179 X 3/4 = 134	243 X 3/4 = 182	16	20 X 28	6 - 9	117 X 3/4 = 88	202 X 3/4 = 152	21	20 X 24	6 - 10
2										
	277 X 3/4 = 208	342 X 3/4 = 257	15	20 X 28	6 - 11	176 X 3/4 = 132	251 X 3/4 = 188	17	20 X 24	6 - 11
1										

FIGURE 6.44. Design of the bent columns—Example 11.

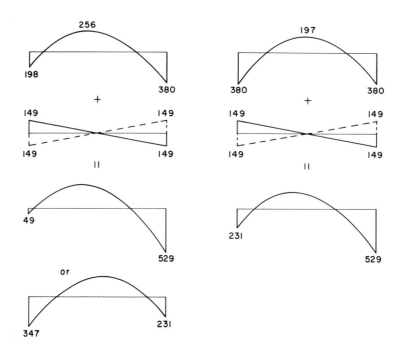

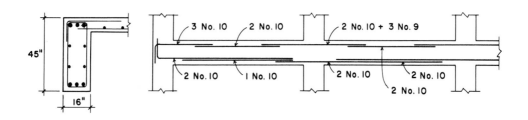

Design Moment		+		256		197
(k-ft)		−	260 (¾ of 347)		397 (¾ of 529)	
Required A_s	top	3.61		5.52		
= 0.0139 M						
(in.²)	bottom		3.56			2.74
	top	3.81	2.54	5.54		2.54
Actual A_s						
	bottom	2.54	3.81	2.54		5.08

FIGURE 6.45. Design of the bent girders—Example 11.

liminary design for the beam. It should, however, be adequate for use in preliminary architectural studies and for sizing the members for a dynamic seismic analysis and a general analysis of the actions of the indeterminate structure.

6.13. EXAMPLE 12—BUILDING F

Figure 6.46a shows a typical upper-floor plan for a multistory apartment building that utilizes shear walls as the bracing system in both directions. In the north–south direction the interior walls between the apartment units are used, together with the two end walls at the stairs. There are thus a total of 14 walls, all approximately 20-ft long in plan.

In the east–west direction the vertical bracing consists of the interior corridor walls. While there is usually a desire to have a minimum of permanent interior wall construction for some occupanies (such as the office building in the preceding section), it is reasonable to consider this structure for buildings such as apartments, hotels, dormitories, jails, and hospitals.

The exterior wall structure consists of a column and beam system. The ends of the shear walls are used as columns in this system. The typical floor structure could be a concrete slab or a deck and joist system. In either of these the shear walls would also be used as bearing walls. The solid concrete slab is a popular system for this situation, primarily because it permits a minimum floor-to-floor distance.

The building section is shown in Figure 6.46b. There are 12 floors of apartments plus a basement and a rooftop structure housing the elevator and ventilating equipment. For analysis we consider the shear wall base to be at the basement-floor level and the top of the building to be at the roof level. Although it must also be braced, and its weight added to the roof load, the penthouse structure is not really part of the general lateral system for the building.

Because of the long narrow plan, this building has considerably different responses in the two directions. Using the *UBC* formulas for an approximate determination of the building periods, we find the following:

In the east–west direction:

$$T = \frac{0.05 h_n}{\sqrt{D}} = \frac{0.05(120)}{\sqrt{175}} = 0.454 \text{ sec}$$

In the north–south direction:

$$T = \frac{0.05(120)}{\sqrt{48}} = 0.866 \text{ sec}$$

These values for T may then be used to find values of the factor C, or the combined factor CS, for the base shear as follows:

In the east–west direction:

$$C = \frac{1}{15 \sqrt{T}} = \frac{1}{15 \sqrt{0.454}} = 0.099$$

and we therefore use the CS factor of 0.14.

In the north–south direction:

$$C = \frac{1}{15 \sqrt{0.866}} = 0.0716$$

for which we compute CS as

$$CS = 1.5 \, C = 1.5 \times 0.0716 = 0.1074$$

The values for base shear may be found as follows:

In the east–west direction:

$$V = ZIKCSW$$
$$= (1)(1)(1.33)(0.14)W = 0.1862W$$

In the north–south direction:

$$V = (1)(1)(1.33)(0.1074)W = 0.1428W$$

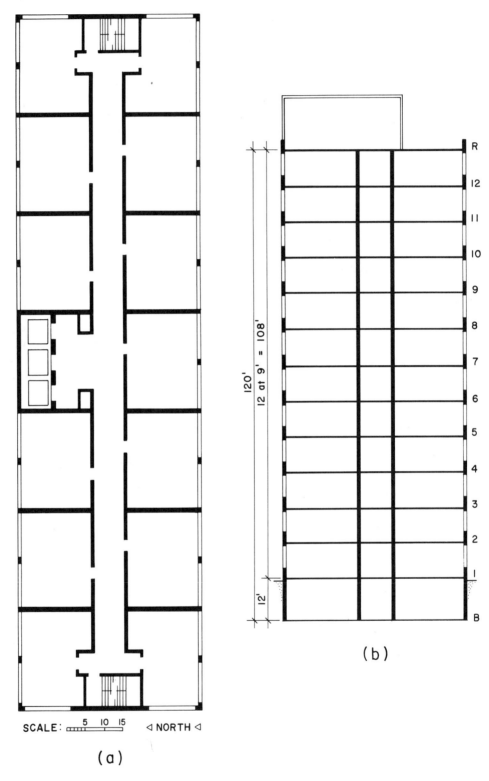

SCALE: 5 10 15 ◁ NORTH ◁

(a)

(b)

FIGURE 6.46. Example 12—Building F: (*a*) typical upper floor plan; (*b*) north–south building section.

Based on the plan shown, we approximate the weight of one typical upper story as follows:

Floor DL: 175 ft × 48 ft × 75 psf = 630 kips
Shear walls: 20 ft × 8.5 ft × 125 psf × 24 = 510 k
Other walls:

$$\text{Interior} = 600 \text{ ft} \times 8.5 \text{ ft} \times 15 \text{ psf}$$
$$= 75 \text{ k}$$
$$\text{Exterior} = 400 \text{ ft} \times 8.5 \text{ ft} \times 25 \text{ psf}$$
$$= 85 \text{ k}$$

Stairs, etc. = 200 ft × 8.5 × 25 psf
$$= 43 \text{ k}$$

Thus, a total of 1345 kips per story is to be used as the unit of W applied at each floor level. This is the value of w_x in the *UBC* formula for redistribution of the loads. Because w_x is constant (almost) at each level, the determination of the F_x values from *UBC* formula 12-7 can be simplified as follows:

$$F_x = \frac{(V - F_t)h_x}{\Sigma h_i}$$

For this determination we find

$$W = 1345 \times 13 \text{ levels} \div 14 \text{ walls}$$
$$= 1249 \text{ k/wall}$$
$$V = 0.1428\, W = 0.1428 \times 1249$$
$$= 178 \text{ k } (N\text{–}S \text{ direction})$$
$$F_t = 0.07\, TV = 0.07 \times 0.866 \times 178$$
$$= 10.8, \text{ say } 11 \text{ k}$$

Then

$$F_x = \frac{(V - F_t)h_x}{\Sigma h_i} = \frac{(178 - 11)h_x}{858}$$
$$= 0.1946\, h_x$$

which is used to find the F_x loads for one shear wall in the north–south direction, as shown in Table 6.10. This loading together with the shear and moment diagrams for one wall are shown in Figure 6.47.

TABLE 6.10 North–South Seismic Loads—Example 12

Building Level	h_x (ft)	F_x (kips)
R	120	23.35
12	111	21.60
11	102	19.85
10	93	18.10
9	84	16.35
8	75	14.60
7	66	12.84
6	57	11.09
5	48	9.34
4	39	7.59
3	30	5.84
2	21	4.09
1	12	2.34
	$\Sigma\, h_i = 858$	

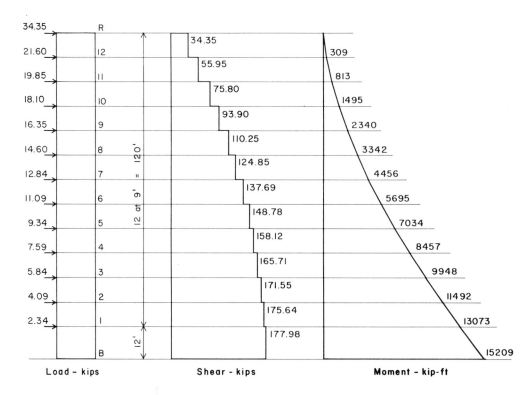

Load – kips	Shear – kips	Moment – kip-ft

FIGURE 6.47. Functioning of the 12-story shear wall.

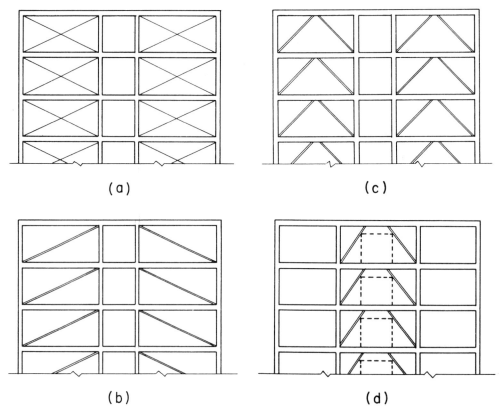

FIGURE 6.48. Example 13—Building F: (*a*) X-braced bents; (*b*) single diagonal-braced bents; (*c*) K-braced bents; (*d*) K-braced core bents.

188

Although the approximate static method of analysis may be reasonable for wind loading, it is recommended that a more exact investigation be made for seismic loading. The approximate analysis just demonstrated may be used for a preliminary determination of feasibility and to establish some data for a more exact analysis.

6.14. EXAMPLE 13—BUILDING F

Truss bracing presents a possibility for the bracing of Building F. A partial section of the upper portion of the structure for such a scheme is shown in Figure 6.48a. Another alternative is for the single diagonal scheme shown in Figure 6.48b. The latter scheme would require much larger members, but these may be desirable for their energy absorption, the reduced building drift, the out-

of-plane bracing of the wall, and other possible reasons. The fact that there are half as many members and connections may be significant, even though the elements are heavier.

A third possibility for the truss bracing is the K-brace system shown in Figure 6.48c. Although increasingly popular for bracing of steel frames, the K-brace system may be a bit of an overkill for this particular structure. Because the K-brace layout permits the use of some space in the center portion of the bay, an alternative may be to use a single, central bay of bracing, as shown in Figure 6.48d. With a drop ceiling in the corridor, it is possible to facilitate the same basic plan as shown for the shear wall structure in Figure 6.46.

Although it is probably necessary to use all of the available walls for shear walls, as was done in Example 12, it is unlikely that

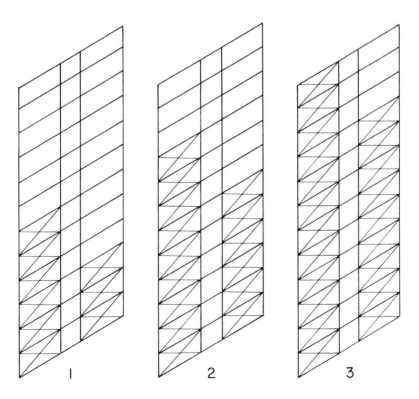

FIGURE 6.49. Stepped bracing system—Example 13.

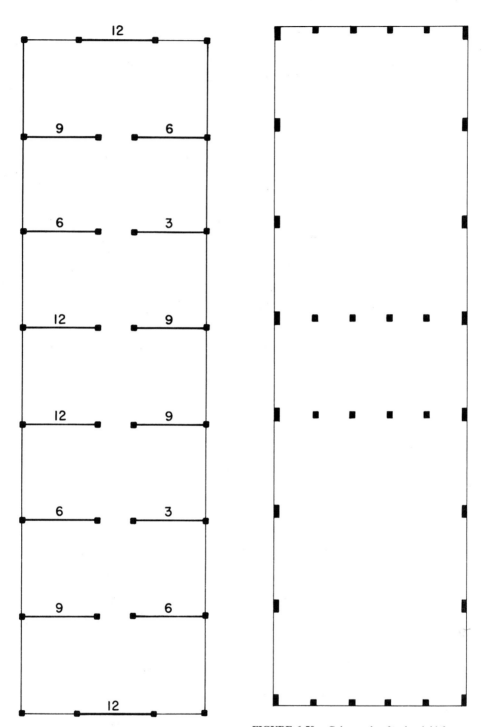

FIGURE 6.49. (*Continued*)

FIGURE 6.50. Column plan for the rigid frame system—Example 14, Building F.

190

all walls need to be developed with diagonal bracing. It is possible to consider the development of trussing in only a few of the walls. It is also possible to consider a staggering of the bracing vertically, as illustrated in Figure 6.49. If bracing is used in all walls, but staggered vertically, a possible arrangement is that shown in the plan in Figure 6.49a.

6.15. EXAMPLE 14—BUILDING F

The plan in Figure 6.50 shows a scheme for a rigid frame system for Building F. The north–south bents are limited to the exterior wall (peripheral) bents for lateral force resistance. There would, of course, be additional vertical structure for the support of the roof and floors; the plan shows only the elements considered for lateral resistance. Because of the long narrow plan, it is not reasonable to use only the two end bents for resistance in the east–west direction. The plan indicates the use of two interior bents near the center of the building. If these are not sufficient, more bents could be developed between apartments. (See the general plan in Figure 6.46.)

As with any building, the choice of the lateral bracing system has implications for architectural planning. In this example, if the scheme shown in Figure 6.50 is used, the layout of the apartments would be much less constrained than it would be with the shear wall system developed in Example 11.

A special problem to consider with the rigid frame system is that of the potential unintended shear wall effect of nonstructural partitioning. This may seriously alter the building's dynamic response, upset distribution of forces, and possibly result in some soft story conditions. The materials used for partitions and the connections at all edges between partitions and the building structure must be developed to avoid these situations.

CHAPTER SEVEN

Design for Structurally Induced Forces

There are many situations in which the vertical effect of gravity loads generates lateral (horizontally directed) forces due to the nature of the structure. This chapter discusses several types of these structures and the structural design and architectural planning concerns that they generate.

7.1. SINGLE-SPAN RIGID FRAMES

Figure 7.1a shows a single-span structure consisting of two columns rigidly connected (for moment transfer) to a horizontal beam. If the column bases are free to move horizontally, the deflection of the beam under vertical loading will rotate the tops of the columns and cause the bases to move outward, as indicated by the dashed line figure. If horizontal restraint is provided with a pin-type connection at the column base, the rotation at the top of the column will result in bending and shear in the columns and an outward pushing force on the supports, as shown in Figure 7.1b. The distribution of moment in the beam and the columns for this condition is shown in Figure 7.1c.

If the column base is fixed against rotation as well as horizontal movement, the behavior of the frame under vertical loading will be as shown in Figures 7.1d and e. Although full rotational restraint is not often feasible, many frames will have some degree of rotational fixity at their base, resulting in a true condition somewhere between those shown in Figures 7.1b and d. It is not our purpose here to discuss the problems of designing moment-resistive column bases, so we limit the concern for resistance to horizontal thrust, as shown in Figure 7.1b.

It is hard to imagine a building in which the outward movement of the column bases as shown in Figure 7.1a could be accommodated. It seems realistic, therefore, to assume that some lateral restraining system must be provided. The three most common ways to achieve lateral restraint are shown in Figure 7.2. Under some conditions it may be possible to develop resistance in the form of lateral movement restraint of the foundations alone. As shown in Figure 7.2a, this requires the development of some combination of passive horizontal soil pressure on the side of the foundation and the sliding friction on the bottom of the footing. The latter is not possible, of course, if a deep foundation is used.

If the footings are shallow (where frost is not a problem) and the soil is highly compressible, reliance on the passive soil pressure is highly questionable. For any significant lateral force, the foundations must be quite deep and probably must be designed in the form of abutments, as described else-

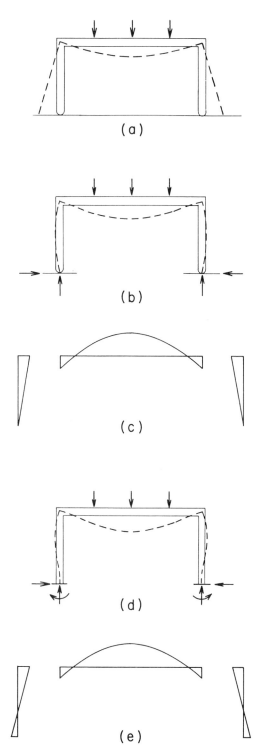

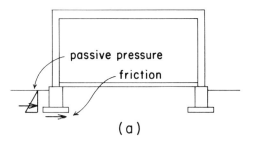

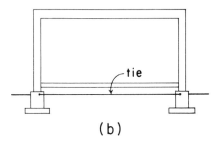

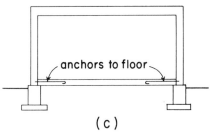

FIGURE 7.2. Development of the horizontal thrust in a single bent.

FIGURE 7.1. Functioning of a single rigid bent under gravity loads.

where. In any event, whatever the actual capacity for resistance, some movement must be expected in the development of high levels of lateral soil pressure; this requires some design for adjustment during construction that permits the movement due to dead load to occur.

If movement must be restrained as fully as possible, or simply if the forces are large, it may be necessary to use the technique illustrated in Figure 7.2b. In this case the two outward thrusts are balanced against each-other by a tie member. This is often the most practical way of achieving a movement-free column base, although some problems must be considered. If the tie is quite long, its tension elongation under high stress may be considerable, requiring some adjustment during construction. If the location of the tie ends at the column bases is too high, it may be difficult to install the tie under the floor structure. The details of the construction of the floor, walls, frame base, and foundation must be worked out to provide for this.

Another way of achieving the tie for the column base is to tie each base separately to the floor structure, as shown in Figure 7.2c. For relatively short-span steel frames this is sometimes accomplished by welding reinforcing bars to the column base plate and extending them into the poured concrete floor slab. This must be coordinated with the locations of poured or cut joints in the slab to be sure that a sufficiently large segment of slab is engaged by the anchoring reinforcing.

It is necessary, of course, to develop the design for gravity load effects with due consideration for the effects of wind or seismic loads. Overturning may require that the column bases resist uplift in addition to the effects just described. Lateral sliding may add to the forces which must be resisted as shown in Figures 7.2a and c, and may add more considerations for the design of the tie member and its connections.

7.2. GABLED ROOFS AND THREE-HINGED STRUCTURES

Double-pitched roofs, commonly called gabled roofs, may be formed in a number of ways. When spans are short, the most simple and direct structure is usually a pair of inclined rafters, as shown in Figure 7.3a. If the two rafters are supported only by each other at the top, the structure is of the three-hinged variety, as indicated in Figure 7.3a, and the stability of the structure requires the development of both vertical and horizontal support forces at the bottom end of the raf-

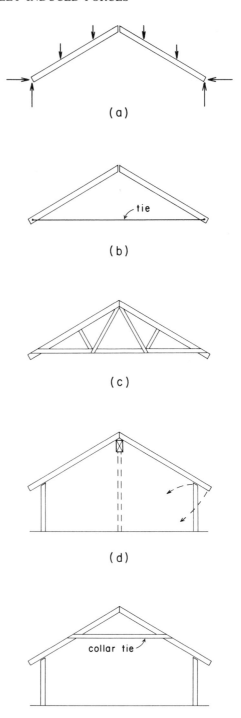

FIGURE 7.3. Actions of gabled structures under gravity loads.

ters. This must have been first discovered several thousand years ago when some early builders tried to put such a roof on top of two walls, only to have the walls topple outward as soon as any weight was placed on the rafters.

As with the rigid frame (Fig. 7.2*b*) a simple solution is to use a tie for balancing the two outward thrusts against each other. If it is desired to have a flat ceiling in the space below, the ceiling joists may often be used to achieve this tie. The rafters and tie will thus form an elementary truss; if the span is very long, this truss may be further subdivided. A simple truss form used commonly in wood-framed construction is that of the W-shape truss (named for the pattern of the interior members) shown in Figure 7.3*c*.

When a ridge beam is used to support the upper ends of the rafters, as shown in Figure 7.3*d*, the outward thrust at the lower ends is essentially removed. This assumes, of course, that the ridge beam is supported by posts or walls and is not merely a member against which the rafters lean for framing purposes. Such a ridge member would ordinarily be used for the structure in Figure 7.3*a*, but would be supported by the rafters rather than vice versa. With the ridge beam there is a possibility for a different problem due to the tendency for the rafter to rotate about its upper end, as shown in Figure 7.3*d*. This is more pronounced if the roof slope is high, and may cause inner movement at the top of the outside wall or post.

Another means for restraining inclined rafters is through the use of a collar tie, as shown in Figure 7.3*e*. In effect, this turns the top joint into a rigid connection, and stability becomes dependent on the bending of the rafters. This solution is reasonably feasible only for very short spans (such as single car garages) and should use rafters of reasonable stiffness.

The three-hinged structure shown in Figure 7.3*a* is a basic type of system that has various possible forms. One such structure

is the two part gabled frame shown in Figure 7.4*a*. This consists of two symmetrical rigid frames pinned at their bases and joined by a pin at the roof peak. With regard to forces at the supports, this structure behaves fundamentally the same as the gabled rafters in Figure 7.3*a*. Options for the development of lateral resistance at the base are basically the same as those shown for the rigid frame in Figure 7.2. Details for the attachment of the

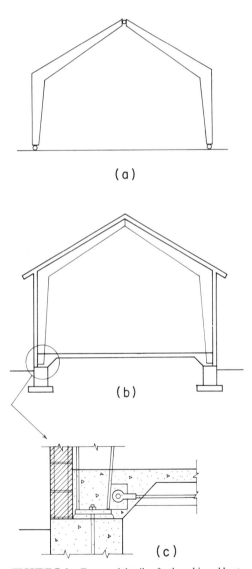

FIGURE 7.4. Form and details of a three-hinged bent.

base of the frame to the support and the anchorage of the base to the floor structure may
take various form, depending on the materials and size of the frame and the general
construction of the walls and floor.

Figure 7.4b shows a typical building section with a modest span frame of welded
steel. With a floor consisting of a poured
concrete slab on grade, the simplest means
for lateral restraint in this case is most likely
a direct tie between the frame legs. Possible
details for the frame base and tie are shown
in Figures 7.4c and d.

If the frame in Figure 7.4b was made of
glue-laminated wood, it would not be possible to simply bury the base in the concrete
to hide the tie and base plate. Thus the direct
tying of the frame legs would probably not
be a solution. In such a situation it would be
necessary to design the connection of the
frame base to the support to fully transmit
the lateral kick to the support and then to tie,
or otherwise brace, the supports.

7.3. ARCHES AND VAULTS

Arches and barrel vaults have support forces
similar to those illustrated for the rigid frame
and the three-hinged systems. One form of
the arch is the three-hinged arch with a pin
connection at the crown and an external stability condition essentially the same as the
gabled rafter or the frame in Figure 7.4. The
arch or vault may also be continuous from
spring point to spring point; in any case, the
need for lateral as well as vertical support is
present.

Figure 7.5a shows the general case for an
arch under vertical gravity loading. If the
arch springs from the ground, the support
will be developed at that level as an abutment
or a tied support; the same basic options as
illustrated for the rigid frame in Figure 7.2.
In various building situations it is sometimes
necessary to raise the arch, or to create a
higher space under it. Figure 7.5b illustrates

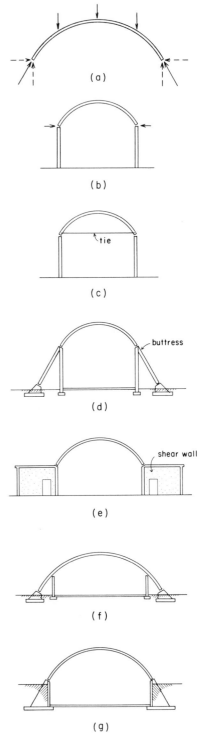

FIGURE 7.5. Resolution of arch thrust.

the situation of an arch or vault that sits on top of supporting walls. The major problem to be resolved in this case is the outward thrust of the arch at the top of the walls. As in previous situations, a direct solution is the use of a tie, as shown in Figure 7.5c. In many cases, however, the arch form will have been chosen for its interior architectural form, and the presence of the ties will be objectionable.

Where they can be accommodated at the building exterior, external braces may be used, as shown in Figure 7.5d. These may take various form such as simple direct struts (as shown), counterfort walls (see discussion of tall retaining walls in Chapter 8), or as the famous flying buttresses of Gothic cathedrals. Two variations on the external buttress are shown in Figures 7.5e and f. Where adjacent spaces occur in the building, it may be possible to use some of the crosswalls as shear walls. Even if these walls do not coincide with the location of the arches, it may be possible to use this scheme by utilizing the roof structure over the adjacent spaces as a horizontal distributing element, as is commonly done with the roof and floor diaphragms in box systems.

A second variation on the external brace is shown in Figure 7.5f. In this case the arch is allowed to spring from low abutments at ground level, but the walls are placed some distance closer to the center. The building interior space—and even the exterior form—is almost the same as with the separate exterior braces.

Depending on site conditions, as well as building planning considerations, it may be possible to use the scheme shown in Figure 7.5g in which the building floor is lowered below the exterior grade. The external building form is thus simply that of a clean arch springing from the ground, whereas the taller interior space is achieved without ties or external elements cluttering the building exterior. Indeed, the external braces do occur, but in the form of counterfort retaining walls.

This is a neat solution, but one that can be used only if windows in the side walls are not required and where siting and ground material conditions are favorable.

Domes present situations similar to arches and vaults, whether the dome is a shell or a framed structure. The round plan of the dome, however, offers a possibility that does not occur with the arch or vault structure. As shown in Figure 7.6, it is often possible to resolve the outer thrusts at the base of the dome by developing a tension ring. This is quite commonly done, with the ring sometimes being part of the dome and other times being developed in the supporting structure.

Where the bottom edge of the dome is not continuous, due to openings or intersecting cross vaults, it is possible to use other methods of bracing. The techniques illustrated for the arch in Figures 7.5d–g can be equally applied to the dome if the tension ring is not possible. However, the ring is usually the best solution when it is an option. In some situations, it may be possible to use one or more rings at points above the dome spring point to partly or totally restrain the outward thrusts. Even when the external bracing system is used, it is often possible to turn the base of the foundations into a ring to avoid dependence on soil pressure for lateral resistance.

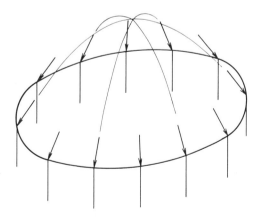

FIGURE 7.6.   Tension ring for dome thrust.

7.4. TENSION STRUCTURES

Tension can be used as the primary resolution in a number of ways for spanning structures. Figure 7.7a shows a simple draped tension element, which may be a cable or a membrane surface. This is basically the same as the gabled rafter or the arch with the load direction reversed; thus the lateral thrusts at the supports are inward instead of outward. In this case a direct solution might be a simple horizontal member between the supports, except that then it would not be a tension tie but a compression strut. If the span is long, the problem of slenderness for the strut becomes a major concern. The strut is there-

fore not a common solution, regardless of considerations of architectural design.

One method of resolving the lateral force at the supports for the draped structure is that shown in Figure 7.7b. This consists of matching external braces similar to those shown for the arch in Figure 7.5d; except that in this case they are tension guys instead of compression struts. If the span is long, the tension anchors required for these guys become major design elements. Furthermore, the guys exert a downward force on the vertical supports, so that the vertical walls or columns must carry considerably more than simply their share of the gravity load on the draped spanning structure. Add these problems to those of the intrusion on the building exterior and thus it is not a very popular solution.

Figure 7.7c shows a slightly different use of the draped tension element. In this situation the roof itself is a separate, flat structure supported in the manner of the deck of a suspension bridge. Used as shown, the cable lateral force is resolved back into a compression in a horizontal direction in the roof structure. This may be possible, but the geometry of the cables and the design of the outer ends of the roof structure must be carefully developed. Rigid arches may be made into a predetermined profile, but flexible cables will take their own form in response to the loads.

A variation on the suspended "bridge" structure is shown in Figure 7.7d. In this case the suspending cables are not draped, but rather are used for direct tension support. For the structure shown, the flat roof system is thus supported in the manner of a continuous beam with multiple supports provided by the mast/columns and the cables. Actually, to control deformations by using lower stresses, it is quite possible that the tension members may be steel bars or shapes rather than cables. As with the structure in Figure 7.7c, the horizontal forces at the bottom end of the suspending members must be

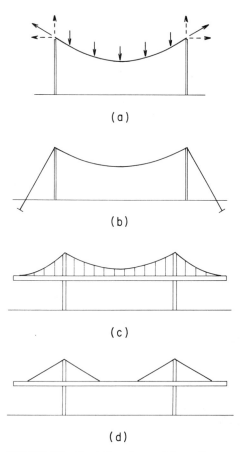

(a)

(b)

(c)

(d)

FIGURE 7.7. Resolution of support forces for spanning cables.

resisted by the roof structure. An advantage in this structure, however, is that the profile of the tension members is truly predetermined because their flexibility is not an issue.

As with the round dome, dished-shape suspended systems may be used with a round edge in plan. The same principle of the continuous ring edge may be used, in this situation it requires a compression ring. Although the compression strut is not as good for the single direction-draped structure (Fig. 7.7*a*), the compression ring is quite feasible and has been often used for the round suspended structure. The major problem for such a structure is usually water runoff and the potential for ponding in the center, rather than lateral forces at the edge.

7.5. PNEUMATIC STRUCTURES

Air pressure as a structural device is usually used in one of three ways.

Inflated Buildings. This consists of a whole enclosure with the enclosing surface held up by air pressure from the inside.

Inflated Buildings—Cable-Stayed. This is a variation on the inflated membrane, with the building form controlled by tension cables that wrap the membrane.

Inflated Structures. This consists of inflating some element to make it rigid (such as a giant air mattress) and using it as a roof or wall.

For the inflated building, the support condition is somewhat similar to that for the arch or dome except that the load direction is reversed. The inflating pressure causes an upward force which must exceed that of gravity, or the structure will not stand. The condition for the supports is thus as shown in Figure 7.8. If the floor level occurs at the point of support, as shown in the figure, the

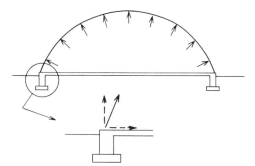

FIGURE 7.8. Support forces in pneumatic structures.

inward lateral force can usually be resisted by the floor. If there is no floor, as in the case of a tentlike structure, or the air-supported structure sits on top of a wall, other means must be used to resist the lateral effect.

For round, or close to round, structures, the support structure may be constituted as a compression ring, similar to that for the round dishlike suspended surface. In some instances this may be done with plans that are ovoid, polygonal, oblong, as well as perfectly circular in plan.

If foundations are shallow, the vertical support force may be a greater problem. The angle at the edge of an inflated membrane structure is usually quite steep, thus making the support force mostly vertical and the lateral component of negligible concern. With cable-stayed structures the situation is usually reversed, with the angle of slope of the surface quite shallow at the edge and the horizontal force component in the cables quite high.

Because of their usual light weight, wind forces on air-supported structures tend to be quite critical. Any development of support systems must be done with the consideration of the combined effects of wind and gravity. Arches and domes, on the other hand, tend to be quite heavy, and the use of systems that are logical for the heavier structures may not be appropriate for the air-supported systems.

7.6. CANTILEVERED STRUCTURES

Canopies, marquees, carport roofs, and similar elements are sometimes formed as cantilevers from the side of a building, as shown in Figure 7.9a. The cantilever requires the development of a resisting moment, which often occurs as a separated pair of opposed forces—outward at the bottom and inward at the top. If these forces are generated at the point where roof or floor structures exist, they may be carried into these structures. If they occur at midheight of the walls, as shown in the figure, the wall structure must be made to resist them.

In some situations entire buildings may be developed as cantilevered structures. These occur on steep hillsides, at edges of cliffs, and sometimes at waterfront sites. Development of supports for such a building is a serious affair. The cantilever may be achieved by using an anchoring structure as a counterweight; that is, by having something that is *not* cantilevered to extend from or grab onto. If this is not possible, the building may be perched on stilts that are

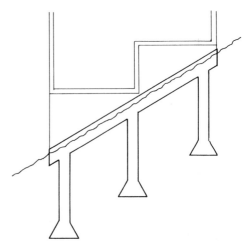

FIGURE 7.10. Downhill frame—grade beam with drilled piers.

either vertical or inclined as shown in Figure 7.9b. The inclined stilt support requires the development of both vertical and lateral resistance at the base of the stilts. In addition, if the stilts occur well back of the cantilever edge, as shown in the illustration, there will be a significant component of lateral outward force at the upper support. This outward (and possibly upward) force is much more difficult to develop than the inward force. It may be necessary to develop a heavy foundation structure at the uphill location as an anchor primarily for its simple weight.

A special structure sometimes used for hillside and beach locations is shown in Figure 7.10. This consists of a set of deep foundation elements—usually driven or cast-in-place piles—that are imbedded in a reasonably dense lower soil stratum and utilized as vertical cantilevers for lateral resistance. A grade level concrete frame is used to tie the piles together and provide direct support for the building. The general stiffness and overall effectiveness of this system are greatly increased if the tops of the piles can be made to form a rigid frame with the grade level structure. The term *downhill frame* is sometimes used to describe this type of structure. It is frequently used where beach front or hillside surface erosion is a potential hazard.

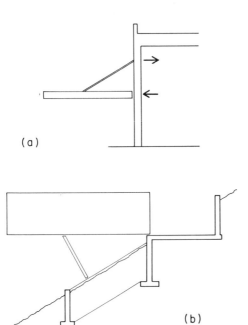

(a)

(b)

FIGURE 7.9. Cantilever structures.

CHAPTER EIGHT

Lateral Forces on Foundations

Lateral force effects on foundations are usually one of two basic types. The first occurs when the soil generates a horizontal pressure, such as that on the outside surface of a basement wall. In the second type of problem the soil is the resistive element, being pushed on by the foundation, and occurs when an abutment for an arch is not tied or anchored to a floor structure. Both of these situations are dealt with in this chapter. Although the general problems are summarized here, foundation design issues are presented in many discussions and illustrations elsewhere in the book.

8.1. HORIZONTAL FORCES IN SOILS

There are a number of situations involving horizontal forces in soils. The three major ones of concern in foundation design are the following:

Active Soil Pressure. Active soil pressure originates with the soil mass; that is, it is pressure exerted *by* the soil on something, such as the outside surface of a basement wall.

Passive Soil Pressure. Passive soil pressure is exerted *on* the soil, for example, that developed on the side of a footing when horizontal forces push on the footing.

Friction. Friction is the sliding effect developed between the soil and the surface of some object in contact with the soil. To develop friction there must be some pressure between the soil and the contact face of the object.

The development of all these effects involves a number of different stress mechanisms and structural behaviors in the various types of soils. A complete treatment of these topics is beyond the scope of this book, and the reader is referred to other references for such a discussion. (See *Foundation Engineering*, Ref. 19, or *Foundation Analysis and Design*, Ref. 18.) The discussion that follows will explain the basic phenomena and illustrate the use of some of the simple techniques for design utilizing data and procedures from existing codes.

Active Soil Pressure. The nature of active soil pressure can be visualized by considering the situation of an unrestrained vertical cut in a soil mass, as shown in Figure 8.1. In most soils, such a cut, as shown at (*a*), will not stand for long. Under the action of various influences, primarily gravity, the soil mass will tend to move to a form as shown at (*b*), producing an angled profile rather than the vertical face.

There are two general forces involved in the change from the vertical to the sloped cut profile. The soil near the top of the cut tends to simply drop vertically under its own

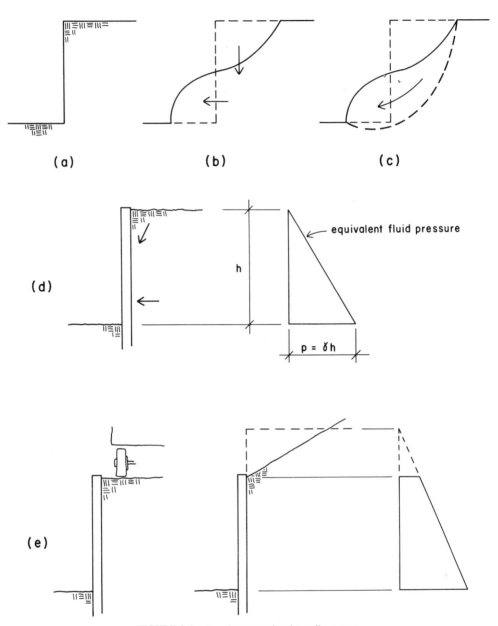

FIGURE 8.1. Development of active soil pressure.

weight. The soil near the bottom of the cut tends to bulge out horizontally from the cut face, being squeezed by the soil mass above it. Another way to visualize this movement is to consider that the whole moving soil mass tends to rotate with respect to a slip plane such as that indicated by the heavy dashed line in Figure 8.1c.

If a restraining structure of some type is introduced at the vertical face, the forces exerted on it by the soil will tend to be those involved in the actions illustrated in Figure 8.1. As shown in Figure 8.1d, the soil mass near the top of the cut will have combined vertical and horizontal effects. The horizontal component of this action will usually be minor, since the mass at this location will move primarily downward, and may develop significant friction on the face of the restraining structure. The soil mass near the bottom of the cut will exert primarily a horizontal force, very similar to that developed by a liquid in a tank. In fact, the most common approach to the design for this situation is to assume that the soil acts as a fluid with a unit density of some percentage of the soil weight, and to consider a horizontal pressure that varies with the height of the cut, as shown in Figure 8.1d.

The simplified equivalent fluid pressure assumption is in general most valid when the retained soil is a well-drained sandy soil. If the soil becomes saturated, the water itself will increase the horizontal pressure, and the buoyancy effect will tend to reduce the resistance to the slip-plane rotation of the soil mass as illustrated in Figure 8.1c. If the soil contains a high percentage of silt or clay, the simple linear pressure variation as a function of the height is quite unrealistic.

In addition to considerations of the soil type and the water content, it is sometimes necessary to deal with a surcharge on the retained soil mass. As shown in Figure 8.1e, the two common situations involving a surcharge occur when the soil mass is loaded by some added vertical force, such as the wheel load of a vehicle, and when the ground profile is not flat, producing the effect of raising its level with respect to the top of the restraining structure. The surcharge tends to increase the pressure near the top of the wall. When the equivalent fluid pressure method is used, the usual procedure is to consider the top of the soil mass (and the zero stress point for the fluid pressure) to be above the top of the structure. This results in a general overall increase in the fluid pressure, which is somewhat conservative in the case of the wheel load whose effect tends to diminish with distance below the contact point. When handled as fluid pressure, the surcharge is sometimes simply visualized either as an increase in the assumed density of the equivalent fluid or as the addition of a certain

height of soil mass above the top of the retaining structure.

Passive Soil Pressure. Passive soil pressure is visualized by considering the effect of pushing some object through the soil mass. If this is done in relation to a vertical cut, as shown in Figure 8.2a, the soil mass will tend to move inward and upward, causing a bulging of the ground surface behind the cut. If the slip-plane type of movement is assumed, the action is similar to that of active soil pressure, with the directions of the soil forces simply reversed. Since the gravity load of the upper soil mass is a useful force in this case, passive soil resistance will generally exceed active pressure for the same conditions.

If the analogy is made to the equivalent fluid pressure, the magnitude of the passive pressure is assumed to vary with depth below the ground surface. Thus for structures whose tops are at ground level, the pressure variation is the usual simple triangular form as shown in the left-hand illustration in Figure 8.2b. If the structure is buried below the ground surface, as is the typical case with footings, the surcharge effect is assumed and the passive pressures are correspondingly increased.

As with active soil pressure, the type of soil and the water content will have some bearing on development of stresses. This is usually accounted for by giving values for specific soils to be used in the equivalent fluid pressure analysis.

Soil Friction. The potential force in resisting the slipping between some object and the soil depends on a number of factors, including the following principal ones:

Form of the Contact Surface. If a smooth object is placed on the soil, there will be a considerable tendency for it to slip. Our usual concern is for a contact surface created by pouring concrete directly onto the soil, which tends to create

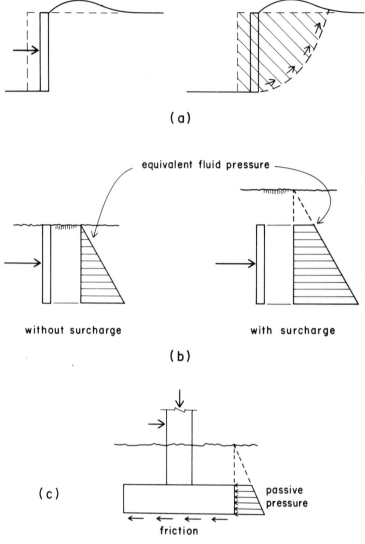

FIGURE 8.2. Development of passive soil pressure.

a very nonsmooth, intimately bonded surface.

Type of Soil.   The grain size, grain shape, relative density, and water content of the soil are all factors that will affect the development of soil friction. Well-graded dense, angular sands and gravels will develop considerable friction. Loose, rounded, saturated, fine sand and soft clays will have relatively low friction resistance. For sand and gravel the friction stress will be reasonably proportional to the compressive pressure on the surface, up to a considerable force. For clays, the friction tends to be independent of the normal pressure, except for the minimum pressure required to develop any friction force.

Pressure Distribution on the Contact Surface.   When the normal surface pressure is not constant, the friction will also tend to be nonuniform over the surface. Thus, instead of an actual stress calculation, the friction is usually evaluated as a total force in relation to the total load generating the normal stress.

Friction seldom exists alone as a horizontal resistive force. Foundations are ordinarily buried with their bottoms some distance below the ground surface. Thus pushing the foundation horizontally will also usually result in the development of some passive soil pressure, as shown in Figure 8.2c. Since these are two totally different stress mechanisms, they will actually not develop simultaneously. Nevertheless, the usual practice is to assume both forces to be developed in opposition to the total horizontal force on the structure.

In situations where simple sliding friction is not reliable or the total resistance offered by the combination of sliding and passive pressure is not adequate for total force resistance, a device called a *shear key* is used. Utilizing such a device is discussed in Section 8.3 in connection with the design of retaining walls. The enhancement of force resistance offered by a shear key is particularly desirable when the soil at the footing bottom is quite slippery (wet clay, etc.) or the footing bottom is a very short distance below grade.

8.2 BASEMENT WALLS

Basement walls usually perform an earth-retaining function. They also often function as vertical load-carrying bearing walls or spanning grade beams or as the base for building shear walls. A complete design must include consideration for all of the load combinations resulting from any of these multiple functions.

For their earth-retaining function, basement walls ordinarily span vertically between levels of support. For a single-story

basement the support at the bottom of the wall is provided by the edge of the concrete basement floor slab, and the support at the top of the wall is provided by the first-floor structure of the building. If an active soil pressure of the fluid type is assumed, the load and structural actions for the wall will be as shown in Fig. 8.3a when the ground level is at the top of the wall. When the ground level is below the top of the wall, the pressure is as shown in (b). A surcharge load at the edge of the building will increase the pressure as shown in (c). If the basement

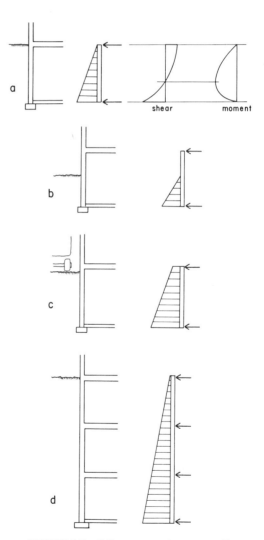

FIGURE 8.3. Soil pressure on basement walls.

is multilevel, the wall will usually function as a multiple span element for the pressure as shown in (d).

For buildings of light construction with relatively short basement walls, the walls are often built of masonry or concrete without reinforcing. Precise analysis of many such walls would show a condition of overstress by current codes, but long experience with few failures is generally accepted as a valid reason for continuing the practice. Nevertheless, when the wall spans vertically more than 10 ft or is subjected to surcharge effects, we recommend the use of walls of reinforced concrete or reinforced fully grouted masonry. And, of course, when the wall has additional structural tasks to perform, they should be included in the design stress analysis.

The following example illustrates the design of a simple vertically spanning basement wall of reinforced concrete. The design conforms to general requirements of the ACI Code (Ref. 5) for cover of reinforcing and minimum reinforcing in both vertical and horizontal directions. The example illustrates the basis for determination of the entries in Table 8.1.

Example: Design of a Basement Wall
Design data and criteria:
   Concrete design strength: $f'_c = 3000$ psi
   Reinforcing: $f_s = 20,000$ psi
   Active soil pressure: 30 lb/ft² per foot of depth below surface
   Surcharge: 300 lb/ft² on ground surface (equivalent to 3 ft of additional soil)

The wall is shown in Figure 8.4. The wall spans vertically between the lateral supports provided by the basement floor and the structure supported on top of the wall. We assume the span to be the clear height of the wall. For ease of pouring the concrete we recommend limiting the wall height to approximately 15 times the thickness. For the 10-in.-thick wall this limits the height to $12\frac{1}{2}$ ft. Subtracting for the basement floor, we will therefore consider the maximum clear height to be 12 ft, and will design the wall for this span.

The ACI Code (Ref. 5) recommends the following minimum reinforcing for the wall:
   Horizontal:

$$A_s = 0.0025A_g = (0.0025)(120)$$

$$= 0.30 \text{ in.}^2/\text{ft}$$

TABLE 8.1.   Reinforced Concrete Basement Walls[a]

	Wall Thickness t (in.)			
	8	10	12	
Wall Height h (ft)	Vertical Reinforcing (Bar Size-Spacing in Inches) $\frac{3}{4}$-in. Clear of Inside of Wall		2 in. Clear of Outside of Wall	
8	4–14	4–13	4–18	4–18
9	4–11	4–13	4–16	4–18
10	5–12	5–16	5–18	4–18
11		5–13	5–15	4–18
12		5–10	5–12	4–18
13	Not recommended		5–10	4–18
14	$h > 15\,t$		6–11	4–18
Horizontal reinforcing	5–15	5–12	5–10 (one face) 4–13 (both faces)	

[a]See Figure 8.5.

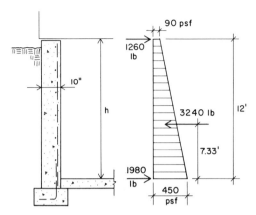

90 psf

1260 lb

10"

h

3240 lb   12'

7.33'

1980 lb

450 psf

FIGURE 8.4. Basement wall design example—wall form and loading condition.

Vertical:

$$A_s = 0.0015 A_g = (0.0015)(120)$$

$$= 0.18 \text{ in.}^2/\text{ft}$$

Thus we would use the following as minimum reinforcing for the wall, unless structural calculations indicate larger areas:

Horizontal:

No. 5 bars at 12 in., $A_s = 0.31 \text{ in.}^2/\text{ft}$.

Vertical:

No. 4 bars at 13 in., $A_s = 0.185 \text{ in}^2/\text{ft}$.

The beam action of the wall is shown in Figure 8.4. Because of the surcharge, the pressure at the top of the wall is $(3)(30) = 90 \text{ lb}/\text{ft}^2$ using the equivalent fluid pressure method. This pressure increases at the rate of $30 \text{ lb}/\text{ft}^2$ per additional foot of depth to the maximum value of $450 \text{ lb}/\text{ft}^2$ at the bottom of the wall. In terms of the span and the unit of the pressure variation, the maximum moment produced for this loading will be approximately

$$M = 0.064 \, ph^3 + 0.375 \, ph^2$$

and for this example,

$$M = (0.064)(30)(12)^3$$
$$+ (0.375)(30)(12)^2$$
$$= 3318 + 1620 = 4938 \text{ lb-ft}$$

This moment may be compared to the balanced moment capacity in order to consider the concrete bending stress and the relative values to be used for k and j:

$$\text{balanced } M = Rbd^2$$

$$= (226)(12)(9)^2 \left(\tfrac{1}{12}\right)$$

$$= 18{,}306 \text{ lb-ft}$$

which indicates that concrete stress is not critical and the section will be considerably underreinforced, permitting a conservative guess of 0.90 or higher for j.

We have used the value of 9 in. for the effective depth of the reinforced concrete section, which assumes the reinforcing to be placed with the minimum clearance of $\tfrac{3}{4}$ in. on the inside face of the wall. With these approximations for j and d, the area of steel required is determined as follows:

$$A_s = \frac{M}{f_s j d} = \frac{(4938)(12)}{(20{,}000)(0.9)(9)}$$

$$= 0.366 \text{ in.}^2/\text{ft}$$

which could be furnished with

No. 5 bars at 10 in., $A_s = 0.37 \text{ in.}^2/\text{ft}$

No. 6 bars at 14 in., $A_s = 0.38 \text{ in.}^2/\text{ft}$

Note from Figure 8.4 that the required support force at the bottom of the wall is 1980 lb. Unless there is considerable dead load on the top of the wall, it will probably be necessary to require that the basement floor slab be placed before the backfill is deposited against the wall.

It is possible, of course, that with a considerable vertical load the wall may have a critical combined stress or load/moment interaction. It is also possible that the vertical load may be sufficiently off center of the wall to produce significant moment, which may add to the bending due to the soil pressure. These conditions, plus any others due to grade beam action, load distributing, and so forth, should be considered in the full design of a basement wall.

Table 8.1 gives reinforcing recommendations for some concrete walls as determined by the procedures illustrated in the preceding example. Figure 8.5 shows the conditions assumed for the walls.

There are many potential detail requirements for basement walls. Although we do not intend to make recommendations for all of the construction requirements for these

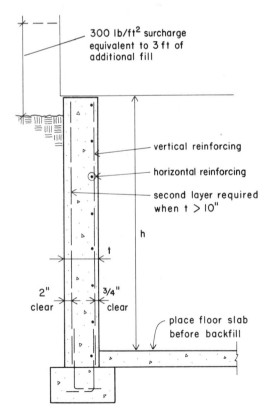

FIGURE 8.5. Reference for Table 8.1.

300 lb/ft² surcharge equivalent to 3 ft of additional fill

vertical reinforcing

horizontal reinforcing

second layer required when t > 10"

h

t

2" clear

3/4" clear

place floor slab before backfill

walls, it is well to be aware of considerations such as the following:

Need for Waterproofing. The degree of concern for water penetration depends on the groundwater situation. When the groundwater level is well below the bottom of the wall, the need is for what is technically called *dampproofing*. This is usually accomplished in two stages. First the wall itself is made as impervious as possible through the use of good mortar joints, vibrating or otherwise working concrete to eliminate air bubbles, segregation, and so forth, and careful detailing and construction to avoid developing cracks in the wall. Then, if necessary, an asphaltic compound is applied to the outside of the wall up to the ground level.

If the wall must actually be *waterproof*, that is, it must resist actual hydrostatic pressure of standing water, it must be treated in a manner essentially similar to that for a flat roof, with a waterproofing membrane of some kind applied to the wall surface. In addition, in the latter case joints in the wall must be watertight. This usually involves the use of some combination of inserted waterstops and applied joint sealing compound. For masonry walls, the exterior surface is sometimes finished with a coating of cement plaster, although this practice is now less common with the advent of quality dampproofing compounds.

Need for Temporary Bracing. In some situations there may be compelling reasons for not pouring the basement floor slab until some later stage of the building construction. If this results in a need for placing the backfill against the walls prior to placing the basement floor slab, the bottoms of the walls must be braced adequately for the lateral earth pressure.

The placing of a keyway slot in the top of the wall footing is an old common practice for providing some such support for the wall. Actually, if the wall is reinforced with vertical bars, the action of the dowels plus the friction due to the wall weight may be sufficient to develop considerable force resistance, and the key slot is really superfluous. And, of course, if the floor slab is placed before backfilling, the key slot is without any function.

8.3. MOMENT-RESISTIVE FOUNDATIONS

In addition to the direct force effects of lateral loads, many foundations must resist moment effects. Some of the situations that produce this effect, as shown in Figure 8.6, are the following:

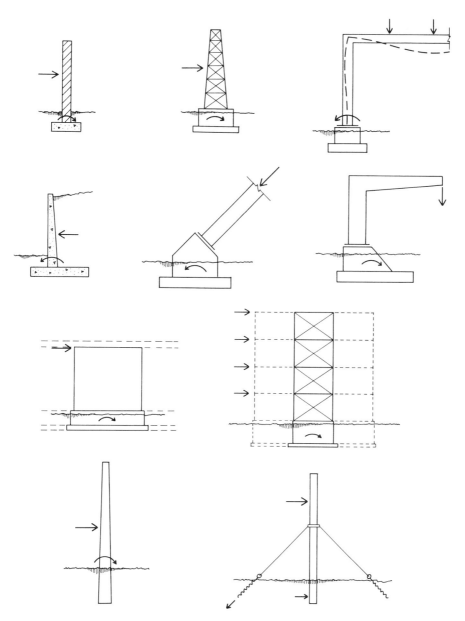

FIGURE 8.6. Structures with moment-resistive foundations.

Freestanding Walls. When a wall is supported only at its base and must resist horizontal forces on the wall, it requires a moment-resistive foundation. Examples are exterior walls used as fences and interior walls that are not full story in height. The horizontal forces are usually due to wind or seismic effects.

Cantilever Retaining Walls. Cantilever retaining walls are essentially freestanding walls that must sustain horizontal earth pressures. The various aspects of behavior and the problems of design of such walls are discussed in Section 8.5.

Bases for Shear Walls and Trussed Frames. The overturning effect at the bottom of a shear wall must be resisted by the foundation. When the wall is relatively isolated in plan, as in the case of some interior walls, the foundation for the wall may be developed in a manner similar to that for a freestanding tower.

Supports for Rigid Frames, Arches, Cable Structures, and so on. The foundations for these types of structures must often sustain horizontal forces and moments, even for vertical gravity loading. The special problems of abutments are discussed in Section 8.7.

Bases for Chimneys, Signs, Towers, Flagpoles, and so on. Any freestanding vertical element supported only at its base must have a moment-resistive foundation. Such a foundation may be quite simple and modest when the element is small, or may be a major engineering undertaking when the element is very tall and the horizontal forces are very high.

Figure 8.7 shows a situation in which a simple rectangular footing is subjected to forces that require the resistance of vertical force, horizontal sliding, and overturning moment. The development of resistance to the horizontal force is discussed in Section 8.1. Our concern here is for the combined effects of the vertical force and overturning

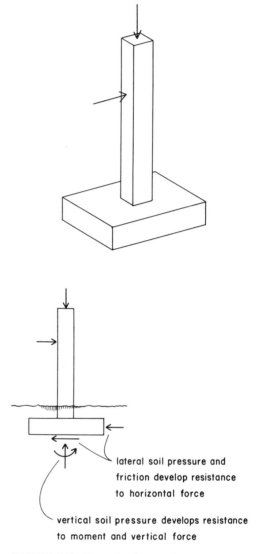

lateral soil pressure and friction develop resistance to horizontal force

vertical soil pressure develops resistance to moment and vertical force

FIGURE 8.7. Force development in moment-resistive foundations.

moment and the resultant combination of vertical soil pressures that they develop.

Figure 8.8 illustrates our usual approach to the combined direct force and moment on a cross section. In this case the "cross section" is the contact face of the footing with the soil. However the combined force and moment may originate, we make a transformation into an equivalent eccentric force that

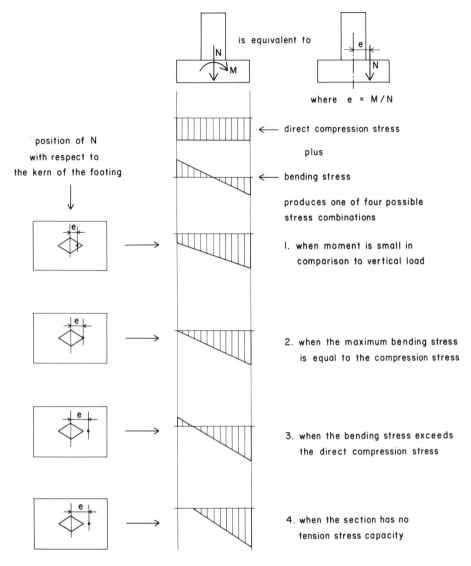

FIGURE 8.8. Analysis for soil stress due to combined vertical compression and overturning moment.

produces the same effects on the cross section. The direction and magnitude of this mythical equivalent e are related to properties of the cross section in order to qualify the nature of the stress combination. The value of e is established by simply dividing the force normal to the cross section by the moment, as shown in the figure. The net, or combined, stress distribution on the section is visualized as the sum of the separate stresses due to the normal force and the moment. For the stresses on the two extreme edges of the footing, the general formula for the combined stress is

$$p = \frac{N}{A} \pm \frac{Nec}{I}$$

We observe three cases for the stress combination obtained from this formula, as shown in the figure. The first case occurs when e is small, resulting in very little bending stress. The section is thus subjected to all compressive stress, varying from a maximum value on one edge to a minimum on the opposite edge.

The second case occurs when the two stress components are equal, so that the minimum stress becomes zero. This is the boundary condition between the first and third cases, since any increase in the eccentricity will tend to produce some tension stress on the section. This is a significant limit for the footing since tension stress is not possible for the soil-to-footing contact face. Thus Case 3 is possible only in a beam or column where tension stress can be developed. The value of e that corresponds to Case 2 can be derived by equating the two components of the stress formula as follows:

$$\frac{N}{A} = \frac{Nec}{I}, \qquad e = \frac{I}{Ac}$$

This value for e establishes what is called the kern limit of the section. The kern is a zone around the centroid of the section within which an eccentric force will not cause tension on the section. The form of this zone may be established for any shape of cross section by application of the formula derived for the kern limit. The forms of the kern zones for three common shapes of section are shown in Figure 8.9.

When tension stress is not possible, eccentricities beyond the kern limit will produce a so-called cracked section, which is shown as Case 4 in Figure 8.8. In this situation some portion of the section becomes unstressed, or cracked, and the compressive stress on the remainder of the section must develop the entire resistance to the force and moment.

Figure 8.10 shows a technique for the analysis of the cracked section, called the *pressure wedge method*. The pressure wedge represents the total compressive force developed by the soil pressure. Analysis of the

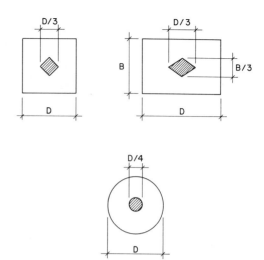

FIGURE 8.9. Kern limits for common shapes.

static equilibrium of this wedge and the force and moment on the section produce two relationships that may be utilized to establish the dimensions of the stress wedge:

1. The total volume of the wedge is equal to the vertical force on the section. (Sum of the vertical forces equals zero.)

2. The centroid of the wedge is located on a vertical line with the force on the section. (Sum of the moments on the section equals zero.)

Referring to Figure 8.10, the three dimensions of the stress wedge are w, the width of the footing; p, the maximum soil pressure; and x, the limit of the uncracked portion of the section. With w known, the solution of the wedge analysis consists of determining values for p and x. For the rectangular footing, the simple triangular stress wedge will have its centroid at the third point of the triangle. As shown in the illustration, this means that x will be three times the dimension a. With the value for e determined, a may be found and the value of x established.

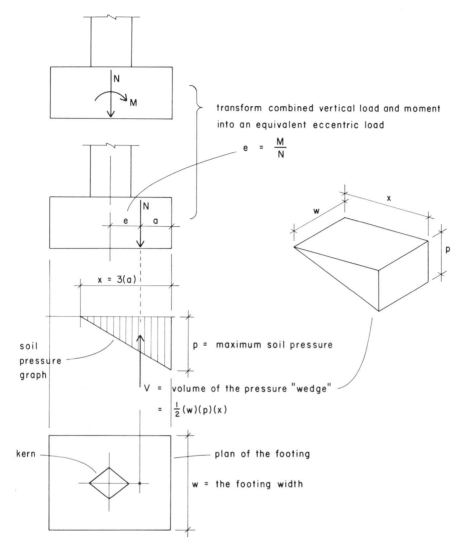

FIGURE 8.10. Analysis of the cracked section by the pressure wedge method.

The volume of the stress wedge may be expressed in terms of its three dimensions as

$$V = \tfrac{1}{2} \, wpx$$

Using the static equilibrium relationship stated previously, this volume may be equated to the force on the section. Then, with the values of w and x established, the value for p may be found as follows:

$$N = V = \tfrac{1}{2} \, wpx$$

$$p = \frac{2N}{wx}$$

All four cases of combined stress shown in Figure 8.8 will cause rotation of the footing due to deformation of the soil. The extent of this rotation and the concern for its effect on the supported structure must be considered carefully in the design of the footing. It is generally desirable that long-term loads (such as dead loads) not develop uneven stress on the footing. This is especially true when the soil is highly deformable or is subject to long-term continued deformation, as is the case with soft, wet clay. Thus it is preferred that stress conditions as shown for cases 2 or 4 in Figure 8.8 be developed only with short-term live loads.

When foundations have significant depth below the ground surface, other forces will develop to resist moment, in addition to the vertical pressure on the bottom of the footing. Figure 8.11a shows the general case for such a foundation. The moment effect of the horizontal force is assumed to develop a rotation of the foundation at some point between the ground surface and the bottom of the footing. The position of the rotated structure is shown by the dashed outline. Resistance to this movement is visualized in terms of the three major soil pressure effects plus the friction on the bottom of the footing.

When the foundation is quite shallow, as shown in Figure 8.11b, the rotation point for the foundation moves down and toward the toe of the footing. It is common in this case to assume the rotation point to be at the toe, and the overturning effect to be resisted only by the weights of the structure, the foundation, and the soil on top of the footing. Resisting force A in this case is considered to function only in assisting the friction to develop resistance to the horizontal force in direct force action.

When a foundation is very deep and is essentially without a footing, as in the situation of a pole, resistance to moment must be developed entirely by the forces A and B, as shown in Figure 8.11c. If the structure is quite flexible, its bending will cause the two forces to develop quite close to the ground surface, making the extension of the element into the ground beyond this point of little use in developing resistance to moment.

8.4. FREESTANDING WALLS

Foundations for freestanding walls are usually quite shallow. When the walls are inside the building, frost protection is usually not a problem. When they occur outside and are not connected to the building it is usually not considered necessary to extend them below the frost line. This is a matter of judgment, however, and may in some cases be restricted by local building codes.

The following example illustrates the design for an exterior masonry wall with a shallow footing.

Example   Footing for a Freestanding Wall
The wall and its footing are as shown in Figure 8.12. Design data and criteria are as follows:

Wall: 8-in. concrete block
Weight = 60 lb/ft^2 of wall surface
Maximum soil pressure: 1000 lb/ft^2
Wind load: 10 lb/ft^2, horizontal on the wall
   surface

Part of the design concerns the stress analysis of the masonry and the adequacy of the anchorage provided by the doweled reinforcing. These must resist the horizontal force and overturn at the top of the footing. We assume these to be adequate in this case and will proceed to investigate the behavior of the foundation.

The three situations to be analyzed are as follows:

1. The maximum soil pressure on the bottom of the footing.
2. The safety factor against sliding, with resistance to sliding developed by friction on the bottom of the footing and passive soil pressure against the face of the footing and the wall.
3. The safety factor against overturning.

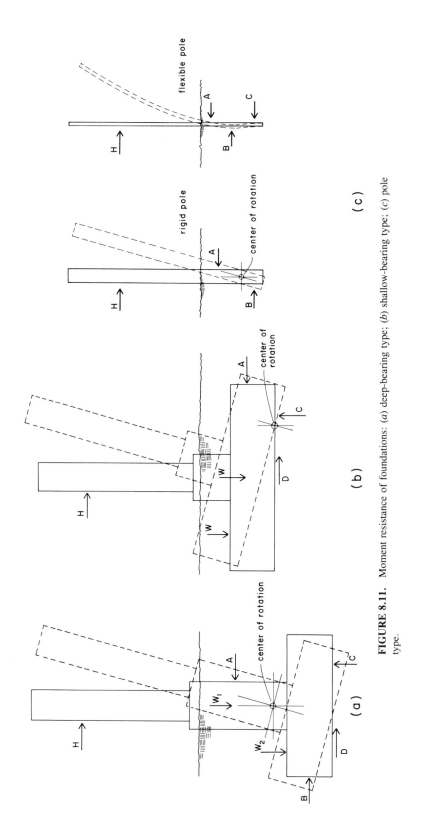

FIGURE 8.11. Moment resistance of foundations: (*a*) deep-bearing type; (*b*) shallow-bearing type; (*c*) pole type.

As in many other situations, the process for designing this footing consists of making some assumptions and guesses to establish enough information to be able to perform the necessary analyses to test the adequacy of the first try. The three facts necessary for the analysis just described are the footing width, the footing thickness, and the depth of the footing below the ground surface. However arrived at, the dimensions given in Figure 8.12a are our first estimates.

Figure 8.12b shows the various forces involved in the three analyses previously described. As labeled in the figure, these are:

H: The total horizontal wind force whose resultant acts at the midheight of the aboveground portion of the wall.

$$H = (10 \text{ lb/ft}^2)(6 \text{ ft}) = 60 \text{ lb}$$

W_1: The weight of the wall.

$$W_1 = (60 \text{ lb/ft}^2)(6.83 \text{ ft}) = 410 \text{ lb}$$

W_2: The weight of the footing.

$$W_2 = (0.67 \text{ ft})(1.5 \text{ ft})(150 \text{ lb/ft}^3)$$

$$= 150 \text{ lb}$$

W_3 and W_4: The weight of the soil on top of the footing (assumed to be 80 lb/ft³).

$$W_3 = W_4$$

$$= (\tfrac{5}{12} \text{ ft})(0.83 \text{ ft})(80 \text{ lb/ft}^3)$$

$$= 28 \text{ lb}$$

F: The friction on the bottom of the footing, as developed by the gravity loads.

S: The passive resistance of the soil to horizontal pressure.

For the overturning analysis we consider only the horizontal wind force and the resistance due to the gravity loads. The rotation point for the overturning moment is assumed to be at the toe of the footing. The calcula-

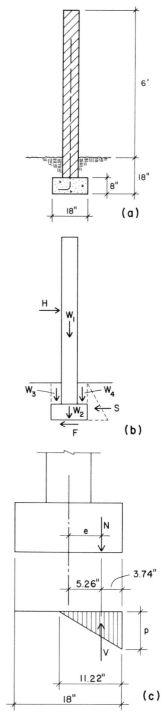

FIGURE 8.12. Freestanding wall design example: (a) proposed design; (b) active and resistive forces; (c) soil stress analysis—cracked section by the pressure wedge method.

TABLE 8.2. Overturn Analysis for the Freestanding Wall

Type of Force	Force (lb)	Moment Arm (in.)	Overturning Moment (lb-in.)	Restoring Moment (lb-in.)
H	60	54	3240	
W_1	410	9		3690
W_2	150	9		1350
W_3	28	15.5		434
W_4	28	2.5		70
Totals	616 lb		3240 lb-in.	5544 lb-in.

$$\text{Safety factor: } \frac{\text{restoring moment}}{\text{overturning moment}} = \frac{5544}{3240} = 1.71$$

tions for the determination of the overturning moment and the restoring moment are given in Table 8.2. Since the safety factor against overturning is found to be in excess of the usual requirement of 1.5, the footing is adequate in this regard.

Friction and passive resistance depend on the type of soil. Criteria vary from reference to reference, so the first source to consider is the applicable building code. We will utilize the data from *UBC* Table 29-B in Appendix C in which soil conditions are generalized into five categories. For the relatively low allowable soil pressure in our example we will assume the soil to be in one of the last two groups in the table and will analyze for both to illustrate the process.

For the cohesionless and generally low plasticity soils in Group 4, the table gives the following design values:

Allowable bearing pressure: 1500 lb/ft^2
Passive resistance: 150 lb/ft^2 per foot of depth
Sliding resistance: 0.25 times the dead load

The total sliding resistance, force F in Figure 8.12b, is thus

$$F = (0.25)(616) = 154 \text{ lb}$$

The total passive resistive force, S in Figure

8.12b, is determined as the area of the triangular stress graph shown in dotted outline in the figure. Using the value from the table, the maximum stress is determined to be

$$p = (1.5 \text{ ft})(150) = 225 \text{ lb/ft}^2$$

and the total resistance is

$$S = \tfrac{1}{2}(1.5)(225) = 169 \text{ lb}$$

The safety factor in this analysis is already included in the table values, which are given as *allowable* values rather than *ultimate* values. We therefore simply compare the sum of F and S with the horizontal wind force H, and observe that sliding is not a critical concern.

For the high clay content soils in Group 5, the *UBC* table gives a passive resistance value of 100 lb/ft^2 per foot of depth. Thus the value of the S force would be two thirds of that calculated previously, or approximately 113 lb. For sliding with this soil group the table gives a value based on the contact area of the footing rather than a coefficient of friction based on the dead load. Using this, we calculate the value for S as

$$S = (1.5 \text{ ft}^2)(130 \text{ lb/ft}^2) = 195 \text{ lb}$$

Note that the footnote to the *UBC* table limits this force to a maximum of one half the total dead load, which is not a critical consideration for our example.

For this soil group the sum of the resistive forces is also clearly in excess of the wind force. Although it is redundant to consider it for our example, the resistive forces could be increased by one third since the load is due to wind.

For the vertical soil pressure on the bottom of the footing we consider the combined effects of the wind and gravity forces. Because the gravity loads are symmetrical on the footing, they contribute only to the vertical force in this case. The combined effect on the footing is thus

$$N = 616 \text{ lb (from Table 8.2)}$$

$$M = 3240 \text{ lb-in. (from Table 8.2)}$$

and the equivalent eccentricity, as discussed in Section 8.3, is

$$e = \frac{M}{N} = \frac{3240}{616} = 5.26 \text{ in.}$$

For the rectangular section of the footing contact face, the kern limit is $18/6 = 3$ in., which indicates that the soil stress condition is Case 4, as shown in Figure 8.8. For the pressure wedge analysis the maximum soil pressure is determined as

$$p = \frac{2N}{wx}$$

in which N = the total vertical force of 594 lb.
  w = the other dimension of the footing "section," or 12 in.
  x = three times the distance of the equivalent eccentric force from the edge of the footing, or as shown in Figure 8.12

$$3(9 - 5.26) = 3(3.74) = 11.22 \text{ in.}$$

Applying these to the formula, the maximum soil pressure is thus

$$p = \frac{2N}{wx} = \frac{(2)(616)}{(12)(11.22)} = 9.150 \text{ psi}$$

$$= (9.150)(144) = 1318 \text{ lb/ft}^2$$

This soil pressure should be compared to a design value based on a one third increase for wind load. Thus the limit for the soil stress is

$$p = (1.333)(1000) = 1333 \text{ lb/ft}^2$$

This indicates that the soil pressure is approximately at the critical level. However, some designers would prefer that the stress distribution on the footing not be permitted to develop the so-called cracked section, that is, that the eccentricity not exceed the kern limit for the section. One argument for this is that the high stress concentration on one side of the footing will produce considerable soil deformation at the edges of the footing. With repeated application of horizontal forces, in both directions, weakened resistance to rocking effects will be developed, as shown in Figure 5.40.

If this argument is accepted, it would be necessary to increase the width of the footing in this example by a considerable amount, since the calculated eccentricity of 5.26 in. greatly exceeds the kern limit of 3 in. If the dimension of 5.26 in. is established as the kern limit, the required footing width would be

$$(6)(5.26) = 31.6 \text{ in.}$$

Because the added footing size will increase the dead load, the revised footing width could be slightly less than this. If we change the footing width to 27 in., the new dead load will be 741 lb and the new eccentricity will be

$$e = \frac{3240}{741} = 4.37 \text{ in.}$$

which is within the kern limit of 4.5 in. for the 27-in. width.

A third design approach to consider for this footing is one in which the resistive moment of the passive soil pressure is included in the analysis. If we take this as the S value of 169 lb for the Group 4 soil, it offers a resisting moment of

$$M = (169)(6) = 1014 \text{ lb-in.}$$

which we subtract from the moment due to wind to obtain a new moment on the footing of

$$M = 3240 - 1014 = 2226 \text{ lb-in.}$$

With this new moment combined with the dead load for the 18-in. wide footing, we obtain a new eccentricity of

$$e = \frac{M}{N} = \frac{2226}{616} \, 3.61 \text{ in.}$$

which is only slightly in excess of the kern limit of 3 in. for the 18-in.-wide footing.

If the footing is widened to 21 in., an analysis that includes the resistance due to passive soil pressure will produce an eccentricity approximately equal to that of the kern

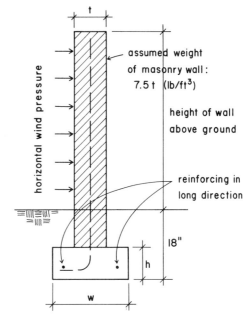

FIGURE 8.13. Reference for Table 8.3.

limit. We consider this to be a reasonable design solution for the footing.

Table 8.3 gives some recommended footings for freestanding walls for wind loads of 10, 15, and 20 lb/ft². Note that *UBC* Section 2311(h) permits a one third reduction in the design wind pressure for fences not over 12 ft high. This reduction may not be permitted

TABLE 8.3. Footings for Freestanding Walls[a]

| Wall Height above Ground (ft) | Horizontal Wind Pressure on Exposed Wall Surface | | | | | | | | | | | |
| | 10 lb/ft² | | | | 20 lb/ft² | | | | 30 lb/ft² | | | |
	t (in.)	h (in.)	w (in.)	Reinf.	t (in.)	h (in.)	w (in.)	Reinf.	t (in.)	h (in.)	w (in.)	Reinf.
4	6	6	15	2 No. 3	6	8	26	2 No. 4	6	8	36	2 No. 5
5	6	6	18	2 No. 3	8	8	31	2 No. 4	8	10	41	3 No. 4
6	8	8	22	2 No. 4	8	10	36	3 No. 4	10	12	45	3 No. 5
7	8	8	25	2 No. 4	10	10	40	3 No. 4	10	12	52	3 No. 5
8	10	10	26	2 No. 4	10	12	44	3 No. 5	12	12	56	4 No. 5
9	10	10	29	2 No. 5	12	12	46	3 No. 5	12	12	62	4 No. 5
10	12	12	31	2 No. 5	12	12	51	3 No. 5	12	14	66	5 No. 5

[a] See Figure 8.13.

by other building codes, however. Footing widths given in the table have been determined on the basis of the procedure recommended in the design example in which the eccentricity is limited to the kern limit, but the passive soil pressure is included in the analysis. The weight of the wall is approximately that obtained with concrete blocks of lighweight aggregate with voids partly filled with grout.

8.5. FREESTANDING RETAINING STRUCTURES

Strictly speaking, any wall that sustains significant lateral soil pressure is a retaining wall. However, the term is usually used with reference to a so-called *cantilever retaining wall*, which is a freestanding wall without lateral support at its top. For such a wall the major design consideration is for the actual dimension of the ground level difference that the wall serves to facilitate. The range of this dimension establishes some different categories for the retaining structure as follows:

Curbs. Curbs are the shortest freestanding retaining structures. The two most common forms are as shown in Figure 8.14a, the selection being made on the basis of whether or not it is necessary to have a gutter on the low side of the curb. Use of these structures is typically limited to grade level changes of about 2 ft or less.

Short Retaining Walls. Vertical walls up to about 10 ft in height are usually built as shown in Figure 8.14b. These consist of a concrete or masonry wall of uniform thickness. The wall thickness, footing width and thickness, vertical wall reinforcing, and transverse footing reinforcing are all designed for the lateral shear and cantilever bending moment plus the vertical weights of the wall, footing, and earth fill.

When the bottom of the footing is a short distance below grade on the low side of the wall and/or the lateral passive resistance of the soil is low, it may be necessary to use an extension below the footing—called a shear key—to increase the resistance to sliding. The form of such a key is shown in Figure 8.14d.

Tall Retaining Walls. As the wall height increases it becomes less feasible to use the simple construction shown in Figure 8.14b or c. The overturning moment increases sharply with the increase in height of the wall. For very tall walls one modification used is to taper the wall thickness. This permits the development of a reasonable cross section for the high bending stress at the base without an excessive amount of concrete. However, as the wall becomes really tall, it is often necessary to consider the use of various bracing techniques, as shown in the other illustrations in Figure 8.15.

The design of tall retaining walls is beyond the scope of this book. They should be designed with a more rigorous analysis of the active soil pressure than that represented by the simplified equivalent fluid stress method. In addition, the magnitudes of forces in the reinforced concrete elements of such walls indicate the use of strength design methods, rather than the less accurate working stress methods.

8.6. DESIGN OF SHORT RETAINING WALLS

Under most circumstances it is reasonable to design short retaining walls (up to 10 ft high) by the equivalent fluid method. The following example illustrates this simplified method of design, using the working stress method for the investigation of the concrete elements.

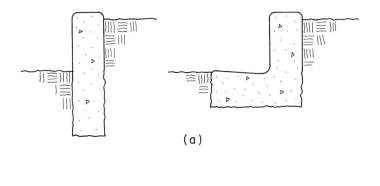

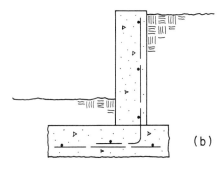

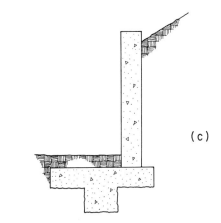

FIGURE 8.14. Low height retaining structures.

Example: Short Concrete Retaining Wall
The wall is to be of reinforced concrete with the profile shown in Figure 8.16a. Design data and criteria are as follows:

Active soil pressure: 30 lb/ft^2 per foot of height

Soil weight: assumed to be 100 lb/ft^3

Maximum allowable soil pressure: 1500 lb/ft^2

Concrete strength: $f_c' = 3000$ psi

Allowable tension on reinforcing: 20,000 psi

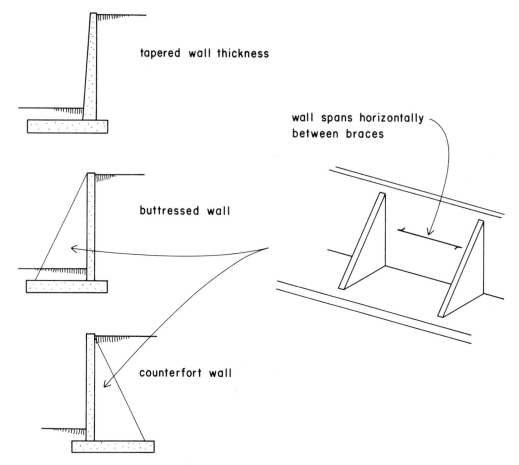

tapered wall thickness

wall spans horizontally
between braces

buttressed wall

counterfort wall

FIGURE 8.15. Tall cantilever retaining walls.

The loading condition used to analyze the stress conditions in the wall is shown in Figure 8.16.

Maximum lateral pressure:

$$p = (30)\,(4.667 \text{ ft}) = 140 \text{ lb/ft}^2$$

Total horizontal force:

$$H_1 = \frac{(140)\,(4.667)}{2} = 327 \text{ lb}$$

Moment at base of wall:

$$M = (327)\,(\tfrac{56}{3}) = 6104 \text{ lb-in.}$$

For the wall we assume an approximate effective d of 5.5 in. The tension reinforcing required for the wall is thus

$$A_s = \frac{M}{f_s jd} = \frac{6104}{(20{,}000)\,(0.9)\,(5.5)}$$
$$= 0.061 \text{ in.}^2/\text{ft}$$

This may be provided by using No. 3 bars at 20-in. centers, which gives an actual A_s of 0.066 in.^{2}/ft. Since the embedment length of these bars in the footing is quite short, they should be selected conservatively and should have hooks at their ends for additional anchorage.

The loading condition used to investigate

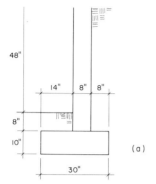

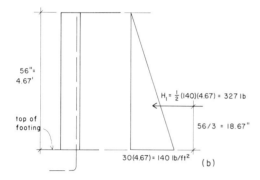

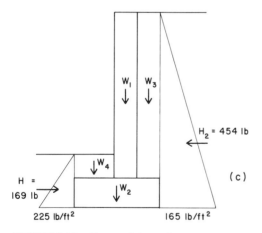

FIGURE 8.16. Short retaining wall design example: (a) wall form; (b) wall analysis; (c) footing analysis.

the soil stresses and the stress conditions in the footing is shown in Figure 8.16. In addition to the limit of the maximum allowable soil-bearing pressure, it is usually required that the resultant vertical force be kept within the kern limit of the footing. The location of

the resultant force is therefore usually determined by a moment summation about the centroid of the footing plan area, and the location is found as an eccentricity from this centroid.

Table 8.4 contains the data and calculations for determining the location of the resultant force that acts at the bottom of the footing. The position of this resultant is found by dividing the net moment by the sum of the vertical forces as follows:

$$e = \frac{5793}{1167} = 4.96 \text{ in.}$$

For the rectangular footing plan area the kern limit will be one sixth of the footing width, or 5 in. The resultant is thus within the kern, and the combined soil stress may be determined by the stress formula

$$p = \frac{N}{A} \pm \frac{M}{S}$$

in which N = the total vertical force
A = the plan area of the footing
M = the net moment about the footing centroid
S = the section modulus of the rectangular footing plan area which is determined as

$$S = \frac{bh^2}{6} = \frac{(1)(2.5)^2}{6} = 1.042 \text{ ft}^3$$

TABLE 8.4 Determination of the Eccentricity of the Resultant Force

Force (lb)		Moment Arm (in.)	Moment (lb-in.)
H_2	454	22	+9988
w_1	466	3	−1398
w_2	312	0	0
w_3	311	11	−3421
w_4	78	8	+624
Σ_w = 1167 lb		Net moment = +5793 lb-in

The limiting maximum and minimum soil pressures are thus determined as

$$p = \frac{N}{A} \pm \frac{M}{S} = \frac{1167}{2.5} \pm \frac{5793/12}{1.042}$$

$$= 467 \pm 463$$

$$= 930 \text{ lb/ft}^2 \text{ maximum}$$

$$\text{and } 4 \text{ lb/ft}^2 \text{ minimum}$$

Since the maximum stress is less than the established limit of 1500 lb/ft², vertical soil pressure is not critical for the wall. For the horizontal force analysis the procedure varies with different building codes. The criteria given in this example for soil friction and passive resistance are those in the *UBC* (Appendix C) for ordinary sandy soils. This code permits the addition of these two resistances without modification. Using these data and technique, the analysis is as follows:

Total active force: 454 lb, as shown in Figure 8.16

Friction resistance [(friction factor) (total vertical dead load)]:

$$(0.25)\,(1167) = 292 \text{ lb}$$

Passive resistance: 169 lb, as shown in Figure 8.16

Total potential resistance:

$$292 + 169 = 461 \text{ lb}$$

(*Note*: Many designers reduce the passive resistance by one third when combining it with sliding.)

Since the total potential resistance is greater than the active force, the wall is not critical in horizontal sliding.

As with most wall footings, it is usually desirable to select the footing thickness to minimize the need for tension reinforcing due to bending. Thus shear and bending stresses are seldom critical, and the only footing stress concern is for the tension reinforcing. The critical section for bending is at the face

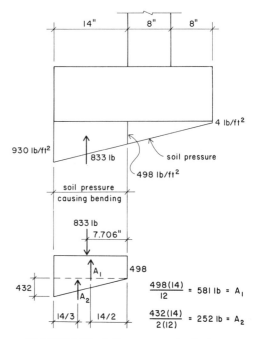

FIGURE 8.17. Soil pressure on the footing.

of the wall, and the loading condition is as shown in Figure 8.17. The trapezoidal stress distribution produces the resultant force of 833 lb, which acts at the centroid of the trapezoid, as shown in the illustration. Assuming an approximate depth of 6.5 in. for the section, the analysis is as follows:

Moment:

$$M = (833)\,(7.706) = 6419 \text{ lb-in}$$

Required area:

$$A_s = \frac{M}{f_s jd} = \frac{6149}{(20,000)\,(0.9)\,(6.5)}$$

$$= 0.055 \text{ in.}^2/\text{ft}$$

This requirement may be satisfied by using No. 3 bars at 24-in. centers. For ease of construction it is usually desirable to have the same spacing for the vertical bars in the wall and the transverse bars in the footing. Thus in this example the No. 3 bars at 20-in. centers previously selected for the wall would probably also be used for the footing bars. The vertical bars can then be held in position by wiring the hooked ends to the transverse footing bars.

Although bond stress is also a potential concern for the footing bars, it is not likely to be critical as long as the bar size is relatively small (less than a No. 6 bar or so).

Reinforcing in the long direction of the footing should be determined in the same manner as for ordinary wall footings. We recommend a minimum of 0.15% of the cross section. For the 10-in.-thick and 30-in.-wide footing this requires

$$A_s = (0.0015)(300) = 0.45 \text{ in.}^2$$

We would therefore use three No. 4 bars with a total area of (3)(0.2) = 0.6 in.^{2}.

In most cases designers consider the stability of a short cantilever wall to be adequate if the potential horizontal resistance exceeds the active soil pressure and the resultant of the vertical forces is within the kern of the footing. However, the stability of the wall is also potentially questionable with regard to the usual overturn effect. If this investigation is considered to be necessary, the procedure is as follows.

The loading condition is the same as that used for the soil stress analysis and shown in Figure 8.16. As with the vertical soil stress analysis, the force due to passive soil resistance is not used in the moment calculation since it is only a potential force. For the

TABLE 8.5   Analysis for Overturning Effect

Force (lb)		Moment Arm (in.)	Moment (lb-in.)
Overturn			
H_2	454	22	9988
Restoring moment			
w_1	466	18	8388
w_2	312	15	4680
w_3	311	26	8086
w_3	78	7	546
			Total 20,686
			lb-in.

overturn investigation the moments are taken with respect to the toe of the footing. The calculation of the overturning and the dead load restoring moments is shown in Table 8.5. The safety factor against overturn is determined as

$$SF = \frac{\text{restoring moment}}{\text{overturning moment}}$$
$$= \frac{20,686}{9988} = 2.07$$

The overturning effect is usually not considered to be critical as long as the safety factor is at least 1.5.

Table 8.6 gives design data for short reinforced concrete retaining walls varying in

TABLE 8.6   Short Concrete Retaining Walls[a]

Wall Height H (ft)	Wall and Footing Dimensions (Ft-in.)				Reinforcing				Actual Maximum Soil Pressure (lb/ft²)
	w	h	t	A	1	2	3	4	
2	1–6	0–6	0–6	0–4	No. 3 at 30	—	—	2 No. 3	750
3	2–0	0–8	0–6	0–6	No. 3 at 24	1 No. 4	—	2 No. 4	800
4	2–6	0–10	0–8	0–8	No. 3 at 20	2 No. 4	No. 3 at 20	3 No. 4	950
5	3–4	1–0	0–9	1–1	No. 4 at 24	3 No. 4	No. 4 at 24	4 No. 4	900
6	4–4	1–3	0–10	1–4	No. 4 at 18	4 No. 4	No. 4 at 18	4 No. 5	925

[a]See Figure 8.18 for reference.

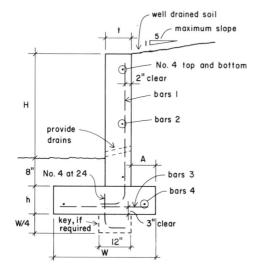

Criteria:

active pressure: ·30 lb/ft²/ft

passive pressure: 150 lb/ft²/ft

coefficient of friction: 0.25

concrete: $f_c' = 2000$ lb/in²

steel: $f_s = 20,000$ lb/in²

FIGURE 8.18. Reference for Table 8.6.

height from 2 to 6 ft. Table data have been developed using the procedures for the design of the concrete wall. Details and criteria for the walls are shown in Figure 8.18. Note that the illustration shows two necessary conditions. The first concerns the profile of the ground surface behnind the wall. If this has a significant slope, there will be an increase in the active soil pressure similar to that due to a surcharge. Table designs are based on consideration of an essentially flat profile, although a very minor slope (up to $1:5$, as shown) will not cause significant increase in pressure. The second requirement is that care be taken to avoid the possibility of highly saturated soil behind the wall. This should be avoided by using a reasonably permeable fill and by placing drains in the wall as shown.

Table 8.7 gives design data for short reinforced masonry retaining walls varying in height from 2 to 6 ft. Table data have been developed using procedures essentially similar to those used for the design of the concrete wall. Details and criteria for the walls

TABLE 8.7 Short Masonry Retaining Walls[a]

Wall Height H (ft)	Nominal t (in.)	Assumed Weight lb/ft² of Wall Surface	w (in.)	h (in.)	A (in.)	1	2	3	Actual Maximum Soil Pressure (lb/ft²)
2	6	55	18	6	4	No. 3 at 48	—	2 No. 3	550
2.67	6	55	22	6	6	No. 3 at 32	—	2 No. 3	600
3.33	8	75	27	8	8	No. 4 at 48	No. 4 at 48	2 No. 4	700
4	8	75	32	10	10	No. 4 at 32	No. 4 at 32	3 No. 4	850
4.67	8	75	40	12	12	No. 4 at 24	No. 3 at 24	4 No. 4	850
5.33	10	95	48	14	15	No. 4 at 24	No. 4 at 24	5 No. 5	825
6	10	95	56	16	18	No. 5 at 24	No. 4 at 24	5 No. 5	850

[a]See Figure 8.19 for reference.

Criteria:

active pressure: 30 lb/ft^2/ft

passive pressure: 150 lb/ft^2/ft

coefficient of friction: 0.25

concrete: $f_c' = 2000$ lb/in^2

steel: $f_s = 20,000$ lb/in^2

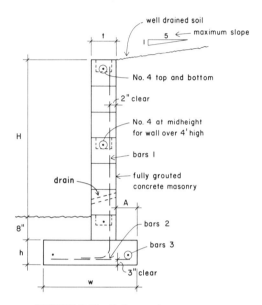

well drained soil

maximum slope

1   5

t

No. 4 top and bottom

2" clear

No. 4 at midheight
for wall over 4' high

H

bars 1

fully grouted
concrete masonry

drain

A

8"

bars 2

bars 3

h

3" clear

w

FIGURE 8.19.   Reference for Table 8.7.

are shown in Figure 8.19. Wall thicknesses
are based on typical nominal block sizes. For
the determination of the wall weight it is
assumed that the blocks are of lightweight
aggregate and have all voids filled with concrete.

8.7 ABUTMENTS

The support of some types of structures, such
as arches, gables, and shells, often requires
the resolution of both horizontal and vertical
forces. When this resolution is accomplished
entirely by the supporting foundation element, the element is described as an abutment. Figure 8.20a shows a simple abutment
for an arch consisting of a rectangular footing and an inclined pier. The design of such
a foundation has three primary concerns as
follows:

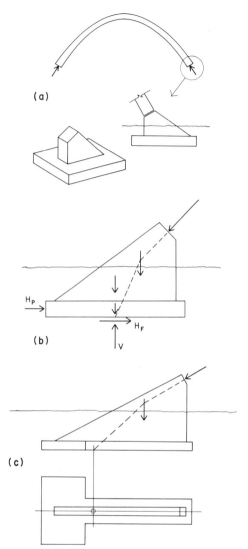

(a)

H_P

H_F

(b)

V

(c)

FIGURE 8.20.   Abutments for arches.

Resolution of the Vertical Force.   This
consists of assuring that the vertical soil
pressure does not exceed the maximum
allowable value for the soil.

Resolution of the Horizontal Force.   If
the abutment is freestanding, resolution
of the horizontal force means the development of sufficient soil friction and passive horizontal pressure.

Resolution of the Moment Effect.   In this
case the aim is usually to keep the re-

sultant force as close as possible to the centroid of the footing plan area. If this is truly accomplished, that is, $e = 0$, there will literally be no moment effect on the footing itself.

Figure 8.20b shows the various forces that act on an abutment such as that shown for the arch in Figure 8.20a. The active forces consist of the load and the weights of the pier, the footing, and the soil above the footing. The reactive forces consist of the vertical soil pressure, the horizontal friction on the bottom of the footing, and the passive horizontal soil pressure against the sides of the footing and pier. The dashed line in the illustration indicates the path of the resultant of the active forces; the condition shown is the ideal one, with the path coinciding with the centroid of the footing plan area at the bottom of the footing.

If the passive horizontal pressure is ignored, the condition shown in Figure 8.20b will result in no moment effect on the bottom of the footing and a uniform distribution of the vertical soil pressure. If the passive horizontal pressure is included in the force summation, the resultant path will move slightly to the right of the footing centroid. However, for the abutment as shown, the resultant of the passive pressure will be quite close to the bottom of the footing, so that the error is relatively small.

If the pier is tall and the load is large with respect to the pier weight or is inclined at a considerable angle from the vertical, it may be necessary to locate the footing centroid at a considerable distance horizontally from the load point at the top of the pier. This could result in a footing of greatly extended length if a rectangular plan form is used. One device that is sometimes used to avoid this is to use a T-shape, or other form, that results in a relocation of the centroid without excessive extension of the footing. Figure 8.20c shows the use of a T-shape footing for such a condition.

When the structure being supported is symmetrical, such as an arch with its supports at the same elevation, it may be possible to resolve the horizontal force component at the support without relying on soil stresses. The basic technique for accomplishing this is to tie the two opposite supports together, as shown in Figure 8.21a, so that the horizontal force is resolved internally (within the structure) instead of externally (by the ground). If this tie is attached at the point of contact between the structure and the pier, as shown in Figure 8.21a, the net load delivered to the pier is simply a vertical force, and the pier and footing could theoretically be developed in the same manner as that for a truss or beam without the horizontal force effect. However, since either wind or seismic loading will produce some horizontal force on the supports, the inclined pier is still the normal form for the supporting structure. The position of the footing, however, would usually be established by locating its centroid directly below the support point, as shown in the illustration.

For practical reasons it is often necessary to locate the tie, if one is used, below the support point for the structure. If this support point is above ground, as it usually is, the existence of the tie above ground is quite likely to interfere with the use of the structure. A possible solution in this problem is to move the tie down to the pier, as shown in Figure 8.21b. In this case the pier weight is added to the load to find the proper location for the footing centroid.

When the footing centroid must be moved a considerable distance from the load point, it is sometimes necessary to add another element to the abutment system. Figure 8.21c shows a structure in which a large grade beam has been inserted between the pier and the footing. The main purpose of this element is to develop the large shear and bending resistance required by the long cantilever distance between the ends of the pier and footing. In the example, however, it also serves to provide for the anchorage of the tie. Because of this location of the tie, the

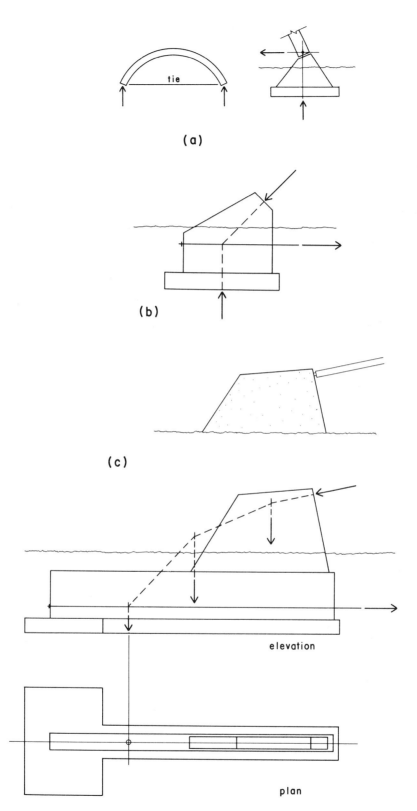

(a)

(b)

(c)

elevation

plan

FIGURE 8.21. Abutments for tied arches.

weights of both the pier and grade beam would be added to the load to find the proper location of the footing centroid. In this way the heavy grade beam further assists the footing by helping to move the centroid closer to the pier and reducing the cantilever distance.

When the horizontal component of the load is large and it is not possible to use a tie, additional passive resistance may be developed by adding a crosswall perpendicular to the pier, as shown in Figure 8.22a. A consideration that must be made in this case is that the resultant of the passive pressure will move up to some significant distance above the bottom of the footing, and thus should be included in the development of the desired location for the footing centroid. If this crosswall is very long or high, the shear and moment produced by the cantilevering action of the crosswall beyond the sides of the pier may be quite significant.

A possible solution in this case is to provide a horizontal slab between the pier and crosswall, as shown in dashed line profile in the isometric view in Figure 8.22a. If there is a useful function for this slab, it may be placed above ground; otherwise it may simply be buried along with the rest of the foundation.

A variation on the footing-plus-crosswall combination is shown in Figure 8.22b. Here an inclined footing is used to develop both vertical and horizontal soil pressure. The crosswall is eliminated and the footing merely changes from horizontal to inclined along its length.

In many situations abutments are parts of the general foundation system for a building and may serve other purposes or be combined with other elements. One example of this is the abutment shown for the arch in Figure 7.5g in which the abutment takes the form of a counterfort brace for the retaining wall that serves as the building wall.

It is also possible to use abutments for tension resistance, as shown in Figure 8.24. This becomes more appropriate as the angle of the tension force becomes low (T_h larger than T_v). Depending on the magnitude of the forces and the nature of the soil, it may be possible to rely only on the dead weight of the abutment and the passive resistance of the soil for development of the vertical and horizontal resistances. Figures 8.24b and c show the use of a crosswall to increase the passive resistance, similar to that shown in Figure 8.22 for the compression-resistive abutment. As the horizontal force becomes larger, it may be possible to consider the use of a compression strut between opposed abutments, which is similar in function to the tension ties shown in Figures 8.21b and c.

8.8. TENSION-RESISTIVE FOUNDATIONS

Tension-resistive foundations are a special, although not unique, problem. Some of the situations that require this type of foundation are the following:

Anchorage of very lightweight structures, such as tents, air-inflated structures, light metal buildings, and so on.

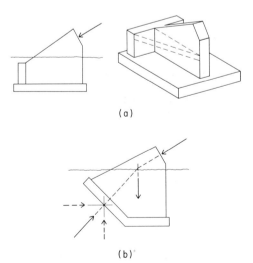

(a)

(b)

FIGURE 8.22. Abutments with enhanced resistance to horizontal movement.

Anchorage of cables for tension structures or for guyed towers.

Anchorage for uplift resistance as part of the development of overturn resistance for the lateral bracing system for a building.

Figure 8.23 illustrates a number of elements that may be used for tension anchorage. The simple tent stake is probably the most widely used temporary tension anchor. It has been used in sizes ranging from large nails up to the huge stakes used for large circus tents. Also commonly used is the screw-ended stake, which offers the advantages of being somewhat more easily inserted and withdrawn, and having less tendency to loosen.

Ordinary concrete bearing foundations offer resistance to tension in the form of their own dead weight. The so-called dead man anchor consists simply of a buried block of concrete similar to a simple footing. Column and wall footings, foundation walls, concrete and masonry piers, and other such heavy elements may be utilized for this type of anchorage. Many lightweight building structures are essentially anchored by being fastened to their heavy foundations.

Where resistance to exceptionally high uplift force is required, special anchoring foundations may be used that develop resistance through a combination of their own dead weight plus the ballast effect of earth fill placed in or on them. Friction piles and piers may also be used for major uplift resistance, although if their shafts are of concrete, care should be taken to reinforce them adequately for the tension force. A special technique is to use a belled pier to resist force by its own dead weight plus that of the soil above it, since the soil must be pushed up by the bell in order to extract the pier. One method for the development of the tension force through the bell end is to anchor a cable to a large plate, which is cast into the bottom of the bell, as shown in Figure 8.23.

The nature of tension forces must be considered as well as their magnitude. Forces

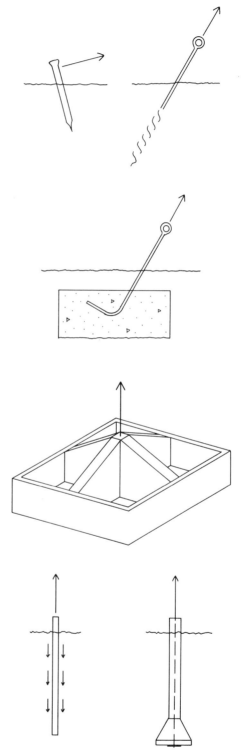

FIGURE 8.23. Various forms of tension anchors.

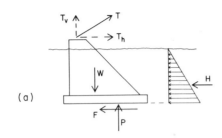

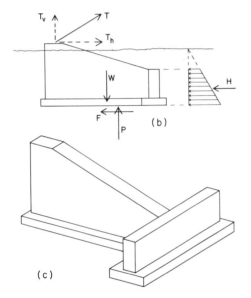

(a)

(b)

(c)

FIGURE 8.24. Tension-resistive abutments.

caused by wind or seismic shock will have a jarring effect that can loosen or progressively weaken anchorage elements. If the surrounding soil is soft and easily compressed, the effectiveness of the anchor may be reduced.

8.9. SHEAR WALL FOUNDATIONS

When shear walls rest on bearing foundations the situation is usually one of the following:

1. The shear wall is part of a continuous wall and is supported by a foundation that extends beyond the shear wall ends.

2. The shear wall is a separate wall and is supported by its own foundation, in the manner of a freestanding tower.

We will consider item 2 first. The basic problems to be solved in the design of such a foundation are the following:

Anchorage of the Shear Wall.   The shear wall anchorage consists of the attachment of the shear wall to the foundation to resist the sliding and the overturning effects due to the lateral loads on the wall. This involves a considerable range of possible situations, depending on the construction of the wall and the magnitude of forces. A number of different situations are illustrated and discussed in the examples in Chapter 6.

Overturning Effect.   The overturning effect is taken into consideration by performing the usual analysis for the overturning moment due to the lateral loads and the determination of the safety factor resulting from the resistance offered by the dead loads and the passive soil pressure.

Horizontal Sliding.   Horizontal sliding is the direct, horizontal force resistance in opposition to the lateral loads. It may be developed by some combination of soil friction and passive soil pressure or may be transferred to other parts of the building structure.

Maximum Soil Pressure and Its Distribution.   The magnitude and form of distribution of the vertical soil pressure on the foundation caused by the combination of vertical load and moment must be compared with the established design limits.

We will illustrate some of the issues involved in dealing with the last three of these problems in the two examples that follow.

Example 1:   Independent Shear Wall Footing—Minor Load.   The wall and proposed foundation are shown in Figure 8.25a. The

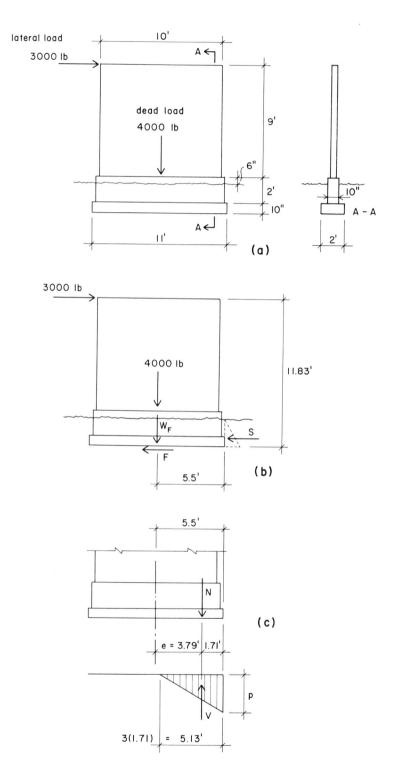

FIGURE 8.25. Shear wall foundation design example.

wall is assumed to function as a bearing wall as well as a shear wall, and the vertical loads applied to the top of the foundation are the sum of the wall weight and the support loads on the wall.

The following are design data and criteria:

> Allowable soil pressure: 1500 lb/ft^2
> Soil type: Group 4, *UBC* Table 29-B, (Appendix C)
> Concrete design strength: $f'_c = 2000$ psi
> Allowable tension on reinforcing: 20,000 psi

The various forces acting on the foundation are shown in Figure 8.25*b*. For the overturning analysis the usual procedure is to assume a rotation about the toe of the footing and to include only the gravity loads in determining the resistive moment. With these assumptions the analysis is as follows:

Overturning moment:

$$M = (3000)(11.83) = 35,490 \text{ lb/ft}$$

Weight of foundation wall:

$$(2)(\tfrac{10}{12})(10.5)(150) = 2625 \text{ lb}$$

Weight of footing:

$$(\tfrac{10}{12})(11)(2)(150) = 2750 \text{ lb}$$

Weight of soil over footing:

$$(1.17)(1.5)(11)(80) = 1544 \text{ lb}$$

Total vertical load:

$$4000 + 2625 + 2750 + 1544 = 10,919 \text{ lb}$$

Resisting moment:

$$(10,919)(5.5) = 60,055 \text{ lb-ft}$$

Safety factor:

$$SF = \frac{60,055}{35,490} = 1.69$$

Since this safety factor is greater than the usual requirement of 1.5, the foundation is not critical for overturning effect.

For the soil group given the soil friction coefficient is 0.25, and the total sliding resistance offered by friction is thus

$$F = (0.25)(10,919) = 2730 \text{ lb}$$

Since we assume that the lateral load on the shear wall is due to either wind or seismic force, this resistance may be increased by one third. Thus, although there is some additional resistance developed by the passive soil pressure on the face of the foundation wall and the footing, it is not necessary to consider it in this example.

For the soil stress analysis we combine the overturning moment as calculated previously with the total vertical load to find the equivalent eccentricity as follows, deducting soil weight for *N:*

$$e = \frac{M}{N} = \frac{35,490}{9375} = 3.79 \text{ ft}$$

This eccentricity is considerably outside the kern limit for the 11-ft-long footing ($\tfrac{11}{6}$, or 1.83 ft) so that the stress analysis must be done by the pressure wedge method, as discussed in Section 8.3. As illustrated in Figure 8.25*c*, the analysis follows.

Distance of the eccentric load from the footing end is

$$5.5 - 3.79 = 1.71 \text{ ft}$$

Therefore

$$x = (3)(1.71) = 5.13 \text{ ft}$$

$$p = \frac{2N}{wx} = \frac{(2)(9375)}{(2)(5.13)} = 1827 \text{ lb/ft}^2$$

Since this is less than the allowable design pressure with the permissible increase of one third [$p = (1.33)(1500) = 2000$], the condition is not critical as long as this type of soil pressure distribution is acceptable. This acceptance is a matter of judgment, based on concern for the rocking effect, as discussed in the example of the freestanding wall and illustrated in Figure 5.40. In this case, with the wall relatively short with respect to the footing length, we would judge the concern to be minor and would therefore accept the foundation as adequate.

The design considerations remaining for this example are concerned with the structural adequacy of the foundation wall and footing. The short wall in this case is probably adequate without any vertical reinforcing, although it would be advisable to provide at least one vertical dowel at each end of the wall, extended with a hook into the footing. The 2-ft-wide footing is adequate without lateral reinforcing. Both the wall and footing, however, should be provided with some minimal longitudinal reinforcing for shrinkage and temperature stresses.

Example 2: Independent Shear Wall Footing—Major Load. The wall and proposed foundation for this example are shown in Figure 8.26a. Additional design data and criteria are as follows:

Allowable soil pressure: 3000 lb/ft^2
Soil type: Group 4, *UBC* Table 29-B (Appendix C).
Concrete design strength: $f_c' = 3000$ psi
Allowable tension on reinforcing: 20,000 psi

In this case the supporting foundation wall and footing are extended some distance past the end of the shear wall to increase the stability and reduce the soil pressures. The forces acting on the structure are shown in Figure 8.26b. Following the usual procedure, we assume the overturning to be resisted only by the gravity forces and the ro-

tation point for overturn to be at the toe of the footing. With these assumptions, the analysis is as follows:

Overturning moment:

$$M = (24)(46) + (40)(34) + (40)(22)$$
$$= 1104 + 1360 + 880 = 3344 \text{ k-ft}$$

Weight of foundation wall:

$$(1.5)(6)(28)(0.150) = 37.8 \text{ k}$$

Weight of footing:

$$(2)(6)(30)(0.150) = 54 \text{ k}$$

Weight of soil over footing:

$$(4.5)(5.5)(30)(0.08) = 59.4 \text{ k}$$

Total vertical load:

$$240 + 37.8 + 54 + 59.4 = 391.2 \text{ k}$$

Resisting moment:

$$M = (391.2)(15) = 5868 \text{ k-ft}$$

Safety factor:

$$\text{SF} = \frac{5868}{3344} = 1.75$$

Since this is greater than the required factor of 1.5, the foundation is not critical for the overturning effect.

For the soil group given, the soil friction coefficient is 0.25, and the total sliding resistance offered by friction is thus

$$F = (0.25)(391.2) = 97.8 \text{ k}$$

Since this is slightly less than the total horizontal load of 104 k, we will proceed with a determination of the additional resistance offered by the passive soil pressure on the

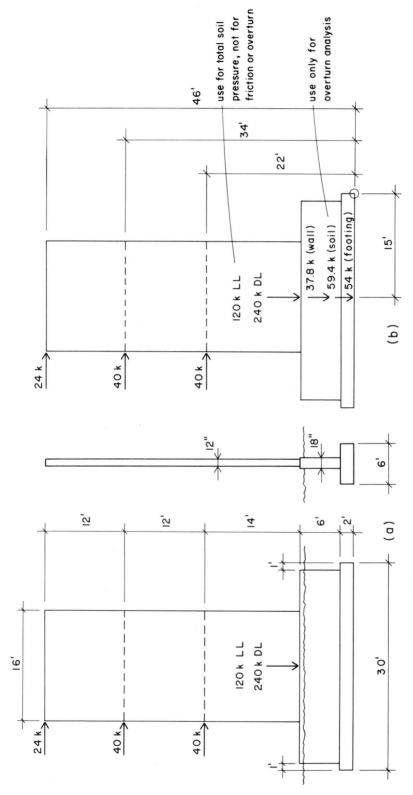

FIGURE 8.26. Investigation of the multistory shear wall: (*a*) the wall and its loading; (*b*) loading for the foundation analysis.

end of the footing and foundation wall. Using the value for passive soil resistance for the Group 4 soil as given in *UBC* Table 29-B (Appendix C), the pressures are as shown in Figure 8.27 and are calculated as follows:

Table value for pressure/ft of depth:

$$150 \text{ lb/ft}^2$$

Maximum pressure at bottom of wall:

$$(5.5)(150) = 825 \text{ lb/ft}^2$$

Pressure at bottom of footing:

$$(7.5)(150) = 1125 \text{ lb/ft}^2$$

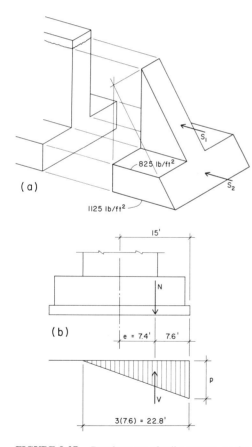

(a)

(b)

FIGURE 8.27. Development of soil pressures on the shear wall foundation: (*a*) horizontal passive pressure; (*b*) vertical pressure.

Total resistive forces:
On the end of the wall:

$$S_1 = \tfrac{1}{2}(1.5)(5.5)(0.825) = 3.4 \text{ k}$$

On the end of the footing:

$$S_2 = (2)(6)\frac{0.825 + 1.125}{2}$$

$$= 11.7 \text{ k}$$

Total force $= S_1 + S_2 = 15.1$ k

This increases the total resistive force due to the combination of sliding friction plus passive soil pressure to 112.9 k, which exceeds the total horizontal load.

For the vertical soil pressure on the bottom of the footing we consider the combined effect of the vertical load and the overturning moment. Although the passive soil pressure offers some resistance to the moment, it is relatively minor in this case and we will ignore it. The vertical load in this case should not include the weight of the soil over the footing, but must include the design live load. The loads and the resulting eccentricity are thus as follows:

Moment:

$$M = 3344 \text{ k-ft}$$

Vertical load:

$$N = 391.2 + 120 - 59.4 = 451.8 \text{ k}$$

Equivalent eccentricity:

$$e = \frac{M}{N} = \frac{3344}{451.8} = 7.40 \text{ ft}$$

This is considerably in excess of the kern limit of 5 ft for the footing and makes the design questionable. However, we will proceed with an analysis for the maximum soil pressure by the pressure wedge method as discussed in Section 8.3. Referring to Figure 8.27*b*, the analysis is as follows.

The distance from the load to the edge of the footing is

$$15 - 7.4 = 7.6 \text{ ft}$$

Then

$$x = 3(7.6) = 22.8 \text{ ft}$$

$$p = \frac{2N}{wx} = \frac{(2)(451,800)}{(6)(22.8)} = 6605 \text{ lb/ft}^2$$

With the increase in allowable stress due to wind or seismic force, this would require a basic allowable soil pressure of

$$p = \tfrac{3}{4}(6605) = 4954 \text{ lb/ft}^2$$

which is greater than the given limit of 3000 lb/ft^2 in this example.

Reduction of the soil pressure requires an increase in the size of the footing. If this increase consists entirely of adding width, the gain is only a linear function of the increase. Increase in length is similar to adding depth to a beam section, which is considerably more effective in increasing bending resistance. However, in this situation increasing the footing length produces an increase in the cantilever distance for the foundation wall. We will therefore compromise with increases in both the width and length, as

shown in Figure 8.28. These changes result in added weight of the foundation as follows:

New wall weight:

$$(1.5)(6)(32)(0.150) = 43.2 \text{ k}$$

New footing weight:

$$(2)(8)(34)(0.150) = 81.6 \text{ k}$$

New vertical load:

$$N = 360 + 43.2 + 81.6 = 484.8 \text{ k}$$

The new combined load analysis is thus as follows:

Eccentricity:

$$e = \frac{M}{N} = \frac{3344}{484.8} = 6.90 \text{ ft}$$

Distance from end of footing:

$$17 - 6.90 = 10.10 \text{ ft}$$

For the pressure wedge:

$$x = (3)(10.1) = 30.3 \text{ ft}$$

Maximum soil pressure:

$$p = \frac{2N}{wx} = \frac{(2)(484,800)}{(8)(30.3)} = 4000 \text{ lb/ft}^2$$

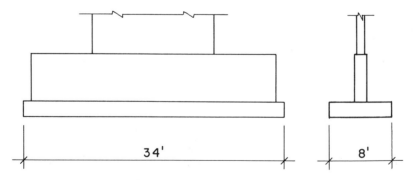

FIGURE 8.28. Modified form of the foundation.

If the wedge type of soil stress distribution is acceptable, this is within the limit for the given soil with the permissible increase for wind and seismic loads. For this example the rocking phenomenon, as discussed for freestanding walls and illustrated in Figure 5.40, may be marginally critical. However, the overall height of the wall above the bottom of the footing is only 1.35 times the length of the footing, so the problem should only be a critical one if the soil is highly compressible or the building structure is highly sensitive to lateral deflections.

In this example we have assumed the shear wall and its foundation to be completely independent of the building structure and have dealt with it as a freestanding tower. This is sometimes virtually the true situation, and the design approach that we have used is a valid one for such cases. However, various relations may occur between the shear wall structure and the rest of the building. One of these possibilities is shown in Figure 8.29. Here the shear wall and its foundation extend some distance below a point at which the building structure offers a bracing force in terms of horizontal constraint to the shear wall. This situation may occur when there is a basement and the first-floor structure is a heavy rigid concrete system. If the floor structure is capable of transferring the necessary horizontal force directly to the outside basement walls, the shear wall foundation may be relieved of the usual sliding resistance function.

As shown in Figure 8.29, when the upper level constraint is present, the rotation point for overturn moves to this point. The forces that contribute to the resisting moment become the gravity load W, the sliding friction F, and the passive soil pressure S. The following example illustrates the analysis for such a structure.

Example: Shear Wall Footing—Upper Level Constraint. As shown in Figure 8.30a, this structure is a modification of the one in the preceding example. We assume the construction to be the same as that shown in Figure 8.26a, except for the added height of the wall and the constraint at the first-floor level. Data and criteria for design remain the same.

The only modification of the vertical loads from those previously determined is the additional basement wall. This added load is

$$w = (12 \text{ ft})(16 \text{ ft})(0.150 \text{ k/ft}^2) = 28.8 \text{ k}$$

Added to the total dead load calculated previously, this results in a new total deal load of

$$W = 391.2 + 28.8 = 420 \text{ k}$$

The overturning analysis in this case begins with a comparison of the overturning moment and the resisting moment due to the dead load. If this does not result in the necessary safety factor of 1.5, we proceed to investigate the added forces that are necessary.

Overturning moment:

$$M = (24)(38) + (40)(26) + (40)(14)$$
$$= 912 + 1040 + 560 = 2512 \text{ k-ft}$$

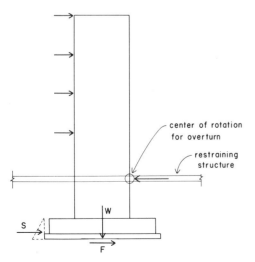

FIGURE 8.29. Tall shear wall with upper level constraint.

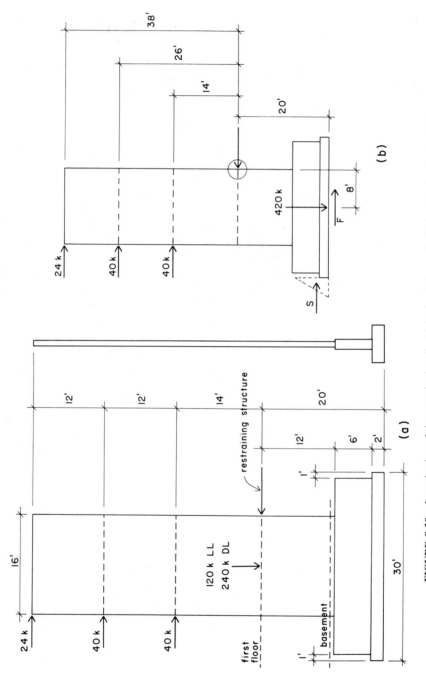

FIGURE 8.30. Investigation of the restrained wall: (*a*) loads on the wall; (*b*) loading for the foundation analysis.

Required dead load moment:

$$(2512)(SF \text{ of } 1.5) = 3768 \text{ k-ft}$$

Actual dead load moment:

$$(420)(8) = 3360 \text{ k-ft}$$

Required additional resisting moment:

$$3768 - 3360 = 408 \text{ k-ft}$$

If we rely on the development of sliding friction for this moment, the necessary friction force is

$$F = \frac{408}{20} = 20.4 \text{ k}$$

which is quite a nominal force in view of the footing size and the magnitude of the dead load.

Since the friction is easily capable of the necessary added moment in this case, we do not need to consider the potential capability of added moment due to passive soil pressure. Were it necessary to do so, we would determine this potential force as was previously done and is illustrated in Figure 8.27.

Considering the equilibrium of the structure as shown with the forces in Figure 8.30b, we can now determine the required force that must be developed by the constraining structure at the first-floor level. This will consist of the sum of the horizontal loads and the required friction force. Thus

$$R = H + F = 104 + 20.4 = 124.4 \text{ k}$$

If we consider the rotational stability of the wall to be maintained in the manner assumed in the preceding calculations, the vertical soil pressure on the footing is relieved of any moment effect. Thus the pressure is simply that due to the vertical loads and is determined as follows:

Total vertical load:

420 k (dead load) + 120 k (live load)

$$= 540 \text{ k}$$

Maximum soil pressure:

$$p = \frac{540}{(6)(30)} = 3 \text{ k/ft}^2$$

Since this is precisely the limit given, the footing is adequate in this example.

Another relationship that may occur between the shear wall structure and the rest of the building is that of some connection between the shear wall footing and other adjacent foundations. This occurs commonly in buildings designed for high seismic risk because it is usually desirable to assure that the foundation system moves in unison during seismic shocks. This may be a useful relationship for the shear wall in that additional horizontal resistance may be developed to add to that produced by the friction and passive soil pressure on the shear wall foundation itself. Thus, if the elements to which the shear wall foundation is tied do not have lateral load requirements, their potential friction and passive pressures may be enlisted to share the loads on the shear wall.

Shear walls on the building exterior often occur as individual wall segments, consisting of solid portions of the wall between openings or other discontinuities in the wall construction. In these situations the foundation often consists of a continuous wall and footing or a grade beam that extends along the entire wall. The effect of the overturning moment on such a foundation is shown in Figure 8.31. The loading tends to develop a shear force and moment in the foundation wall, both of which are one half of the forces in the wall. If the foundation wall is capable of developing this shear and bending, it functions as a distributing member, spreading the overturning effect along an extended length of the foundation.

The overturning effect just described must be added to other loadings on the wall for a

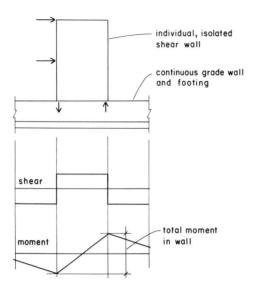

individual, isolated
shear wall

continuous grade wall
and footing

shear

moment

total moment
in wall

FIGURE 8.31. Isolated shear wall on a continuous foundation.

complete investigation of the foundation wall and footing stresses. It is likely that the continuous foundation wall also functions as a distributing member for the gravity loads.

8.10. TOWERS

When a vertical freestanding structure has height-to-width ratio exceeding three or so, it takes on the nature of a tower. Most highrise buildings fall in this category, although the tallest and the most slender ones seldom have an aspect ratio (height/width) greater than six. The most slender structures are usually not buildings but those for signs, flagpoles, water towers, or broadcast transmission towers. For the towerlike structure, the three basic means for providing support are as shown in Figure 8.32.

Two major problems with most towerlike structures are the lateral deflection at the top and the resistance of overturning moment at the base. For the pole-type structure (Figure 8.32a) the critical concerns are for the flexibility of the pole, the compressibility of the soil in the upper strata, and the amount of

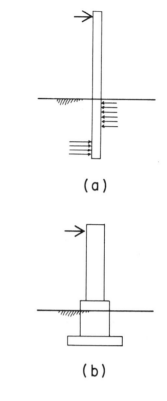

(a)

(b)

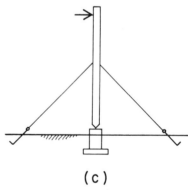

(c)

FIGURE 8.32. Lateral support for towers: (*a*) pole type; (*b*) shallow-bearing foundation; (*c*) guy cables.

embedment of the pole in the ground. "Design" of the pole structure is very much a matter of using empirical, experience-based rules of thumb. (See Section 8.11.)

For the guyed tower, critical concerns are for the flexibility and dynamic behavior of the tower, the positioning of the guys, the tension stretching of the guys, and the tension anchors at the base of the guys. Because these are very special structures, we will not attempt to deal with them here.

Building structures are usually of the type shown in Figure 8.32b. If the foundation is a shallow-bearing type of footing, the aspect ratio of the height above the footing base to the footing width is a critical concern. (See Figure 8.33.) Whatever the tower shape or construction may be, if this ratio exceeds five or so and the soil is even slightly compressible, various problems may occur. These problems are discussed in Section 8.3 for the single-footing structure. For large buildings, support is usually by multiple column footings, but the same general behavior of the building structure and combined footings is similarly considered.

Large tall buildings are often supported on deep foundations of piles or piers rather than on bearing footings. Although the same general concerns exist, it is sometimes possible to develop some amount of tension anchorage using friction piles or the dead weight of large piers.

The horizontal deflection at the top of a vertically cantilevered structure, such as that shown in Figure 8.34, is produced by a number of things. These include:

The flexing of the tower structure itself.

Yield in the tower-to-base connection.

Structural deformations in the tower base.

Tilt of the base due to the uneven soil stresses caused by the combined vertical load and moment.

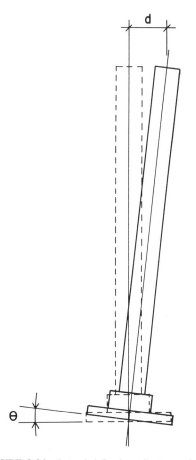

FIGURE 8.34. Lateral deflection of a tower due to base rotation.

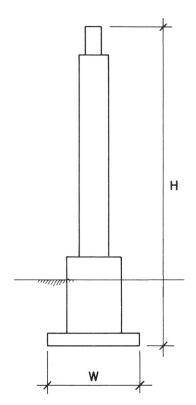

FIGURE 8.33. Aspect ratio for towers: H/W.

If the tower foundation is a bearing footing, some rotation of the base is inevitable, unless the footing is placed on solid rock. As the tower height increases, this rotation can become quite critical. For example, with a 300-ft-tall tower, a rotation of only 0.5 degree at the base will produce a horizontal movement of approximately 30 in. at the top of the tower.

Towers of modest size can be designed with the simplified procedures illustrated in this chapter for freestanding walls and short cantilever retaining walls. However, very tall or very slender towers, or those that must be supported on highly compressible soil, require more rigorous investigation of both the tower and its foundation.

8.11. POLES

When a slender, vertically cantilevered element develops resistance to lateral force by its simple embedment in the ground, it is described as a pole or a polelike structure. Wood fence posts and utility poles for power lines are examples of these structures. The general nature of such a structure is discussed in Section 8.3 and illustrated in Figure 8.11c.

Building code requirements generally deal with the pole structure as being one of two situations, as illustrated in Figure 8.35. If construction exists at grade level, the lateral movement of the pole may be constrained at this location, so that a rotation of the pole occurs at grade level and the development of resistance to lateral load is as shown in Figure 8.35a. If grade level constraint is minor or nonexistent, lateral resistance will be developed by opposing soil pressures on the buried portion of the pole, as shown in Figure 8.35b.

The following example illustrates the use of design criteria for the unconstrained pole taken from the *Uniform Building Code* and the *City of Los Angeles Building Code*.

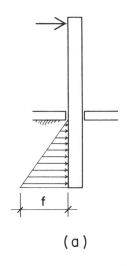

(a)

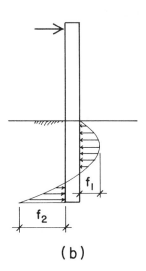

(b)

FIGURE 8.35.

Example. A 12-in.-diameter round wood pole is used as shown in Figure 8.36. The soil around the buried pole is generally a medium compacted silty sand. Investigate the adequacy of the 10-ft embedment.

Solution: Using criteria from Section 91.2311 of the *City of Los Angeles Building Code* (see Appendix C), a determination is made of the two critical soil stresses f_1 and f_2, as shown in Figure 8.35. These computed stresses are then compared to the allowable

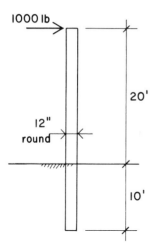

1000 lb

20'

12"
round

10'

FIGURE 8.36.

pressures. Using the formulas from the code, we find

$$f_2 = \frac{7.62\,P(2h + d)}{bd^2} = \frac{7.62\,(1000)(50)}{(1)(10)^2}$$

$$= 3810 \text{ psf}$$

$$f_1 = \frac{2.85\,P}{bd} + \frac{f_2}{4} = \frac{2.85\,(1000)}{(1)(10)} + \frac{3810}{4}$$

$$= 285 + 953 = 1238 \text{ psf}$$

From Table 28-B of the Los Angles Code the allowable lateral-bearing pressure for the compact silty sand is 233 psf per foot of depth. For f_1 the depth is taken as one third the total; thus

allowable $p = \frac{10}{3} \times 233 \times \frac{4}{3} = 1036$ psf

(Assuming the lateral force is due to wind

or seismic load, and the increase of one third is permitted.)

For f_2 the allowable pressure is

$$p = 10 \times 233 \times \tfrac{4}{3} = 3107 \text{ psf}$$

As both of the computed pressures exceed the allowable values, it is observed that the embedment is not adequate.

Solving for the required depth of embedment is not very direct with the formulas from the Los Angeles Code. On the other hand, the *UBC* provides a formula for the direct determination of the depth of embedment as follows (see Appendix C):

From *UBC*, Section 2907 (g) 2,

$$d = \frac{A}{2}\left(1 + \sqrt{1 + \frac{4.36h}{A}}\right)$$

$$A = \frac{2.34\,P}{S_1 b}$$

From *UBC* Table 29-B, p for silty sand $=$ 150 psf per foot of depth; thus

$$S_1 = 150 \times \frac{10}{3} \times \frac{4}{3} = 667 \text{ psf}$$

$$A = \frac{2.34\,(1000)}{(667)(1)} = 3.51$$

$$d = \frac{3.51}{2}\left(1 + \sqrt{1 + \frac{4.36\,(20)}{3.51}}\right)$$

$$= 14.24 \text{ ft}$$

which also indicates that the proposed embedment is not adequate.

CHAPTER NINE

Special Problems

9.1. EFFECTS OF VOLUME CHANGE

Volume change resulting from fluctuation of temperature, moisture content, or other effects induces movements. Under various circumstances these movements may present difficulties, including the potential for development of lateral forces.

Thermal Change

Thermal change occurs primarily from daily and seasonal changes in the air temperature. This is generally most critical for the elements that constitute the building's exposed surfaces. Critical concerns include the following:

1. *Size of the Building.* The amount of volume change will generally be proportional to the size of the building. Dimensions of movements will be greater if the building is wider or higher. If the building is quite small, little provision may be required. If the building is very long or tall, extreme measures may be required.

2. *Continuous Structures or Surfaces.* If the building structure or the surface construction is made with a form of continuous construction (such as poured concrete or masonry), movements due to thermal change will be cumulative between breaks in the continuous elements. Assemblages with considerable jointing or other discontinuities

will tend to absorb the small incremental changes. For the materials that are normally continuous, cumulative movement may be reduced or eliminated by the introduction of control joints that constitute breaks in the continuity.

3. *Differential Expansion.* Although large potential movements can be a major concern, small movements may also be critical, especially when attached elements of the construction move differently. Some situations where this may occur are the following:

a. When different materials are attached. Aluminum trim elements supported by steel structures are a common example of this. This is not often a source of distress to the structure, but must be considered for the effect of the movements on the attached elements or the jointing.

b. When an exposed skin is attached to a covered structure. Assuming a temperature-controlled interior, there will be a time lag of temperature change, with the surface elements changing more rapidly. This may be compounded if the materials are different, as discussed in item 3a. This is also seldom a source of concern for the structure but rather of concern for the surface elements and their attachment.

c. Exposed exterior structure and enclosed interior structure. When structural elements (usually columns or spandrels) are exposed, they will experience greater thermal change than the enclosed interior elements of the structure. This is a potential source of major stress if the building is long or tall, the climate temperature range is great, and the structure is relatively continuous in nature.

d. Structure partly above and partly below ground. The building foundations normally experience little thermal change in mild climates, with the ground temperature a short distance below the surface experiencing little seasonal change. If there is considerable cumulative movement in the construction above ground, there may be significant structural interaction—again, most critical for long buildings of continuous construction in cold climates.

4. *Long Construction Period.* When the time for the completion of construction stretches out (as it most often does), there are some special considerations that may be required. A common one occurs when the structure is erected during the coldest portion of the year. When the building is later enclosed and heated, or simply when summer comes, there may be thermal movements that were not considered in the design because the entire structure was expected to be enclosed. Since the construction schedule is seldom known at the time of the design of the construction, consideration of this problem is often forgotten. A common example is a steel beam supported by relatively rigid masonry or concrete construction. A beam of even modest length, if erected in cold temperature and rigidly fastened in place, may likely cause failure of the supporting materials.

In some instances it is possible—and possibly the simplest solution—to simply design the structure for the stresses caused by thermal actions, and adding them to those for other loading combinations. Where the details of the construction necessary to alleviate the effects are costly, disruptive to the construction process, or disturbing to the appearance of the building, this is a reasonable approach. Often, however, it is necessary, or more desirable, to reduce or eliminate the thermal effects by one means or another. Some common techniques for achieving this are the following:

1. *Planned Discontinuity.* The general planning of the building may be developed with the deliberate intention of avoiding continuous construction. Thus the magnitudes of cumulative movement are kept small, even though the building is large.

2. *Provision of Deliberate Construction Breaks.* If continuous construction is unavoidable, it may be possible to use expansion joints at reasonable intervals to contain the expansion within some tolerable limit. The specific dimension between such joints will depend on the materials of the construction and the local climate. Joints so used may also function as seismic separation joints or controls for other types of structural movement.

3. *Use of Movement-Tolerating Joints.* Joints that permit controlled slipping, flexing, stretching, or other movement may be used to avoid the transfer of forces or the cumulative effect of thermal changes. These may be used between elements of the structure or between the structure and the attached parts of the construction.

4. *Staged Jointing during Construction.* Where the use of permanent movement-tolerating joints may not be desirable, it may be possible to use them on a temporary basis during construction. Thus the problem of the long construction period may be solved by leaving joints untightened until the structure is enclosed and heated, and then making the final connection.

Change of Moisture Content

Wood and products made from wood (paper, cardboard, and fiberboard) are subject to significant changes in volume due to fluctuations of moisture content. For elements of solid wood, there is a greater change in the direction perpendicular to the wood grain than along the grain. Although the greatest change occurs during the time of curing of the wood as it dries out from its condition in the live tree, changes may also occur with long duration shifts in the percent of moisture in the air around the wood. In northern climates interiors tend to be quite low in moisture during cold months, whereas humid summer conditions present the opposite situation. Elements of the building construction can experience long duration major change in moisture content with accompanying changes in volume.

In general, moisture change does not present a major source of lateral loads. The considerable jointing of wood structures allows for incremental development of dimensional changes, without major cumulative effects. In addition, any provisions made for thermal change will usually also provide for changes due to moisture content. However, thermal and moisture changes are not always linked, and provision for one may not be required where the other is. The interior moisture changes mentioned previously for northern climates can occur with little change in interior temperatures. Thus a condition not considered critical for thermal change should nevertheless be considered for expansion control caused by moisture change. Obviously, local climate conditions, as well as the materials and details of the building construction, must be carefully studied for good design.

Shrinkage

Shrinkage occurs in wood with the reduction of moisture content; the major effect occurs as the wood cures from its live condition.

Shrinkage also occurs significantly during the drying of wet plaster, mortar, and concrete. For ordinary concrete not in a permanent submerged situation, the volume change is usually between 1 and 2%.

Good construction practices with plaster, masonry, and concrete require numerous provisions for the effects of shrinkage. The three basic techniques are to provide reinforcement (for the tension developed), to build sufficiently small increments so that large cumulative changes are avoided, and to provide control joints. As with moisture change in general, provisions made for thermal change will also work to reduce shrinkage effects. However, although thermal and air moisture content changes may vary with the local climate or the interior climate control, shrinkage is universal and must be provided for, even where other conditions are not critical.

9.2. LATERAL DRIFT

Lateral deflections are discussed for various types of structures and various loadings in other portions of this book. Lateral movements of the building structure may be critical for one or more of the following reasons.

Visible Movement. Exceptionally tall and slender structures may be seen to sway by persons inside or outside the building. While presenting a possibly disquieting experience, this is not necessarily a dangerous situation. Some movement is inevitable, but its theoretical computation as well as the setting of meaningful limitations are quite difficult for the average building. Once-in-a-lifetime movements due to major forces may be tolerable, but frequent occurrences due to average loadings are most likely objectionable. Experience is pretty much the only guide for design in this case.

Sensible Movements. Occupants of a building may not be able to see movement, but may experience the swaying effect. This is the way that most people know that an earthquake has occurred. Although this is also disquieting, it is inevitable and really objectionable only if it is of excessive magnitude or occurs frequently under ordinary loading conditions.

Distortions of Building Elements. Damage due to major movements is more often critical for other parts of the building than for the building structure. Plaster wall and ceiling surfaces, window glass, ceramic tile, and nonstructural masonry are all relatively intolerant of significant distortions. Although these rigid materials may suffer damage, other elements may also be affected. Rigid piping, operable windows, doors, and elevators are generally not able to remain functional with major distortions of the building. As in other situations where movements present problems, control jointing or other devices may be necessary if movement cannot be prevented sufficiently.

Objectionable Interactions. Structural movements are often considered with regard to the movement of some individual component of the structural system. Many problems, however, occur as interactions—between the structure and other parts of the building or between separate parts of the structure. Many of these situations are discussed in other sections of the book with regard to battering, multimassed buildings, unsymmetrical buildings, load sharing, interactive elements, and so on.

Codes are of limited help in design for lateral movements. (See discussion of story drift.) Experience and judgment are mostly required, although some general considerations may be made for techniques to reduce movements by a general stiffening of the lateral bracing structure as follows.

1. *Use Stiffer Materials.* This may involve a choice of basic materials (concrete or masonry versus wood) or of a stiffer grade of the same material (higher E value). Deflections of rigid frames, tall shear walls, and long horizontal diaphragms will be most affected.

2. *Increase Member Stiffness by Increasing I/L.* This may be done by increasing I or reducing L. For example, use a rectangular rather than a square shape for a wood or concrete column (increased I) or use closer spacing of columns in a bent (reduced L for the bent beams). This mostly affects rigid frames.

3. *Fix the Base of Frame Columns.* As discussed in Section 6.3, this greatly reduces story drift. The supports, of course, must be capable of developing the required fixity.

4. *Select a Stiffer Bracing System.* In general, shear walls and trusses are stiffer than rigid frames. However, the rigid frame with deep, short span beams and many closely spaced columns may be quite stiff.

5. *Avoid Forms That Increase Movement.* Tall, narrow shear walls and long, narrow horizontal diaphragms are examples of poor form.

6. *Use Positive, Unyielding Jointing.* This most affects trussed bents, but may also be a factor for shear walls and horizontal diaphragms.

9.3. HORIZONTAL MOVEMENTS DUE TO VERTICAL LOADS

Lateral movements occur mostly under lateral loads. There are various situations, however, in which some horizontal movement occurs in structures that are subjected to vertical loads. An example is the movement of the columns of a rigid frame, as discussed in Section 5.4. Figure 9.1*a* illustrates a common occurrence with tied rafters or the bottom chords of trusses. If the supports are as shown, outward movement at the supports is inevitable due to the tension

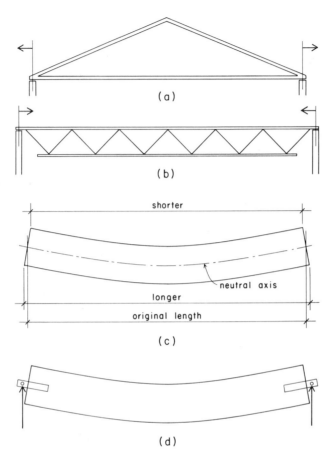

FIGURE 9.1. Horizontal support movements with deep spanning structures.

elongation of the horizontal bottom member. This is reversed in the case of the parallel chord truss when support is provided for the top chords, as shown in Figure 9.1b. In this case, inward movement is inevitable because of the compression shortening of the top chord.

Another situation of this type occurs with very long span trusses or girders. As these members are generally quite deep, the end rotation causes an outward movement at the bottom and an inward movement at the top, as shown in Figure 9.1c. For this situation one possible solution is to provide support that approaches that of a pin joint at the neutral axis where no length change occurs.

Obviously, the size of the structure has a great deal to do with the magnitude of the movements just illustrated. For modest size structures the movements may be absorbed in joint distortions. However, some detailing similar to that used for control of thermal expansion effects may be indicated. In some situations a technique that may be used is to leave the joint only partly fastened until all dead load movement has occurred. If the joint is then fully tightened, the movements to be considered will be only those due to live load—especially effective if live load is low in comparison with dead load.

9.4. LONG TIME EFFECTS

Buildings exist for the most part over a long time, and various effects occur as a result of long time. Dead load is in effect permanent, so that structures that sustain high percentages of dead load are the most affected by the time duration of loads. Wind and earthquake effects are generally of quite short duration in their critical magnitudes, although repetitions of lower magnitude effects may also be critical. The following are some problems for concern with regard to time over the life of the building.

Soil Movements.   Soils with high clay content that are subject to high stress may deform on a more or less continuous basis. This is especially critical for structures in which the movements may result in tilting or horizontal displacement. Cantilever retaining walls and untied abutments must be carefully designed for these effects, and preferably not placed on soft clays or other continuously deformable materials. Movements may also occur due to seasonal soaking of the soil or heavy irrigation. Silty soils with high void ratios and very fine sands may be adversely affected in these situations.

Creep of Concrete.   Long-term creep effects in concrete may result in progressive movements over time. Where dead load is high or soil pressures constant over time, considerable deflection may occur. Tilt of tall cantilever retaining walls and inward bulging of concrete basement walls are examples of this phenomenon. Increased stiffness or use of bracing may be possible remedies.

Dimensional Change of Wood.   Moisture reduction due to curing, long time fluctuations of moisture, and general aging of the material tend to result in some dimensional changes in solid wood elements: beams sag, columns twist, and walls and floors warp and curl. Where these can result in objectionable conditions—other than visual ones—measures should be taken to reduce the effects. Use of better cured wood for construction, bracing with steel elements, and substitution of glue-laminated products are some of the measures.

Progressive Loosening.   As discussed in Chapters 4 and 5, it is desirable to use connections that do not experience loosening over time. Connecting techniques vary in this aspect, and appropriate ones should be selected where their permanent tightness is critical to the maintaining of a general stiffness and tightness of the bracing system.

BIBLIOGRAPHY

1. *Uniform Building Code*, 1985 ed., International Conference of Building Officials, 5360 South Workman Mill Road, Whittier, CA 90601. (Called simply the *UBC*.)

2. *American National Standard Minimum Design Loads for Building and Other Structures*, American National Standards Institute, 1430 Broadway, New York, NY 10018, 1982.

3. *The BOCA Basic National Building Code/1984*, 9th ed., Building Officials and Code Administrators International, Inc., 4051 W. Flossmoor Road, Country Club Hills, IL 60477-5795, 1984 (with 1985 supplement). (Called simply the BOCA Code.)

4. *Manual of Steel Construction*, 8th ed., American Institute of Steel Construction, Chicago, 1980. (Called simply the *AISC Manual*.)

5. *Building Code Requirements for Reinforced Concrete*, ACI 318-83, American Concrete Institute, Detroit, MI, 1983. (Called simply the ACI Code.)

6. *National Design Specification for Wood Construction*, National Forest Products Association, Washington, D.C., 1982.

7. *Timber Construction Manual*, 3rd ed., American Institute of Timber Construction, Wiley, New York, 1985.

8. *CRSI Handbook*, 4th ed., Concrete Reinforcing Steel Institute, Schaumburg, IL, 1982.

9. *City of Los Angeles Building Code*, 1976 ed., Building News Inc., 3055 Overland Avenue, Los Angeles, CA, 1976.

10. *Masonry Design Manual*, 3rd ed., Masonry Institute of America, 2550 Beverly Boulevard, Los Angeles, CA 90057, 1979.

11. *Wind Forces on Buildings and Structures: an introduction*, E. L. Houghton and N. B. Carruthers, Wiley, New York, 1976.

12. Wolfgang Scheuller, *High-Rise Building Structures*, Wiley, New York, 1977.

13. Christopher Arnold and Robert Reitherman, *Building Configuration and Seismic Design*, Wiley, New York, 1982.

14. James Ambrose and Dimitry Vergun, *Seismic Design of Buildings*, Wiley, New York, 1985.

15. S. W. Crawley and R. M. Dillon, *Steel Buildings Analysis and Design*, 3rd ed., Wiley, New York, 1984.

16. P. F. Rice and E. S. Hoffman, *Structural Design: Guide to the ACI Building Code*, 2nd ed., Van Nostrand, New York, 1979.

17. R. R. Schneider and W. L. Dickey, *Reinforced Masonry Design*, Prentice-Hall, Englewood Cliffs, NJ, 1980.

18. Joseph E. Bowles, *Foundation Analysis and Design*, 3rd ed., McGraw-Hill, New York, 1982.

19. R. B. Peck, W. E. Hanson, and T. H. Thornburn, *Foundation Engineering*, 2nd ed., Wiley, New York, 1974.

20. James Ambrose, *Simplified Design of Building Foundations*, Wiley, New York, 1981.

21. Jack C. McCormac, *Structural Analysis*, 4th ed., Harper & Row, New York, 1984.

22. W. C. Huntington and R. E. Mickadeit, *Building Construction: Materials and Types of Construction*, 5th ed., Wiley, New York, 1981.

23. C. G. Ramsey and H. R. Sleeper, *Architectural Graphic Standards*, 7th ed., Wiley, New York, 1980.

GLOSSARY

The material presented here constitutes a brief dictionary of words and terms frequently encountered in discussions of the design of structures to withstand wind and earthquakes. Many of the words and terms have reasonably well-established meanings in the scientific and engineering literature. In those cases we have tried to be consistent with the accepted usage. In some cases, however, words and terms are given somewhat different meanings by different authors, by different professional groups, in different fields of study, in different countries, and so on. In these situations we have given the definitions as used by the authors of this work so that the reader may be clear as to our meaning.

In some instances words or terms are commonly misused with regard to their precise meaning. We have generally used such words and terms as they are broadly understood, but we have given both the correct and popular definitions in some cases.

To be as clear as possible in its requirements, the *Uniform Building Code* (Ref. 1) occasionally gives its own definitions. Reference should be made to these definitions in interpreting *UBC* requirements.

For a fuller explanation of some of these words and terms, the reader should use the Index to find the related discussion in the text.

Abutment. Originally, the end support of an arch or vault. Now, any support that receives both vertical and lateral loading.

Acceleration. The rate of change of the velocity, expressed as the first derivative of the velocity (dv/dt) or as the second derivative of the displacement (d^2s/dt^2). Acceleration of the ground surface is more significant than its displacement during an earthquake because it relates more directly to the force effect. $F = ma$ as a dynamic force.

Active lateral pressure. See *Lateral pressure*.

Aerodynamic. Fluid flow effects of air, similar to current effects in running water.

Anchorage. Refers to attachment for resistance to movement; usually a result of uplift, overturn, sliding, or horizontal separation. Tiedown, or hold down, refers to anchorage against uplift or overturn. Positive anchorage generally refers to direct fastening that does not easily loosen.

Aseismic. The correct word for description of resistance to seismic effects. Building design actually consists of *aseismic* design, although the term *seismic design* is more commonly used.

Base shear. See the *UBC* definition of *base* in Section 2312(b).

Battering. Describes the effect that occurs when two elements in separate motion bump into each other repeatedly, such as two adjacent parts of a structure during an earthquake. Also called *pounding* or *hammering*.

Bent. A planar framework, or some portion of one, that is designed for resistance to both vertical and horizontal forces in the plane of the frame.

Box system. A structural system in which lateral loads are not resisted by a vertical load-bearing space frame but rather by shear walls or a braced frame.

Braced frame. Literally, any framework braced against lateral forces. Codes use the term for a frame braced by trussing (triangulation).

Bracing. In structural design usually refers to the resistance to movements caused by lateral forces or by the effects of buckling, torsional rotation, sliding, and so on.

Brittle fracture. Sudden ultimate failure in tension or shear. The basic structural behavior of so-called brittle materials.

Buffeting. Refers to wind effects caused by turbulent air flow or by changes in the wind direction that result in whipping, rocking, and so on.

Cohesionless. General lack of cohesiveness; noncohesive. The typical character of clean sands and gravels.

Cohesive. General character of a soil in which the soil particles adhere to each other to produce a nondisintegrating mass. The typical character of fine-grained soils: silts and clays.

Collector. A force transfer element that functions to collect loads from a horizontal diaphragm and distribute them to the vertical elements of the lateral resistive system.

Continuity. Most often used to describe structures or parts of structures that have behavior characteristics influenced by the monolithic, continuous nature of adjacent elements, such as continuous, vertical multistory columns, continuous, multispan beams, and rigid frames.

Core bracing. Vertical elements of a lateral-bracing system developed at the location

of permanent interior walls for stairs, elevators, duct shafts, or rest rooms.

Critical damping. The amount of damping that will result in a return from initial deformation to the neutral position without reversal.

Damping. The effect that causes a decrease in the amplitude of succeeding cycles of harmonic motion (vibration). May be deliberately increased by devices such as shock absorbers. Occurs naturally in structures as energy is lost through internal strains and friction in joints.

Dead Load. See *Load*.

Deep foundation. Foundation system that utilizes elements to achieve a considerable extension of the construction below the level of the bottom of the supported structure. Elements most commonly used are *piles* or *piers*.

Deflection. Generally refers to the lateral movement of a structure caused by loads, such as the vertical sag of a beam, the bowing of a surface under wind pressure, or the lateral sway of a rigid frame. The total horizontal deflection at the top of a structure caused by lateral loads is also called *drift*.

Degree of freedom. See *Freedom*.

Density. See *Mass*.

Diaphragm. A surface element (deck, wall, etc.) used to resist forces in its own plane by spanning or cantilevering. See *Horizontal diaphragm* and *Shear wall*.

Displacement. Movement away from some fixed reference point. Motion is described mathematically as a displacement-time function. See *Acceleration and Velocity*.

Drag. Generally refers to wind effects on surfaces parallel to the wind direction. Ground drag refers to the effect of the ground surface in slowing the wind velocity near ground level.

Drag strut. A structural member used to transfer lateral load across the building and into some part of the vertical system. See also *Collector*.

Drift. See *Deflection*.

Ductile. Describes the load–strain behavior that results from the plastic yielding of materials or connections. To be significant, the plastic strain prior to failure should be considerably more than the elastic strain up to the point of plastic yield.

Ductile moment-resisting space frame. Frame that complies with the requirements of Section 2312(j) of the *UBC*.

Dynamic. Usually used to characterize load effects or structural behaviors that are nonstatic in nature. That is, they involve time-related considerations such as vibrations, energy effects versus simple force, and so on.

Earthquake. The common term used to describe sensible ground movements, usually caused by subterranean faults or explosions. The point on the ground surface immediately above the subterranean shock is called the *epicenter*. The magnitude of the energy released at the location of the shock is the basis for the rating of the shock on the *Richter scale*.

Elastic. Used to describe two aspects of stress–strain behavior. The first is a constant stress–strain proportionality, or constant modulus of elasticity, as represented by a straight line form of the stress–strain graph. The second is the limit within which all the strain is recoverable; that is, there is no permanent deformation. The latter phenomenon may occur even though the stress–strain relationship is nonlinear.

Energy. Capacity for doing work; what is used up when work is done. Occurs in various forms; mechanical, heat, chemical, electrical, and so on.

Epicenter. See *Earthquake*.

Equilibrium. A balanced state or condition, usually used to describe a situation in which opposed effects neutralize each other to produce a net effect of zero.

Equivalent static force analysis. The technique by which a dynamic effect is translated into a hypothetical (equivalent) static effect that produces a similar result.

Essential facilities. Code term for a facility that should remain functional after a disaster such as a major earthquake; affects establishment of the *I* factor for base shear.

Fault. The subterranean effect that produces an earthquake. Consists of a slippage, cracking, sudden strain release, and so on. See *Earthquake*.

Flexible. See *Stiffness*.

Flutter. Flapping, vibration type of movement of an object in high wind. Essentially a resonant behavior. See *Vibration*.

Footing. A shallow, bearing-type foundation element consisting typically of concrete that is poured directly into an excavation.

Force. An effort that tends to change the shape or the state of motion of an object.

Freedom. In structures usually refers to the lack of some type of resistance or constraint. In static analysis the connections between members and the supports of the structure are qualified as to type, or degree, of freedom. Thus the terms *fixed support, pinned support*, and *sliding support* are used to qualify the types of movement resisted. In dynamic analysis the degree of freedom is an important factor in determining the dynamic response of a structure.

Freestanding wall. See *Wall*.

Frequency. In harmonic motion (bouncing springs, vibrating strings, swinging pendulums, etc.), the number of complete cycles of motion per unit of time. See *Vibration*.

Fundamental period. See *Period*.

Gable roof. Double sloping roof formed by joined rafters or rigid frames with a ridge or peak at their connection. A *gable* is the upper triangular portion of the wall at the end of the roof.

Grade. The level of the ground surface. Usually refers to the *finished grade*, which is the recontoured surface after the completion of construction.

Grade beam. A horizontal element in a foundation system that serves some spanning or load-distributing function.

Gust. An increase, or surge, of short duration in the wind velocity.

Hammering. See *Battering*.

Header. Usually used to describe a horizontal element over an opening in a wall or at the edge of an opening in a roof or floor.

Hertz. Same as cycles per second.

Hold down. See *Anchorage*.

Horizontal diaphragm. See *Diaphragm*. Usually a roof or floor deck used as part of the lateral resistive structural system for a building.

Inelastic. See *Stress–strain behavior*.

Interrupted shear wall. Shear wall that is not continuous in its solid construction from its top to the ground.

Kern limit. Limiting dimension for the eccentricity of a compression force, if tension stress is to be avoided.

Lateral. Literally means to the side or from the side. Often used in reference to something that is perpendicular to a major axis or direction. With reference to the vertical direction of the gravity forces, wind, earthquakes, and horizontally directed soil pressures are called lateral effects.

Lateral pressure. Horizontal soil pressure of two kinds:

1. *Active* lateral pressure is that exerted by a retained soil upon the retaining structure.
2. *Passive* lateral pressure is that exerted by soil against an object that is attempting to move in a horizontal direction.

Let-in bracing. Diagonal boards nailed to studs to provide trussed bracing in the wall plane. In order not to interfere with the surfacing materials of the wall, they are usually notched in, or let in, to the stud faces.

Live load. See *Load*.

Load. The active force (or combination of forces) exerted upon a structure. *Dead load* is permanent load due to gravity, which includes the weight of the structure itself. *Live load* is any load component that is not permanent, including those due to wind, seismic effects, temperature effects, and gravity forces that are not permanent.

Mass. The dynamic property of an object that causes it to resist changes in its state of motion. This resistance is called *inertia*. The magnitude of the mass per unit volume of the object is called its *density*. Dynamic force is defined by $F = ma$, or force equals mass times acceleration. Weight is defined as the force produced by the acceleration of gravity; thus $W = mg$.

Moment-resisting space frame. A vertical load carrying space frame in which the members and joints are capable of resisting forces primarily by flexure (*UBC* definition).

Natural period. See *Period*.

Normal. 1. The ordinary, usual, unmodified state of something. 2. Perpendicular, such as pressure normal to a surface, stress normal to a cross section, and so on.

Occupancy. In building code language refers to the use of a building as a residence, school, office, and so on.

Occupancy importance factor (I). *UBC* term used in the basic equation for seismic force: $V = ZIKCSW$. Accounts for possible increased concern for certain occupancies.

Overturn. The toppling, or tipping over, effect of lateral loads.

Parapet. The extension of a wall plane or the roof edge facing above the roof level.

Pedestal. A short pier or upright compression member. Is actually a short column with a ratio of unsupported height to least lateral dimension of three or less.

Period (of vibration.) The total elapsed time for one full cycle of vibration. For an elastic structure in simple, single-mode vibration, the period is a constant (called the *natural* or *fundamental period*) and is independent of the magnitude of the amplitude, of the number of cycles, and of most damping or resonance effects. See *Vibration*.

Peripheral bracing. Vertical elements of a lateral bracing system located at the building perimeter.

Pier. 1. A short, stocky column with height not greater than three times its least lateral dimension. The *UBC* defines a masonry wall as a pier if its plan length is less than three times the wall thickness. 2. A deep foundation element that is placed in an excavation rather than being driven as a pile. Although it actually refers to a particular method of excavation, the term *caisson* is also commonly used to describe a pier foundation.

Pile. A deep foundation element, consisting of a linear, shaftlike member that is placed by being driven dynamically into the ground. *Friction piles* develop resistance to both downward load and upward (pullout) load through friction between the soil and the surface of the pile shaft. *End-bearing piles* are driven so that their ends are seated in low-lying strata of rock or very hard soil.

Plastic hinge. Region where ultimate moment strength of a member may be developed and maintained with corresponding significant inelastic rotation as a result of ductile yielding of steel.

Positive anchorage. See *Anchorage*.

Pounding. See *Battering*.

Pressure. A force distributed over, and normal to, a surface.

Relative stiffness. See *Stiffness*.

Reserve energy. Energy a ductile system is capable of absorbing by plastic strains.

Resonance. See *Vibration*.

Retaining wall. A structure used to brace a vertical cut, or a change in elevation of the ground surface. The term is usually used to refer to a *cantilever retaining wall*, which is a freestanding structure consisting only of a wall and its footing, although basement walls also serve a retaining function.

Richter scale. A log-based measuring system for evaluation of the relative energy level of an earthquake at its center of origin.

Rigid bent. A two-dimensional (planar) rigid (moment-resisting) frame structure.

Rigid frame. Framed structure in which the joints between members are made to transmit moments between the ends of the connected members. Called a *bent* when the frame is planar and a *moment-resisting space frame* when the frame is three dimensional.

Risk. The degree of probability of loss due to some potential hazard. The risk of an earthquake in a particular geographic area is the basis for the Z factor in the *UBC* equation for seismic force: $V = ZIKCSW$.

Rotation. Motion in a circular path. Also used to describe a twisting, or torsional, effect. See *Torsion*.

Seismic. Pertaining to ground shock. See *Aseismic*.

Separation. Often used in structural design to denote situations in which parts of a structure are made to act independently. Partial separation refers to a controlled separation that allows for some interactions but permits independence for other actions, such as a connection that transmits vertical forces but not horizontal ones. The separation may be dimensionally controlled to allow for a specific amount of movement.

Shear. A force effect that is lateral (perpendicular) to the major axis of a structure, or one that involves a slipping effect, as opposed to a push–pull effect. Wind and earthquake forces are sometimes visualized as shear effects on a building because they are perpendicular to the major vertical (gravity) axis of the building.

Shear wall. A vertical diaphragm.

Site response factor (S). A *UBC* term used in the basic equation for seismic force: $V = ZIKCSW$. Accounts for the effect of the period of the ground mass under the building.

Space frame. An ambiguous term used variously to describe three-dimensional structures. The *UBC* uses a particular definition in Section 2312 in classifying structural systems.

Spectrum. In seismic analysis generally refers to the curve that describes the actual dynamic force effect on a structure as a function of variation in its fundamental period. Response spectra are the family of curves produced by various degrees of damping. This represents the basis for determining the *C* factor in the *UBC* equation for seismic force: $V = ZIKCSW$.

Stability. Refers to the inherent capability of a structure to develop force resistance as a property of its form, orientation, articulation of its parts, type of connections, methods of support, and so on. Is not directly related to quantified strength or stiffness, except when the actions involve the buckling of elements of the structure.

Static. The state that occurs when the velocity is zero; thus no motion is occurring. Is generally used to refer to situations in which no change is occurring.

Stiffness. In structures refers to resistance to deformation, as opposed to strength which refers to resistance to force. A lack of stiffness indicates a flexible structure. Relative stiffness usually refers to the comparative deformation of two or more structural elements that share a load.

Strain. Deformation resulting from stress. Is usually measured as a percentage of deformation, called *unit strain* or *unit deformation*, and is thus dimensionless.

Strength design. One of the two fundamental design techniques for assuring a margin of safety for a structure. *Stress design*, also called *working stress design*, is performed by analyzing stresses produced by the estimated actual usage loads, and assigning limits for the stresses that are below the ultimate capacity of the materials by some margin. *Strength design*, also called *ultimate strength design*, is performed by multiplying the actual loads by the desired factor of safety

(the universal average factor being two) and proceeding to design a structure that will have that load as its ultimate failure load.

Stress. The mechanism of force within the material of a structure; visualized as a pressure effect (tension or compression) or a shear effect on the surface of a unit of the material, and quantified in units of force per unit area. *Allowable, permissible*, or *working* stress refers to a stress limit that is used in stress design methods. *Ultimate* stress refers to the maximum stress that is developed just prior to failure of the material.

Stress–strain behavior. The relation of stress to strain in a material or a structure. Is usually visually represented by a stress-strain graph covering the range from no load to failure. Various aspects of the form of the graph define particular behavioral properties. A straight line indicates an elastic relationship; a curve indicates inelastic behavior. A sudden bend in the graph usually indicates a plastic strain or yield which results in some permanent deformation. The slope of the graph is defined as the modulus of elasticity of the material.

Surcharge. Vertical load applied at the ground surface or simply above the level of the bottom of a footing. The weight of soil above the bottom of the footing is surcharge for the footing.

Tiedown. See *Anchorage*.

Three-hinged structure. An arch, gabled rafter or rigid frame structure with two hinged end supports and a third, interior, pin at its peak. Forces on supports due to thermal change are avoided and the structure is statically determinate.

Torsion. Moment effect involving twisting or rotation that is in a plane perpendicular to the major axis of an element. Lateral loads produce torsion on a building when they tend to twist it about its vertical axis. This occurs when the centroid of the load does not coincide with the center of stiffness of the vertical elements of the lateral load-resisting structural system.

Ultimate strength. Usually used to refer to the maximum static force resistance of a structure at the time of failure. This limit is the basis for the so-called strength design methods, as compared to the stress design methods that use some established stress limit, called the design stress, working stress, permissible stress, and so on.

Uplift. Refers to a net upward force effect; may be due to wind suction, overturning moment, or upward vertical seismic acceleration.

Velocity. The time rate of a motion, also commonly called *speed*.

Vertical diaphragm. See *Diaphragm*. Also called a shear wall.

Vibration. The cyclic, rhythmic motion of a body such as a spring. Occurs when the body is displaced from some neutral position and seeks to restore itself to a state of equilibrium when released. In its pure form it occurs as a harmonic motion with a characteristic behavior described by the cosine form of the displacement–time graph of the motion. The magnitude of linear displacement from the neutral position is called the *amplitude*. The time elapsed for one full cycle of motion is called the *period*. The number of cycles occurring in one second is called the *frequency*. Effects that tend to reduce the amplitude of succeeding cycles are called *damping*. The increase of amplitude in successive cycles is called a *resonant effect*.

Wall. A vertical, planar building element. *Foundation* walls are those that are partly or totally below ground. *Bearing* walls are used to carry vertical loads in direct compression. *Grade* walls are those that are used to achieve the transition between the building that is above the ground and the foundations that are below it; grade is used to refer to the level of the ground surface at the edge of the building. (See also *Grade beam*.) *Shear* walls are those used to brace the building against horizontal forces due to wind or seismic shock. *Freestanding* walls are walls whose tops are not laterally braced. *Retaining* walls are walls that resist horizontal soil pressure.

Working stress. See *Stress*.

Working stress design. See *Strength design*.

Yield. See *Stress–strain behavior*.

Zone. Usually refers to a bounded area on a surface, such as the ground surface or the plan of a level of a building.

APPENDIX A

Dynamic Effects

A good lab course in physics should provide a reasonable understanding of the basic ideas and relationships involved in dynamic behavior. A better preparation is a course in engineering dynamics that focuses on the topics in an applied fashion, dealing directly with their applications in various engineering problems. The material in this section consists of a brief summary of basic concepts in dynamics that will be useful to those with a limited background and that will serve as a refresher for those who have studied the topics before.

A.1. KINEMATICS

The general field of dynamics may be divided into the areas of *kinetics* and *kinematics*. *Kinematics* deals exclusively with motion, that is, with time–displacement relationships and the geometry of movements. *Kinetics* adds the consideration of the forces that produce or resist motion.

Motion can be visualized in terms of a moving point, or in terms of the motion of a related set of points that constitute a body. The motion can be qualified geometrically and quantified dimensionally. In Figure A.1a the point is seen to move along a path (its geometric character) a particular distance. The distance traveled by the point between any two separate locations on its path is called *displacement*. The idea of motion is that this displacement occurs over time, and

the general mathematical expression for the time–displacement function is

$$s = f(t)$$

Velocity is defined as the rate of change of the displacement with respect to time. As an instantaneous value, the velocity is expressed as the ratio of an increment of displacement (ds) divided by the increment of time (dt) elapsed during the displacement. Using the calculus, the velocity is thus defined as

$$v = \frac{ds}{dt}$$

That is, the velocity is the first derivative of the displacement.

If the displacement occurs at a constant rate with respect to time, it is said to have *constant velocity*. In this case the velocity may be expressed more simply without the calculus as

$$v = \frac{\text{total displacement}}{\text{total elapsed time}}$$

When the velocity changes over time, its rate of change is called the *acceleration* (a). Thus, as an instantaneous change

$$a = \frac{dv}{dt} = \frac{d^2s}{dt^2}$$

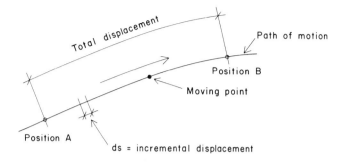

(a) Motion of a Point

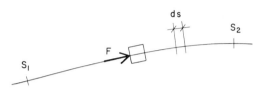

$$\text{Work} = \int_{S_1}^{S_2} F_t \ ds \quad (F \text{ variable with time})$$

$$= F(S_2 - S_1) \quad (F \text{ constant with time})$$

(b) Kinetics of a Moving Object

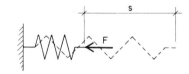

Potential (stored) energy:

$$E = F \cdot k \cdot s$$

$$k = \text{spring constant}$$

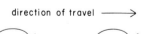

direction of travel ⟶

v_1 (at t_1)　　　v_2 (at t_2)

Kinetic energy:

$$E = \frac{1}{2} m (v_1^2 - v_2^2)$$

or, if $v_2 = 0$:

$$E = \frac{1}{2} m v_1^2$$

(c) Forms of Mechanical Energy

FIGURE A.1. Aspects of dynamic actions.

That is, the acceleration is the first derivative of the velocity or the second derivative of the displacement with respect to time.

Except for the simplest cases, the derivation of the equations of motion for an object generally requires the use of the calculus in the operation of these basic relationships. Once derived, however, motion equations are generally in algebraic form and can be used without the calculus for application to problems. An example is the set of equations that describe the motion of a free-falling object acted on by the earth's gravity field. Under idealized conditions (ignoring air friction, etc.) the distance of fall from a rest position will be

$$s = f(t) = 16.1t^2 \quad (s \text{ in ft}, \, t \text{ in sec})$$

This equation indicates that the rate of fall (the velocity) is not a constant but increases with the elapsed time, so that the velocity at any instant of time may be expressed as

$$v = \frac{ds}{dt} = \frac{d(16.1t^2)}{dt} = 32.2t \, (v \text{ in ft/sec})$$

and the acceleration as

$$a = \frac{dv}{dt} = \frac{d(32.2t)}{dt} = 32.2 \text{ ft/sec}^2$$

which is the acceleration of gravity.

Kinematics also includes the study of the various forms of motion: translation, rotation, plane motion, motion of deformable bodies, and so on. A study of the mechanics of motion is very useful in the visualization of the deformation of a structure by static as well as dynamic forces.

A.2. KINETICS

As stated previously, kinetics includes the additional consideration of the forces that cause motion. This means that in addition to the variables of displacement and time, we must consider the mass of the moving objects. From Newtonian physics the simple definition of mechanical force is

$$F = ma = \text{mass} \times \text{acceleration}$$

Mass is the measure of the property of inertia, which is what causes an object to resist change in its state of motion. The more common term for dealing with mass is *weight*, which is a force defined as

$$W = mg$$

where g is the constant acceleration of gravity (32.2 ft/sec^2).

Weight is literally a dynamic force, although it is the standard means of measurement of force in statics when the velocity is assumed to be zero. Thus, in static analysis we express forces simply as

$$F = W$$

and in dynamic analysis, when using weight as the measure of mass, we express force as

$$F = ma = \frac{W}{g} a$$

If a force moves an object, work is done. *Work* is defined as the product of the force multiplied by the displacement (distance traveled). If the force is constant during the displacement, work may be simply expressed as

$$w = Fs = \text{force} \times \text{total distance traveled}$$

If the force varies with time, the relationship is more generally expressed with the calculus as

$$w = \int_{s2}^{s1} F_t \, ds$$

indicating that the displacement is from position s_1 to position s_2, and the force varies in some manner with respect to time.

Figure A.1*b* illustrates these basic relationships. In dynamic analysis of structures the dynamic "load" is often translated into work units in which the distance traveled is actually the deformation of the structure.

Energy may be defined as the capacity to do work. Energy exists in various forms such as heat, mechanical, and chemical. For structural analysis the concern is with mechanical energy, which occurs in one of two forms. *Potential energy* is stored energy, such as that in a compressed spring or an elevated weight. Work is done when the spring is released or the weight is dropped. *Kinetic energy* is possessed by bodies in motion; work is required to change their state of motion, that is, to slow them down or speed them up. (See Fig. A.1*c*.)

In structural analysis energy is considered to be indestructible, that is, it cannot be destroyed, although it can be transferred or transformed. The potential energy in the compressed spring can be transferred into kinetic energy if the spring is used to propel an object. In a steam engine the chemical energy in the fuel is transformed into heat and then into pressure of the steam and finally into mechanical energy delivered as the engine's output.

An essential idea is that of the conservation of energy, which is a statement of its indestructibility in terms of input and output. This idea can be stated in terms of work by saying that the work done on an object is totally used and that it should therefore be equal to the work accomplished plus any losses due to heat, air friction, and so on. In structural analysis we make use of this concept by using a "work equilibrium" relationship similar to the static force equilibrium relationship. Just as all the forces must be in balance for static equilibrium, so the work input must equal the work output (plus losses) for "work equilibrium."

A.3. HARMONIC MOTION

A special kinematic problem of major concern in structural analysis for dynamic effects is that of *harmonic motion*. The two elements generally used to illustrate this type of motion are the swinging pendulum and the bouncing spring. Both the pendulum and the spring have a neutral position where they will remain at rest in static equilibrium. If one displaces either of them from this neutral position by pulling the pendulum sideways or compressing or stretching the spring, they will tend to move back to the neutral position. Instead of stopping at the neutral position, however, they will be carried past it by their momentum to a position of displacement in the opposite direction. This sets up a cyclic form of motion (swinging of the pendulum; bouncing of the spring) that has some basic characteristics.

Figure A.2*a* illustrates the typical motion of a bouncing spring. Using the calculus and the basic motion and force equations, the displacement–time relationship may be derived as

$$s = A \cos Bt$$

The cosine function produces the basic form of the graph, as shown in Figure A.2*b*. The maximum displacement from the neutral position is called the *amplitude*. The time elapsed for one full cycle is called the *period*. The number of full cycles in a given unit of time is called the *frequency* (usually expressed in cycles per second) and is equal to the inverse of the period. Every object subject to harmonic motion has a fundamental period (also called natural period), which is determined by its weight, stiffness, size, and so on.

Any influence that tends to reduce the amplitude in successive cycles is called a *damping effect*. Heat loss in friction, air resistance, and so on, are natural damping effects. Shock absorbers, counterbalances, cushion-

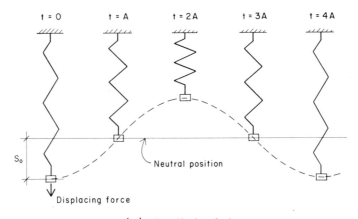

(a) The Moving Spring

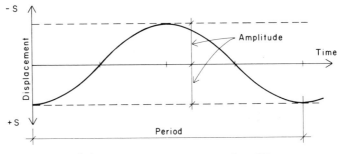

(b) Plot of the Equation: S = A cos BT

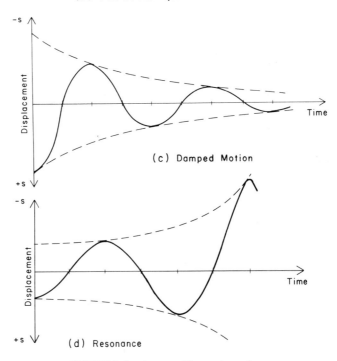

(c) Damped Motion

(d) Resonance

FIGURE A.2. Aspects of harmonic motion.

ing materials, and other devices can also be used to damp the amplitude. Figure A.2c shows the form of a damped harmonic motion, which is the normal form of most such motions, because perpetual motion is not possible without a continuous reapplication of the original displacing force.

Resonance is the effect produced when the displacing effort is itself harmonic with a cyclic nature that corresponds with the period of the impelled object. An example is someone bouncing on a diving board in rhythm with the board's fundamental period, thus causing a reinforcement, or amplification, of the board's free motion. This form of motion is illustrated in Figure A.2d. Unrestrained resonant effects can result in intolerable amplitudes, producing destruction or damage of the moving object or its supports. A balance of damping and resonant effects can sometimes produce a constant motion with a flat profile of the amplitude peaks.

Loaded structures tend to act like springs. Within the elastic stress range of the materials, they can be displaced from a neutral (unloaded) position and, when released, will go into a form of harmonic motion. The fundamental period of the structure as a whole, as well as the periods of its parts, are major properties that affect responses to dynamic loads.

A.4. DYNAMIC EFFECTS IN BUILDINGS

Load sources that involve motion, such as wind, earthquakes, walking people, moving vehicles, and vibrating heavy machinery, have the potential to cause dynamic effects on structures. Analyzing for their effects requires consideration of essential dynamic properties of the structure. These properties are determined by the size, weight, relative stiffness, fundamental period, type of support, and degree of elasticity of the materials

of the structure and by various damping influences that may be present.

Dynamic load sources deliver an energy load to the structure that may be in the form of an impact, such as that caused by the moving air bumping into the stationary building. In this case the energy load is derived from the kinetic energy of the moving air, which is a product of its mass and velocity. In the case of an earthquake, or the vibration of heavy machinery, the load source is not a force as such but rather something that induces motion of the structure, in which case the mass of the building is actually the load source.

An important point to note is that the effects of a dynamic load on a structure are determined by the structure's response as well as by the nature of the load. Thus the same dynamic load can produce different effects in different structures. Two buildings standing side by side can have significantly different responses to the same earthquake shock if they have major differences in their dynamic properties.

Dynamic effects on structures may be of several types. Some of the principal effects are the following:

Total energy load is the balance between the peak magnitude of the load and the maximum work required by the structure and is known as the *work equilibrium concept*. Work done to the structure by the load equals the work done by the structure in resisting the load.

Unstabilizing effects occur if the dynamic load produces a stability failure of the structure. Thus a freestanding wall may topple over, an unbraced post and beam system may collapse sideways, and so forth, because of the combined effects of gravity and the dynamic load.

Harmonic effects of various types may be set up in the structure, especially if the load source is cyclic in nature, such as the footsteps of marching troops. Earthquake motions are basically cyclic, in the form of vibration or shaking of the surface of the ground. Relations between these motions and the harmonic properties of the structure can result in various effects, such as the flutter of objects at a particular wind velocity, the resonant bouncing of floors, and the resonant reinforcing of the swaying of buildings during an earthquake.

Using up of the structure's energy capacity can occur if the energy of the load exceeds the limit for the structure. Actually, there are several degrees, or stages, of energy capacity, instead of a single limit. Four significant stages are the following:

1. The *resilience limit*, or the limit beyond which some form of permanent damage—however slight—may occur.
2. The *minor damage limit*, the damage being either relatively insignificant or easily repairable.
3. The *major damage limit*, short of total destruction but with loss of some minor elements. The structure as a whole remains intact, but some major repairs may be required to restore it to its original level of capacity.
4. The *toughness limit*, or the maximum, ultimate capacity represented by the destruction of the structure.

Failure under repeated loadings can result in some cases when structures progressively use up their dynamic resistance. The structures may successfully resist a single peak load of some dynamic effort, only to fail later under a similar, or even smaller, loading. This failure is usually due to the fact that the first loading used up some degree of structural failure, such as ductile yielding or brittle cracking, which absorbed enough energy to prevent total failure but was only a one time usable strength.

A major consideration in design for dynamic loads is what the response of the structure means to the building as a whole. Thus, although the structure may remain in-

tact, that may be only a minor accomplishment if there is significant damage to the building as a whole. A high-rise building may swing and sway in an earthquake without there being any significant damage to the structure, but if the occupants are tossed about, the ceilings fall, the windows shatter, the partitions and curtain walls collapse, the plumbing bursts, and the elevators derail, it can hardly be said that the building was adequately designed.

In many cases analysis and design for dynamic effects are not done by working directly with the dynamic relationships but simply by using recommendations and rules of thumb that have been established by experience. Some testing or theoretical analysis may have helped in deriving ideas or data, but much of what is used is based on the observations and records from previous disasters. Even when actual calculations are performed, they are mostly done with data and relationships that have been translated into simpler static terms—so-called equivalent static analysis and design. The reasons for this practice have to do frankly with the degree of complexity of dynamic analysis. Even with the use of programmable calculators or computers, the work is quite laborious in all but the simplest of situations.

A.5. EQUIVALENT STATIC EFFECTS

Use of equivalent static effects essentially permits simpler analysis and design by eliminating the complex procedures of dynamic analysis. To make this possible the load effects and the structure's responses must be translated into static terms.

For wind load the primary translation consists of converting the kinetic energy of the wind into an equivalent static pressure, which is then treated in a manner similar to that for a distributed gravity load. Additional considerations are made for various aerodynamic effects, such as ground surface drag, building shape, and suction, but these do not change the basic static nature of the work.

For earthquake effects the primary translation consists of establishing a hypothetical horizontal static force that is applied to the structure to simulate the effects of sideward motions during ground movements. This force is calculated as some percentage of the dead weight of the building, which is the actual source of the kinetic energy loading once the building is in motion—just as the weight of the pendulum and the spring keeps them moving after the initial displacement and release. The specific percentage used is determined by a number of factors, including some of the dynamic response characteristics of the structure.

An apparently lower safety factor is used when designing for the effects of wind and earthquake because an increase of one third is permitted in allowable stresses. This is actually not a matter of a less-safe design but is merely a way of compensating for the fact that one is actually adding static (gravity) effects and *equivalent* static effects. The total stresses thus calculated are really quite hypothetical because in reality one is adding

static strength effects to dynamic strength effects, in which case 2 + 2 does not necessarily make 4.

Regardless of the number of modifying factors and translations, there are some limits to the ability of an equivalent static analysis to account for dynamic behavior. Many effects of damping and resonance cannot be accounted for. The true energy capacity of the structure cannot be accurately measured in terms of the magnitudes of stresses and strains. There are some situations, therefore, in which a true dynamic analysis is desirable, whether it is performed by mathematics or by physical testing. These situations are actually quite rare, however. The vast majority of building designs present situations for which a great deal of experience exists. This experience permits generalizations on most occasions that the potential dynamic effects are really insignificant or that they will be adequately accounted for by design for gravity alone or with use of the equivalent static techniques.

Use of the seismic design criteria of the *UBC* (Ref. 1)—most of which is keyed to an analysis for equivalent static effects—is explained in detail in Section 4.4.

APPENDIX B

Investigation and Design of Reinforced Concrete—Working Stress Method

The following is a brief presentation of the formulas and procedures used in the working stress method. It is recommended that this method be used only for approximate designs for preliminary studies or for designs with low strength concrete (f'_c = 3000 psi or less) and low amounts of reinforcement (percent of steel of 1.0 or less).

B.1. FLEXURE—RECTANGULAR SECTION WITH TENSION REINFORCEMENT ONLY

Referring to Figure B.1, the following are defined:

b = the width of the concrete compression zone.

d = the effective depth of the section for stress analysis; from the centroid of the steel to the edge of the compression zone.

A_s = the cross-sectional area of the reinforcing.

p = the percentage of reinforcing, defined as

$$p = \frac{A_s}{bd}$$

n = the elastic ratio =

$$\frac{E \text{ of the steel reinforcing}}{E \text{ of the concrete}}.$$

kd = the height of the compression stress zone; used to locate the neutral axis of the stressed section; expressed as a percentage (k) of d.

jd = the internal moment arm between the net tension force and the net compression force; expressed as a percentage (j) of d.

f_c = the maximum compressive stress in the concrete.

f_s = the tensile stress in the reinforcing.

The compression force C may be expressed as the volume of the compression stress "wedge," as shown in the figure.

$$C = \tfrac{1}{2}(kd)(b)(f_c) = \tfrac{1}{2} kf_c bd$$

Using the compression force, the moment resistance of the section may be expressed as

$$M = Cjd = (\tfrac{1}{2} kf_c bd)(jd) = \tfrac{1}{2} kjf_c bd^2 \tag{1}$$

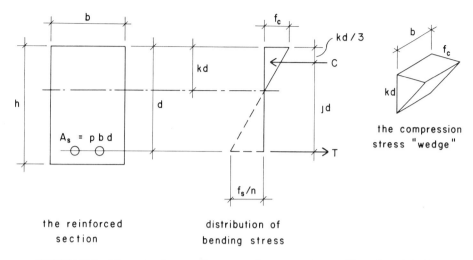

FIGURE B.1. Moment resistance of a rectangular concrete beam with tension reinforcing.

This may be used to derive an expression for the concrete stress:

$$f_c = \frac{2M}{kjbd^2} \qquad (2)$$

The resisting moment may also be expressed in terms of the steel and the steel stress as

$$M = Tjd = (A_s)(f_s)(jd)$$

This may be used for determination of the steel stress or for finding the required area of steel:

$$f_s = \frac{M}{A_s jd} \qquad (3)$$

$$A_s = \frac{M}{f_s jd} \qquad (4)$$

A useful reference is the so-called balanced section, which occurs when the exact amount of reinforcing used results in the simultaneous limiting stresses in the concrete and steel. The properties which establish this relationship may be expressed as follows:

balanced $k = \dfrac{1}{1 + f_s/nf_c} \qquad (5)$

$$j = 1 - \frac{k}{3} \qquad (6)$$

$$p = \frac{f_c k}{2f_s} \qquad (7)$$

$$M = Rbd^2 \qquad (8)$$

in which

$$R = \tfrac{1}{2} kjf_c \qquad (9)$$

(derived from formula 1). If the limiting compression stress in the concrete ($f_c = 0.45 f'_c$) and the limiting stress in the steel are entered in formula 5, the balanced section value for k may be found. Then the corresponding values for j, p, and R may be found. The balanced p may be used to determine the maximum amount of tensile reinforcing that may be used in a section without the addition of compressive reinforcing. If less tensile reinforcing is used, the moment will be limited by the steel stress, the maximum stress in the concrete will be below the limit of $0.45 f'_c$, the value

TABLE B.1 Balanced Section Properties for Rectangular Concrete Sections with Tension Reinforcing Only

| f_s | | f'_c | | n | k | j | p | R | |
ksi	MPa	ksi	MPa					k-in.	kN-m
16	110	2.0	13.79	11.3	0.389	0.870	0.0109	0.152	1045
		2.5	17.24	10.1	0.415	0.862	0.0146	0.201	1382
		3.0	20.68	9.2	0.437	0.854	0.0184	0.252	1733
		4.0	27.58	8.0	0.474	0.842	0.0266	0.359	2468
20	138	2.0	13.79	11.3	0.337	0.888	0.0076	0.135	928
		2.5	17.24	10.1	0.362	0.879	0.0102	0.179	1231
		3.0	20.68	9.2	0.383	0.872	0.0129	0.226	1554
		4.0	27.58	8.0	0.419	0.860	0.0188	0.324	2228
24	165	2.0	13.79	11.3	0.298	0.901	0.0056	0.121	832
		2.5	17.24	10.1	0.321	0.893	0.0075	0.161	1107
		3.0	20.68	9.2	0.341	0.886	0.0096	0.204	1403
		4.0	27.58	8.0	0.375	0.875	0.0141	0.295	2028

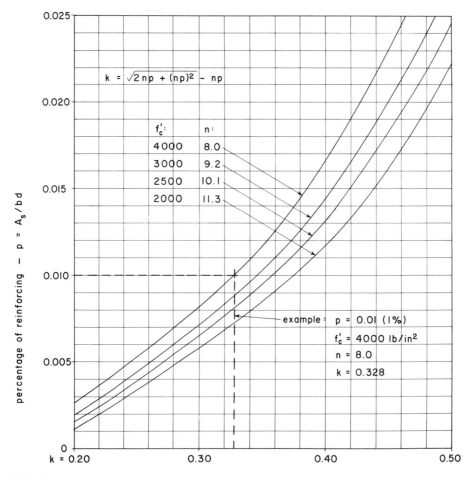

FIGURE B.2. k factors for rectangular concrete beams with tension reinforcing only—as a function of p and n.

of k will be slightly lower than the balanced value, and the value of j slightly higher than the balanced value. These relationships are useful in design for the determination of approximate requirements for cross sections.

Table B.1 gives the balanced section properties for various combinations of concrete strength and limiting steel stress. The values of n, k, j, and p are all without units. However, R must be expressed in particular units; the units used in the table are kip-inches (k-in.) and kilonewton-meters (kN-m).

When the area of steel used is less than the balanced p, the true value of k may be determined by the following formula:

$$k = \sqrt{2np - (np)^2} - np \qquad (10)$$

Figure B.2 may be used to find approximate k values for various combinations of p and n.

B.2. REINFORCED CONCRETE COLUMNS

The practicing structural designer customarily uses tables or a computer-aided procedure to determine the dimensions and reinforcing for concrete columns. The complexity of analytical formulas and the large number of variables make it impractical to perform design for a large number of columns solely by hand computation. The provisions relating to the design of columns in the 1983 ACI Code are quite different from those of the working stress design method in the 1963 Code. The current code does not permit design of columns by the working stress method, but it rather requires that the service load capacity of columns be determined as 40% of that computed by strength design procedures.

Due to the nature of most concrete structures, current design practices generally do not consider the possibility of a concrete column with axial compression alone. That is to say, the existence of some bending moment is always considered together with the axial force. Figure B.3a illustrates the nature of the so-called *interaction response* for a concrete column with a range of combinations of axial load plus bending moment. In general, the three basic ranges of this behavior are as follows:

1. *Large Axial Force, Minor Moment.* For this case, the moment has little effect, and the resistance to pure axial force is only negligibly reduced.

2. *Significant Values for Both Axial Force and Moment.* For this case, the analysis for design must include the full combined force effects, that is, the interaction of the axial force and the bending moment.

3. *Large Bending Moment, Minor Axial Force.* For this case, the column behaves essentially as a doubly reinforced (tension and compression reinforced) member, with its capacity for moment resistance affected only slightly by the axial force.

In Figure B.3a the solid line on the graph represents the true response of the column—a form of behavior verified by many load tests on laboratory specimens. The dashed line figure on the graph represents the generalization of the three types of response just described.

The terminal points of the interaction response—pure axial compression or pure bending moment (P_0 and M_0 on the graph)—may be reasonably easily determined. The interaction responses between these two limits require complex analyses, which are beyond the scope of this book.

Reinforced concrete columns for buildings generally fall into one of the following categories:

1. Square tied columns.

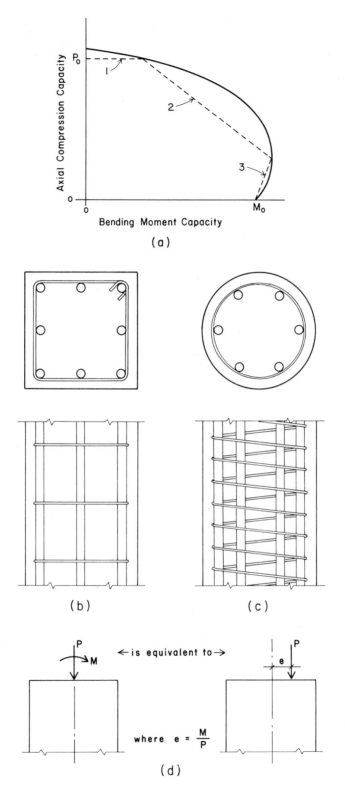

FIGURE B.3. Reinforced concrete columns: (*a*) form of the response to combined compression and bending; (*b*) tied column; (*c*) spiral column; (*d*) development of equivalent eccentricity.

272

2. Round spiral columns.

3. Oblong tied columns.

4. Columns of other geometries (hexagonal, L-shaped, T-shaped, etc.) with either ties or spirals.

In tied columns the longitudinal reinforcing is held in place by loop ties made of small-diameter reinforcing bars, commonly No. 3 or No. 4. Such a column is represented by the square section shown in Figure B.3b. This type of reinforcing can quite readily accommodate other geometries as well as the square. The design of such a column is discussed in Section B.3.

In spiral columns the longitudinal reinforcing is placed in a circle, with the whole group of bars enclosed by a continuous cylindrical spiral made from steel rod or large-diameter steel wire. Although this reinforcing system obviously works best with a round column section, it can be used also with other geometries. A round column of this type is shown in Figure B.3c.

Experience has shown the spiral column to be slightly stronger than an equivalent tied column with the same amount of concrete and reinforcing. For this reason, code provisions allow slightly more load on spiral columns. Spiral reinforcing tends to be expensive, however, and the round bar pattern does not always mesh well with other construction details in buildings. Thus tied columns are often favored where restrictions on the outer dimensions of the sections are not severe.

Code provisions and practical construction considerations place the following restrictions on column dimensions and choice of reinforcing.

Column Size. The current code does not contain limits for column dimensions. For practical reasons, the following limits are recommended. Rectangular tied columns should be limited to a minimum area of 100 in.^{2} and a side dimension of 10 in. if square

and 8 in. if oblong. Spiral columns should be limited to a minimum size of 12 in. if either round or square.

Reinforcing. Minimum bar size is No. 5. The minimum number of bars is four for tied columns, five for spiral columns. The minimum amount of area of steel is 1% of the gross column area. A maximum area of steel of 8% of the gross area is permitted, but bar spacing limitations make this difficult to achieve; 4% is a more practical limit. Section 10.8.4 of the 1983 ACI Code stipulates that for a compression member with a larger cross section than required by considerations of loading, a reduced effective area not less than one-half the total area may be used to determine minimum reinforcement and design strength.

Ties. Ties shall be at least No. 3 for bars No. 10 and smaller. No. 4 ties should be used for bars that are No. 11 and larger. Vertical spacing of ties shall be not more than 16 times the bar diameter, 48 times the tie diameter, or the least dimension of the column. Ties shall be arranged so that every corner and alternate longitudinal bar is held by the corner of a tie with an included angle of not greater than 135°, and no bar shall be farther than 6 in. clear from such a supported bar. Complete circular ties may be used for bars placed in a circular pattern.

Concrete Cover. A minimum of 1.5 in. is needed when the column surface is not exposed to weather or in contact with the ground; 2 in. should be used for formed surfaces exposed to the weather or in contact with ground; 3 in. are necessary if the concrete is cast against earth.

Spacing of Bars. Clear distance between bars shall not be less than 1.5 times the bar diameter, 1.33 times the maximum specified size for the coarse aggregate, or 1.5 in.

B.3. DESIGN OF TIED COLUMNS

In most building structures, concrete columns will sustain some computed bending moment in addition to the axial compression load (see Fig. B.3c). Even when a computed moment is not present, however, it is well to consider some amount of accidental eccentricity or other source of moment. It is recommended, therefore, that the maximum safe load be limited to that given for a minimum eccentricity of 10% of the column dimension.

Figure B.4 gives safe loads for a selected number of sizes of square tied columns. Loads are given for various degrees of eccentricity, which is a means for expressing axial load and bending moment combinations. The computed moment on the column is translated into an equivalent eccentric loading, as shown in Figure B.3d. Data for the curves were computed by using 40% of

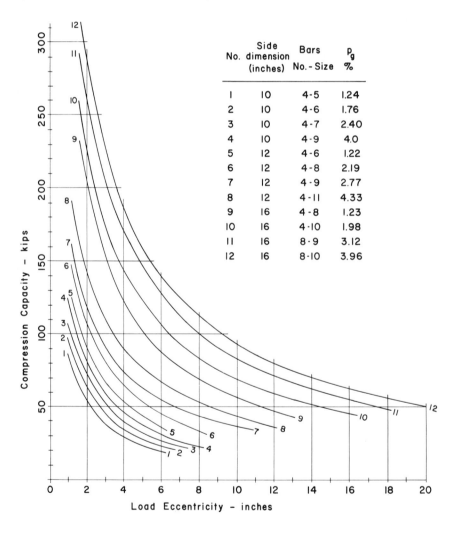

No.	Side dimension (inches)	Bars No. - Size	P_g %
1	10	4-5	1.24
2	10	4-6	1.76
3	10	4-7	2.40
4	10	4-9	4.0
5	12	4-6	1.22
6	12	4-8	2.19
7	12	4-9	2.77
8	12	4-11	4.33
9	16	4-8	1.23
10	16	4-10	1.98
11	16	8-9	3.12
12	16	8-10	3.96

FIGURE B.4.   Safe service loads for square tied columns with $f'_c = 4$ ksi and $f_y = 60$ ksi.

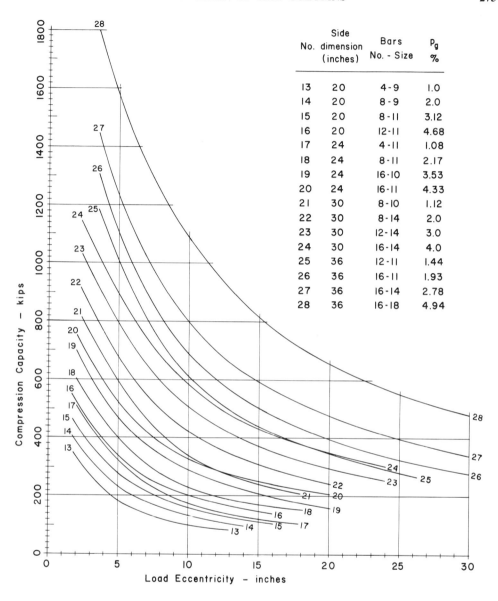

No.	Side dimension (inches)	Bars No. - Size	P_g %
13	20	4-9	1.0
14	20	8-9	2.0
15	20	8-11	3.12
16	20	12-11	4.68
17	24	4-11	1.08
18	24	8-11	2.17
19	24	16-10	3.53
20	24	16-11	4.33
21	30	8-10	1.12
22	30	8-14	2.0
23	30	12-14	3.0
24	30	16-14	4.0
25	36	12-11	1.44
26	36	16-11	1.93
27	36	16-14	2.78
28	36	16-18	4.94

FIGURE B.4. (*Continued*)

the load determined by strength design methods, as required by the 1983 ACI Code.

The curves in Figure B.4 do not begin at zero eccentricity. In addition, the requirement that only 40% of the load determined by strength methods be used places a rather high safety factor on the working stress method. To say the least, the Code does not favor the working stress method in this case.

The following examples illustrate the use of Figure B.4 for the design of tied columns.

Example 1. A column with $f_c' = 4$ ksi and steel with $f_y = 60$ ksi sustains an axial compression load of 400 k. Find the minimum practical column size if reinforcing is a maximum of 4% and the maximum size if reinforcing is a minimum of 1%.

Solution: Using Figure B.4b, we find from the sizes given:

> Minimum column is 20 in.^{2} with eight No. 9 (curve No. 14).
>
> Maximum capacity is 410 kips, p_g = 2.0%.
>
> Maximum size is 24 in.^{2} with four No. 11 (curve no. 17).
>
> Maximum capacity is 510 kips, p_g = 1.08%.

It should be apparent that it is possible to use an 18-in. or 19-in. column as the minimum size and to use a 22-in. or 23-in. column as the maximum size. Since these sizes are not given in the figure, we cannot verify them for certain without using strength design procedures.

Example 2. A square tied column with f'_c = 4 ksi and steel with f_y = 60 ksi sustains an axial load of 400 k and a bending moment of 200 k-ft. Determine the minimum size column and its reinforcing.

Solution: We first determine the equivalent eccentricity as shown in Figure B.3c. Thus

$$e = \frac{M}{P} = \frac{200 \times 12}{400} = 6 \text{ in.}$$

Then, from Figure B.4b, we find:

> Minimum size is 24 in. square with 16 No. 10 bars.
>
> Capacity at 6-in. eccentricity is 410 k.

Usually a number of possible combinations of reinforcing bars may be assembled to satisfy the steel area requirement for a given column. Aside from providing for the area, the number of bars must also work reasonably in the layout of the column. Figure B.5 shows a number of tied columns with various number of bars. When a column is small, the preferred choice is usually that of the simple four-bar layout, with one bar in each corner and a single peripheral tie. As the column gets larger, the distance between the corner bars gets larger, and it is best to use more bars so that the reinforcing is spread out around the column periphery. For a symmetrical layout and the simplest of tie layouts, the best choice is for numbers that are multiples of four, as shown in Figure B.5a. The number of additional ties required for these layouts depends on the size of the column and the considerations discussed in Section B.2.

An unsymmetrical bar arrangement is not necessarily bad, even though the column and its construction details are otherwise not oriented differently on the two axes. In situations where moments may be greater on one axis, the unsymmetrical layout is actually preferred; in fact, the column shape will also be more effective if it is unsymmetrical, as shown for the oblong shapes in Figure B.5c.

Round columns may be designed and built as spiral columns as described in Section B.2, or they may be developed as tied columns with the bars placed in a circle and held by a series of round circumferential ties. Because of the cost of spirals, it is often more economical to use the tied columns; thus they are often used unless the additional strength or other behavioral characteristics of the spiral column are required. In such cases, the column is usually designed as a square column using the square shape that can be included within the round form. It is thus possible to use a four-bar column for small-diameter, round column forms.

Figure B.6 gives safe loads for round columns that are designed as tied columns. Load values have been adapted from values determined by strength design methods. The curves in Figure B.6 are similar to those for the square columns in Figure B.4, and their use is similar to that demonstrated in Examples 1 and 2.

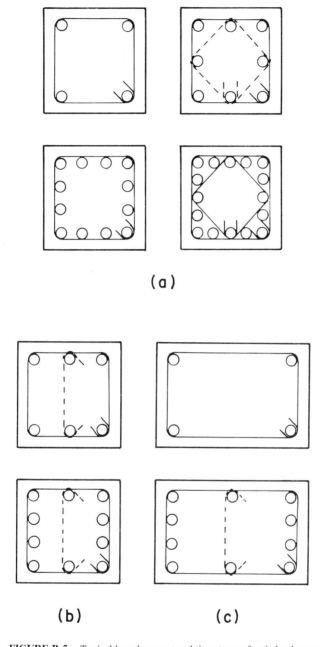

(a)

(b)   (c)

FIGURE B.5. Typical bar placement and tie patterns for tied columns.

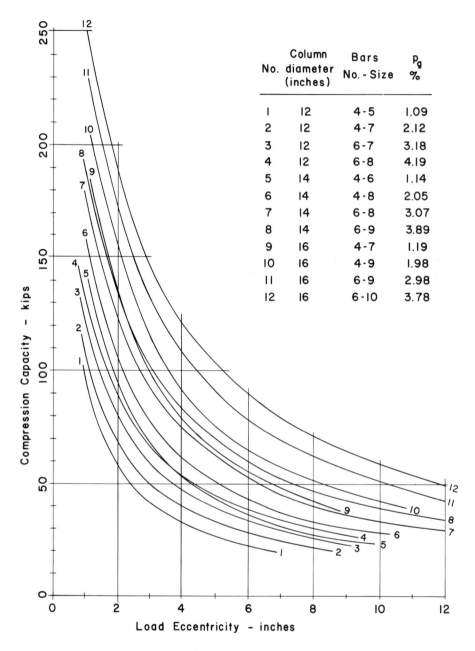

Column No.	diameter (inches)	Bars No. - Size	p_g %
1	12	4-5	1.09
2	12	4-7	2.12
3	12	6-7	3.18
4	12	6-8	4.19
5	14	4-6	1.14
6	14	4-8	2.05
7	14	6-8	3.07
8	14	6-9	3.89
9	16	4-7	1.19
10	16	4-9	1.98
11	16	6-9	2.98
12	16	6-10	3.78

FIGURE B.6. Safe service loads for round tied columns with $f'_c = 4$ ksi and $f_y = 60$ ksi.

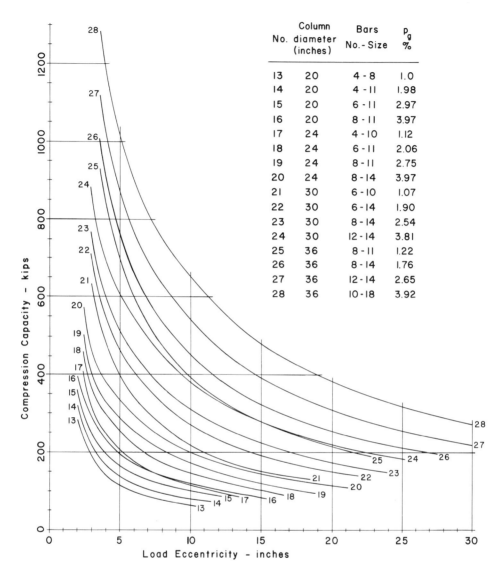

No.	Column diameter (inches)	Bars No. - Size	p_g %
13	20	4 - 8	1.0
14	20	4 - 11	1.98
15	20	6 - 11	2.97
16	20	8 - 11	3.97
17	24	4 - 10	1.12
18	24	6 - 11	2.06
19	24	8 - 11	2.75
20	24	8 - 14	3.97
21	30	6 - 10	1.07
22	30	6 - 14	1.90
23	30	8 - 14	2.54
24	30	12 - 14	3.81
25	36	8 - 11	1.22
26	36	8 - 14	1.76
27	36	12 - 14	2.65
28	36	10 - 18	3.92

FIGURE B.6. (*Continued*)

279

APPENDIX C

Building Code Requirements

The material in this section consists of selected reprints from the *Uniform Building Code* (Ref. 1) and the *City of Los Angeles Building Code* (Ref. 9). While most of this material is similar to that found in any building code, local practices and circumstances produce unique requirements and recommendations in most city, county, and state codes.

Excerpts from the *Uniform Building Code*, 1985 edition, are reprinted with permission of the publisher, International Conference of Building Officials, 5360 South Workmanmill Road, Whittier, CA 90601.

Excerpts from the *City of Los Angeles Building Code*, 1976 edition, are reprinted with permission of the publisher, Building News, Inc., 3055 Overland Avenue, Los Angeles, CA 90034.

Design Methods

Sec. 2303. (a) General. All buildings and portions thereof shall be designed and constructed to sustain, within the stress limitations specified in this code, all dead loads and all other loads specified in this chapter or elsewhere in this code. Impact loads shall be considered in the design of any structure where impact loads occur.

EXCEPTION: Unless otherwise required by the building official, buildings or portions thereof which are constructed in accordance with the conventional framing requirements specified in Chapter 25 of this code shall be deemed to meet the requirements of this section.

(b) Rationality. Any system or method of construction to be used shall be based on a rational analysis in accordance with well-established principles of mechanics. Such analysis shall result in a system which provides a complete load path capable of transferring all loads and forces from their point of origin to the load-resisting elements. The analysis shall include, but not be limited to, the following:

1. **Distribution of horizontal shear.** The total lateral force shall be distributed to the various vertical elements of the lateral force-resisting system in proportion to their rigidities considering the rigidity of the horizontal bracing system or diaphragm. Rigid elements that are assumed not to be part of the lateral force-resisting system may be incorporated into buildings, provided that their effect on the action of the system is considered and provided for in the design.

2. **Horizontal torsional moments.** Provision shall be made for the increased forces induced on resisting elements of the structural system resulting from torsion due to eccentricity between the center of application of the lateral forces and the center of rigidity of the lateral force-resisting system. Forces shall not be decreased due to torsional effects. For accidental torsion requirements for seismic design, see Section 2312 (e) 4.

3. **Stability against overturning.** Every building or structure shall be designed to resist the overturning effects caused by the lateral forces specified in this chapter. See Section 2311 (e) for wind and Section 2312 (f) for seismic.

4. **Anchorage.** Anchorage of the roof to walls and columns, and of walls and columns to foundations, shall be provided to resist the uplift and sliding forces which result from the application of the prescribed forces. For additional requirements for masonry or concrete walls, see Section 2310.

(c) Critical Distribution of Live Loads. Where structural members are arranged so as to create continuity, the loading conditions which would cause maximum shear and bending moments along the member shall be investigated.

(d) Stress Increases. All allowable stresses and soil-bearing values specified in this code for working stress design may be increased one-third when considering wind or earthquake forces either acting alone or when combined with vertical loads. No increase will be allowed for vertical loads acting alone.

(e) Load Factors. Load factors for ultimate strength design of concrete and plastic design of steel shall be as indicated in the appropriate chapters on the materials.

(f) Load Combinations. Every building component shall be provided with strength adequate to resist the most critical effect resulting from the following combination of loads (floor live load shall not be included where its inclusion results in lower stresses in the member under investigation):[1]

1. Dead plus floor live plus roof live (or snow).[2]
2. Dead plus floor live plus wind (or seismic).
3. Dead plus floor live plus wind plus snow/2.[2]
4. Dead plus floor live plus snow plus wind/2.[2]
5. Dead plus floor live plus snow[3] plus seismic.

Special Design

Sec. 2308. (a) General. In addition to the design loads specified in this chapter, the design of all structures shall consider the special loads set forth in Table No. 23-B and in this section.

(b) Retaining Walls. Retaining walls shall be designed to resist the lateral pressure of the retained material in accordance with accepted engineering practice. Walls retaining drained earth may be designed for pressure equivalent to that exerted by a fluid weighing not less than 30 pounds per cubic foot and having a depth equal to that of the retained earth. Any surcharge shall be in addition to the equivalent fluid pressure.

Retaining walls shall be designed to resist sliding or overturning by at least 1.5 times the lateral force or overturning moment.

Anchorage of Concrete or Masonry Walls

Sec. 2310. Concrete or masonry walls shall be anchored to all floors and roofs which provide lateral support for the wall. Such anchorage shall provide a positive direct connection capable of resisting the horizontal forces specified in this chapter or a minimum force of 200 pounds per lineal foot of wall, whichever is greater. Walls shall be designed to resist bending between anchors where the anchor spacing exceeds 4 feet. Required anchors in masonry walls of hollow units or cavity walls shall be embedded in a reinforced grouted structural element of the wall. See Sections 2312 (j) 2 C and 2312 (j) 3 A.

Wind Design

Sec. 2311. (a) General. Every building or structure and every portion thereof shall be designed and constructed to resist the wind effects determined in accordance with the requirements of this section. Wind shall be assumed to come from any horizontal direction. No reduction in wind pressure shall be taken for the shielding effect of adjacent structures.

Structures sensitive to dynamic effects, such as buildings with a height-width ratio greater than five, structures sensitive to wind-excited oscillations, such as vortex shedding or icing, and buildings over 400 feet in height, shall be, and any structure may be, designed in accordance with approved national standards.

(b) **Basic Wind Speed.** The minimum basic wind speed for determining design wind pressure shall be taken from Figure No. 4. Where terrain features and local records indicate that 50-year wind speeds at standard height are higher than those shown in Figure No. 4, these higher values shall be the minimum basic wind speeds.

(c) **Exposure.** An exposure shall be assigned at each site for which a building or structure is to be designed. Exposure C represents the most severe exposure and has terrain which is flat and generally open, extending one half mile or more from the site. Exposure B has terrain which has buildings, forest or surface irregularities 20 feet or more in height covering at least 20 percent of the area extending one mile or more from the site.

(d) **Design Wind Pressures.** Design wind pressures for structures or elements of structures shall be determined for any height in accordance with the following formula:

$$p = C_e C_q q_s I \dots\dots\dots\dots\dots\dots\dots(11\text{-}1)$$

WHERE:

p = Design wind pressure.

C_e = Combined height, exposure and gust factor coefficient as given in Table No. 23-G.

C_q = Pressure coefficient for the structure or portion of structure under consideration as given in Table No. 23-H.

q_s = Wind stagnation pressure at the standard height of 30 feet as set forth in Table No. 23-F.

I = Importance factor as set forth in Section 2311 (h).

(e) **Primary Frames and Systems.** The primary frames or load-resisting system of every structure shall be designed for the pressures calculated using Formula (11-1) and the pressure coefficients, C_q, of either Method 1 or Method 2. In addition, design of the overall structure and its primary load-resisting system shall conform to Section 2303.

The base overturning moment for the entire structure, or for any one of its individual primary lateral resisting elements, shall not exceed two thirds of the dead-load-resisting moment. The weight of earth superimposed over footings may be used to calculate the dead-load-resisting moment.

1. **Method 1 (Normal Force Method).** Method 1 shall be used for the design of gabled rigid frames and may be used for any structure. In the Normal Force Method, the wind pressures shall be assumed to act simultaneously normal to all exterior surfaces. For pressures on leeward walls, C_q shall be evaluated at the mean roof height.

2. **Method 2 (Projected Area Method).** Method 2 may be used for any structure less than 200 feet in height except those using gabled rigid frames. This method may be used in stability determinations for any structure less than 200 feet high. In the Projected Area Method, horizontal pressures shall be assumed to act upon the full vertical projected area of the structure, and the vertical pressures shall be assumed to act simultaneously upon the full horizontal projected area.

(f) **Elements and Components of Structures.** Design wind pressures for each element or component of a structure shall be determined from Formula (11-1) and C_q values from Table No. 23-H, and shall be applied perpendicular to the surface. For outward acting forces the value of C_e shall be obtained from Table No. 23-G based on the mean roof height and applied for the entire height of the structure. Each element or component shall be designed for the more severe of the following loadings:

1. The pressures determined using C_q values for elements and components acting over the entire tributary area of the element.

2. The pressures determined using C_q values for local areas at discontinuities such as corners, ridges and eaves. These local pressures shall be applied over a distance from a discontinuity of 10 feet or 0.1 times the least width of the structure, whichever is less.

The wind pressures from Subsections (e) and (f) need not be combined.

(g) **Miscellaneous Structures.** Greenhouses, lath houses, agricultural buildings or fences 12 feet or less in height shall be designed in accordance with Section 2311. However, three fourths of q_s, but not less than 10 pounds per square foot, may be substituted for q_s in Formula (11-1). Pressures on local areas at discontinuities need not be considered.

(h) **Importance Factor.** A factor of 1.15 shall be used for essential facilities which must be safe and usable for emergency purposes after a windstorm in order to preserve the health and safety of the general public. Such facilities shall include:

1. Hospitals and other medical facilities having surgery or emergency treatment areas.

2. Fire and police stations.

3. Municipal government disaster operation and communication centers deemed to be vital in emergencies.

4. Buildings where the primary occupancy is for assembly use for more than 300 people.

A factor of 1.0 shall be used for all other buildings.

Earthquake Regulations

Sec. 2312. (a) General. Every building or structure and every portion thereof shall be designed and constructed to resist stresses produced by lateral forces as provided in this section. Stresses shall be calculated as the effect of a force applied horizontally at each floor or roof level above the base. The force shall be assumed to come from any horizontal direction.

Structural concepts other than set forth in this section may be approved by the building official when evidence is submitted showing that equivalent ductility and energy absorption are provided.

Where prescribed wind loads produce higher stresses, such loads shall be used in lieu of the loads resulting from earthquake forces.

(b) **Definitions.** The following definitions apply only to the provisions of this section:

BASE OF STRUCTURE is the level at which the earthquake motions are assumed to be imparted to the structure or the level at which the structure as a dynamic vibrator is supported. This level does not necessarily coincide with the ground level.

BOX SYSTEM is a structural system without a complete vertical load-carrying space frame. In this system the required lateral forces are resisted by shear walls or braced frames as hereinafter defined.

BRACED FRAME is a truss system or its equivalent which is provided to resist lateral forces in the frame system and in which the members are subjected primarily to axial stresses.

DUCTILE MOMENT-RESISTING SPACE FRAME is a moment-resisting space frame complying with the requirements for a ductile moment-resisting space frame as given in Section 2312 (j).

ESSENTIAL FACILITIES—See Section 2312 (k).

LATERAL FORCE-RESISTING SYSTEM is that part of the structural system assigned to resist the lateral forces prescribed in Section 2312 (d).

MOMENT-RESISTING SPACE FRAME is a vertical load-carrying space frame in which the members and joints are capable of resisting forces primarily by flexure.

SHEAR WALL is a wall designed to resist lateral forces parallel to the wall.

SPACE FRAME is a three-dimensional structural system without bearing walls, composed of interconnected members laterally supported so as to function as a complete self-contained unit with or without the aid of horizontal diaphragms or floor-bracing systems.

VERTICAL LOAD-CARRYING SPACE FRAME is a space frame designed to carry all vertical loads.

(c) **Symbols and Notations.** The following symbols and notations apply only to the provisions of this section:

C = Numerical coefficient as specified in Section 2312 (d).

C_p = Numerical coefficient as specified in Section 2312 (g) and as set forth in Table No. 23-J.

D = The dimension of the structure, in feet, in a direction parallel to the applied forces.

δ_i = Deflection at level i relative to the base, due to applied lateral forces, Σf_i, for use in Formula (12-3).

F_i, F_n, F_x = Lateral force applied to level i, n or x, respectively.

F_p = Lateral forces on a part of the structure and in the direction under consideration.

F_t = That portion of V considered concentrated at the top of the structure in addition to F_n.

f_i = Distributed portion of a total lateral force at level i for use in Formula (12-3).

g = Acceleration due to gravity.

h_i, h_n, h_x = Height in feet above the base to level i, n or x, respectively.

I = Occupancy Importance Factor as set forth in Table No. 23-K.

K = Numerical coefficient as set forth in Table No. 23-I.

Level i

l = Level of the structure referred to by the subscript i.

i = 1 designates the first level above the base.

Level n = That level which is uppermost in the main portion of the structure.

Level x = That level which is under design consideration.

x = 1 designates the first level above the base.

N = The total number of stories above the base to level n.

S = Numerical coefficient for site-structure resonance.

T = Fundamental elastic period of vibration of the building or structure in seconds in the direction under consideration.

T_s = Characteristic site period.

V = The total lateral force or shear at the base.

W = The total dead load as defined in Section 2302, including the partition loading specified in Section 2304 (d) where applicable.

EXCEPTION: W shall be equal to the total dead load plus 25 percent of the floor live load in storage and warehouse occupancies. Where the design snow load is 30 psf or less, no part need be included in the value of W. Where the snow load is greater than 30 psf, the snow load shall be included; however, where the snow load duration warrants, the building official may allow the snow load to be reduced up to 75 percent.

w_i, w_x = That portion of W which is located at or is assigned to level i or x, respectively.

W_p = The weight of a portion of a structure or nonstructural component.

Z = Numerical coefficient dependent upon the zone as determined by Figures No. 1, No. 2 and No. 3 in this chapter. For locations in Zone No. 1, Z = 3/16. For locations in Zone No. 2, Z = 3/8. For locations in Zone No. 3, Z = 3/4. For locations in Zone No. 4, Z = 1.

(d) **Minimum Earthquake Forces for Structures.** Except as provided in Section 2312 (g) and (i), every structure shall be designed and constructed to resist minimum total lateral seismic forces assumed to act nonconcurrently in the direction of each of the main axes of the structure with the following formula:

$$V = ZIKCSW \quad \ldots\ldots\ldots\ldots\ldots(12\text{-}1)$$

The value of K shall be not less than that set forth in Table No. 23-I. The value of C and S are as indicated hereafter except that the product of CS need not exceed 0.14.

The value of C shall be determined in accordance with the following formula:

$$C = \frac{1}{15\sqrt{T}} \dots\dots (12-2)$$

The value of C need not exceed 0.12.

The period T shall be established using the structural properties and deformational characteristics of the resisting elements in a properly substantiated analysis such as the following formula:

$$T = 2\pi\sqrt{\left(\sum_{i=1}^{n} w_i\delta_i^2\right) \div \left(g\sum_{i=1}^{n} f_i\delta_i\right)} \dots\dots (12-3)$$

where the values of f_i represent any lateral force distributed approximately in accordance with the principles of Formulas (12-5), (12-6) and (12-7) or any other rational distribution. The elastic deflections, δ_i, shall be calculated using the applied lateral forces, f_i.

In the absence of a determination as indicated above, the value of T for buildings may be determined by the following formula:

$$T = \frac{0.05h_n}{\sqrt{D}} \dots\dots (12-3A)$$

Or in buildings in which the lateral force-resisting system consists of ductile moment-resisting space frames capable of resisting 100 percent of the required lateral forces and such system is not enclosed by or adjoined by more rigid elements tending to prevent the frame from resisting lateral forces:

$$T = 0.10N \dots\dots (12-3B)$$

The value of S shall be determined by one of the following methods, but shall be not less than 1.0.

Method A:

for $T/T_s = 1.0$ or less $\quad S = 1.0 + \frac{T}{T_s} - 0.5\left[\frac{T}{T_s}\right]^2 \dots\dots (12-4)$

for T/T_s greater than 1.0 $\quad S = 1.2 + 0.6\frac{T}{T_s} - 0.3\left[\frac{T}{T_s}\right]^2 \dots\dots (12-4A)$

WHERE:

T in Formulas (12-4) and (12-4A) shall be established by a properly substantiated analysis but T shall be not less than 0.3 second.

The range of values of T_s may be established from properly substantiated geotechnical data, in accordance with U.B.C. Standard No. 23-1, except that T_s shall not be taken as less than 0.5 second nor more than 2.5 seconds. T_s shall be that value within the range of site periods, as determined above, that is nearest to T.

When T_s is not properly established, the value of S shall be 1.5.

EXCEPTION: Where T has been established by a properly substantiated analysis and exceeds 2.5 seconds, the value of S may be determined by assuming a value of 2.5 seconds for T_s.

Method B:

The value of S may be determined in accordance with the following:

SOIL PROFILE COEFFICIENT

	Soil Profile Type		
	S_1	S_2	S_3
Factor S	1.0	1.2	1.5

Soil Profile Type S_1: Rock of any characteristic, either shale-like or crystalline in nature (such material may be characterized by a shear wave velocity greater than 2500 feet per second); or stiff soil conditions where the soil depth is less than 200 feet and the soil types overlying rock are stable deposits of sands, gravels or stiff clays.

Soil Profile Type S_2: Deep cohesionless or stiff clay soil conditions, including sites where the soil depth exceeds 200 feet and the soil types overlying rock are stable deposits of sands, gravels or stiff clays.

Soil Profile Type S_3: Soft to medium-stiff clays and sands, characterized by 30 feet or more of soft to medium-stiff clay with or without intervening layers of sand or other cohesionless soils.

In locations where the soil properties are not known in sufficient detail to determine the soil profile type or where the profile does not fit any of the three types, Soil Profile Type S_3 shall be used.

(e) **Distribution of Lateral Forces. 1. Structures having regular shapes or framing systems.** The total lateral force V shall be distributed over the height of the structure in accordance with Formulas (12-5), (12-6) and (12-7).

$$V = F_t + \sum_{i=1}^{n} F_i \dots\dots (12-5)$$

The concentrated force at the top shall be determined according to the following formula:

$$F_t = 0.07TV \dots\dots (12-6)$$

F_t need not exceed 0.25V and may be considered as 0 where T is 0.7 second or less. The remaining portion of the total base shear V shall be distributed over the height of the structure including level n according to the following formula:

$$F_x = \frac{(V - F_t) w_x h_x}{\sum\limits_{i=1}^{n} w_i h_i} \quad \dots \dots \dots \dots (12\text{-}7)$$

At each level designated as x, the force F_x shall be applied over the area of the building in accordance with the mass distribution on that level.

2. **Setbacks.** Buildings having setbacks wherein the plan dimension of the tower in each direction is at least 75 percent of the corresponding plan dimension of the lower part may be considered as uniform buildings without setbacks, provided other irregularities as defined in this section do not exist.

3. **Structures having irregular shapes or framing systems.** The distribution of the lateral forces in structures which have highly irregular shapes, large differences in lateral resistance or stiffness between adjacent stories, or other unusual structural features, shall be determined considering the dynamic characteristics of the structure.

4. **Accidental torsion.** In addition to the requirements of Section 2303 (b) 2, where the vertical resisting elements depend on diaphragm action for shear distribution at any level, the shear-resisting elements shall be capable of resisting a torsional moment assumed to be equivalent to the story shear acting with an eccentricity of not less than 5 percent of the maximum building dimension at that level.

(f) **Overturning.** At any level the incremental changes of the design overturning moment, in the story under consideration, shall be distributed to the various resisting elements in the same proportion as the distribution of the shears in the resisting system. Where other vertical members are provided which are capable of partially resisting the overturning moments, a redistribution may be made to these members if framing members of sufficient strength and stiffness to transmit the required loads are provided.

Where a vertical resisting element is discontinuous, the overturning moment carried by the lowest story of that element shall be carried down as loads to the foundation.

(g) **Lateral Force on Elements of Structures and Nonstructural Components.** Parts or portions of structures, nonstructural components and their anchorage to the main structural system shall be designed for lateral forces in accordance with the following formula:

$$F_p = ZIC_p W_p \quad \dots \dots \dots \dots (12\text{-}8)$$

The values of C_p are set forth in Table No. 23-J. The value of the I coefficient shall be the value used for the building.

EXCEPTIONS: 1. The value of I for panel connectors shall be as given in Section 2312 (j) 3 C.

2. The value of I for anchorage of machinery and equipment required for life safety systems shall be 1.5.

The distribution of these forces shall be according to the gravity loads pertaining thereto.

For applicable forces on diaphragms and connections for exterior panels, refer to Sections 2312 (j) 2 C and 2312 (j) 3 C.

(h) **Drift and Building Separations.** Lateral deflections or drift of a story relative to its adjacent stories shall not exceed 0.005 times the story height unless it can be demonstrated that greater drift can be tolerated. The displacement calculated from the application of the required lateral forces shall be multiplied by (1.0/K) to obtain the drift. The ratio (1.0/K) shall be not less than 1.0.

All portions of structures shall be designed and constructed to act as an integral unit in resisting horizontal forces unless separated structurally by a distance sufficient to avoid contact under deflection from seismic action or wind forces.

(i) **Alternate Determination and Distribution of Seismic Forces.** Nothing in Section 2312 shall be deemed to prohibit the submission of properly substantiated technical data for establishing the lateral forces and distribution by dynamic analyses. In such analyses the dynamic characteristics of the structure must be considered.

(j) **Structural Systems.** 1. **Ductility requirements.** A. All buildings designed with a horizontal force factor K = 0.67 or 0.80 shall have ductile moment-resisting space frames.

B. Buildings more than 160 feet in height shall have ductile moment-resisting space frames capable of resisting not less than 25 percent of the required seismic forces for the structure as a whole.

EXCEPTION: Buildings more than 160 feet in height in Seismic Zones Nos. 1 and 2 may have concrete shear walls designed in accordance with Section 2627 or braced frames designed in conformance with Section 2312 (j) 1 G of this code in lieu of a ductile moment-resisting space frame, provided a K value of 1.00 or 1.33 is utilized in the design.

C. In Seismic Zones No. 2, No. 3 and No. 4 all concrete space frames required by design to be part of the lateral force-resisting system and all concrete frames located in the perimeter line of vertical support shall be ductile moment-resisting space frames.

EXCEPTION: Frames in the perimeter line of the vertical support of buildings designed with shear walls taking 100 percent of the design lateral forces need only conform with Section 2312 (j) 1 D.

D. In Seismic Zones No. 2, No. 3 and No. 4 all framing elements not required by design to be part of the lateral force-resisting system shall be investigated and shown to be adequate for vertical load-carrying capacity and induced moment due to 3/K times the distortions resulting from the code-required lateral forces. The rigidity of other elements shall be considered in accordance with Section 2303 (b) 1.

resist the forces determined in accordance with the following formula:

$$F_{px} = \frac{\displaystyle\sum_{i=x}^{n} F_i}{\displaystyle\sum_{i=x}^{n} w_i} w_{px} \quad \cdots\cdots\cdots\cdots\cdots (12\text{-}9)$$

WHERE:

F_i = the lateral force applied to level i.

w_i = the portion of W at level i.

w_{px} = the weight of the diaphragm and the elements tributary thereto at level x, including 25 percent of the floor live load in storage and warehouse occupancies.

The force F_{px} determined from Formula (12-9) need not exceed $0.30ZIw_{px}$. When the diaphragm is required to transfer lateral forces from the vertical resisting elements above the diaphragm to other vertical resisting elements below the diaphragm due to offsets in the placement of the elements or to changes in stiffness in the vertical elements, these forces shall be added to those determined from Formula (12-9).

However, in no case shall lateral force on the diaphragm be less than $0.14ZIw_{px}$.

Diaphragms supporting concrete or masonry walls shall have continuous ties between diaphragm chords to distribute, into the diaphragm, the anchorage forces specified in this chapter. Added chords may be used to form subdiaphragms to transmit the anchorage forces to the main cross ties. Diaphragm deformations shall be considered in the design of the supported walls. See Section 2312 (j) for special anchorage requirements of wood diaphragms.

3. **Special requirements. A. Wood diaphragms providing lateral support for concrete or masonry walls.** Where wood diaphragms are used to laterally support concrete or masonry walls the anchorage shall conform to Section 2310. In Zones No. 2, No. 3 and No. 4 anchorage shall not be accomplished by use of toenails or nails subjected to withdrawal; nor shall wood framing be used in cross-grain bending or cross-grain tension.

B. **Pile caps and caissons.** Individual pile caps and caissons of every building or structure shall be interconnected by ties, each of which can carry by tension and compression a minimum horizontal force equal to 10 percent of the larger pile cap or caisson loading, unless it can be demonstrated that equivalent restraint can be provided by other approved methods.

C. **Exterior elements.** Precast or prefabricated nonbearing, nonshear wall panels or similar elements which are attached to or enclose the exterior shall be designed to resist the forces determined from Formula (12-8) and shall accommodate movements of the structure resulting from lateral forces or temperature changes. The concrete panels or other similar elements shall be supported by means of cast-in-place concrete or mechanical connections and fasteners in accordance with the following provisions:

E. **Moment-resisting space frames** and ductile moment-resisting space frames may be enclosed by or adjoined by more rigid elements which would tend to prevent the space frame from resisting lateral forces where it can be shown that the action or failure of the more rigid elements will not impair the vertical and lateral load-resisting ability of the space frame.

F. **Necessary ductility** for a ductile moment-resisting space frame shall be provided by a frame of structural steel with moment-resisting connections (complying with Section 2722 for buildings in Seismic Zones No. 3 and No. 4 or Section 2723 for buildings in Seismic Zones No. 1 and No. 2) or by a reinforced concrete frame (complying with Section 2625 for buildings).

EXCEPTION: Buildings with ductile moment-resisting space frames in Seismic Zones No. 1 and No. 2 having an importance factor I greater than 1.0 shall comply with Section 2625 or 2722.

G. **In Seismic Zones No. 3 and No. 4** and for buildings having an importance factor I greater than 1.0 located in Seismic Zone No. 2, all members in braced frames shall be designed for 1.25 times the force determined in accordance with Section 2312 (d). Connections shall be designed to develop the full capacity of the members or shall be based on the above forces without the one-third increase usually permitted for stresses resulting from earthquake forces.

EXCEPTION: Elevated water tanks as described in Item No. 5 of Table No. 23-I.

Compression struts and connections for cross bracing of elevated water tanks shall be designed to develop the yield capacity of the cross bracing.

Braced frames in buildings shall be composed of axially loaded bracing members of A36, A441, A500 Grades B and C, A501, A572 (Grades 42 and 50) or A588 structural steel, or reinforced concrete members conforming to the requirements of Section 2625.

H. **Reinforced concrete shear walls** for all buildings shall conform to the requirements of Section 2625.

I. **In structures** where $K = 0.67$ and $K = 0.80$, the special ductility requirements for structural steel or reinforced concrete specified in Section 2312 (j) 1 F, shall apply to all structural elements below the base which are required to transmit to the foundation the forces resulting from lateral loads.

2. **Design requirements. A. Minor alterations.** Minor structural alterations may be made in existing buildings and other structures, but the resistance to lateral forces shall be not less than before such alterations were made, unless the building as altered meets the requirements of this section.

B. **Reinforced masonry or concrete.** All elements within structures located in Seismic Zones No. 2, No. 3 and No. 4 which are of masonry or concrete shall be reinforced so as to qualify as reinforced masonry or concrete under the provisions of Chapters 24 and 26. Principal reinforcement in masonry shall be spaced 2 feet maximum on center in buildings using a moment-resisting space frame.

C. **Diaphragms.** Floor and roof diaphragms and collectors shall be designed to

TABLE NO. 23-F—WIND STAGNATION PRESSURE (q_s) AT STANDARD HEIGHT OF 30 FEET

Basic wind speed (mph)[1]	70	80	90	100	110	120	130
Pressure q_s (psf)	13	17	21	26	31	37	44

[1]Wind speed from Section 2311 (b).

TABLE NO. 23-G—COMBINED HEIGHT, EXPOSURE AND GUST FACTOR COEFFICIENT (C_e)

HEIGHT ABOVE AVERAGE LEVEL OF ADJOINING GROUND, IN FEET	EXPOSURE C	EXPOSURE B
0- 20	1.2	0.7
20- 40	1.3	0.8
40- 60	1.5	1.0
60-100	1.6	1.1
100-150	1.8	1.3
150-200	1.9	1.4
200-300	2.1	1.6
300-400	2.2	1.8

TABLE NO. 23-H—PRESSURE COEFFICIENTS (C_q)

STRUCTURE OR PART THEREOF	DESCRIPTION	C_q FACTOR
1. Primary frames and systems	Method 1 (Normal Force Method)	
	Windward wall	0.8 inward
	Leeward wall	0.5 outward
	Leeward roof or flat roof	0.7 outward
	Windward roof	
	Slope<9:12	0.7 outward
	Slope 9:12 to 12:12	0.4 inward
	Slope >12:12	0.7 inward
	Wind parallel to ridge	
	Enclosed structures	0.7 outward
	Open structures[1]	1.2 outward
	Method 2 (Projected Area Method)	
	On vertical projected area	
	Structures 40 feet or less in height	1.3 horizontal any direction
	Structures over 40 feet in height	1.4 horizontal any direction
	On horizontal projected area	
	Enclosed structure	0.7 upward
	Open structure[1]	1.2 upward

Connections and panel joints shall allow for a relative movement between stories of not less than two times story drift caused by wind or ($3.0/K$) times the calculated elastic story displacement caused by required seismic forces, or $1/2$ inch, whichever is greater. Connections to permit movement in the plane of the panel for story drift shall be properly designed sliding connections using slotted or oversized holes or may be connections which permit movement by bending of steel or other connections providing equivalent sliding and ductility capacity.

Bodies of connectors shall have sufficient ductility and rotation capacity so as to preclude fracture of the concrete or brittle failures at or near welds.

The body of the connector shall be designed for one and one-third times the force determined by Formula (12-8). Fasteners attaching the connector to the panel or the structure such as bolts, inserts, welds, dowels, etc., shall be designed to ensure ductile behavior of the connector or shall be designed for four times the load determined from Formula (12-8).

Fasteners embedded in concrete shall be attached to or hooked around reinforcing steel or otherwise terminated so as to effectively transfer forces to the reinforcing steel.

The value of the coefficient I shall be 1.0 for the entire connector assembly in Formula (12-8).

(k) **Essential Facilities.** Essential facilities are those structures or buildings which must be safe and usable for emergency purposes after an earthquake in order to preserve the health and safety of the general public. Such facilities shall include but not be limited to:

1. Hospitals and other medical facilities having surgery or emergency treatment areas.

2. Fire and police stations.

3. Municipal government disaster operation and communication centers deemed to be vital in emergencies.

The design and detailing of equipment which must remain in place and be functional following a major earthquake shall be based upon the requirements of Section 2312 (g) and Table No. 23-J. In addition, their design and detailing shall consider effects induced by structure drifts of not less than ($2.0/K$) times the story drift caused by required seismic forces nor less than the story drift caused by wind. Special consideration shall also be given to relative movements at separation joints.

(l) **Earthquake-recording Instrumentations.** For earthquake-recording instrumentations see Appendix, Chapter 23, Division II.

Footnotes – Table No. 23-H:

[1]A structure with more than 30 percent of any one side open shall be considered an open structure. Nonimpact-resistant glazing shall be considered as an opening.

[2]Local pressures shall apply over a distance from the discontinuity of 10 feet or 0.1 times the least width of the structure, whichever is smaller.

[3]The design wind forces shall be calculated based on the area of all exposed members and elements projected on a vertical plane normal to the wind direction. The forces shall be assumed to act parallel to the wind direction.

TABLE NO. 23-I—HORIZONTAL FORCE FACTOR K FOR BUILDINGS OR OTHER STRUCTURES[1]

TYPE OR ARRANGEMENT OF RESISTING ELEMENTS	VALUE[2] OF K
1. All building framing systems except as hereinafter classified	1.00
2. Buildings with a box system as specified in Section 2312 (b) EXCEPTION: Buildings not more than three stories in height with stud wall framing and using plywood horizontal diaphragms and plywood vertical shear panels for the lateral force system may use $K = 1.0$.	1.33
3. Buildings with a dual bracing system consisting of a ductile moment-resisting space frame and shear walls or braced frames using the following design criteria: a. The frames and shear walls or braced frames shall resist the total lateral force in accordance with their relative rigidities considering the interaction of the shear walls and frames b. The shear walls or braced frames acting independently of the ductile moment-resisting portions of the space frame shall resist the total required lateral forces c. The ductile moment-resisting space frame shall have the capacity to resist not less than 25 percent of the required lateral force	0.80
4. Buildings with a ductile moment-resisting space frame designed in accordance with the following criteria: The ductile moment-resisting space frame shall have the capacity to resist the total required lateral force	0.67
5. Elevated tanks plus full contents, on four or more cross-braced legs and not supported by a building	2.5[3]
6. Structures other than buildings and other than those set forth in Table No. 23-J	2.00

[1]Where wind load as specified in Section 2311 would produce higher stresses, this load shall be used in lieu of the loads resulting from earthquake forces.

[2]See Figures Nos. 1, 2 and 3 in this chapter and definition of Z as specified in Section 2312 (c).

[3]The minimum value of KC shall be 0.12 and the maximum value of KC need not exceed 0.25

Elevated tanks which are supported by buildings or do not conform to type or arrangement of supporting elements as described above shall be designed in accordance with Section 2312 (g) using $C_p = .3$.

TABLE NO. 23-H—PRESSURE COEFFICIENTS (C_q)—(Continued)

STRUCTURE OR PART THEREOF	DESCRIPTION	C_q FACTOR
2. Elements and components	Wall elements	
	All structures	1.2 inward
	Enclosed structures	1.1 outward
	Open structures	1.6 outward
	Parapets	1.3 inward or outward
	Roof elements	
	Enclosed structures	
	Slope<9:12	1.1 outward
	Slope 9:12 to 12:12	1.1 outward or inward
	Slope>12:12	1.1 outward or inward 0.8 inward
	Open structures[1]	
	Slope<9:12	1.6 outward
	Slope 9:12 to 12:12	1.6 outward or inward 0.8 inward
	Slope>12:12	1.6 outward or inward 1.1 inward
3. Local areas at discontinuities[2]	Wall corners	2.0 outward
	Canopies or overhangs at eaves or rakes	2.8 upward
	Roof ridges at ends of buildings or eaves and roof edges at building corners	3.0 upward
	Eaves or rakes without overhangs away from building corners and ridges away from ends of building	2.0 upward
	Cladding connections Add 0.5 to outward or upward C_q for appropriate location	
4. Chimneys, tanks and solid towers	Square or rectangular	1.4 any direction
	Hexagonal or octagonal	1.1 any direction
	Round or elliptical	0.8 any direction
5. Open-frame towers[3] Rectangular		2.0 any direction
Triangular		1.8 any direction
6. Signs, flagpoles, lightpoles, minor structures		1.4 any direction

Where a number of storage rack units are interconnected so there are a minimum of four vertical elements in each direction on each column line designed to resist horizontal forces, the design coefficients may be as for a building with K values from Table No. 23-J, $CS = 0.2$ for use in the formula $V = ZIKCSW$ and W equal to the total dead load plus 50 percent of the rack-rated capacity. Where the design and rack configurations are in accordance with this paragraph, the design provisions in U.B.C. Standard No. 27-11 do not apply.

[3]For flexible and flexibly mounted equipment and machinery, the appropriate values of C_p shall be determined with consideration given to both the dynamic properties of the equipment and machinery and to the building or structure in which it is placed but shall be not less than the listed values. The design of the equipment and machinery and their anchorage is an integral part of the design and specification of such equipment and machinery.

For essential facilities and life safety systems, the design and detailing of equipment which must remain in place and be functional following a major earthquake shall consider drifts in accordance with Section 2312 (k).

[4]Ceiling weight shall include all light fixtures and other equipment which is laterally supported by the ceiling. For purposes of determining the lateral force, a ceiling weight of not less than 4 pounds per square foot shall be used.

[5]The force shall be resisted by positive anchorage and not by friction.

[6]See also Section 2309 (b) for minimum load and deflection criteria for interior partitions.

[7]Does not apply to ceilings constructed of lath and plaster or gypsum board screw or nail attached to suspended members that support a ceiling at one level extending from wall to wall.

[8]W_p for access floor systems shall be the dead load of the access floor system plus 25 percent of the floor live load and a 10 psf partition load.

TABLE NO. 23-K—VALUES FOR OCCUPANCY IMPORTANCE FACTOR I

TYPE OF OCCUPANCY	I
Essential facilities[1]	1.5
Any building where the primary occupancy is for assembly use for more than 300 persons (in one room)	1.25
All others	1.0

[1]See Section 2312 (k) for definition and additional requirements for essential facilities.

TABLE NO. 23-J—HORIZONTAL FORCE FACTOR C_p FOR ELEMENTS OF STRUCTURES AND NONSTRUCTURAL COMPONENTS

PART OR PORTION OF BUILDINGS	DIRECTION OF HORIZONTAL FORCE	VALUE OF C_p[1]
1. Exterior bearing and nonbearing walls, interior bearing walls and partitions, interior nonbearing walls and partitions—see also Section 2312 (j) 3 C. Masonry or concrete fences over 6 feet high	Normal to flat surface	0.3[6]
2. Cantilever elements: a. Parapets	Normal to flat surfaces	0.8
b. Chimneys or stacks	Any direction	0.8
3. Exterior and interior ornamentations and appendages	Any direction	0.8
4. When connected to, part of, or housed within a building: a. Penthouses, anchorage and supports for chimneys, stacks and tanks, including contents[3] b. Storage racks with upper storage level at more than 8 feet in height, plus contents[2] c. All equipment or machinery[3] d. Fire sprinkler system	Any direction	0.3
e. Supports and bracing, equipment racks and piping for hazardous production material		0.45
5. Suspended ceiling framing systems (applies to Seismic Zones Nos. 2, 3 and 4 only)—see also Section 4701 (e)	Any direction	0.3[4,7]
6. Connections for prefabricated structural elements other than walls, with force applied at center of gravity of assembly	Any direction	0.3[5]
7. Access floor systems	Any direction	0.3[8]

[1]C_p for elements laterally self-supported only at the ground level may be two thirds of value shown.

[2]W_p for storage racks shall be the weight of the racks plus contents. The value of C_p for racks over two storage support levels in height shall be 0.24 for the levels below the top two levels. In lieu of the tabulated values, steel storage racks may be designed in accordance with U.B.C. Standard No. 27-11.

(Continued)

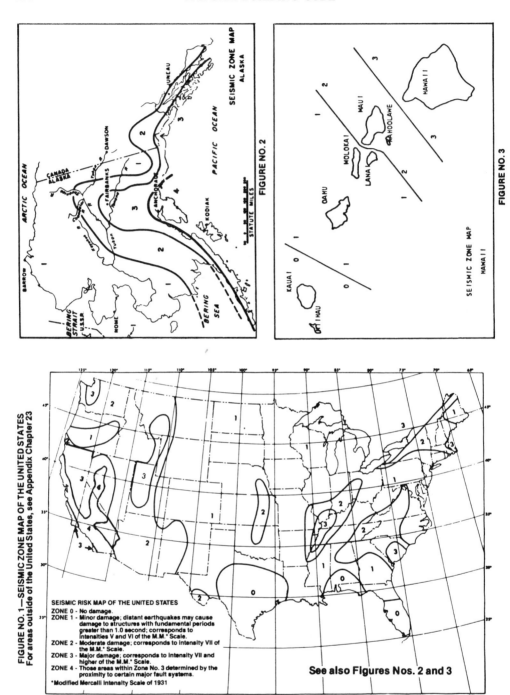

FIGURE NO. 2

FIGURE NO. 3

FIGURE NO. 1—SEISMIC ZONE MAP OF THE UNITED STATES
For areas outside of the United States, see Appendix Chapter 23

SEISMIC RISK MAP OF THE UNITED STATES
ZONE 0 - No damage.
ZONE 1 - Minor damage; distant earthquakes may cause
         damage to structures with fundamental periods
         greater than 1.0 second; corresponds to
         intensities V and VI of the M.M.* Scale.
ZONE 2 - Moderate damage; corresponds to intensity VII of
         the M.M.* Scale.
ZONE 3 - Major damage; corresponds to intensity VII and
         higher of the M.M.* Scale.
ZONE 4 - Those areas within Zone No. 3 determined by the
         proximity to certain major fault systems.
*Modified Mercalli Intensity Scale of 1931

See also Figures Nos. 2 and 3

TABLE NO. 24-E—ALLOWABLE SHEAR ON ANCHOR BOLTS[1] FOR CLAY AND CONCRETE MASONRY

DIAMETER (Inches)	TOTAL EMBEDMENT[2] (Inches)	ALLOWABLE SHEAR[3] (Lbs.)
1/4	4	270
3/8	4	410
1/2	4	550
5/8	4	750
3/4	5	1100
7/8	6	1500
1	7	1850[4]
1 1/8	8	2250[4]

[1]An anchor bolt is a bolt that has a right angle extension of at least three diameters. A standard machine bolt is acceptable.

[2]Of the total required embedment, a minimum of five bolt diameters must be perpendicular to the masonry surface.

[3]No reduction in values required for uninspected masonry.

[4]Applicable for units having a net area strength of 2500 psi or more.

Wood Diaphragms

Sec. 2513. (a) General. Lumber, plywood and particleboard diaphragms may be used to resist horizontal forces in horizontal and vertical distributing or resisting elements, provided the deflection in the plane of the diaphragm, as determined by calculations, tests or analogies drawn therefrom, does not exceed the permissible deflection of attached distributing or resisting elements. See U.B.C. Standard No. 25-9 for a method of calculating the deflection of a blocked plywood diaphragm.

Permissible deflection shall be that deflection up to which the diaphragm and any attached distributing or resisting element will maintain its structural integrity under assumed load conditions, i.e., continue to support assumed loads without danger to occupants of the structure.

Connections and anchorages capable of resisting the design forces shall be provided between the diaphragms and the resisting elements. Openings in diaphragms which materially affect their strength shall be fully detailed on the plans and shall have their edges adequately reinforced to transfer all shearing stresses.

Size and shape of diaphragms shall be limited as set forth in Table No. 25-I.

In buildings of wood frame construction where rotation is provided for, the depth of the diaphragm normal to the open side shall not exceed 25 feet nor two thirds the diaphragm width, whichever is the smaller depth. Straight sheathing shall not be permitted to resist shears in diaphragms acting in rotation.

EXCEPTIONS: 1. One-story, wood-framed structures with the depth normal to the open side not greater than 25 feet may have a depth equal to the width.

2. Where calculations show that diaphragm deflections can be tolerated, the depth normal to the open end may be increased to a depth-to-width ratio not greater than 11/2:1 for diagonal sheathing or 2:1 for special diagonal sheathed or plywood or particleboard diaphragms.

FIGURE NO. 4—BASIC WIND SPEEDS IN MILES PER HOUR

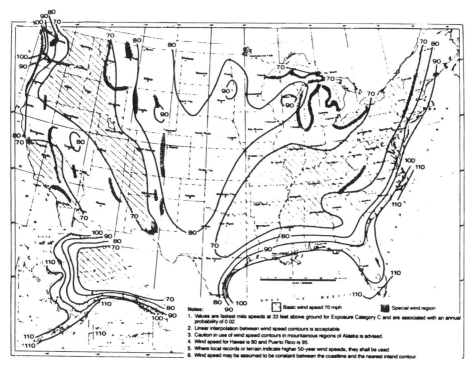

Notes:

1. Values are fastest mile speeds at 33 feet above ground for Exposure Category C and are associated with an annual probability of 0.02.
2. Linear interpolation between wind speed contours is acceptable.
3. Caution in use of wind speed contours in mountainous regions of Alaska is advised.
4. Wind speed for Hawaii is 80 and Puerto Rico is 95.
5. Where local records or terrain indicate higher 50-year wind speeds, they shall be used.
6. Wind speed may be assumed to be constant between the coastline and the nearest inland contour.

Basic wind speed 70 mph   Special wind region

In masonry or concrete buildings, lumber, plywood and particleboard diaphragms shall not be considered as transmitting lateral forces by rotation.

Diaphragm sheathing nails or other approved sheathing connectors shall be driven flush but shall not fracture the surface of the sheathing.

(b) **Diagonally Sheathed Diaphragms.** 1. **Conventional construction.** Such lumber diaphragms shall be made up of 1-inch nominal sheathing boards laid at an angle of approximately 45 degrees to supports. Sheathing boards shall be directly nailed to each intermediate bearing member with not less than two 8d nails for 1-inch by 6-inch nominal boards and three 8d nails for boards 8 inches or wider; and, in addition, three 8d nails and four 8d nails shall be used for 6-inch and 8-inch boards, respectively, at the diaphragm boundaries. End joints in adjacent boards shall be separated by at least one joist or stud space, and there shall be at least two boards between joints on the same support. Boundary members at edges of diaphragms shall be designed to resist direct tensile or compressive chord stresses and shall be adequately tied together at corners.

Conventional lumber diaphragms of Douglas fir-larch or southern pine may be used to resist shear due to wind or seismic forces not exceeding 300 pounds per lineal foot of width. The allowable strength shall be adjusted by the factors 0.82 and 0.65 where nails are used with sheathing and framing of Group III or IV wood species as listed in Table No. 25-17-J of U.B.C. Standard No. 25-17.

2. **Special construction.** Special diagonally sheathed diaphragms shall conform to conventional construction and, in addition, shall have all elements designed in conformance with the provisions of this code.

Each chord or portion thereof may be considered as a beam loaded with a uniform load per foot equal to 50 percent of the unit shear due to diaphragm action. The load shall be assumed as acting normal to the chord, in the plane of the diaphragm and either toward or away from the diaphragm. The span of the chord, or portion thereof, shall be the distance between structural members of the diaphragm, such as the joists, studs and blocking, which serve to transfer the assumed load to the sheathing.

Special diagonally sheathed diaphragms shall include conventional diaphragms sheathed with two layers of diagonal sheathing at 90 degrees to each other and on the same face of the supporting members.

Special diagonally sheathed diaphragms of Douglas fir-larch or southern pine may be used to resist shears due to wind or seismic loads, provided such shears do not stress the nails beyond their allowable safe lateral strength and do not exceed 600 pounds per lineal foot of width. The allowable strength shall be adjusted by the factors 0.82 and 0.65 where nails are used with sheathing and framing of Group III or IV wood species as listed in Table No. 25-17-J of U.B.C. Standard No. 25-17.

(c) **Plywood Diaphragms.** Horizontal and vertical diaphragms sheathed with plywood may be used to resist horizontal forces not exceeding those set forth in Table No. 25-J-1 for horizontal diaphragms and Table No. 25-K-1 for vertical diaphragms, or may be calculated by principles of mechanics without limitation by using values of nail strength and plywood shear values as specified elsewhere in this code. Plywood for horizontal diaphragms shall be as set forth in Table No. 25-S-1 and No. 25-S-2 for corresponding joist spacing and loads. Plywood in shear walls shall be at least 5/16 inch thick for studs spaced 16 inches on center and 3/8 inch thick where studs are spaced 24 inches on center.

Maximum spans for plywood subfloor underlayment shall be as set forth in Table No. 25-T-1. Plywood used for horizontal and vertical diaphragms shall conform to U.B.C. Standard No. 25-9.

All boundary members shall be proportioned and spliced where necessary to transmit direct stresses. Framing members shall be at least 2-inch nominal in the dimension to which the plywood is attached. In general, panel edges shall bear on the framing members and butt along their center lines. Nails shall be placed not less than 3/8 inch in from the panel edge, shall be spaced not more than 6 inches on center along panel edge bearings, and shall be firmly driven into the framing members. No unblocked panels less than 12 inches wide shall be used.

Where plywood is applied on both faces of a shear wall in accordance with Table No. 25-K-1, allowable shear for the wall may be taken as twice the tabulated shear for one side, except that where the shear capacities are not equal, the allowable shear shall be either the shear for the side with the higher capacity or twice the shear for the side with the lower capacity, whichever is greater.

(d) **Particleboard Diaphragms.** Horizontal and vertical diaphragms sheathed with particleboard may be used to resist horizontal forces not exceeding those set forth in Table No. 25-J-2 for horizontal diaphragms and Table No. 25-K-2 for vertical diaphragms.

All boundary members shall be proportioned and spliced where necessary to transmit direct stresses. Framing members shall be at least 2-inch nominal in the dimension to which the particleboard is attached. In general, panel edges shall bear on the framing members and butt along their center lines. Nails shall be placed not less than 3/8 inch in from the panel edge, shall be spaced not more than 6 inches on center along panel edge bearings, and shall be firmly driven into the framing members. No unblocked panels less than 12 inches wide shall be used.

Fiberboard Sheathing Diaphragms

Sec. 2514. Wood stud walls sheathed with fiberboard sheathing complying with U.B.C. Standard No. 25-24 may be used to resist horizontal forces not exceeding those set forth in Table No. 25-P. The fiberboard sheathing, 4 feet by 8 feet, shall be applied vertically to wood studs not less than 2-inch nominal in thickness spaced 16 inches on center. Nailing shown in Table No. 25-P shall be provided at the perimeter of the sheathing board and at intermediate studs. Blocking not less than 2-inch nominal in thickness shall be provided at horizontal joints within wall height exceeds length of sheathing panel, and sheathing shall be fastened to the blocking with nails sized as shown in Table No. 25-P spaced 3 inches on centers each side of joint. Nails shall be spaced not less than 3/8 inch from edges and ends of sheathing. Marginal studs of shear walls or shear-resisting elements shall be adequately anchored at top and bottom and designed to resist all forces. The maximum height-width ratio shall be 1 1/2:1.

Wood Combined with Masonry or Concrete

Sec. 2515. (a) **Dead Load.** Wood members shall not be used to permanently support the dead load of any masonry or concrete.

EXCEPTIONS: 1. Masonry or concrete nonstructural floor or roof surfacing not more than 4 inches thick may be supported by wood members.

2. Any structure may rest upon wood piles constructed in accordance with the requirements of Chapter 29.

Studs shall have full bearing on a plate or sill not less than 2 inches in thickness having a width not less than that of the wall studs.

3. **Bracing.** All exterior walls and main cross-stud partitions shall be effectively and thoroughly braced at each end, or as near thereto as possible, and at least every 25 feet of length, by one of the following methods:

A. Nominal 1-inch by 4-inch continuous diagonal braces let into top and bottom plates and intervening studs, placed at an angle not more than 60 degrees nor less than 45 degrees from the horizontal, and attached to the framing in conformance with Table No. 25-Q.

B. Wood boards of 5/8-inch net minimum thickness applied diagonally on studs spaced not over 24 inches on center.

C. Plywood sheathing with a thickness not less than 5/16 inch for 16-inch stud spacing and not less than 3/8 inch for 24-inch stud spacing in accordance with Tables No. 25-M-1 and No. 25-N-1.

D. Fiberboard sheathing 4-foot by 8-foot panels not less than 1/2 inch thick applied vertically on studs spaced not over 16 inches on center when installed in accordance with Section 2514 and Table No. 25-P.

E. Gypsum board (sheathing 1/2 inch thick by 4 feet wide, wallboard or veneer base) on studs spaced not over 24 inches on center and nailed at 7 inches on center with nails as required by Table No. 47-I.

F. Particleboard wall sheathing panels shall be in accordance with Table No. 25-N-2.

G. Portland cement plaster on studs spaced 16 inches on center installed in accordance with Table No. 47-I.

H. Hardboard panel siding when installed in accordance with Section 2516 (g) 6 and Table No. 25-O.

For methods B, C, D, E, F, G and H the braced panel must be at least 48 inches in width, covering three stud spaces where studs are spaced 16 inches apart and covering two stud spaces where studs are spaced 24 inches apart.

Solid sheathing of one of the materials specified in Items B through D and Item F, gypsum wallboard in Item E applied to supports at 16 inches on center, portland cement plaster in Item G, or hardboard panel siding in Item H, shall be applied to the exterior walls of the first story of all wood framed buildings three stories in height. In Seismic Zones Nos. 3 and 4 such braced wall sections shall be located at each end, or as near thereto as possible, and shall comprise at least 40 percent of the linear length of the wall.

Solid sheathing of one of the materials specified in Items B through D and Item F, gypsum wallboard in Item E applied to supports at 16 inches on center, portland cement plaster in Item G, or hardboard panel siding in Item H, shall be applied on either face of the exterior walls of the first story of all wood framed, two-story buildings and the second story of three-story buildings located in Seismic Zones No. 3 and No. 4. Braced wall sections shall be located at each end or as near thereto as possible and comprise at least 25 percent of the linear length of the wall.

All vertical joints of panel sheathing shall occur over studs. Horizontal joints shall occur over blocking equal in size to the studding except where waived by the installation requirements for the specific sheathing materials.

3. Masonry or concrete fireplace with a factory-built chimney conforming to Chapter 37 may be supported by wood framing.

4. Veneer of brick, concrete or stone applied as specified in Section 3006 (b) may be supported by approved treated wood foundations when the maximum height of veneer does not exceed 25 feet above the foundation. Such veneer used as an interior wall finish may also be supported on wood floors which are designed to support the additional load, and be designed to limit the deflection and shrinkage to 1/500 of the span of the supporting members.

(b) **Horizontal Force.** Wood members shall not be used to resist horizontal forces contributed by masonry or concrete construction in buildings over one story in height.

EXCEPTION: Wood floor and roof members may be used in horizontal trusses and diaphragms to resist horizontal forces imposed by wind, earthquake or earth pressure, provided such forces are not resisted by rotation of the truss or diaphragm.

2517

(g) **Wall Framing.** 1. **Size, height and spacing.** The size, height and spacing of studs shall be in accordance with Table No. 25-R-3 except that Utility grade studs shall not be spaced more than 16 inches on center, nor support more than a roof and ceiling, nor exceed 8 feet in height for exterior walls and load-bearing walls or 10 feet for interior nonload-bearing walls.

2. **Framing details.** Studs shall be placed with their wide dimension perpendicular to the wall. Not less than three studs shall be installed at each corner of an exterior wall.

EXCEPTION: At corners a third stud may be omitted through the use of wood spacers or backup cleats of 3/8-inch-thick plywood, 1-inch-thick lumber or other approved devices which will serve as an adequate backing for the attachment of facing materials.

Bearing and exterior wall studs shall be capped with double top plates installed to provide overlapping at corners and at intersections with other partitions. End joints in double top plates shall be offset at least 48 inches.

EXCEPTION: A single top plate may be used, provided the plate is adequately tied at joints, corners and intersecting walls by at least the equivalent of 3-inch by 6-inch by 0.036-inch-thick galvanized steel that is nailed to each wall or segment of wall by six 8d nails or equivalent, provided the rafters, joists or trusses are centered over the studs with a tolerance of no more than 1 inch.

When bearing studs are spaced at 24-inch intervals and top plates are less than two 2 by 6 or two 3 by 4 members and when the floor joists, floor trusses or roof trusses which they support are spaced at more than 16-inch intervals, such joists or trusses shall bear within 5 inches of the studs beneath or a third plate shall be installed.

Interior nonbearing partitions may be capped with a single top plate installed to provide overlapping at corners and at intersections with other walls and partitions. The plate shall be continuously tied at joints by solid blocking at least 16 inches in length and equal in size to the plate or by 1/8-inch by 1 1/2-inch metal ties with spliced sections fastened with two 16d nails on each side of the joint.

TABLE NO. 25-I—MAXIMUM DIAPHRAGM DIMENSION RATIOS

MATERIAL	HORIZONTAL DIAPHRAGMS Maximum Span-Width Ratios	VERTICAL DIAPHRAGMS Maximum Height-Width Ratios
1. Diagonal sheathing, conventional	3:1	2:1
2. Diagonal sheathing, special	4:1	3½:1
3. Plywood and particleboard, nailed all edges	4:1	3½:1
4. Plywood and particleboard, blocking omitted at intermediate joints	4:1	2:1

TABLE NO. 25-G—SAFE LATERAL STRENGTH AND REQUIRED PENETRATION OF BOX AND COMMON WIRE NAILS DRIVEN PERPENDICULAR TO GRAIN OF WOOD

SIZE OF NAIL	STANDARD LENGTH (Inches)	WIRE GAUGE	PENETRATION REQUIRED (Inches)	LOADS (Pounds)[1][2][3] Douglas Fir Larch or Southern Pine	Other Species
BOX NAILS					
6d	2	12½	1¼	51	
8d	2½	11½	1¼	63	
10d	3	10½	1½	76	See U.B.C. Standard No. 25-17
12d	3¼	10½	1½	76	
16d	3½	10	1½	82	
20d	4	9	1⅝	94	
30d	4½	9	1⅝	94	
40d	5	8	1¾	108	
COMMON NAILS					
6d	2	11½	1¼	63	
8d	2½	10¼	1½	78	
10d	3	9	1⅝	94	See U.B.C. Standard No. 25-17
12d	3¼	9	1⅝	94	
16d	3½	8	1¾	108	
20d	4	6	2⅛	139	
30d	4½	5	2¼	155	
40d	5	4	2½	176	
50d	5½	3	2¾	199	
60d	6	2	2⅞	223	

[1] The safe lateral strength values may be increased 25 percent where metal side plates are used.

[2] For wood diaphragm calculations these values may be increased 30 percent. (See U.B.C. Standard No. 25-17.)

[3] Tabulated values are on a normal load-duration basis and apply to joints made of seasoned lumber used in dry locations. See U.B.C. Standard No. 25-17 for other service conditions.

TABLE NO. 25-J-1—ALLOWABLE SHEAR IN POUNDS PER FOOT FOR HORIZONTAL PLYWOOD DIAPHRAGMS WITH FRAMING OF DOUGLAS FIR-LARCH OR SOUTHERN PINE[1]

PLYWOOD GRADE	Common Nail Size	Minimum Nominal Penetration in Framing (In inches)	Minimum Nominal Plywood Thickness (In inches)	Minimum Nominal Width of Framing Member (In inches)	BLOCKED DIAPHRAGMS — Nail spacing at diaphragm boundaries (all cases), at continuous panel edges parallel to load (Cases 3 and 4) and at all panel edges (Cases 5 and 6)				UNBLOCKED DIAPHRAGM — Nails spaced 6" max. at supported end	
					6	4	2½[2]	2[2]	Load perpendicular to unblocked edges and continuous panel joints (Case 1)	Other configurations (Cases 2, 3 & 4)
					Nail spacing at other plywood panel edges					
					6	6	4	3		
STRUCTURAL I	6d	1¼	⁵⁄₁₆	2 / 3	185 / 210	250 / 280	375 / 420	420 / 475	165 / 185	125 / 140
	8d	1½	⅜	2 / 3	270 / 300	360 / 400	530 / 600	600 / 675	240 / 265	180 / 200
	10d	1⅝	¹⁵⁄₃₂	2 / 3	320 / 360	425 / 480	640 / 720	730[2] / 820	285 / 320	215 / 240
C-D, C-C, STRUCTURAL II and other grades covered in U.B.C. Standard No. 25-9	6d	1¼	⁵⁄₁₆	2 / 3	170 / 190	225 / 250	335 / 380	380 / 430	150 / 170	110 / 125
			⅜	2 / 3	185 / 210	250 / 280	375 / 420	420 / 475	165 / 185	125 / 140
	8d	1½	⅜	2 / 3	240 / 270	320 / 360	480 / 540	545 / 610	215 / 240	160 / 180
			¹⁵⁄₃₂	2 / 3	270 / 300	360 / 400	530 / 600	600 / 675	240 / 265	180 / 200
	10d	1⅝	¹⁵⁄₃₂	2 / 3	290 / 325	385 / 430	575 / 650	655[2] / 735	255 / 290	190 / 215
			¹⁹⁄₃₂	2 / 3	320 / 360	425 / 480	640 / 720	730[2] / 820	285 / 320	215 / 240

[1]These values are for short-time loads due to wind or earthquake and must be reduced 25 percent for normal loading. Space nails 10 inches on center for floors and 12 inches on center for roofs along intermediate framing members.

Allowable shear values for nails in framing members of other species set forth in Table No. 25-17-J of U.B.C. Standards shall be calculated for all grades by multiplying the values for nails in STRUCTURAL I by the following factors: Group III, 0.82 and Group IV, 0.65.

[2]Framing shall be 3-inch nominal or wider and nails shall be staggered where nails are spaced 2 inches or 2½ inches on center, and where 10d nails having penetration into framing of more than 1⅝ inches are spaced 3 inches on center.

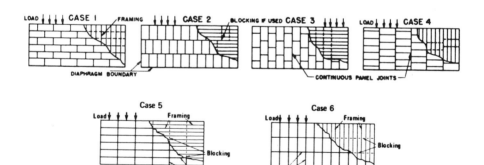

NOTE: Framing may be located in either direction for blocked diaphragms.

TABLE NO. 25-J-2—ALLOWABLE SHEAR IN POUNDS PER FOOT FOR HORIZONTAL PARTICLEBOARD DIAPHRAGMS WITH FRAMING OF DOUGLAS FIR-LARCH OR SOUTHERN PINE[1]

PANEL GRADE	COMMON NAIL SIZE	MINIMUM NAIL PENETRATION IN FRAMING (Inches)	MINIMUM NOMINAL PANEL THICKNESS (Inch)	MINIMUM NOMINAL WIDTH OF FRAMING MEMBER (Inches)	BLOCKED DIAPHRAGMS Nail Spacing (In.) at diaphragm boundaries (all cases), at continuous panel edges parallel to load (Cases 3 & 4), and at all panel edges (Cases 5 & 6) 6	4	2½[2]	2[2]	UNBLOCKED DIAPHRAGMS Nails Spaced 6″ max. at Supported Edges Case 1 (No unblocked edges or continuous joints parallel to load)	All other configurations (Cases 2, 3 4, 5 & 6)
					Nail Spacing (In.) at other panel edges (Cases 1, 2, 3 & 4) 6	6	4	3		
2-M-W	6d	1¼	⁵⁄₁₆	2	170	225	335	380	150	110
				3	190	250	380	430	170	125
			³⁄₈	2	185	250	375	420	165	125
				3	210	280	420	475	185	140
	8d	1½	³⁄₈	2	240	320	480	545	215	160
				3	270	360	540	610	240	180
			⁷⁄₁₆	2	255	340	505	575	230	170
				3	285	380	570	645	255	190
			½	2	270	360	530	600	240	180
				3	300	400	600	675	265	200
	10d	1⅝	½	2	290	385	575	655[2]	255	190
				3	325	430	650	735	290	215
			⅝	2	320	425	640	730[2]	285	215
				3	360	480	720	820	320	240
2-M-3	10d	1⅝	¾	2	320	425	640	730[2]	285	215
				3	360	480	720	820	320	240

[1]These values are for short-time loads due to wind or earthquake and must be reduced 25 percent for normal loading. Space nails 10 inches on center for floors and 12 inches on center for roofs along intermediate framing members.

Allowable shear values for nails in framing members of other species set forth in Table No. 25-17-J of U.B.C. Standards shall be calculated for all grades by multiplying the values for nails by the following factors: Group III, 0.82 and Group IV, 0.65.

[2]Framing shall be 3-inch nominal or wider and nails shall be staggered where nails are spaced 2 inches or 2½ inches on center, and where 10d nails having penetration into framing of more than 1⅝ inches are spaced 3 inches on center.

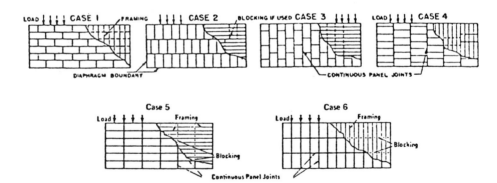

Note: Framing may be located in either direction for blocked diaphragms.

TABLE NO. 25-K-1—ALLOWABLE SHEAR FOR WIND OR SEISMIC FORCES IN POUNDS PER FOOT FOR PLYWOOD SHEAR WALLS WITH FRAMING OF DOUGLAS FIR-LARCH OR SOUTHERN PINE[1][4]

PLYWOOD GRADE	MINIMUM NOMINAL PLYWOOD THICKNESS (Inches)	MINIMUM NAIL PENETRATION IN FRAMING (Inches)	NAIL SIZE (Common or Galvanized Box)	PLYWOOD APPLIED DIRECT TO FRAMING — Nail Spacing at Plywood Panel Edges				NAIL SIZE (Common or Galvanized Box)	PLYWOOD APPLIED OVER ½-INCH GYPSUM SHEATHING — Nail Spacing at Plywood Panel Edges			
				6	4	3	2[2]		6	4	3	2[2]
STRUCTURAL I	5/16	1¼	6d	200	300	390	510	8d	200	300	390	510
	3/8	1½	8d	230[3]	360[3]	460[3]	610[3]	10d	280	430	550[2]	730[2]
	15/32	1½	8d	280	430	550	730	10d	280	430	550[2]	730
	15/32	1⅝	10d	340	510	665[2]	870	—	—	—	—	—
C-D, C-C STRUCTURAL II and other grades covered in U.B.C. Standard No. 25-9	5/16	1¼	6d	180	270	350	450	8d	180	270	350	450
	3/8	1¼	6d	200	300	390	510	8d	200	300	390	510
	3/8	1½	8d	220[3]	320[3]	410[3]	530[3]	10d	260	380	490[2]	640
	15/32	1½	8d	260	380	490	640	10d	260	380	490[2]	640
	15/32	1⅝	10d	310	460	600[2]	770	—	—	—	—	—
	19/32	1⅝	10d	340	510	665[2]	870	—	—	—	—	—
			NAIL SIZE (Galvanized Casing)					NAIL SIZE (Galvanized Casing)				
Plywood panel siding in grades covered in U.B.C. Standard No. 25-9	5/16	1¼	6d	140	210	275	360	8d	140	210	275	360
	3/8	1½	8d	130[3]	200[3]	260[3]	340[3]	10d	160	240	310[2]	410

[1]All panel edges backed with 2-inch nominal or wider framing. Plywood installed either horizontally or vertically. Space nails at 6 inches on center along intermediate framing members for 3/8-inch plywood installed with face grain parallel to studs spaced 24 inches on center and 12 inches on center for other conditions and plywood thicknesses. These values are for short-time loads due to wind or earthquake and must be reduced 25 percent for normal loading.

Allowable shear values for nails in framing members of other species set forth in Table No. 25-17-J of U.B.C. Standards shall be calculated for all grades by multiplying the values for common and galvanized box nails in STRUCTURAL I and galvanized casing nails in other grades by the following factors: Group III, 0.82 and Group IV, 0.65.

[2]Framing shall be 3-inch nominal or wider and nails shall be staggered where nails are spaced 2 inches on center, and where 10d nails having penetration into framing of more than 1⅝ inches are spaced 3 inches on center.

[3]The values for 3/8-inch-thick plywood applied direct to framing may be increased 20 percent, provided studs are spaced a maximum of 16 inches on center or plywood is applied with face grain across studs.

[4]Where plywood is applied on both faces of a wall and nail spacing is less than 6 inches on center on either side, panel joints shall be offset to fall on different framing members or framing shall be 3-inch nominal or thicker and nails on each side shall be staggered.

300

TABLE NO. 25-K-2—ALLOWABLE SHEAR FOR WIND OR SEISMIC FORCES IN POUNDS PER FOOT FOR PARTICLEBOARD SHEAR WALLS WITH FRAMING OF DOUGLAS FIR-LARCH OR SOUTHERN PINE[1][4]

PANEL GRADE	MINIMUM NOMINAL PANEL THICKNESS (In.)	MINIMUM NAIL PENETRATION IN FRAMING (In.)	Nail Size (Common or galvanized box)	PANELS APPLIED DIRECT TO FRAMING — Nail Spacing at Panel Edges (In.)				Nail Size (Common or galvanized box)	PANELS APPLIED OVER ½" GYPSUM SHEATHING — Nail Spacing at Panel Edges (In.)			
				6	4	3	2[2]		6	4	3	2[2]
2-M-W	5/16	1¼	6d	180	270	350	450	8d	180	270	350	450
	3/8			200	300	390	510		200	300	390	510
	3/8	1½	8d	220[3]	320[3]	410[3]	530[3]	10d	260	380	490[2]	640
	7/16			240[3]	350[3]	450[3]	585[3]					
	½			260	380	490	640					
	½	1⅝	10d	310	460	600[2]	770	—	—	—	—	—
	5/8			340	510	665[2]	870	—	—	—	—	—

[1]All panel edges backed with 2-inch nominal or wider framing. Panels installed either horizontally or vertically. Space nails at 6 inches on center along intermediate framing members for 3/8-inch panel installed with the long dimension parallel to studs spaced 24 inches on center and 12 inches on center for other conditions and panel thicknesses. These values are for short-time loads due to wind or earthquake and must be reduced 25 percent for normal loading.

Allowable shear values for nails in framing members of other species set forth in Table No. 25-17-J of U.B.C. Standards shall be calculated for all grades by multiplying the values for common and galvanized box nails by the following factors: Group III, 0.82 and Group IV, 0.65.

[2]Framing shall be 3-inch nominal or wider and nails shall be staggered where nails are spaced 2 inches on center, and where 10d nails having penetration into framing of more than 1⅝ inches are spaced 3 inches on center.

[3]The allowable shear values may be increased to the values shown for ½-inch-thick sheathing with the same nailing, provided:
(a) The studs are spaced a maximum of 16 inches on center, or
(b) The panels are applied with the long dimension perpendicular to studs.

[4]Where plywood is applied on both faces of a wall and nail spacing is less than 6 inches on center on either side, panel joints shall be offset to fall on different framing members, or framing shall be 3-inch nominal or thicker and nails on each side shall be staggered.

TABLE NO. 25-P—ALLOWABLE SHEARS FOR WIND OR SEISMIC LOADING ON VERTICAL DIAPHRAGMS OF FIBERBOARD SHEATHING BOARD CONSTRUCTION FOR TYPE V CONSTRUCTION ONLY[1]

SIZE AND APPLICATION	NAIL SIZE	SHEAR VALUE 3-INCH NAIL SPACING AROUND PERIMETER AND 6-INCH AT INTERMEDIATE POINTS
1. ½" x 4' x 8'	No. 11 gauge galvanized roofing nail 1½" long, 7/16" head	125[2]
2. 25/32" x 4' x 8'	No. 11 gauge galvanized roofing nail 1¾" long, 7/16" head	175

[1]Fiberboard sheathing diaphragms shall not be used to brace concrete or masonry walls.

[2]The shear value may be 175 for ½-inch x 4-foot x 8-foot fiberboard nail-base sheathing.

TABLE NO. 25-Q—NAILING SCHEDULE

CONNECTION	NAILING[1]
1. Joist to sill or girder, toenail	3-8d
2. Bridging to joist, toenail each end	2-8d
3. 1" x 6" subfloor or less to each joist, face nail	2-8d
4. Wider than 1" x 6" subfloor to each joist, face nail	3-8d
5. 2" subfloor to joist or girder, blind and face nail	2-16d
6. Sole plate to joist or blocking, face nail	16d at 16" o.c.
7. Top plate to stud, end nail	2-16d
8. Stud to sole plate	4-8, toenail or 2-16d, end nail
9. Double studs, face nail	16d at 24" o.c.
10. Doubled top plates, face nail	16d at 16" o.c.
11. Top plates, laps and intersections, face nail	2-16d
12. Continuous header, two pieces	16d at 16" o.c. along each edge
13. Ceiling joists to plate, toenail	3-8d
14. Continuous header to stud, toenail	4-8d
15. Ceiling joists, laps over partitions, face nail	3-16d
16. Ceiling joists to parallel rafters, face nail	3-16d
17. Rafter to plate, toenail	3-8d
18. 1" brace to each stud and plate, face nail	2-8d
19. 1" x 8" sheathing or less to each bearing, face nail	2-8d
20. Wider than 1" x 8" sheathing to each bearing, face nail	3-8d
21. Built-up corner studs	16d at 24" o.c.
22. Built-up girder and beams	20d at 32" o.c. at top and bottom and staggered 2-20d at ends and at each splice

(Continued)

CONNECTION	NAILING[1]
23. 2" planks	2-16d at each bearing
24. **Plywood and particleboard:[5]**	
Subfloor, roof and wall sheathing (to framing):	
½" and less	6d[2]
19/32"-¾"	8d[3] or 6d[4]
⅞"-1"	8d[2]
1⅛"-1¼"	10d[3] or 8d[4]
Combination Subfloor-underlayment (to framing):	
¾" and less	6d[4]
⅞"-1"	8d[4]
1⅛"-1¼"	10d[3] or 8d[4]
25. **Panel Siding (to framing):**	
½" or less	6d[6]
⅝"	8d[6]
28. **Fiberboard Sheathing:[7]**	
½"	No. 11 ga. 8 / 6d[3] / No. 16 ga. 9
25/32"	No. 11 ga. 8 / 8d[3] / No. 16 ga. 9

[1]Common or box nails may be used except where otherwise stated.

[2]Common or deformed shank.

[3]Common.

[4]Deformed shank.

[5]Nails spaced at 6 inches on center at edges, 12 inches at intermediate supports (10 inches at intermediate supports for floors), except 6 inches at all supports where spans are 48 inches or more. For nailing of plywood and particleboard diaphragms and shear walls, refer to Section 2513 (c). Nails for wall sheathing may be common, box or casing.

[6]Corrosion-resistant siding or casing nails conforming to the requirements of Section 2516 (j) 1.

[7]Fasteners spaced 3 inches on center at exterior edges and 6 inches on center at intermediate supports.

[8]Corrosion-resistant roofing nails with 7/16-inch-diameter head and 1½-inch length for ½-inch sheathing and 1¾-inch length for 25/32-inch sheathing conforming to the requirements of Section 2516 (j) 1.

[9]Corrosion-resistant staples with nominal 7/16-inch crown and 1⅛-inch length for ½-inch sheathing and 1½-inch length for 25/32-inch sheathing conforming to the requirements of Section 2516 (j) 1.

2. Design criteria: A. Nonconstrained. The following formula may be used in determining the depth of embedment required to resist lateral loads where no constraint is provided at the ground surface, such as rigid floor or rigid ground surface pavement.

$$d = \frac{A}{2}\left(1 + \sqrt{1 + \frac{4.36h}{A}}\right)$$

WHERE:

$$A = \frac{2.34P}{S_1 b}$$

P = Applied lateral force in pounds.

S_1 = Allowable lateral soil-bearing pressure as set forth in Table No. 29-B based on a depth of one third the depth of embedment.

S_3 = Allowable lateral soil-bearing pressure as set forth in Table No. 29-B based on a depth equal to the depth of embedment.

b = Diameter of round post or footing or diagonal dimension of square post or footing (feet).

h = Distance in feet from ground surface to point of application of "P."

d = Depth of embedment in earth but not over 12 feet for purpose of computing lateral pressure.

B. Constrained. The following formula may be used to determine the depth of embedment required to resist lateral loads where constraint is provided at the ground surface, such as a rigid floor or pavement.

$$d^2 = 4.25 \frac{Ph}{S_3 b}$$

C. Vertical load. The resistance to vertical loads is determined by the allowable soil-bearing pressure set forth in Table No. 29-B.

3. Backfill. The backfill in the annular space around columns not embedded in poured footings shall be by one of the following methods:

A. Backfill shall be of concrete with an ultimate strength of 2000 pounds per square inch at 28 days. The hole shall be not less than 4 inches larger than the diameter of the column at its bottom or 4 inches larger than the diagonal dimension of a square or rectangular column.

B. Backfill shall be of clean sand. The sand shall be thoroughly compacted by tamping in layers not more than 8 inches in depth.

4. Limitations. The design procedure outlined in this subsection shall be subject to the following limitations:

The frictional resistance for retaining walls and slabs on silts and clays shall be limited to one half of the normal force imposed on the soil by the weight of the footing or slab.

Posts embedded in earth shall not be used to provide lateral support for structural or nonstructural materials such as plaster, masonry or concrete unless bracing is provided that develops the limited deflection required.

TABLE NO. 26-G—ALLOWABLE SHEAR AND TENSION ON BOLTS (In Pounds)[1] [2]

DIAMETER (In Inches)	MINIMUM EMBEDMENT (In Inches)[3]	MINIMUM CONCRETE STRENGTH (In psi)		
		SHEAR[4]		TENSION[5]
		2000	3000	2000 to 5000
1/4	2½	500	500	200
3/8	3	1100	1100	500
1/2	4	2000	2000	950
5/8	4	2750	3000	1500
3/4	5	2940	3560	2250
7/8	6	3580	4150	3200
1	7	3580	4150	3200
1 1/8	8	3580	4500	3200
1 1/4	9	3580	5300	3200

[1]Values are for natural stone aggregate concrete and bolts of at least A307 quality. Bolts shall have a standard bolt head or an equal deformity in the embedded portion.

[2]Values are based upon a bolt spacing of 12 diameters with a minimum edge distance of 6 diameters. Such spacing and edge distance may be reduced 50 percent with an equal reduction in value. Use linear interpolation for intermediate spacings and edge margins.

[3]An additional 2 inches of embedment shall be provided for anchor bolts located in the top of columns for buildings located in Seismic Zones Nos. 2, 3 and 4.

[4]Values shown are for work with or without special inspection.

[5]Values shown are for work without special inspection. Where special inspection is provided values may be increased 100 percent.

2907

(f) **Foundation Plates or Sills.** Foundation plates or sills shall be bolted to the foundation or foundation wall with not less than 1/2-inch nominal diameter steel bolts embedded at least 7 inches into the concrete or reinforced masonry or 15 inches into unreinforced grouted masonry and spaced not more than 6 feet apart. There shall be a minimum of two bolts per piece with one bolt located within 12 inches of each end of each piece. Foundation plates and sills shall be the kind of wood specified in Section 2516 (c).

(g) **Designs Employing Lateral Bearing. 1. General.** Construction employing posts or poles as columns embedded in earth or embedded in concrete footings in the earth may be used to resist both axial and lateral loads. The depth to resist lateral loads shall be determined by means of the design criteria established herein or other methods approved by the building official.

TABLE NO. 47-I—ALLOWABLE SHEAR FOR WIND OR SEISMIC FORCES IN POUNDS PER FOOT FOR VERTICAL DIAPHRAGMS OF LATH AND PLASTER OR GYPSUM BOARD FRAME WALL ASSEMBLIES[1]

TYPE OF MATERIAL	THICKNESS OF MATERIAL	WALL CONSTRUCTION	NAIL SPACING[2] MAXIMUM (In Inches)	SHEAR VALUE	MINIMUM NAIL SIZE[3]
1. Expanded metal, or woven wire lath and portland cement plaster	⅞″	Unblocked	6	180	No. 11 gauge, 1½″ long, 7/16″ head No. 16 gauge staple, ⅞″ legs
2. Gypsum lath, plain or perforated	⅜″ Lath and ½″ Plaster	Unblocked	5	100	No. 13 gauge, 1⅛″ long, 19/64″ head, plasterboard blued nail
3. Gypsum sheathing board	½″ x 2′ x 8′	Unblocked	4	75	No. 11 gauge, 1¾″ long, 7/16″ head, diamond-point, galvanized
	½″ x 4′	Blocked	4	175	
	½″ x 4′	Unblocked	7	100	
4. Gypsum wallboard or veneer base	½″	Unblocked	7	100	5d cooler or parker nails
			4	125	
		Blocked	7	125	
			4	150	
	⅝″	Blocked	4	175	6d cooler or parker nails
		Blocked Two-ply	Base ply 9 Face ply 7	250	Base ply—6d cooler or parker nails Face ply—8d cooler or parker nails

[1]These vertical diaphragms shall not be used to resist loads imposed by masonry or concrete construction. See Section 4713 (b). Values are for short-time loading due to wind or earthquake and must be reduced 25 percent for normal loading.

[2]Applies to nailing at all studs, top and bottom plates and blocking.

[3]Alternate nails may be used if their dimensions are not less than the specified dimensions.

TABLE NO. 29-B—ALLOWABLE FOUNDATION AND LATERAL PRESSURE

CLASS OF MATERIALS[2]	ALLOWABLE FOUNDATION PRESSURE LBS. SQ. FT.[3]	LATERAL BEARING LBS./SQ. FT./ FT. OF DEPTH BELOW NATURAL GRADE[4]	LATERAL SLIDING[1]	
			COEF-FICIENT[5]	RESISTANCE LBS./SQ. FT.[6]
1. Massive Crystalline Bedrock	4000	1200	.79	
2. Sedimentary and Foliated Rock	2000	400	.35	
3. Sandy Gravel and/or Gravel (GW and GP)	2000	200	.35	
4. Sand, Silty Sand, Clayey Sand, Silty Gravel and Clayey Gravel (SW, SP, SM, SC, GM and GC)	1500	150	.25	
5. Clay, Sandy Clay, Silty Clay and Clayey Silt (CL, ML, MH and CH)	1000[7]	100		130

[1]Lateral bearing and lateral sliding resistance may be combined.

[2]For soil classifications OL, OH and PT (i.e., organic clays and peat), a foundation investigation shall be required.

[3]All values of allowable foundation pressure are for footings having a minimum width of 12 inches and a minimum depth of 12 inches into natural grade. Except as in Footnote 7 below, increase of 20 percent allowed for each additional foot of width and/or depth to a maximum value of three times the designated value.

[4]May be increased the amount of the designated value for each additional foot of depth to a maximum of 15 times the designated value. Isolated poles for uses such as flagpoles or signs and poles used to support buildings which are not adversely affected by a ½-inch motion at ground surface due to short-term lateral loads may be designed using lateral bearing values equal to two times the tabulated values.

[5]Coefficient to be multiplied by the dead load.

[6]Lateral sliding resistance value to be multiplied by the contact area. In no case shall the lateral sliding resistance exceed one half the dead load.

[7]No increase for width is allowed.

SEC. 91.2309 — RETAINING WALLS

(a) **Design.** Retaining walls shall be designed to resist the lateral pressure of the retained material determined in accordance with accepted engineering principles.

The soil characteristics and design criteria necessary for such a determination shall be obtained from a special foundation investigation performed by an agency acceptable to the Department. The Department shall approve such characteristics and criteria only after receiving a written opinion from the investigation agency together with substantiating evidence.

EXCEPTION: Freestanding walls which are not over 15' in height or basement walls which have spans of 15' or less between supports may be designed in accordance with Subsection (b) of this Section.

TABLE NO. 23-E

Surface Slope of Retained Material* Horiz. to Vert.	Equivalent Fluid Weight lb/ft³
LEVEL	30
5 to 1	32
4 to 1	35
3 to 1	38
2 to 1	43
1½ to 1	55
1 to 1	80

* Where the surface slope of the retained earth varies, the design slope shall be obtained by connecting a line from the top of the wall to the highest point on the slope, whose limits are within the horizontal distance from the stem equal to the stem height of the wall.

(b) **Arbitrary Design Method.** Walls which retain drained earth and come within the limits of the exception to Subsection (a) of this section may be designed for an assumed earth pressure equivalent to that exerted by a fluid weighing not less than one-third of the horizontal force so obtained may be assumed at the plane of application of the force.

Table 23-E. A vertical component equal to one-third of the horizontal force so obtained may be assumed at the plane of application of the force.

The depth of the retained earth shall be the vertical distance below the ground surface measured at the wall face for stem design or measured at the heel of the footing for overturning and sliding.

(c) **Surcharge.** Any superimposed loading, except retained earth, shall be considered as surcharge and provided for in the design. Uniformly distributed loads may be considered as equivalent added depth of retained earth. Surcharge loading due to continuous or isolated footings shall be determined by the following formulas or by an equivalent method approved by the Superintendent of Building.

Resultant Lateral Force

$$R = \frac{0.3\ Ph^3}{x^2 + h^3}$$

Location of Lateral Resultant

$$d = x\left[\left(\frac{x^2}{h^3} + 1\right)\left(\tan^{-1}\frac{h}{x}\right) - \left(\frac{x}{h}\right)\right]$$

Where:

R = Resultant lateral force measured in pounds per foot of wall width.

P = Resultant surcharge load of continuous or isolated footings measured in pounds per foot of length parallel to the wall.

x = Distance of resultant load from back face of wall measured in feet.

h = Depth below point of application of surcharge loading to top of wall footing measured in feet.

d = Depth of lateral resultant below point of application of surcharge loading measured in feet.

$\left(\tan^{-1}\dfrac{h}{x}\right)$ = The angle in radians whose tangent is equal to $\left(\dfrac{h}{x}\right)$.

Loads applied within a horizontal distance equal to the wall stem height, measured from the back face of the wall, shall be considered as surcharge.

For isolated footings having a width parallel to the wall less than three feet, "R" may be reduced to 1/6 the calculated value.

The resultant lateral force "R" shall be assumed to be uniform for the length of footing parallel to the wall, and to diminish uniformly to zero at the distance "x" beyond the ends of the footing.

Vertical pressure due to surcharge applied to the top of the wall footing may be considered to spread uniformly within the limits of the stem and planes making an angle of 45° with the vertical.

(d) **Bearing Pressure and Overturning.** The maximum vertical bearing pressure under any retaining wall shall not exceed that allowed in Division 28 of this Article except as provided for by a special foundation investigation. The resultant of vertical loads and lateral pressures shall pass through the middle one-third of the base.

(e) **Friction and Lateral Soil Pressures.** Retaining walls shall be restrained against sliding by friction of the base against the earth, by lateral resistance of the soil, or by a combination of the two. Allowable friction and lateral soil values shall not exceed those allowed in Division 28 of this Article except as provided by a special foundation investigation.

When used, keys shall be assumed to lower the plane of frictional resistance and the depth of lateral bearing to the level of the bottom of the key. Lateral bearing pressures shall be assumed to act on a vertical plane located at the toe of the footing.

(f) **Construction.** No retaining wall shall be constructed of wood.

(g) **Special Conditions.** Whenever, in the opinion of the Superintendent of Building, the adequacy of the foundation material to support a wall is questionable, an unusual surcharge condition exists, or whenever the retained earth is so stratified or of such a character as to invalidate normal design assumptions, he may require a special foundation investigation before approving any permit for such a wall.

TABLE NO. 28-B — ALLOWABLE FRICTIONAL & BEARING VALUES FOR ROCK[1]

Type	Friction Coefficient	Allowable Lateral Bearing lbs. per sq. ft.	per ft. Max. Value
Massive Crystalline Bedrock	1.0	4,000	20,000
Foliated Rocks	.8	1,600	8,000
Sedimentary Rocks	.6	1,200	6,000
Soft or Broken Bedrocks	.4	400	2,000

1. Coefficient to be multiplied by the Dead Load.

ALLOWABLE FRICTIONAL & LATERAL BEARING VALUES FOR SOILS

Frictional Resistance — Gravels and Sands[1]

Soil Type	Friction Coefficient
Gravel, Well Graded	0.6
Gravel, Poorly Graded	0.6
Gravel, Silty	0.5
Gravel, Clayey	0.4
Sand, Well Graded	0.4
Sand, Poorly Graded	0.4
Sand, Silty	0.4
Sand, Clayey	0.4

1. Coefficient to be multiplied by the Dead Load.

ALLOWABLE FRICTIONAL RESISTANCE (lbs. per sq. ft.) — Clay and Silt[1]

Soil Type	Loose or Soft	Compact or Stiff
Silt, Inorganic	250	500
Silt, Organic	250	500
Silt, Elastic	200	400
Clay, Lean	500	1000
Clay, Fat	200	400
Clay, Organic	150	300
Peat	0	0

2. Frictional values to be multiplied by the width of footing subjected to positive soil pressure. In no case shall the frictional resistance exceed ½ the dead load on the area under consideration.

ALLOWABLE LATERAL BEARING PER FT. OF DEPTH BELOW NATURAL GROUND SURFACE (lbs. per sq. ft.) (Natural Soils or approved compacted fill)

Soil Type	Loose or Soft	Compact or Stiff	Max. Values
Gravel, Well Graded	200	400	8000
Gravel, Poorly Graded	200	400	8000
Gravel, Silty	167	333	8000
Gravel, Clayey	167	333	8000
Sand, Well Graded	183	367	6000
Sand, Poorly Graded	77	200	6000
Sand, Silty	100	233	4000
Sand, Clayey	133	300	4000
Silt, Inorganic	67	133	3000
Silt, Organic	33	67	2000
Silt, Elastic	33	67	1500
Clay, Lean	267	967	3000
Clay, Fat	33	167	1500
Clay, Organic			500
Peat	0	0	0

GENERAL CONDITIONS OF USE

1. Frictional and lateral resistance of soils may be combined, provided the lateral bearing resistance does not exceed ⅔ of allowable lateral bearing.
2. A ⅓ increase in frictional and lateral bearing values will be permitted to resist loads caused by wind pressure or earthquake forces.
3. Isolated poles such as flag poles or signs may be designed using lateral bearing values equal to two times the tabulated values.
4. Lateral bearing values are permitted only when concrete is deposited against natural ground or compacted fill, approved by the Superintendent of Building.

SEC. 91.2311 — POLES

(a) Design. Flag poles, sign poles, columns or other poles cantilevering from and receiving lateral stability from the ground shall have their lateral support designed in accordance with the following formulas or other methods approved by the Superintendent of Building. Bearing stresses so obtained shall not exceed the values permitted by Section 91.2803 (d).

CASE I — POLES WITH LATERAL RESTRAINT AT THE GROUND SURFACE

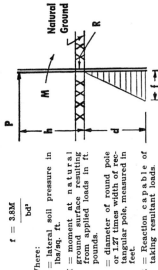

$$f = \frac{3.8M}{bd^2}$$

Where:

f = lateral soil pressure in lbs/sq. ft.

M = moment at natural ground surface resulting from applied loads in ft. pounds.

b = diameter of round pole or 1.27 times width of rectangular pole, measured in feet.

R = Reaction capable of taking resultant loads.

CASE II — POLES WITHOUT LATERAL RESTRAINT AT THE GROUND SURFACE

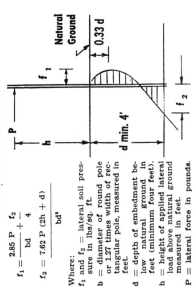

$$f_1 = \frac{2.85\,P}{bd} + \frac{f_2}{4}$$

$$f_2 = \frac{7.62\,P\,(2h + d)}{bd^2}$$

Where:

f_1 and f_2 = lateral soil pressure in lbs/sq. ft.

b = diameter of round pole or 1.27 times width of rectangular pole, measured in feet.

d = depth of embedment below natural ground in feet (minimum four feet).

h = height of applied lateral load above natural ground measured in feet.

P = lateral force in pounds.

APPENDIX D

Factors for Masonry

The following tables present factors that are used for the evaluation of relative stiffness of masonry piers (short segments of masonry walls). This relates to the determination of load distribution for a series of interacting piers. Use of these data is illustrated in the design examples in Chapter 6. Table data are reprinted from the *Concrete Masonry Design Manual* (Ref. 10) with permission of the publishers.

D.1. BENDING IN MASONRY WALLS

The following example illustrates the use of Figure D.1. Other uses are illustrated in Chapter 6.

Investigate the wall and the required reinforcing for the following data:

Wall height = 16.7 ft.

8-in. block: $t = 7.625$ in.

Use single row of reinforcing in center: d = 3.813 in., $n = 40$, allowable $f_m = 250 \times 1.33 = 333$ psi.

Grade 40 bars: $f_s = 1.33 \times 20{,}000 = 26{,}667$ psi.

Wind pressure is 20 psf.

Find

$$M = \frac{wL^2}{8} = \frac{20(16.7)^2}{8} \times 12$$

$$= 8367 \text{ in.-lb}$$

$$K = \frac{M}{bd^2} = \frac{8367}{12(3.813)^2} = 48$$

Enter the diagram (Fig. D.1) at the left with $K = 48$, proceed to the right to intersect f_m = 333 psi, read at the bottom $np = 0.073$. Then

$$p = \frac{0.073}{n} = \frac{0.073}{40} = 0.001825$$

$$A_s = pbd = 0.001825 \times 12 \times 3.813$$

$$= 0.0835 \text{ in.}^2/\text{ft}$$

Try No. 5 at 40 in.:

$$A_s = \frac{12}{40} \times 0.31 = 0.093 \text{ in.}^2/\text{ft}$$

Check f_s using approximate $j = 0.90$:

$$f_s = \frac{M}{f_s jd} = \frac{8367}{(0.093)(0.9)(3.813)}$$

$$= 26{,}217 \text{ psi}$$

The reinforcing is adequate unless a combined stress must be investigated.

TABLE D.1. Rigidity Coefficients for Cantilevered Masonry Walls

h/d	Rc	h/d	Rc	h/d	Rc	h/d	Rc	h/d	Rc	h/d	Rc
9.90	.0006	5.20	.0043	1.85	.0810	1.38	.1706	0.91	.4352	0.45	1.4582
9.80	.0007	5.10	.0046	1.84	.0821	1.37	.1737	0.90	.4452	0.44	1.5054
9.70	.0007	5.00	.0049	1.83	.0833	1.36	.1768	0.89	.4554	0.43	1.5547
9.60	.0007	4.90	.0052	1.82	.0845	1.35	.1800	0.88	.4659	0.42	1.6063
9.50	.0007	4.80	.0055	1.81	.0858	1.34	.1832	0.87	.4767	0.41	1.6604
9.40	.0007	4.70	.0058	1.80	.0870	1.33	.1866	0.86	.4899	0.40	1.7170
9.30	.0008	4.60	.0062	1.79	.0883	1.32	.1900	0.85	.4994	0.39	1.7765
9.20	.0008	4.50	.0066	1.78	.0896	1.31	.1935	0.84	.5112	0.38	1.8380
9.10	.0008	4.40	.0071	1.77	.0909	1.30	.1970	0.83	.5233	0.37	1.9098
9.00	.0008	4.30	.0076	1.76	.0923	1.29	.2007	0.82	.5359	0.36	1.9738
8.90	.0009	4.20	.0081	1.75	.0937	1.28	.2044	0.81	.5488	0.35	2.0467
8.80	.0009	4.10	.0087	1.74	.0951	1.27	.2083	0.80	.5621	0.34	2.1237
8.70	.0009	4.00	.0093	1.73	.0965	1.26	.2122	0.79	.5758	0.33	2.2051
8.60	.0010	3.90	.0100	1.72	.0980	1.25	.2162	0.78	.5899	0.32	2.2913
8.50	.0010	3.80	.0108	1.71	.0995	1.24	.2203	0.77	.6044	0.31	2.3828
8.40	.0010	3.70	.0117	1.70	.1010	1.23	.2245	0.76	.6194	0.30	2.4802
8.30	.0011	3.60	.0127	1.69	.1026	1.22	.2289	0.75	.6349	0.29	2.5838
8.20	.0012	3.50	.0137	1.68	.1041	1.21	.2333	0.74	.6509	0.28	2.6945
8.10	.0012	3.40	.0149	1.67	.1058	1.20	.2378	0.73	.6674	0.27	2.8130
8.00	.0012	3.30	.0163	1.66	.1074	1.19	.2425	0.72	.6844	0.26	2.9401
7.90	.0013	3.20	.0178	1.65	.1091	1.18	.2472	0.71	.7019	0.25	3.0769
7.80	.0013	3.10	.0195	1.64	.1108	1.17	.2521	0.70	.7200	0.24	3.2246
7.70	.0014	3.00	.0214	1.63	.1125	1.16	.2571	0.69	.7388	0.23	3.3845
7.60	.0014	2.90	.0235	1.62	.1143	1.15	.2622	0.68	.7581	0.22	3.5583
7.50	.0015	2.80	.0260	1.61	.1162	1.14	.2675	0.67	.7781	0.21	3.7479
7.40	.0015	2.70	.0288	1.60	.1180	1.13	.2729	0.66	.7987	0.20	3.9557
7.30	.0016	2.60	.0320	1.59	.1199	1.12	.2784	0.65	.8201	.195	4.0673
7.20	.0017	2.50	.0357	1.58	.1218	1.11	.2841	0.64	.8422	.190	4.1845
7.10	.0017	2.40	.0400	1.57	.1238	1.10	.2899	0.63	.8650	.185	4.3079
7.00	.0018	2.30	.0450	1.56	.1258	1.09	.2959	0.62	.8886	.180	4.4379
6.90	.0019	2.20	.0508	1.55	.1279	1.08	.3020	0.61	.9131	.175	4.5751
6.80	.0020	2.10	.0577	1.54	.1300	1.07	.3083	0.60	.9384	.170	4.7201
6.70	.0020	2.00	.0658	1.53	.1322	1.06	.3147	0.59	.9647	.165	4.8736
6.60	.0021	1.99	.0667	1.52	.1344	1.05	.3213	0.58	.9919	.160	5.0364
6.50	.0022	1.98	.0676	1.51	.1366	1.04	.3281	0.57	1.0201	.155	5.2095
6.40	.0023	1.97	.0685	1.50	.1389	1.03	.3351	0.56	1.0493	.150	5.3937
6.30	.0025	1.96	.0694	1.49	.1412	1.02	.3422	0.55	1.0797	.145	5.5904
6.20	.0026	1.95	.0704	1.48	.1436	1.01	.3496	0.54	1.1112	.140	5.8008
6.10	.0027	1.94	.0714	1.47	.1461	1.00	.3571	0.53	1.1439	.135	6.0261
6.00	.0028	1.93	.0724	1.46	.1486	0.99	.3649	0.52	1.1779	.130	6.2696
5.90	.0030	1.92	.0734	1.45	.1511	0.98	.3729	0.51	1.2132	.125	6.5306
5.80	.0031	1.91	.0744	1.44	.1537	0.97	.3811	0.50	1.2500	.120	6.8136
5.70	.0033	1.90	.0754	1.43	.1564	0.96	.3895	0.49	1.2883	.115	7.1208
5.60	.0035	1.89	.0765	1.42	.1591	0.95	.3981	0.48	1.3281	.110	7.4555
5.50	.0037	1.88	.0776	1.41	.1619	0.94	.4070	0.47	1.3696	.105	7.8215
5.40	.0039	1.87	.0787	1.40	.1647	0.93	.4162	0.46	1.4130	.100	8.2237
5.30	.0041	1.86	.0798	1.39	.1676	0.92	.4255				

TABLE D.2. Rigidity Coefficients for Fixed Masonry Walls

h/d	R_f	h/d	R_f	h/d	R_f	h/d	R_f	h/d	R_f	h/d	R_f
9.90	.0025	5.20	.0160	1.85	.2104	1.38	.3694	0.91	.7177	0.45	1.736
9.80	.0026	5.10	.0169	1.84	.2128	1.37	.3742	0.90	.7291	0.44	1.779
9.70	.0027	5.00	.0179	1.83	.2152	1.36	.3790	0.89	.7407	0.43	1.825
9.60	.0027	4.90	.0189	1.82	.2176	1.35	.3840	0.88	.7527	0.42	1.874
9.50	.0028	4.80	.0200	1.81	.2201	1.34	.3890	0.87	.7649	0.41	1.924
9.40	.0029	4.70	.0212	1.80	.2226	1.33	.3942	0.86	.7773	0.40	1.978
9.30	.0030	4.60	.0225	1.79	.2251	1.32	.3994	0.85	.7901	0.39	2.034
9.20	.0031	4.50	.0239	1.78	.2277	1.31	.4047	0.84	.8031	0.38	2.092
9.10	.0032	4.40	.0254	1.77	.2303	1.30	.4100	0.83	.8165	0.37	2.154
9.00	.0033	4.30	.0271	1.76	.2330	1.29	.4155	0.82	.8302	0.36	2.219
8.90	.0034	4.20	.0288	1.75	.2356	1.28	.4211	0.81	.8442	0.35	2.287
8.80	.0035	4.10	.0308	1.74	.2384	1.27	.4267	0.80	.8585	0.34	2.360
8.70	.0037	4.00	.0329	1.73	.2411	1.26	.4324	0.79	0.873	0.33	2.437
8.60	.0038	3.90	.0352	1.72	.2439	1.25	.4384	0.78	0.888	0.32	2.518
8.50	.0039	3.80	.0377	1.71	.2468	1.24	.4443	0.77	0.904	0.31	2.605
8.40	.0040	3.70	.0405	1.70	.2497	1.23	.4504	0.76	0.920	0.30	2.697
8.30	.0042	3.60	.0435	1.69	.2526	1.22	.4566	0.75	0.936	0.29	2.795
8.20	.0043	3.50	.0468	1.68	.2556	1.21	.4628	0.74	0.952	0.28	2.900
8.10	.0045	3.40	.0505	1.67	.2586	1.20	.4692	0.73	0.969	0.27	3.013
8.00	.0047	3.30	.0545	1.66	.2617	1.19	.4757	0.72	0.987	0.26	3.135
7.90	.0048	3.20	.0590	1.65	.2648	1.18	.4823	0.71	1.005	0.25	3.265
7.80	.0050	3.10	.0640	1.64	.2679	1.17	.4891	0.70	1.023	0.24	3.407
7.70	.0052	3.00	.0694	1.63	.2711	1.16	.4959	0.69	1.042	0.23	3.560
7.60	.0054	2.90	.0756	1.62	.2744	1.15	.5029	0.68	1.062	0.22	3.728
7.50	.0056	2.80	.0824	1.61	.2777	1.14	.5100	0.67	1.082	0.21	3.911
7.40	.0058	2.70	.0900	1.60	.2811	1.13	.5173	0.66	1.103	0.20	4.112
7.30	.0061	2.60	.0985	1.59	.2844	1.12	.5247	0.65	1.124	.195	4.220
7.20	.0063	2.50	.1081	1.58	.2879	1.11	.5322	0.64	1.146	.190	4.334
7.10	.0065	2.40	.1189	1.57	.2914	1.10	.5398	0.63	1.168	.185	4.454
7.00	.0069	2.30	.1311	1.56	.2949	1.09	.5476	0.62	1.191	.180	4.580
6.90	.0072	2.20	.1449	1.55	.2985	1.08	.5556	0.61	1.216	.175	4.714
6.80	.0075	2.10	.1607	1.54	.3022	1.07	.5637	0.60	1.240	.170	4.855
6.70	.0078	2.00	.1786	1.53	.3059	1.06	.5719	0.59	1.266	.165	5.005
6.60	.0081	1.99	.1805	1.52	.3097	1.05	.5804	0.58	1.292	.160	5.164
6.50	.0085	1.98	.1824	1.51	.3136	1.04	.5889	0.57	1.319	.155	5.334
6.40	.0089	1.97	.1844	1.50	.3175	1.03	.5977	0.56	1.347	.150	5.514
6.30	.0093	1.96	.1864	1.49	.3214	1.02	.6066	0.55	1.376	.145	5.707
6.20	.0097	1.95	.1885	1.48	.3245	1.01	.6157	0.54	1.407	.140	5.914
6.10	.0102	1.94	.1905	1.47	.3295	1.00	.6250	0.53	1.438	.135	6.136
6.00	.0107	1.93	.1926	1.46	.3337	0.99	.6344	0.52	1.470	.130	6.374
5.90	.0112	1.92	.1947	1.45	.3379	0.98	.6441	0.51	1.504	.125	6.632
5.80	.0118	1.91	.1969	1.44	.3422	0.97	.6540	0.50	1.539	.120	6.911
5.70	.0124	1.90	.1991	1.43	.3465	0.96	.6641	0.49	1.575	.115	7.215
5.60	.0130	1.89	.2013	1.42	.3510	0.95	.6743	0.48	1.612	.110	7.545
5.50	.0137	1.88	.2035	1.41	.3555	0.94	.6848	0.47	1.651	.105	7.908
5.40	.0144	1.87	.2058	1.40	.3600	0.93	.6955	0.46	1.692	.100	8.306
5.30	.0152	1.86	.2081	1.39	.3647	0.92	.7065				

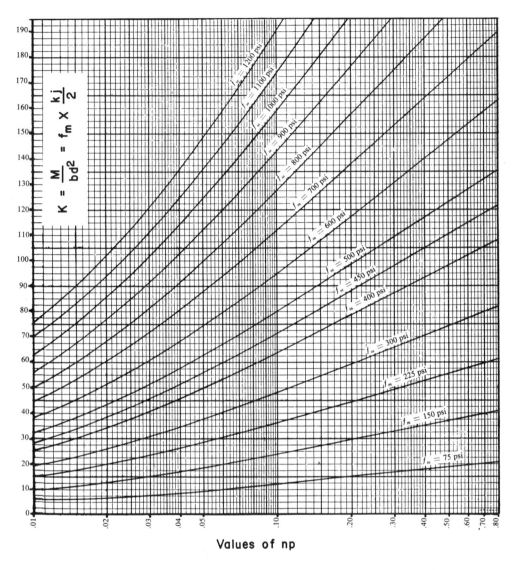

$$K = \frac{M}{bd^2} = f_m \times \frac{kj}{2}$$

$f'_m = 1200$ psi
$f'_m = 1100$ psi
$f'_m = 1000$ psi
$f'_m = 900$ psi
$f'_m = 800$ psi
$f'_m = 700$ psi
$f'_m = 600$ psi
$f'_m = 500$ psi
$f'_m = 450$ psi
$f'_m = 400$ psi
$f'_m = 300$ psi
$f'_m = 225$ psi
$f'_m = 150$ psi
$f'_m = 75$ psi

Values of np

FIGURE D.1. Flexural coefficient k-chart for reinforced masonry. From *Masonry Design Manual* (Ref.10) with permission of the publishers, Masonry Institute of America.

APPENDIX E

Weight of Elements of Building Construction

This chapter contains material that will assist in the determination of the weight of various parts of the building as is required in the process of finding the lateral inertial force. Table E.1 contains data for the determination of the weight of specific materials where a unique assemblage must be evaluated. Table E.2 presents the average weights of commonly used elements of construction. For simpler and faster approximations of weights in preliminary calculations, Table E.3 presents average weights of ordinary total assemblages of typical construction.

TABLE E.1. Weight of Materials

Material	Weight lb/ft^3	Specific Gravity[a]
Soil		
Top soil		
Dry, loose	75	1.21
Moist, packed	100	1.61
Sand, gravel		
Dry, loose	90–100	1.53
Moist, packed	110–120	1.85
Clay		
Dry	65	1.05
Wet	100–110	1.69
Wood		
Cedar	22	0.35
Fir, northern	35	0.56
Fir, white	25	0.40
Hemlock	30	0.48
Oak, red	40	0.65
Pine, white	25	0.40
Pine, yellow, long-leaf	45	0.73
Poplar	30	0.48
Redwood	25	0.40
Spruce	25	0.40
Metal		
Aluminum	165	2.66
Copper	556	8.97
Lead	710	11.45
Steel	490	7.90
Masonry		
Brick		
Finished, pressed	130–150	2.26
Common, soft	110–120	1.85
Concrete block		
Normal weight, voids empty	90	1.45
Lightweight, voids empty	65	1.05
Lightweight, voids 25% filled	85	1.37
Lightweight, voids 100% filled	140	2.26

TABLE E.1. Weight of Materials (*Continued*)

Material	Weight lb/ft^3	Specific Gravity[a]
Concrete		
Normal, gravel	145	2.34
(with average reinforcing)	150	2.42
Lightweight		
Structural	110	1.77
Masonry units	90	1.45
Insulating	30–40	0.56
Miscellaneous		
Asphalt paving	100	1.61
Glass	160	2.58
Plaster		
Cement, stucco	120	1.94
Gypsum	40	0.65
Water	62	1.00

[a] Average weight divided by weight of water at 62 lb/ft^3.

TABLE E.2. Weight of Elements of Building Construction

	lb/ft^2	kN/m^2
Roofs		
3-ply ready roofing (roll, composition)	1	0.05
3-ply felt and gravel	5.5	0.26
5-ply felt and gravel	6.5	0.31
Shingles		
Wood	2	0.10
Asphalt	2–3	0.10–0.15
Clay tile	9–12	0.43–0.58
Concrete tile	8–12	0.38–0.58
Slate, $\frac{1}{4}$ in.	10	0.48
Fiber glass	2–3	0.10–0.15
Aluminum	1	0.05
Steel	2	0.10
Insulation		
Fiber glass batts	0.5	0.025
Rigid foam plastic	1.5	0.075
Foamed concrete, mineral aggregate	2.5/in.	0.0047/mm
Wood rafters		
2 × 6 at 24 in.	1.0	0.05
2 × 8 at 24 in.	1.4	0.07
2 × 10 at 24 in.	1.7	0.08
2 × 12 at 24 in.	2.1	0.10
Steel deck, painted		
22 ga	1.6	0.08
20 ga	2.0	0.10
18 ga	2.6	0.13
Skylight		
Glass with steel frame	6–10	0.29–0.48
Plastic with aluminum frame	3–6	0.15–0.29
Plywood or softwood board sheathing	3.0/in.	0.0057/mm
Ceilings		
Suspended steel channels	1	0.05
Lath		
Steel mesh	0.5	0.025
Gypsum board, $\frac{1}{2}$ in.	2	0.10
Fiber tile	1	0.05
Drywall, gypsum board, $\frac{1}{2}$ in.	2.5	0.12
Plaster		
Gypsum, acoustic	5	0.24
Cement	8.5	0.41
Suspended lighting and air distribution Systems, average	3	0.15

TABLE E.2. Weight of Elements of Building Construction

	lb/ft^2	kN/m^2
Floors		
Hardwood, $\frac{1}{2}$ in.	2.5	0.12
Vinyl tile, $\frac{1}{8}$ in.	1.5	0.07
Asphalt mastic	12/in.	0.023/mm
Ceramic tile		
$\frac{3}{4}$ in.	10	0.48
Thin set	5	0.24
Fiberboard underlay, $\frac{5}{8}$ in.	3	0.15
Carpet and pad, average	3	0.15
Timber deck	2.5/in.	0.0047/mm
Steel deck, stone concrete fill, average	35–40	1.68–1.92
Concrete deck, stone aggregate	12.5/in.	0.024/mm
Wood joists		
2 × 8 at 16 in.	2.1	0.10
2 × 10 at 16 in.	2.6	0.13
2 × 12 at 16 in.	3.2	0.16
Lightweight concrete fill	8.0/in.	0.015/mm
Walls		
2 × 4 studs at 16 in., average	2	0.10
Steel studs at 16 in., average	4	0.20
Lath, plaster; see Ceilings		
Gypsum drywall, $\frac{5}{8}$ in. single	2.5	0.12
Stucco, $\frac{7}{8}$ in., or wire and paper or felt	10	0.48
Windows, average, glazing + frame		
Small pane, single glazing, wood or metal frame	5	0.24
Large pane, single glazing, wood or metal frame	8	0.38
Increase for double glazing	2–3	0.10–0.15
Curtain walls, manufactured units	10–15	0.48–0.72
Brick veneer		
4 in., mortar joints	40	1.92
$\frac{1}{2}$ in., mastic	10	0.48
Concrete block		
Lightweight, unreinforced—4 in.	20	0.96
6 in.	25	1.20
8 in.	30	1.44
Heavy, reinforced, grouted—6 in.	45	2.15
8 in.	60	2.87
12 in.	85	4.07

TABLE E.3. Average Values of Total Dead Weight for Typical Building Construction

Description of Construction	Weight[a] lb/ft^2
Roofs	
1. Light wood frame, shingles, no ceiling	5
2. Light wood frame, 3-ply felt + gravel, gypsum drywall ceiling	12
3. Medium span wood or steel trusses, plywood deck, 3-ply felt + gravel, no ceiling	15
4. Steel open-web joists, metal deck, lightweight concrete insulating fill, 3-ply felt + gravel, suspended drywall ceiling	18–25
5. Glue-laminated wood girders, timber purlins, plywood deck, clay or concrete tile shingles, no ceiling	25–30
6. Steel beams, otherwise same as item 5	22–30
7. Precast concrete plank, 3-ply felt + gravel, 2-in. concrete fill, no ceiling	22–30
6-in.-thick units	50
8-in.-thick units	65
10-in.-thick units	80
8. Precast concrete double-tees, 2-in concrete fill, 3-ply felt + gravel, no ceiling	80–100
9. Poured-in-placed concrete slab and beams, insulating concrete fill, 3-ply felt + gravel, suspended drywall ceiling	100–125
Floors	
10. Wood joist, plywood deck, carpet, drywall ceiling	10
11. Steel- or wood-trussed joists, plywood deck, 2-in. concrete fill, carpet, drywall ceiling	30
12. Steel beam, steel deck, concrete fill, suspended lay-in the ceiling	60–70
13. Precast concrete plank, 2-in. concrete fill, carpet, suspended drywall ceiling	
6-in.-thick units	50
8-in.-thick units	65
10-in.-thick units	80
14. Poured-in-place concrete slab and beams, 2-in. concrete fill, suspended lay-in tile ceiling	100–125

TABLE E.3. Average Values of Total Dead Weight for Typical Building Construction

Description of Construction	Weight[a] lb/ft^2
Walls	
15. Exterior, wood studs, stucco, drywall	15–20
16. Exterior, wood studs, wood siding, drywall	10–15
17. Exterior, brick veneer, wood studs, plywood, drywall (real bricks)	60
18. Exterior, fake brick (thin tile), plywood, wood studs, drywall	25
19. Exterior, reinforced concrete block, 8-in. units, 25% voids filled, average reinforcing, insulation, furred-out drywall	60
20. Steel frame, aluminum + glass windows (curtain wall), 25% windows—small size	25
21. Windows, wood or metal frame, small panes of glass (5–10 ft^2/window)	5
22. Interior, wood stud, drywall both sides	8
23. Interior, wood stud, cement plaster both sides	20

[a]Average weight per square foot of surface.

Index